Capturing Carbon and Conserving Biodiversity

Capturing Carbon and Conserving Biodiversity

The Market Approach

Edited by Ian R. Swingland

 THE ROYAL SOCIETY

Earthscan Publications Ltd
London • Sterling, VA

First published in the UK and USA in 2003
by Earthscan Publications Ltd

Originating from contributions first published in the
Philosophical Transactions of The Royal Society, Series A

ISBN: 1 85383 951 5 paperback
        1 85383 950 7 hardback

Typesetting by T&T Productions Ltd, London
Printed and bound in the UK by Creative Print and Design Wales, Ebbw Vale
Cover design by Danny Gillespie
For a full list of publications please contact:

Earthscan Publications Ltd
120 Pentonville Road, London, N1 9JN, UK
Tel: +44 (0)20 7278 0433
Fax: +44 (0)20 7278 1142
Email: earthinfo@earthscan.co.uk
Web: **www.earthscan.co.uk**

22883 Quicksilver Drive, Sterling, VA 20166-2012, USA

Earthscan is an editorially independent subsidiary of Kogan Page Ltd and
publishes in association with WWF-UK and the International Institute for
Environment and Development

A catalogue record for this book is available from the British Library

Library of Congress Cataloging-in-Publication Data

applied for

This book is printed on elemental chlorine free paper

To Fiona,
who has supported me unselfishly and with love
through this and many other endeavours

Contents

Part 2 **Environmental Services**

Part 3 **The Future Model**

List of figures and tables

Figures

Tables

About the contributors

Andrew S. Ball is Reader in Microbiology at the Department of Biological Sciences, University of Essex, Wivenhoe Park, Colchester, CO4 3SQ, UK, *andrew@essex.ac.uk*

Eric C. Bettelheim is Executive Chairman of Sustainable Forestry Management Ltd and Consultant at Mishcon de Reya, 12 Red Lion Square, Summit House, London, WC1R 4QD, UK, *eric.bettelheim@mishcon.co.uk*

Richard A. Betts is Senior Ecosystem Scientist at the Met Office, Hadley Centre for Climate Prediction and Research, London Road, Bracknell, RG12 2SY, UK, *richard.betts@metoffice.com*

Robert Bonnie is Managing Director of the Center for Conservation Incentives, Environmental Defense, 1875 Connecticut Avenue, NW, Washington, DC, USA, *rbonnie@environmentaldefense.org*

Sandra Brown is Senior Program Officer/Senior Scientist at Winrock International, 1621 N Kent St, Suite 1200, Arlington, VA 22209, USA, *sbrown@winrock.org*

Melissa Carey is Climate Change Policy Specialist at Environmental Defense, 1875 Connecticut Avenue, NW, Washington, DC, USA *mcarey@environmentaldefense.org*

Gonzalo Castro is Team Leader for Biodiversity at the Global Environment Facility, The World Bank, Washington, DC 20433, USA, *gcastro@worldbank.org*

Thomas N. Chase is Assistant Professor in the Cooperative Institute for Research in Environmental Sciences and Department of Geography, University of Colorado, Boulder, CO 80309, USA, *tchase@cires.colorado.edu*

Joseph L. Eastman is a member of the Research Faculty, University of Maryland Baltimore County, Hydrological Sciences Branch, NASA/GSFC Code 974, Building 33, Room A402, Greenbelt, MD 20771, USA, *jleastman@attbi.com*

John P. Fay is GIS Manager at the Center for Conservation Biology, Stanford University, Stanford, CA 94305, USA, *jpfay@stanford.edu*

Peter C. Frumhoff is Director and Senior Scientist at the Global Environment Program, Union of Concerned Scientists, 2 Brattle Square, Cambridge, MA 02238-9105, USA, *pfrumhoff@ucsusa.org*

John Grace is Professor of Environmental Biology and Head of the School of GeoSciences, University of Edinburgh, Edinburgh, EH9 3JG, UK, *jgrace@ed.ac.uk*

Robin Hanbury-Tenison is President of the Rain Forest Club, Cabilla Manor, Bodmin, Cornwall, PL30 4DW, UK, *robin@cabilla.co.uk*

Jared J. Hardner is Managing Partner at Hardner & Gullison Associates, L.L.C., Palo Alto, CA 94302, USA, *jared@hg-llc.com*

Agnes Kiss is Environment Lead Specialist, Africa, Environment and Social Development Unit, The World Bank, Washington, DC 20433, USA, *akiss@worldbank.org*

Izabella Koziell is an Environment Adviser of the Department for International Development, UK Government in Kenya, *i-koziell@dfid.gov.uk*

Natasha Landell-Mills is Senior Research Associate at the International Institute for Environment and Development, 3 Endsleigh St, London, WC1H 0DD, UK, *natasha.landell-mills@iied.org*

Nigel Leader-Williams is Professor of Biodiversity Management and Director of the Durrell Institute of Conservation and Ecology, University of Kent, Canterbury, CT2 7NS, UK, *n.leader-williams@ukc.ac.uk*

Li Xiaoyun is a professor at the China Agricultural University, Beijing, China, *xiaoyun@mail.cau.edu.cn*

Yadvinder Malhi is a Royal Society University Research Fellow at the School of GeoSciences, University of Edinburgh, Edinburgh, EH9 3JG, UK, *ymalhi@ed.ac.uk*

Michelle M. Manion is Senior Analyst at the Global Environment Program, Union of Concerned Scientists, 2 Brattle Square, Cambridge, MA 02238-9105, USA, *mmanion@ucsusa.org*

Gregg Marland is Distinguished Staff Scientist of the Environmental Sciences Division, Oak Ridge National Laboratory, Oak Ridge, TN 37831-6335, USA, *gum@ornl.gov*

Rafael L. Marques is an Economist at Chicago Climate Exchange, Inc., 111 W. Jackson Blvd., Suite 1404, Chicago, IL 60604, USA, *rmarques@chicagoclimateexchange.com*

Patrick Meir is Lecturer in Biogeography at the School of GeoSciences, University of Edinburgh, Edinburgh, EH9 3JG, UK, *pmeir@ed.ac.uk*

Norman Myers is Honorary Visiting Fellow at Green College, University of Oxford, Upper Meadow, Douglas Downes Close, Headington, Oxford, OX3 8NT, UK, *myers1n@aol.com*

Kenneth Newcombe is Senior Manager of Carbon Finance and Fund Manager of the Prototype Carbon Fund, The World Bank, Washington, DC 20433, USA, *knewcombe@worldbank.org*

Eduard Niesten is Economist at Hardner & Gullison Associates, L.L.C., Palo Alto, CA 94302, USA, *eddy@hg-llc.com*

John O. Niles is Project Manager of the Climate and Biodiversity Alliance, 1919 M St, Suite 600, Washington, DC 20036, USA, *jniles@conservation.org*

Dev dutta S. Niyogi is Research Assistant Professor at the Department of Marine, Earth, and Atmospheric Sciences, North Carolina State University, Raleigh, NC 27695-8208, USA, *dev_niyogi@ncsu.edu*

Jacob Olander is Director of EcoDecision Cia. Ltda., Calle La Pinta 236 y Rabida, Quito, Ecuador, *jolander@ecnet.ec*

Gilonne d'Origny is a lawyer at International Alert, 1 Glyn Street, London, SE11 5HT, UK, *gdorigny@international-alert.org*

Annie Petsonk is International Counsel at Environmental Defense, 1875 Connecticut Avenue, NW, Washington, DC, USA, *apetsonk@environmentaldefense.org*

Roger A. Pielke Sr is Professor of Atmospheric Science and President of the American Association of State Climatologists, Department of Atmospheric Science at Colorado State University, Fort Collins, CO 80523, USA, *pielke@atmos.colostate.edu*

Ghillean T. Prance is Visiting Professor at the School of Plant Sciences, University of Reading, Whiteknights, Reading, RG6 6AS, UK, *gtolmiep@aol.com*

Jules N. Pretty is Professor of Environment and Society in the Department of Biological Sciences and Director of the Centre for Environment and Society at the University of Essex, Colchester, CO4 3SQ, UK, *jpretty@essex.ac.uk*

N. H. Ravindranath is a professor at the Centre for ASTRA and Centre for Ecological Sciences Indian Institute of Science, Bangalore, India, *ravi@ces.iisc.ernet.in*

Alan Renwick is Head of the Rural Business Unit, Department of Land Economy, University of Cambridge, Cambridge, CB3 9EP, UK, *awr11@cam.ac.uk*

Steven W. Running is Director of the Numerical Terradynamic Simulation Group, School of Forestry, University of Montana, Missoula, MT 59812, USA, *swr@ntsg.umt.edu*

Richard L. Sandor is Chairman and Chief Executive Officer of Chicago Climate Exchange, Inc., and Research Professor at the Kellogg Graduate School of Management, Northwestern University, USA, *rsandor@chicagoclimateexchange.com*

Lindsay S. Saunders is Development Consultant and Director of Resource Strategies NZ Ltd, St Heliers, Auckland, New Zealand, *l_saunders_sw@compuserve.com*

Reimund Schwarze is Senior Researcher at the German Institute for Economic Research (DIW Berlin) and Head of the Sustainable Development Research Group, Koenigin-Luise-Str. 4, D-14195 Berlin, Germany, *rschwarze@diw.de*

Ian R. Swingland is the Emeritus Professor of Conservation Biology at The Durrell Institute of Conservation and Ecology, and Director of Sustainable Forestry Management Ltd, Herons Hall, Nash, Canterbury, CT3 2JX, UK, *ian@herons-hall.co.uk*

Michael J. Walsh is Senior Vice President of Chicago Climate Exchange, Inc., 111 W. Jackson Blvd., Suite 1404, Chicago, IL 60604, USA, *mwalsh@chicagoclimateexchange.com*

H. W. Whittington was Professor of Electrical Power Engineering in the Department of Electronics and Electrical Engineering at the University of Edinburgh, until his untimely and tragic death on 11 March 2002

Preface

For decades I have watched conservation efforts fail, forests disappear, people dispossessed, deserts created and landscapes devastated all over the globe. During my time at the University of Oxford (where I was classified as an evolutionary ecologist) in the late 1970s and, more particularly, while studying giant tortoises on a desert atoll for two of those years, I began to see that the value of biodiversity, properly governed and reinvested, could not only conserve it but provide sustainable returns to all beneficiaries. The main obstacle to this outcome was that those in power, governments included, lacked the capacity to deliver it and, in most cases, the interest to do so unless it also benefited them personally. So I questioned what delivery system might have a chance of succeeding? Thus my long adventure into the use of market-driven instruments and governance started nearly three decades ago.

Five years ago Robin Hanbury-Tenison, a founder of the worldwide organization supporting tribal peoples, Survival International, and I made a television film for Channel 4 about Gunung Mulu National Park in the heart of Borneo, an area we had been to 20 years earlier on a large Royal Geographical Society expedition. Our return to Mulu and our reunion with one of the local inhabitants, a Penan named Nyapun, convinced us that our worst fears for the rainforest and its people were being realized. Back in London, Robin and I met up with Eric Bettelheim, a close mutual friend and lawyer, and the three of us decided to form a partnership to make a difference to the way things were done. Against the received wisdom of the 'greens', we favoured market mechanisms to change the destructive course on which the world seemed set. The three flexibility mechanisms of the Kyoto Protocol—Joint Implementation, the Clean Development Mechanism and emissions trading—offered the best opportunity.

By October 2001 it was clear that misinformation and misguided political lobbying by a few pressure groups and conservation charities were seriously distorting the debate. Worse, their fixation on a single issue of reducing the use of fossil fuels led them to reject carbon sinks as part of the solution to climate change. This policy threatened to continue the damage to the world's most important habitats. They ignored the wider and negative repercussions on the environment as a whole of their monomania on the issue of fossil fuels.

As proponents of market mechanisms, Eric, Robin, and I realized that the facts about carbon, climate, biodiversity and people needed to be presented in an unbiased way. With the support of The Royal Society, the United Kingdom's academy of science, and joined by Ghillean Prance, John Grace and Lindsay Saunders, we recruited 44 authors from many specialities and professions—academics, conservationists, scientists, economists and lawyers—from around the world to produce a theme issue for the *Philosophical Transactions of The Royal Society*. It was a very productive and pleasurable experience, working with world-class professionals, and I was heartened that the new President of The Royal Society, Lord Robert May, was so supportive, as were Michael Thompson and Cathy Brennan, who first suggested a theme issue. Having relied heavily on email, I have still not had the pleasure of meeting most of the authors.

This Earthscan volume has been updated since the publication of the original work in August 2002 and expanded to include an Introduction which discusses the most recent arguments, especially those concerning carbon sinks. It addresses the current onslaught on the existing, yet far-from-ideal, international agreements by the usual culprits who continue their misguided efforts to remove the better parts of the Kyoto Protocol, and advocate restrictions, bureaucratic regulation and top-down controls which haven't worked over the last 50 years. When we would expect them to be batting for conservation, they seem determined to damage any chance of using the market system to help. Together with all my co-authors I hope that this book will help to persuade policy-makers and opinion formers to pause and think again and to adopt a better course for all of our sakes.

Ian Swingland
March 2003

Acknowledgements

I would like to thank the following without whom this book would not have happened or been done in only four hectic months by email; or who were responsible for stimulating me into thinking it was possible to use markets and business to drive the natural world better than we have so far if we use the right approaches, methods and rules:

George Hughes (formerly Natal Park Board); Hamey Mishra, Tahir Qadri and Bruce Carrad (Asian Development Bank); Naomi Pena (Pew Center on Global Climate Change); Sandra Brown (Winrock International); Peter Frumhoff (Union of Concerned Scientists); Richard Burge (Countryside Alliance); Cathy Brennan, Debbie Vaughn, Phil Hurst and Matthew Llewellin (The Royal Society, London); Eric Bettelheim (Mishcon de Reya); Agi Kiss (The World Bank); John Grace (Edinburgh University); Ghillean Prance (Reading University); Lindsay Saunders (Saunders Consulting); Robin Hanbury-Tenison; and my colleagues at the Institute I founded, The Durrell Institute of Conservation and Ecology.

This book was originally published as an issue of the *Philosophical Transactions of The Royal Society*, Series A, in August 2002, but has been materially changed and updated.

List of acronyms and abbreviations

A&R	afforestation and reforestation
AAU	assigned amount unit
AGO	Australian Greenhouse Office
AIJ	Activities Implemented Jointly
ARD	afforestation, reforestation and deforestation
BP	before present
BP	*formerly* British Petroleum
C	carbon
C	centigrade
CAA	carbon annuity account
CAAA	Clean Air Act Amendments (US)
CAMPFIRE	Communal Areas Management Programme for Indigenous Resources (Zimbabwe)
CBD	Convention on Biological Diversity
CCD	Convention to Combat Desertification
CCX	Chicago Climate Exchange
CDCF	Community Development Carbon Fund (The World Bank)
CDM	Clean Development Mechanism
CER	certified emissions reduction
CH_4	methane
CHP	combined heat and power
CITES	Convention on International Trade in Endangered Species of Wild Fauna and Flora
CO_2	carbon dioxide
COP	Conference of the Parties
CRP	Conservation Reserve Program (US)
CST	Committee on Science and Technology (CCD)
DBH	diameter-at-breast-height
DGGE	denaturing gradient gel electrophoresis
DIC	dissolved inorganic carbon
DNA	deoxyribonucleic acid
DOC	dissolved organic carbon
EIA	environmental-impact assessment
EQIP	Environmental Quality Incentives Program (US)
ERU	emissions-reduction unit
EU	European Union
FAO	Food and Agriculture Organization of the United Nations
FCA	full carbon accounting

FHA	Federal Housing Authority (US)
g	gram
G-7	group of seven leading industrialized nations (Canada, France, Germany, Italy, Japan, UK, US)
GCM	general circulation model
GCP	gross domestic product
GEF	Global Environment Facility
GHG	greenhouse gas
GPP	gross primary production
GNMA	Government National Mortgage Association (US)
Gt	gigatonne
GW	gigawatt
GWP	global-warming potential
ha	hectare
HFC	hydrofluorocarbon
IBRD	International Bank for Reconstruction and Development
IDA	International Development Association
IFAD	International Fund for Agricultural Development
IFC	International Finance Corporation
IPCC	Intergovernmental Panel on Climate Change
IYE	International Year of Ecotourism
J	joule
kW	kilowatt
kyr	kiloyear (1000 years)
IIED	International Institute for Environment and Development
INPE	National Institute for Space Research (Brazil)
IUCN	World Conservation Union
JI	Joint Implementation
LUCF	land-use change and forestry
LULUCF	land use, land-use change and forestry
m	metre
M	million
MDB	multilateral development bank
MEA	multilateral environmental agreement
MMTCE	million metric tonnes of carbon equivalent
Mt	megatonne
Myr	megayear (1 million years)
MW	megawatt
N	nitrogen
NGO	non-governmental organization
N_2O	nitrous oxide
NO_x	nitrogen oxides
NPP	net primary production
NPV	net present value
NRDC	Natural Resources Defense Council (US)
NSW	New South Wales
NTFP	non-timber forest product

nW	nanowatt
O_2	oxygen
OECD	Organisation for Economic Co-operation and Development
OWC	oscillating water column
PA	protected area
PAN	Protected Area Network
PAYG	pay as you go
PCF	Prototype Carbon Fund (The World Bank)
pCO_{2air}	partial pressure of CO_2 in air
pCO_{2sea}	partial pressure of CO_2 in sea
Pg	petagram
PNW	Pacific Northwest
ppb	parts per billion
ppm	parts per million
ppt	parts per trillion
QA/QC	quality assurance and quality control
RCCP	regional climate-change potential
RIL	reduced-impact logging
RMU	removal unit
R/S	root-to-shoot ratio
SBSTA	Subsidiary Body for Scientific and Technological Advice (UNFCCC)
SBSTTA	Subsidiary Body on Scientific, Technical and Technological Advice (CBD)
SF_6	sulphur hexafluoride
SO_2	sulphur dioxide
SOM	soil organic matter
SOP	standard operating procedure
SRC	short rotation coppice
t	tonne
TAPCHAN	tapered channel device
TEPCO	Tokyo Electric Power Company
Tg	teragram
TNC	The Nature Conservancy
TWh	terawatt hour
UK	United Kingdom
UN	United Nations
UNCED	United Nations Conference on Environment and Development (also known as the Earth Summit)
UNCTAD	United Nations Conference on Trade and Development
UNDP	United Nations Development Programme
UNEP	United Nations Environment Programme
UNFCCC	United Nations Framework Convention on Climate Change
UNIDO	United Nations Industrial Development Organization
US	United States
USDA	United States Department of Agriculture
USEPA	United States Environmental Protection Agency

USGS	United States Geological Survey
VA	Veterans Administration (US)
VLC	variable-length contract
WBCSD	World Business Council for Sustainable Development
WSSD	World Summit on Sustainable Development
WTO	World Trade Organization
yr	year
ZT	zero tillage

Introduction

IAN R. SWINGLAND, ERIC C. BETTELHEIM AND JOHN O. NILES

Conventional donation-driven conservation

In order to preserve the rapidly diminishing natural world it previously seemed logical that we should intervene and pay to protect it, and exclude people. Thus the past 50 years have been spent industriously engaged in research, planning, stocking zoos, creating protected areas and removing villages and settlements, disturbing the sustainable balance of hunters with their prey populations of plants and animals (thereby stimulating the invention of poaching), exacerbating poverty and introducing disease where none existed before. All motivated by a donation-driven western culture permeated by the idea that so-called expert and political committees could and should plan what would happen, and draw lines on maps as boundaries between people and the rest of the animal and plant world. Well-meaning it may have been, but disastrous it has proved.

In the past, remedial action has focused on on-site and off-site conservation approaches. The establishment of protected areas has been the primary focus of on-site conservation. Off-site conservation has focused on conservation of, for example, germplasm or certain plants or animals away from their site of origin, in botanical gardens, zoos or gene banks. Until recently, the financing and management of protected areas remained the responsibility of the public sector. However, over the last few decades, severe cutbacks in the availability of public resources have severely undermined the effectiveness of such strategies. This, coupled with ever-increasing pressures on the land and resources held within protected areas, especially in developing countries, has constrained the lasting success of such approaches.

Social equity and financial stability

The manner of how biodiversity can pay for itself through benign systems of sustainable extraction, where people can receive some equitable share by right, not patronage, is addressed in this book. Some projects are moving down this path in a number of countries but much is still to be done. Biodiversity yields many sustainable development benefits yet, paradoxically, human societies continue to undermine this valuable resource base, instigating large-scale biodiversity losses and species extinctions (see Chapter 15). Most worrying, however, is that the situation is deteriorating faster than resources can be mobilized to counteract the destructive processes, hence the commonly expressed view that we are in the midst of a sixth 'mass extinction'.

The disenfranchisement of people and their isolation from their natural habitat through conventional approaches to conservation, i.e. exclusion in the cause of conservation and natural resource planning, not only fuelled resentment and resource fragmentation but also accelerated inevitable failure. The donation-driven 'model' was not sustainable, either economically or environmentally. It relied on the continuing goodwill of donors and the consistency of the charitable bodies' commitment to maintain the funding support for each and every project indefinitely. Withdrawal of such funding, or a change of mind by the donors, inevitably left the people and the wildlife in a worse position than before. Charitable conservation organizations must maintain their overheads (rent, salaries, airfares, etc.) to survive. If whales, for example, stop attracting donations from the public and elsewhere then they shift to, say, great apes, leaving the cetaceans beached. There is no doubt that 'pump-priming' a project for a short period, so it can earn its own living thereafter, is the best use of donations or direct payment, but as a method of maintaining continuity, ecologically or socio-economically, it is a disaster.

Alternative incentive-based mechanisms, governance and communities

Consequently, the conservation sector has been forced to look at alternative methods of biodiversity conservation, and especially methods that can generate viable and desired livelihood or development returns over the long term, while at the same time conserving biodiversity. Given that the root causes of biodiversity loss are linked to increasing populations and poverty on one hand, and high levels of consumption or economic development on the other, finding alternatives is not an easy task. Demanding that people radically change their life-styles or give up their aspirations for a better life is futile. In the face of this enormous challenge, the 1990s spawned a series of innovative approaches, which focus mainly on providing suitable social and economic incentives for conservation. It is now widely recognized that, given the lack of public funding, biodiversity conservation must start to pay for itself, otherwise biodiversity, and perhaps even the human race, are in jeopardy. Hence the growing interest taken in opportunities for biodiversity conservation that might arise from market-driven approaches to sustainable land use and management.

Market-based approaches to environmental management are increasingly important not least because they offer a chance to reconcile humanity's need for development and the biosphere's need for stability. Market mechanisms can encourage environmental protection and promote greater economic efficiency while saving taxpayers money. In the forestry sector, policy-makers are beginning to heed this advice by shrinking command and control systems in favour of incentive mechanisms that seek to align private gain with the public good (see Chapter 16). In some cases, governments are promoting the creation of markets where none existed before. In others, markets are evolving of their own accord. In such times of change, it is difficult to stand back and take stock. Yet, it is during such times that guidance is most needed. In the rush to introduce market-based solutions to environmental problems, a particular concern is how markets impact the poor.

Chapter 14 concentrates on the fact that the United Nations Framework Convention on Climate Change (UNFCCC) focuses on a large ecosystem and does not specifically recognize the need to conserve species, while other treaties do recognize the importance of biodiversity. Species, including *Homo sapiens*, are the building blocks of ecosystems, and they provide a means of capturing market values from ecosystems. Achieving successful conservation globally will require the systems under which species and ecosystems are conserved to be more inclusive than statutory protected areas. Equal emphasis needs to be placed on including effective regimes that also encompass private and communal ownership through incentive-based approaches. If globalized industries, such as nature-based tourism or sustainable use, are to provide meaningful incentives locally, a key requirement is to reduce leakage of revenue earned as a result of conserving species, such that local development concerns are addressed. Current biodiversity conventions that address these needs are largely aspirational, while globalized industries such as tourism mainly promote their green credentials through voluntary codes of conduct. Greatly improved linkages are needed between international conservation concerns and ensuring effective solutions to sustainability, which inevitably rest at national and sub-national levels, through systems of rights, tenure, benefits and incentives.

But what has yet to be worked out in nearly every programme is how there is to be a stable governance system, which works and is satisfactory to the local people, the public sector (i.e. governments and politicians) and the private sector. The question of intellectual property rights, for example, is fraught with concerns that communal knowledge may be hijacked. Private interests and governmental interference also complicates an important area of income to people and conservation. The most critical questions, however, concern real property rights, land ownership and government land use policies.

Carbon-emission trading and social capital

New incentives for protection and on-site use of forests and the services they provide raise hopes for the reversal of tropical and temperate deforestation. Past management of forests appropriated the rights of forest communities, providing incentives to convert natural forest into financial capital through logging, while destroying the underlying physical property. Carbon-emission trading aims to provide a means to convert the forest property into financial capital, while protecting the physical property of forests, providing new incentives for sustainable on-site forest management (see Chapter 10). The potential for carbon-emission trading as a contributor to these new incentives is tempered by often irrational declarations such as that it is another tool for capitalists and neo-colonialists seeking to exploit the developing world.

There are legitimate reasons for concern, as the history of exploitation of indigenous people, the appropriation of their rights, the loss of forests and their benefits is well documented and examined in Chapter 12. This exploitation resulted in the exclusion of forest communities from the basic tenets for development created by the wealth generated by traded property. However, one virtue of trade is that it can be made subject to constraints. Through international treaties and agreements, it can be constrained and national governments and private interests obliged to observe rules. The value of tradable carbon credits will be discounted or invalid if they do not meet these criteria, providing all parties with strong incentives to achieve the performance standards relating to both processes and contracts. For carbon trading to develop social capital from natural capital requires the admission of forest communities into the polity and management of forest resources.

The contributors to this book argue for responsible carbon-emission trading based on the clear and appropriate definition of carbon entitlements, with the proviso that trading respects the rights and needs of local and indigenous people. Emissions trading now seems inevitable and there should be proper rules to control this trade where it affects forests and their inhabitants. It is imperative that the poor and indigenous people are not excluded from these systems. They may benefit greatly provided the trading systems and the property systems they depend on are accountable, transparent and inclusive of those features which we propose.

The development of the Kyoto Protocol and perverse incentives

As with markets for many other goods and services, a carbon market may generate negative environmental externalities (see Chapter 19). Possible interpretations and application of Kyoto Protocol provisions under the sixth and seventh Conference of the Parties (COP-6*bis* and COP-7) to the UNFCCC raise concerns that rules governing forestry with respect to the Kyoto Protocol carbon market may increase pressure on native forests and their biodiversity in developing countries. Two specific concerns with Kyoto provisions for forestry measures are uppermost. First, whether, under the Clean Development Mechanism (CDM), by restricting allowable forestry measures to afforestation and reforestation, and explicitly excluding protection of threatened native forests, the Kyoto Protocol will enhance incentives for degradation and clearing of forests in developing countries. Second, whether carbon crediting for forest management in Annex I (industrialized) regions under Article 3.4 creates a dynamic that can encourage displacement of timber harvests from Annex I countries to developing nations. Given current timber extraction patterns in developing regions, additional harvest pressure would certainly entail a considerable cost in terms of biodiversity loss. In both cases, the concerns about deleterious impacts to forests and biodiversity are justified, although the scale of such impacts is difficult to predict. In order both to ensure reliable progress in managing carbon concentrations and to avoid unintended consequences with respect to forest biodiversity, the further development of the Kyoto carbon market must explicitly correct these perverse incentives.

The history of climate-change negotiations over the last decade provides a vivid illustration of an underlying transformation of the environmental movement from consciousness-raising to practical implementation. This has been the case particularly with respect to the debates on the role that carbon sinks and emissions trading are to play in addressing global warming. Moreover, issues surrounding carbon and biodiversity are inextricably linked, and this connection raises the temperature even further.

Carbon sinks and emissions trading versus ideology

Chapter 1 describes how every year forest gross photosynthesis cycles approximately one-twelfth of the atmospheric stock of carbon dioxide (CO_2), accounting for 50% of terrestrial photosynthesis. This cycling has remained almost constant since the end of the last ice age but, since the Industrial Revolution, has undergone substantial disruption due to the injection of 480 PgC into the atmosphere through fossil-fuel combustion and land-use change, including forest clearance. Tropical deforestation is resulting in a release of 1.7 PgC yr^{-1} into the atmosphere. However, there is also strong evidence for a 'sink' for carbon in natural vegetation (carbon absorption), which can be explained partly by the regrowth of forests on abandoned lands, and partly by a global change factor, the most likely cause being 'fertilization' resulting from the increase in atmospheric CO_2. In the 1990s this biosphere sink was estimated to be sequestering 3.2 PgC yr^{-1} and is likely to have substantial effects on the dynamics, structure and biodiversity of all forests.

Ecological orthodoxy suggests that old-growth forests should be close to dynamic equilibrium (Phillips *et al.* 2002*a*). This view has been challenged by recent findings that show old-growth neotropical forests contribute a substantial carbon sink (*ca.* 0.5 Gt per year) and are accumulating carbon and biomass, possibly in response to the increasing atmospheric concentrations of CO_2 (Phillips *et al.* 2002*b*). However, it is unclear whether the recent increase in tree biomass has been accompanied by a shift in community composition. Such changes could reduce or enhance the carbon storage potential of old growth forests in the long term. A new international research and monitoring network to quantify the carbon balance and forest change in Amazonia has been started (Malhi *et al.* 2002*a*).

An extensive global carbon sequestration programme has the potential to make a particularly significant contribution to controlling the rise in CO_2 emissions in the next few decades. In the course of the century, however, even the maximum amount of carbon that could be sequestered will be dwarfed by the magnitude of (projected) fossil-fuel emissions. Chapter 6 points out that forest carbon sequestration should only be viewed as a component of a mitigation strategy, not as a substitute for changes in energy supply, use and technology that will be required if atmospheric CO_2 concentrations are to be stabilized.

It is fair to say that those debates over carbon sinks and emissions trading have generated more heat than light and been based more on ideology than sound science. The controversy is based primarily on two arguments: sinks may allow developed nations to delay or avoid actions to reduce fossil-fuel emissions; and the technical and operational difficulties are too threatening to the successful implementation of land-use and forestry projects for providing carbon offsets.

This book discusses the importance of including carbon sinks in efforts to address global warming and the consequent social, environmental and economic benefits to host countries. Activities highlighted in Chapter 2 in tropical forestlands provide the lowest cost methods for reducing emissions and reducing atmospheric concentrations of greenhouse gases (GHGs). A major concern about land use, land-use change and forestry (LULUCF) projects under the CDM is the potential for leakage. Leakage refers to a net increase of GHG emissions in an area outside the project resulting from the CDM activity. Chapter 8 provides an overview of leakage, its definitions and its causes. It describes ways in which LULUCF projects may suffer from leakage and attempts to assess the magnitude of leakage risks for different LULUCF project types. It also summarizes some of the approaches, both in terms of policies and project development, to address LULUCF leakage.

Steps could be taken by climate policy-makers to ensure that conservation and restoration of biodiversity-rich natural forests in developing countries are rewarded rather than penalized. To correct incentives to clear natural forests through CDM crediting for afforestation and reforestation, for the first commitment period policy-makers should establish an early base year, such as 1990, such that lands cleared after that year would be ineligible for crediting. Some have argued that such a restriction should apply to all LULUCF projects in the CDM (Schulze *et al.* 2003). Such arguments fail to take full account of the costs of overly inflexible policies. For biodiversity and local communities to truly benefit, Chapter 19 argues that exceptions should be made for CDM projects that are explicitly designed to promote natural forest restoration and that pass rigorous environmental impact review. Restoration efforts are typically most effective on lands that are adjacent to standing forests and hence likely to have been recently cleared. For these projects, establishing a more recent base year, such as 2000, would be preferable.

For the second and subsequent commitment periods, climate policy-makers should act to restrain inter-annex leakage and its impacts by ensuring that crediting for forest management in industrialized countries is informed by modelling efforts to anticipate the scale of leakage associated with different Annex I LULUCF policy options, and coupled with incentives to protect and restore natural forests in developing countries (see Chapter 9). The latter should include expanding the options permitted under the CDM to carbon crediting for projects that protect threatened forests from deforestation and forest degradation. Ultimately, carbon market incentives for forest clearing can be reduced and incentives for forest conservation most effectively strengthened by fully capturing carbon emissions associated with deforestation and forest degradation in developing countries under a future emissions cap.

The current asymmetry in treatment of forests favours the rich against the poor and monoculture over biodiversity.

Kyoto, carbon accounting and conservation

The major international treaties to address ecosystem protection lack meaningful binding obligations and the financial instruments to affect large-scale conservation (see Chapter 18). The Kyoto Protocol's emissions-trading framework creates economic incentives for nations to reduce GHG emissions cost-effectively. Incorporating GHG impacts from land-use activities into this system would create a market for an important ecosystem service provided by forests and agricultural lands: sequestration of atmospheric carbon. This would spur conservation efforts while reducing the 20% of anthropogenic CO_2 emissions produced by land-use change, particularly tropical deforestation. The Kyoto negotiations surrounding land-use activities have been hampered by a lack of robust carbon inventory data. Moreover, the Protocol's provisions make it difficult to incorporate carbon-sequestering land-use activities into the emissions-trading framework without undermining the atmospheric GHG reductions contemplated in the treaty. Subsequent negotiations since 1997 failed to produce a crediting system that provides meaningful incentives for enhanced carbon sequestration. Notably, credit for reducing rates of tropical deforestation was explicitly excluded from the Protocol. Ultimately, an effective GHG emissions-trading framework will require full carbon accounting for all emissions and sequestration from terrestrial ecosystems. Improved inventory systems and capacity building for developing nations will, therefore, be necessary.

Carbon pools that are based on field measurements should be incorporated into the calculation of carbon benefits (see Chapter 7). This system allows for trade-offs between expected carbon benefits, costs and desired precision, while maintaining the integrity of the net carbon benefits. Techniques and methods for accurately and precisely measuring individual carbon pools in forestry projects exist, are based on peer-reviewed principles of forest inventory, soil sampling and ecological surveys, and have been well tested in many parts of the world. Experience with many forestry projects in tropical countries has shown that with the use of these techniques carbon stocks can readily be estimated to be within less than $\pm10\%$ of the mean. The various objections raised as to the inclusion of carbon sinks to ameliorate climate change can be addressed by existing techniques and technology. Carbon sinks provide a practical available method of achieving meaningful reductions in atmospheric concentrations of CO_2 and at the same time contribute to national sustainable development goals.

Compromises

The controversy over the issues of carbon sinks and emissions trading nearly aborted the Kyoto Protocol (see Chapter 17). The lengthy and intense debate over the roles that each is to play under the Protocol and the consequent political compromises have resulted in a complex set of provisions and an arcane nomenclature. The distinction drawn between the uses of carbon sinks in developed countries under Joint Implementation (JI) and their use in developing countries under the CDM is a particular source of intricacy. It is at least arguable that key elements of the compromises reached at COP-6 and COP-7 in this regard are inconsistent with the terms of the Protocol and are *ultra vires* the UNFCCC. This is a source of both uncertainty and potential legal challenge.

Not only do the recent decisions create needless complexity, they also clearly discriminate against developing nations. Among the recent political compromises is the creation of a third type of non-bankable but tradeable unit with respect to forest management, which is only available to Annex I countries. The result is an anomalous one in which a variety of otherwise equivalent carbon credits can be generated under three different regimes including the CDM which is subject to an elaborate regulatory overlay that discriminates against carbon sequestration by developing countries. For example, complying developed countries can essentially self-certify sequestration projects. In contrast, projects in developing countries must obtain prior approval from a subsidiary body, the CDM Executive Board, mandated to require detailed information and impose substantive and procedural hurdles not required or imposed by its companion body, the Article 6 Supervisory Committee on Joint Implementation Projects.

The parallel and related debate over the third 'flexibility' mechanism, emissions trading, compounded the complexity of an already asymmetric and bifurcated system. The new requirements devoted to 'environmental integrity' not only have raised the costs of compliance of developing country projects but also virtually ignore the fundamental principle of sustainable economic growth and development embodied in the Convention and related international agreements. The regulations for carbon sinks now being formulated at Conferences of the Parties will have a significant impact on their use worldwide. Of key importance, in addition to their successful integration of carbon sinks and emissions trading into other international treaties, is the development of practically achievable and objective standards and an efficient and transparent approval process consistent with the terms of the Convention and the Protocol. Most important of all is a rebalancing that restores the primacy of addressing climate change in the context of sustainable economic growth and development.

Markets

The convergence of environmental and financial markets discussed in Chapter 3, and the evolution of market-based environmental programmes, is an example of the evolutionary process witnessed in a variety of markets, and summarizes the emergence of GHG mitigation markets and their potential role in advancing land stewardship, biodiversity and other environmental services. Emissions trading has been developed to meet the demand to reduce pollution while avoiding economic disruption. Consistent with the pattern of market evolution, the US programme to reduce the damage from acid rain established a standardized environmental commodity, developed 'evidence of ownership' necessary for financial instruments and provided the infrastructure to efficiently transfer title. The success of the system in reducing pollution at low cost has provided a model for other market-based environmental protection initiatives.

The demand for cost-effective action to reduce the threat of climate change has initiated the same evolutionary process for markets to reduce GHG emissions. Many of the land- and forest-management practices that can capture and store atmospheric CO_2 can also provide other environmental benefits, such as biodiversity preservation and enhanced water quality. The presence of a carbon-trading market will introduce a clear financial value for capture and mitigation of CO_2 emissions, thus introducing a new source of funding for land stewardship and forest rehabilitation. The market is now emerging through a variety of 'bottom-up' developments being undertaken through governmental, multilateral, private sector and non-governmental organization (NGO) initiatives. The extension of markets to other emerging environmental issues is now underway, and the linkages between environmental sustainability and capital markets are being more deeply understood (see Chapter 20). Early evidence indicates that environmental sustainability can be compatible with maximization of shareholder and stakeholder value.

Developing countries and their 'goldmine'(?)

The many opportunities for mitigating atmospheric carbon emissions in developing countries include reforesting degraded lands, implementing sustainable agricultural practices on existing lands and slowing tropical deforestation. Analysis in Chapter 4 shows that over the next 10 years, 48 major tropical and subtropical developing countries have the potential to reduce the atmospheric carbon burden by about 2.3 billion tonnes of carbon. Given a central price of US$10 per tonne of carbon and a discount rate of 3%, this mitigation would generate a net present value of about US$16.8 billion collectively for these countries. Achieving these potentials would require a significant global effort, covering more than 50 million hectares of land, to implement carbon-friendly practices in agriculture, forest and previously forested lands. Chapter 11 reviews 40 sustainable agriculture and renewable-resource-management projects in China and India under the three mechanisms estimated a carbon mitigation potential of 64.8 MtC yr^{-1} from 5.5 Mha. The potential income for carbon mitigation is US$324 million at US$5 per tonne of carbon. The potential exists to increase this by orders of magnitude, and so contribute significantly to GHG abatement. Most agricultural mitigation options also provide several ancillary benefits.

These estimates of host-country income potentials take no account of the additional benefits of carbon sequestration in forest soils undergoing reforestation, increased use of biomass and reduced use of fossil-fuel inputs and reduced agricultural emissions. In all events, realizing these incomes would necessitate substantially greater policy support and investment in sustainable land uses than is currently the case.

Ethical carbon funds

The World Bank initiated the Prototype Carbon Fund (PCF) in April 2000 to help spur the development of a global carbon market and to 'learn by doing' how to use carbon-purchase transactions across a range of energy-sector technologies (and some forestry applications) to achieve environmentally credible and cost-effective emissions reductions that benefit developing countries and economies in transition (see Chapter 5). Building on the success of the PCF (US$145 million raised from public and private sector investors), The World Bank launched the Community Development Carbon Fund (CDCF) at the World Summit on Sustainable Development (WSSD) in Johannesburg, South Africa, in September 2002. The CDCF seeks to provide carbon finance to small-scale energy and biocarbon projects in the least developed countries. In November 2002, The World Bank launched the BioCarbon Fund, a public-private partnership (target size US$100 million) providing an opportunity for farmers and rural communities in the developing world to find new value in their agricultural lands and forests as they earn income from sequestering or conserving carbon. Whereas the PCF deals mainly with energy related projects, the BioCarbon Fund will focus on sink-related projects. These funds will target synergies between carbon markets and objectives such as biodiversity conservation, combating desertification and small-scale community-driven development.

Experience from the PCF shows that developing countries can have a comparative advantage in supplying this global market, as emissions reductions can be achieved in developing countries in the range of US$3–US$5 per ton of CO_2 equivalent, compared with a marginal abatement cost of US$10–US$15 per ton of CO_2 equivalent in most countries within the Organisation for Economic Co-operation and Development (OECD). However, realizing this economic potential over the next decade, and targeting the market to the rural poor, will require substantial assistance with project development and government legal and institutional capacity building. Specific needs include raising awareness of the potential of carbon markets at all levels (particularly in energy and land-use sectors), clarifying property rights, particularly in the case of communally held land and resources, ensuring the existence of an attractive investment climate, eliminating policies that create perverse incentives and constraints, and mitigating logistical, political and 'reputational' risks that could deter private-sector investors. It will also be necessary to find ways to reconcile the short-term needs of the rural poor and the typically long-term revenue stream associated with carbon sequestration.

Politics versus success

It is also time for a dispassionate review of where the political process has led us thus far and time to provide the scientific basis for action. The great achievement of those who pioneered the UNFCCC and its companion treaties the Montreal Protocol on Substances that Deplete the Ozone Layer, the Convention on Biological Diversity (CBD), the Convention to Combat Desertification (CCD) and the Convention on Wetlands of International Importance (known as the Ramsar Convention), was to have both alerted the world's politicians and the general public to the need to address these issues and to do so by way of international cooperation. Their greatest weakness, however, was a failure to distinguish between the arguably necessary rhetoric and realistic methods of implementation. Exaggeration of the available scientific evidence, commonly disguised by invocation of the precautionary principle, disregard of the economic and human costs involved in radical change, and distrust of markets and the private sector, often combined either to frustrate their goals or to lead to unintended and sometimes perverse consequences. The WSSD in 2002 publicly acknowledged the failure of governments to deliver and the need for partnership with the private sector, but we must go further and abandon the thought processes of the past that led to that failure.

As the contributions to this book make clear, the issues of carbon sequestration and emissions trading present all of these elements. The case made here for the maximum use of terrestrial carbon sinks, particularly in the developing world, is overwhelming. The benefits of such a strategy to the rural poor, indigenous people, habitat preservation, biodiversity, watershed protection and the climate as a whole is revealed here in persuasive detail. That such a strategy is also, particularly when combined with emissions trading, the lowest-cost approach makes it hard to understand why some environmentalists and policy-makers involved in the negotiations have chosen to do their utmost to prevent it. A sober reassessment of what they have wrought so far is clearly called for. The ultimate goal, in the context of climate change as elsewhere, must be the adoption of those strategies and techniques that will result in genuinely sustainable economic growth and development; in other words, an approach that successfully combines humankind's need for human development and a need for a healthy environment that conserves biodiversity in perpetuity.

The signing of the UNFCCC in 1992 marked not only the foundation of the world's concern with climate change, it also marked its abandonment of command and control as methods of human organization. The human as well as the economic costs of central planning were demonstrated beyond doubt to be too high to be sustained by any society for very long. The year 2002 was supposed to be the year when the same lesson was to be learnt and taken to heart by those concerned with the environment. Neither humankind nor the natural environment for which it is responsible can afford further such experiments. Unless the enormous value of the biosphere and the services it provides can be made tangible to all through free markets and prices, we are all too likely to continue to squander them. What everyone owns, no one owns; and no one conserves it.

In this book, world leaders in their disciplines set out comprehensively and eloquently the right way forward, both in respect to climate change and the other key indicators of a healthy planet.

References

Malhi, Y. (and 25 others) 2002 An international network to monitor the structure, composition and dynamics of Amazonian forests (RAINFOR). *J. Vegetat. Sci.* **13**, 439–450.

Phillips, O. L. (and 17 others) 2002*a* Increasing dominance of large lianas in Amazonian forests. *Nature* **418**, 770–774.

Phillips, O. L. (and 13 others) 2002*b* Changes in growth of tropical forests: evaluating potential biases. *Ecologic. Applic.* **12**, 576–587.

Schulze, E.-D., Mollicone, D., Achard, F., Matteucci, G., Federici, S., Eva, H. D. & Valentini, R. 2003 Climate change: making deforestation pay under the Kyoto Protocol? *Science* **299**, 1669.

Part 1

CARBON AND CLIMATE CHANGE

Chapter 1

Forests, carbon and global climate

Yadvinder Malhi, Patrick Meir and Sandra Brown

Introduction

In recent centuries, human activities have fundamentally altered many of the Earth's biogeochemical cycles. Among the first recognized and most prominent of these changes has been the modification of the global carbon cycle. The dramatic release of carbon trapped by both prehistoric ecosystems (i.e. fossil fuels) and modern-day vegetation has led to a 31% increase in concentrations of atmospheric carbon dioxide (CO_2) from a preindustrial concentration of $ca.$ 280 ppm to 368 ppm in 2000. This concentration has certainly not been exceeded during the past 420 000 years, and probably not during the past 20 million years. Moreover, *the rate of increase* in CO_2 concentration during the past century is at least an order of magnitude greater than the world has seen for the last 20 kyr (Prentice *et al.* 2001). CO_2 is the most important of the greenhouse gases that are increasingly trapping solar heat and warming the global climate. In addition to climatic warming, this extra CO_2 may have a number of effects on terrestrial ecosystems, from increasing plant growth rates and biomass to modifying ecosystem composition by altering the competitive balance between species.

The focus of this chapter will be on the role of forests and forest management in this global carbon cycle. In their pre-agricultural state, forests are estimated to have covered $ca.$ 57 million km^2 (Goldewijk 2001), and contained $ca.$ 500 PgC (1 PgC = 1 GtC = 10^{15} g of carbon) in living biomass and a further 700 PgC in soil organic matter (Figure 1.3), in total holding more than twice the total amount of carbon in the preindustrial atmosphere and circulating 10% of atmospheric CO_2 back and forth into the biosphere every year through gross photosynthesis. A reduction of global forest cover has accompanied human history since the dawn of the agricultural revolution 8000 years ago, but by 1700 only $ca.$ 7% of global forest area had been lost (Ramankutty & Foley 1999; Goldewijk 2001). The intensity and scale of human alteration of the biosphere has accelerated since the industrial revolution, and by 1990 $ca.$ 20–30% of original forest area had been lost. This loss of forest cover has contributed 45% of the increase in atmospheric CO_2 observed since 1850. In recent decades, carbon emissions from fossil fuels have surpassed those from deforestation, but land-use change still contributes *ca.* 25% of current human-induced carbon emissions. However, just as the loss of forests has significantly contributed to the atmospheric 'carbon disruption', so good forest management, the prevention of deforestation, and the regrowth of forests have a significant potential to lessen the carbon disruption.

In this review we place into context the role of forests in the global carbon cycle and climate change. In the first section we examine the preindustrial 'natural' carbon cycle, both in recent millennia and during the ice ages. We then review the anthropogenic 'carbon disruption', examining the influences of both land-use change and fossil-fuel combustion on the global carbon cycle, and the causes, magnitudes and uncertainties of the natural 'carbon sinks' in both oceans and terrestrial ecosystems. Finally, we peer into the future and examine the influence that forest management and protection can play on the climate of the 21st century.

The natural global carbon cycle

The global carbon cycle before the industrial carbon disruption

As our planet emerged from the last glacial maximum 11 000 years ago, the climate first warmed and became wetter, but subsequently underwent a slight cooling and aridification 8000 years before present (BP). Human populations and activities increased substantially during this epoch, the Holocene, but, until the Industrial Revolution, atmospheric CO_2 concentration varied only a little, increasing overall from a post-glacial minimum of 260–285 ppm in the late 19th century (Figure 1.2).

The relative constancy in CO_2 concentrations during the previous few millennia implies a rough constancy in the global carbon cycle. Figure 1.1 identifies the main global stocks of carbon and the principal fluxes among them for the natural or 'pre-carbon disruption' era. There are four main carbon stores, which are, in decreasing order of size, the geological, the oceanic, the terrestrial and the atmospheric reservoirs. Although the smallest component, it is changes in the atmospheric carbon store that ultimately provide the direct link between changes in the global carbon cycle and changes in climate.

The thick arrows in Figure 1.1 denote the most important fluxes from the point of view of the contemporary CO_2 balance of the atmosphere: they represent gross primary production (i.e. absorption of carbon from the atmosphere through photosynthesis) and respiration (release of carbon to the atmosphere) by the land surface, and physical sea–air exchange. Under 'natural' conditions these two main carbon transfer pathways between the atmosphere and the land or the oceans are in approximate balance over an annual cycle, and represent a total exchange of 210 PgC yr^{-1}, of which the larger share (120 PgC yr^{-1}) is taken by the land (Prentice *et al.* 2001). This annual exchange is more than 25 times the total amount of carbon annually released into the atmosphere through human activities. Forests are responsible for about half of total terrestrial photosynthesis, and hence for *ca.* 60 PgC yr^{-1}. The processes governing this exchange are biological and physical, and hence

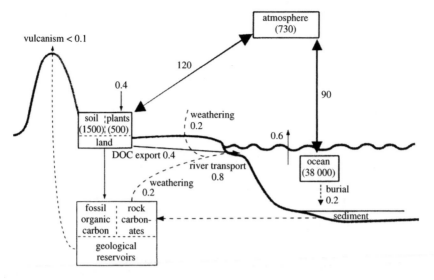

Figure 1.1. Main components of the carbon cycle. The thick arrows represent gross primary production and respiration by the biosphere and physical sea–air exchange. The thin arrows denote natural fluxes which are important over longer time-scales. Dashed lines represent fluxes of carbon as calcium carbonate. The units for all fluxes are PgC yr^{-1}; the units for all compartments are PgC.

are responsive to climate. Consequently, a fractional net change in them resulting from small changes in climate (e.g. temperature) could match the magnitude of the human-linked emissions causing them.

A number of additional fluxes also occur as part of the natural carbon cycle (Figure 1.1). The transfer by plants of 0.4 PgC yr^{-1} of inert carbon from the atmosphere to the soil is balanced by the outflow of dissolved organic carbon (DOC) through rivers to the sea (Schlesinger 1990). This outflow is joined by a flux of 0.4 PgC yr^{-1} of dissolved inorganic carbon (DIC) derived from the weathering of rock carbonates, which combine with atmospheric CO_2 to form DIC. In total, 0.8 PgC yr^{-1} flow through rivers to the sea, where all of the DOC and half of the DIC are ultimately respired to the atmosphere. This leaves 0.2 PgC yr^{-1} to be deposited in deep-sea sediments as fixed carbonates, the remains of dead marine organisms. These deposits are the precursors of carbonate rocks. Over still longer time-scales, organic matter is buried as fossil organic matter (including fossil fuels), and CO_2 is released into the atmosphere as a result of tectonic activity, such as vulcanism (Williams *et al.* 1992; Bickle 1994). These longer time-scale processes exert an important influence on atmospheric CO_2 concentrations on geological time-scales (millions of years), but have had little influence at the time-scale corresponding to human expansion (100 000 years).

Changes in atmospheric CO_2 *over long and short time-scales*

The description of the carbon cycle in Figure 1.1 is most relevant to the relatively constant climate of the Late Holocene, but atmospheric CO_2 concentra-

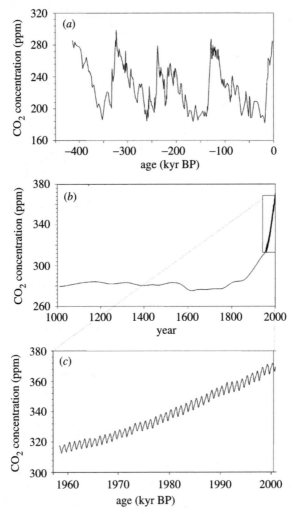

Figure 1.2. Variation in atmospheric CO_2 concentration on different time-scales. (a) CO_2 concentrations during glacial–interglacial transitions, obtained from measurements of CO_2 in deep-ice bubbles, from the Vostok Antarctic ice core (Petit *et al.* 1999; Fischer *et al.* 1999). (b) CO_2 concentrations during the last millennium, obtained from ice-cores at the Law Dome, Antarctica (Etheridge *et al.* 1996). (c) Direct measurements of CO_2 concentration in the Northern and Southern Hemispheres (Keeling & Whorf 2000).

tions have not always been so stable (Figure 1.2). Very high concentrations of over 3000 ppm probably existed during at least two very early periods, 400 and 200 Myr BP (Berner 1997). As photosynthetic machinery evolved and became globally dominant, CO_2 was drawn out of the atmosphere and there is geochemical evidence pointing to concentrations of less than 300 ppm by *ca.* 20 million years BP (Pagani *et al.* 1999; Pearson & Palmer 1999, 2000). It is likely, therefore, that atmospheric CO_2 concentrations in the current century are significantly higher than at any time during the last 20 million years.

On more recent time-scales measurements of the constituents of deep-ice bubbles in the Antarctic have provided information on glacial–interglacial transitions. The high-quality measurements of the CO_2 record from the Vostock ice core give us clear-sighted vision of the past four glacial cycles, over a period of 420 kyr (Petit *et al.* 1999: Fischer *et al.* 1999). The results show atmospheric CO_2 concentrations varied between 180 and 300 ppm, with lower values during glacial epochs (Figure 1.2*a*). It is likely that more C is stored on land during interglacials, and the observed higher atmospheric CO_2 during these periods must be accounted for by oceanic processes of C release. Overall, planetary orbital variations are clearly the pacemaker of such multi-millennial changes in climate, but coincidental changes in CO_2 concentration have played a key role in locking-in these 100 kyr cycles by amplifying their effects, rather than by initiating them (Lorius & Oeschger 1994; Shackleton 2000).

The terrestrial carbon cycle

The storage of carbon on land is partitioned between soil and vegetation. Globally, soils contain more than 75% of all terrestrial carbon stocks, although their contribution to the total varies with latitude and land use (Figure 1.3*a*). Forests and wooded grasslands/savannahs are by far the biggest carbon storehouses, respectively accounting for *ca.* 47% and 25% of the global total. Other ecosystems tend to maintain comparatively little aboveground carbon, with the stock in soil varying between 100 and 225 PgC (Figure 1.3*b*).

In forested ecosystems, carbon accumulates through the absorption of atmospheric CO_2 and its assimilation into biomass. Carbon is stored in various pools in a forest ecosystem: above- and below-ground living biomass, including standing timber, branches, foliage and roots; and necromass, including litter, woody debris, soil organic matter and forest products. Approximately 50% of the dry biomass of trees is carbon. Any activity that affects the amount of biomass in vegetation and soil has the potential to sequester carbon from, or release carbon into, the atmosphere. In total, boreal forests account for more carbon than any other terrestrial ecosystem (26%), while tropical and temperate forests account for 20% and 7%, respectively (Dixon *et al.* 1994; Prentice *et al.* 2001). There are, however, considerable variations among forest types in where carbon accumulates. Up to 90% of the carbon in boreal ecosystems is stored in soil, while in tropical forests the total is split fairly evenly above and below ground. The primary reason for this difference is temperature, which at high latitudes restricts soil-organic-matter decomposition and nutrient recycling, but at low latitudes encourages rapid decomposition and subsequent recycling of nutrients. In wetlands carbon in plant biomass is also a small proportion of the total carbon present: slow decomposition rates in water-laden soils (e.g. peaty soils) has led to a high carbon density in these environments (Figure 1.3*b*).

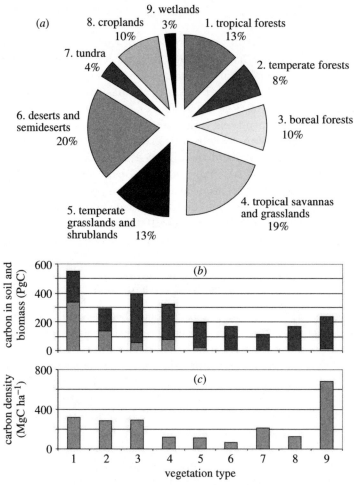

Figure 1.3. Global area and carbon content of different vegetation types. (*a*) The area of each vegetation type as a percentage of the global total (13.73×10^9 ha). The legend in panel (*a*) is used in (*b*) and (*c*): (*b*) total carbon (PgC) in soil (dark shading) and vegetation (light shading); (*c*) total carbon density (MgC ha^{-1}). Data from Roy *et al.* (2001) and Dixon *et al.* (1994).

Between 30 and 50% of the total amount of carbon absorbed by vegetation (gross primary production (GPP)) is used to support plant metabolic processes and is released back to the atmosphere as a by-product of respiration (Amthor & Baldocchi 2001). The remaining carbon is fixed as organic matter above or below the ground and is termed net primary production (NPP). Vegetation types vary in their NPP according to climate, soil type and species composition. Although broadleaf temperate forests are highly productive for part of the year, seasonality constrains their NPP, and this is effect is felt more strongly at higher latitudes.

Clearly, carbon is processed at different rates through different vegetation types. This value, expressed as the average residence time for assimilated car-

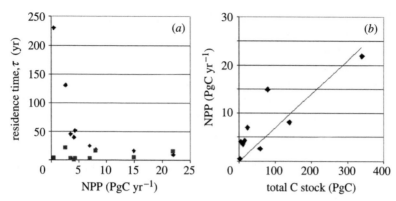

Figure 1.4. The relationships between (*a*) net primary productivity (NPP, PgC yr^{-1}) and the residence time for carbon in soil (diamonds) and biomass (squares), and (*b*) between NPP and total (soil plus biomass) carbon stock. The vegetation types are those used in Figure 1.3. Data from Roy *et al.* (2001) and Dixon *et al.* (1994); the relationship in the right-hand panel is significant (NPP = 0.07 C stock, $r^2 = 0.6$, $P < 0.05$).

bon (τ, in years), can be estimated by dividing the total stock by the NPP. The result is different for soil and vegetation (Figure 1.4*a*). With plant biomass, there is no strong relationship between NPP and τ, with τ ranging in non-crops between 3 and 22 years. However, there is a strong relationship between NPP and τ for soil: in tropical forests, where NPP is high, carbon residence time in soil is relatively short (*ca.* 10 years), while in colder environments, where NPP can be an order of magnitude lower, residence times are much longer (*ca.* 2–300 years). If we focus on plant biomass alone, the sink capacity of different types of vegetation is proportional to the product of their NPP and residence time, which turns out to be proportional to the existing biomass carbon stock. Figure 1.4*b* shows there is also a linear relationship between NPP and the carbon stock in plant biomass, a consequence of residence times in biomass being approximately constant across woody ecosystems.

The 'carbon disruption' and the Anthropocene

In the previous section we described the quasi-equilibrium state of the global carbon cycle that prevailed throughout the Holocene, and for most of human history. In recent centuries, however, human economic activity and population have accelerated enormously. Although these activities had profound local environmental effects, such as large-scale urban and industrial pollution, until recently the Earth as a whole appeared to be a vast resource of raw materials and sink for waste products. This perspective began to change in the late 20th century. One of the most important agents contributing to this change of perspective was the appearance of a measurement that served as a quantifiable index that humans were altering the Earth's fundamental biogeochemical cycles at a global scale. This index was the concentration of CO_2 in the atmosphere as measured at Mauna Loa in Hawaii since 1958, and is illustrated in Figure 1.2*c*.

The data show that atmospheric CO_2 concentrations have risen inexorably, with some seasonal and interannual variations. They indicate that the quasi-equilibrium Holocene state of the global carbon cycle, one of the most fundamental of the great global cycles, is being disrupted. This 'carbon disruption' was one of the first signals that biogeochemical cycles were being disrupted at a global scale, and subsequently evidence has emerged of similar disruption to other biogeochemical cycles. For example, the release of SO_2 to the atmosphere by coal and oil burning, globally *ca.* 160 Tg yr^{-1}, is at least twice as large as the sum of all natural emissions; more nitrogen is now fixed synthetically and applied as fertilizers in agriculture than is fixed naturally in all terrestrial ecosystems (Vitousek *et al.* 1997); and mechanized fishing removes more than 25% of the primary production of the oceans in the upwelling regions and 35% in the temperate continental-shelf regions (Pauly & Christensen 1995).

Such large-scale disruption has led to the suggestion that the modern era could be thought of as a new geological era, the Anthropocene (Crutzen 2002), with a proposed starting date in the late 18th century, coinciding with James Watt's invention of the steam engine in 1784. This represents a fundamental change of viewpoint, and a recognition that human activities and the functioning of the Earth system are now intimately entwined.

In this section we review the history and nature of the 'carbon disruption' that has been a herald of the Anthropocene. Although the rise in CO_2 may have a direct effect on terrestrial ecosystems, the most well-known effect is its potential to be the major gas driving greenhouse warming. Before examining these effects we will review the history and magnitude of emissions.

Fossil-fuel combustion

Figure 1.5 shows the annual rate of CO_2 emissions through fossil-fuel combustion and cement production since 1750, divided between regions (Marland *et al.* 2001). By 1998, a total of 270 Pg of carbon had been emitted by these processes. Europe (including Russia) was responsible for 41% of this total, and North America for a further 31%, figures that point clearly to where the greatest burden of responsibility lies for initiating a solution to this problem. More recently, emissions from the East Asian industrial region have increased rapidly, and currently Europe, North America and East Asia each account for 25% of global fossil-fuel emissions. In terms of process, coal combustion has accounted for 51.2% of global emissions, oil for 34.4%, gas for 11.3% and cement production 1.9% of total emissions. Recently, oil and gas have risen in prominence, and the current (1998) partition of emissions is coal 35.7%, oil 42.0%, gas 18.5% and cement production 3.1%.

Fossil-fuel combustion represents the return to the atmosphere of carbon that was originally trapped by the biosphere and then transferred to geological reservoirs, effectively being removed from the fast carbon cycle. The other principal source of carbon in the modern carbon disruption has been the direct transfer of carbon from the biosphere to the atmosphere, principally through the conversion of forests into croplands and pasture. This is a process

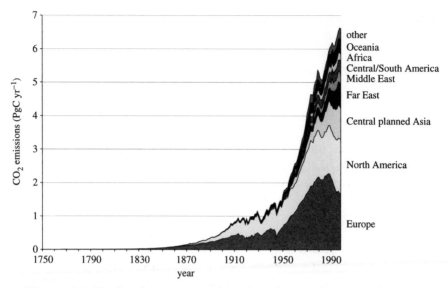

Figure 1.5. Total carbon emissions from fossil-fuel combustion and cement
production since 1750, divided by region. Data from Marland (2001).

older than human civilization, but the rate of change has accelerated rapidly
in recent centuries.

Land-use change

Since the discovery of fire management, most human societies have relied on
modifications of natural landscapes with consequent changes in the carbon
storage densities of forests, savannahs and grasslands (Perlin 1989). In particular, most temperate forests of Europe and China, and the monsoon and dry
forests of India, have been progressively cleared with the spread of pasture
and cropland since 7000 yr BP (Williams 1990) and only a fraction of the
original forest area survived into the industrial era. Long-term clearance of
tropical rain forests was much less, with notable localized exceptions such as
the areas occupied by Mayan civilization in the Americas (Whitmore *et al.*
1990) and the Khmer civilization in Cambodia.

Goldewijk (2001) built a spatially explicit historical database of potential
vegetation cover and historical land use to estimate the areas of natural vegetation cover lost to cropland and pasture (see Table 1.1). By 1700, forest cover
had declined by *ca.* 7%, with similar losses in steppes and shrublands. Since
the industrial revolution and the era of European global colonization these
processes have accelerated sharply, and by 1990 forest area had declined by
30%, steppes/savannahs/grasslands by 50%, and shrublands by 75%.

These figures only cover total conversion to pasture and cropland, and do
not include the degradation of apparently intact natural ecosystems, which
has also led to a substantial release of carbon. DeFries (1999) compared current and potential vegetation maps with land-use-change data from Houghton
(1999) to estimate that agricultural expansion prior to 1850 resulted in the

Table 1.1. *Areal extent of natural and anthropogenic ecosystems at various periods of history, with percentage declines relative to pre-agricultural areal extent*

	Undisturbed area	1700 area	1700 % change	1850 area	1850 % change	1990 area	1990 % change
forest/woodland	58.6	54.4	−7.17	50.00	−14.68	41.50	−29.18
steppe/savanna/ grassland	34.3	32.1	−6.41	28.70	−16.33	17.50	−48.98
shrubland	9.8	8.7	−11.22	6.80	−30.61	2.50	−74.49
tundra/desert	31.4	31.1	−0.96	30.40	−3.18	26.90	−14.33
cropland	0	2.7		5.40		14.70	
pasture	0	5.2		12.80		31.00	

Note: All areas shown $\times 10^6$ km^2.

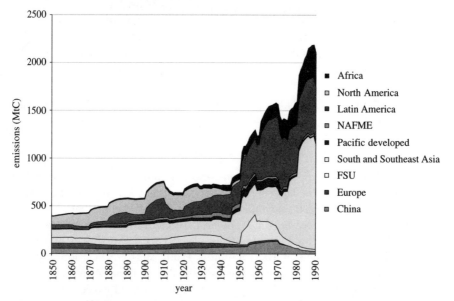

Figure 1.6. Estimated net carbon emissions from land-use change, divided by region. Data from Houghton (1999) and R. A. Houghton (2002, personal communication). The key follows the vertical distribution of shading in the figure.

loss of 48–57 PgC, compared with 124 PgC from land-use change since 1850 (see below).

Figure 1.6 shows the net carbon emissions since 1850 caused by land-use change, as estimated by Houghton (1999; R. A. Houghton 2002, personal communication). Because deforestation, logging and regrowth are more difficult to monitor than industrial activity, and the net carbon emissions from deforestation more difficult to quantify, there is greater uncertainty in this figure than in Figure 1.5. Houghton estimates that a total of 124 GtC was emitted between 1850 and 1990. There are remarkable variations over time. In particular, temperate deforestation rates have slowed greatly and there has even been

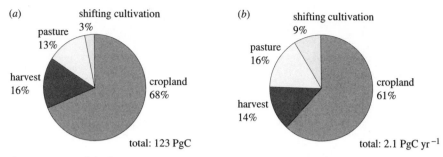

Figure 1.7. (*a*) Estimated total net carbon emissions from land-use change, 1850–1990. (*b*) Estimated annual emissions from land-use change in 1990. Data from Houghton (1999) and R. A. Houghton (2002, personal communication).

a recent net expansion of forest cover in North America and Europe, whereas deforestation in the tropics has surged since the 1950s, which accounts for almost all current emissions. Different regions have surged at different times in response to political priorities: for example, sub-tropical Latin America in the 1900s, the Soviet Union in the 1950s and 1960s, the tropical Americas in the 1960s and 1980s, and tropical Asia in the 1980s.

The division of land-use change between various processes is illustrated in Figure 1.7. The major types of land-use change that affect carbon storage are:

- the permanent clearance of forest for pastures and arable crops;

- shifting cultivation that may vary in extent and intensity as populations increase or decline;

- logging with subsequent forest regeneration or replanting; and

- abandonment of agriculture and replacement by regrowth or planting of secondary forest (i.e. deforestation, afforestation and reforestation).

Many of these processes (shifting cultivation, logging, clearing for pasture and abandonment) involve dynamics between forest destruction and subsequent recovery, although the net effect has been a loss of carbon from forests. A review of these processes is provided by Houghton (1996).

Of the various processes, the expansion of croplands at the expense of natural ecosystems has dominated and continues to dominate the net efflux of carbon from the terrestrial biosphere, with the regions of highest activity being the tropical forests of Southeast Asia (0.76 PgC yr^{-1} in 1990) and Africa (0.34 PgC yr^{-1} in 1990). The conversion of forest into cattle pasture has gradually increased in importance and is concentrated almost entirely in Latin America (0.34 PgC yr^{-1} in 1990 compared with 0.16 PgC yr^{-1} from cropland expansion in the same region). Net emissions from wood harvesting are dominated by logging in Southeast Asia (0.19 PgC yr^{-1} in 1990; 66% of total emissions from harvesting), and China (0.07 PgC yr^{-1} in 1990; 23% of total emissions). In the 19th century, shifting cultivation was in decline because of the abandonment of agricultural lands (often under tragic conditions) by indigenous peoples in the Americas and Southeast Asia. Since the mid-20th

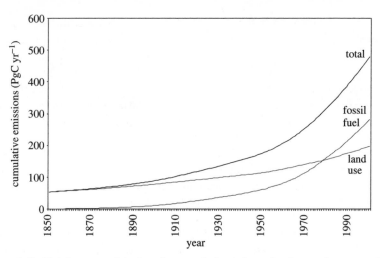

Figure 1.8. Total accumulated carbon emissions from land-use change and fossil-fuel combustion, 1850–2000. Data sources as in Figures 1.5 and 1.6, with land-use-change values for 1991–2000 assumed to be constant at 1990 values.

century, however, increasing population pressures have led to an increase in cultivation area and a decrease in rotation times, and shifting cultivation has become an increasing source of carbon. In North America and Europe, there has been a gradual abandonment of agricultural lands and regrowth of forests that have resulted in a carbon sink.

The results presented above are derived by Houghton (1999) from estimates of land-cover change derived from the Food and Agriculture Organization (FAO). Recent studies in a number of countries have suggested that the FAO may be overestimating land-cover change (e.g. Steininger *et al.* (2001) for Bolivia, Houghton *et al.* (2000) for Brazil). Conversely, there are a number of processes that may be contributing to carbon emissions but that are not included in these calculations. These include forest degradation without loss of forest cover; illegal, unmonitored logging; and hidden ground fires (Nepstad *et al.* 1999) and may add *ca.* 0.4 GtC yr^{-1} to the estimate of net carbon emissions (Fearnside 2000).

The cumulative CO_2 emissions since 1850 (including fossil-fuel change and land-use change) are shown in Figure 1.8. In total, *ca.* 480 GtC had been emitted to the atmosphere as a result of human activity by the end of 2000 (91% of this since 1850, 50% of this since only 1968). The overall contribution from fossil-fuel combustion only surpassed that from land-use change in the 1970s, but fossil-fuel combustion now accounts for 75% of current emissions.

Impacts of the 'carbon disruption'

The atmosphere

High-precision measurements of the concentration of atmospheric CO_2, pioneered at Mauna Loa in Hawaii (Keeling & Whorf 2000), and now made at a number of stations around the world, show an unequivocal increase in concentration over nearly half a century (Figure 1.2c). CO_2 concentrations are fairly uniform across the globe because the mixing time-scale for the lower global atmosphere is approximately one year, while the lifetime for CO_2 in the atmosphere is much longer, varying from 5 to 200 years. However, slightly higher concentrations are found in the Northern Hemisphere than in the Southern, a planetary-scale 'smoking gun' reminding us of the high rates of fossil-fuel combustion in northern mid-latitudes. The rate of increase in atmospheric CO_2 is dramatic: it has averaged *ca.* 0.4% per year since 1980, although net emissions to the atmosphere vary annually between *ca.* 2 and 6 PgC yr^{-1}, mainly as a result of changes in oceanic and terrestrial uptake that overlie the continuous human-related outflow of CO_2. The effects of El Niño events, for example, can temporarily result in high rates of CO_2-release to the atmosphere because of reduced terrestrial uptake in tropical ecosystems experiencing increased temperatures, droughts, fires and cloudiness (Prentice *et al.* 2001). At a finer, sub-annual, time-step, the repeated sinusoidal pattern in CO_2 concentration (Figure 1.2c) shows us that hemisphere-scale behaviour in gross ecosystem metabolism can also be detected as natural systems respond to seasonality in climate.

Although the increase in atmospheric CO_2 concentration may affect the biosphere directly, the main cause for concern about rising CO_2 is its role as a greenhouse gas (GHG). GHGs allow short-wave solar radiation to pass into the Earth's atmosphere, but they absorb some of the long-wave thermal radiation that is emitted back out towards space. This has a warming effect on our atmosphere, and is termed 'positive radiative forcing'. CO_2 is not the most effective GHG, but it exists at relatively high concentrations, and consequently contributes the largest proportion of the total radiative forcing from GHGs. Other GHGs such as methane and nitrous oxide are more efficient at trapping radiant energy. They can be compared with CO_2 by calculating 'CO_2 equivalents': the warming potential of each gas compared with CO_2 over a specified time horizon, often 100 years. Methane (CH_4) and nitrous oxide (N_2O) have 23 and 296 times the warming potential of CO_2, respectively, but their atmospheric concentrations are much lower. Other GHGs, such as hydrofluorocarbons, have warming potentials that are an order of magnitude higher still (Table 1.2).

The relative constancy in atmospheric CO_2 concentration during the millennium leading up to the end of the 19th century (Figure 1.2b) is also reflected in the temperature trace. Figure 1.9 shows Northern Hemisphere temperatures obtained from thermometers and proxy measurements from 1000 up to 1998. A small but continuous cooling from 1000 is abruptly broken around 1900, and temperatures rise from then until the present. Overall, the global mean temperature has gone up by 0.6 °C$\pm$0.2 °C, 95% confidence) since 1861. 1998 is considered to have been the warmest year on record, and crucially, temperatures are now sufficiently high to exceed the bounds of uncertainty associated with the proxy measurements made for historical times (Figure 1.9). During the same period the atmospheric CO_2 concentration has also risen steeply

Table 1.2. *Direct global warming potentials of greenhouse gases affected by human activities*

Gas	Lifetime (yr)	Warming potential (CO_2 equivalent)	Concentration in 1998	Rate of change of concentration	Preindustrial concentration
CO_2		1	365 ppm	1.5 ppm yr^{-1}	280
CH_4	12	23	1745 ppb	7.0 ppb yr^{-1}	700
N_2O	114	296	314 ppb	0.8 ppb yr^{-1}	270
HFC-23	260	12 000	14 ppt	0.55 ppt yr^{-1}	*ca.* 0

Note: The time horizon used to estimate the CO_2-equivalent warming potential for each gas is 100 years (the atmospheric residence time for CO_2 varies from 5 to 200 years). Warming potential is an index used to express relative global warming contribution due to atmospheric emission of a kilogram of a particular greenhouse gas compared with the emission of a kilogram of CO_2. Concentration units are expressed by volume.

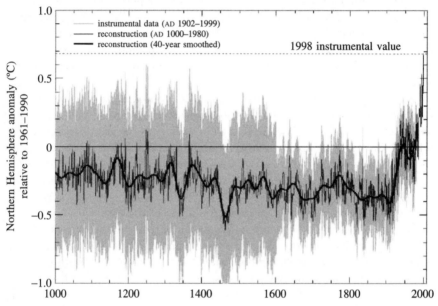

Figure 1.9. Northern Hemisphere temperatures for the last millennium (1000–1998). Direct measurements are shown as a thin grey line. Other data are reconstructed from proxy measurements: tree rings, corals, ice cores and historical records. The thick black line is a 40-year smoothed average; the shaded grey is the uncertainty in the temperature (two standard errors).

(Figure 1.2*b*). The 31% increase in atmospheric CO_2 since 1750 is now thought to be responsible for 60% of all GHG-induced warming.

It is not surprising, therefore, that the modelling of climate scenarios for the next 100 years is strongly dependent on the amount of CO_2 that is predicted to be released into the atmosphere. Since fossil-fuel combustion currently contributes three-quarters of all CO_2 emissions (Figure 1.10) the socio-economic model underpinning fuel-consumption estimates strongly influences future climate scenarios. Using the full range of potential economic scenar-

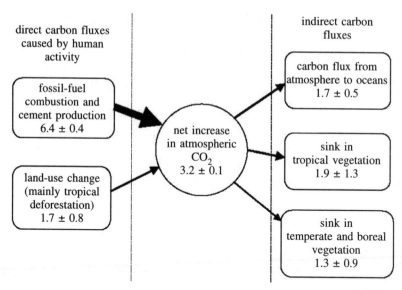

Figure 1.10. An estimate of the human-induced carbon cycle in the 1990s (units are PgC yr^{-1}). The carbon flows from fossil-fuel emissions to the atmosphere and the net carbon flows to the ocean and land are known with relatively high confidence. The partitioning of the net land sink between human activity and 'natural' carbon sinks is less certain, as is the partition between tropical and temperate regions.

ios, the IPCC (2001) projected future temperature increases over the next 100 years to range from 1.5 to 5.8 °C, and the atmospheric CO_2 concentration to rise from the current value of 368 to between 500 and 1000 ppm. Very approximately, these model outputs suggest that *every* 3 Pg *of C emissions will result in an extra* 1 ppm *atmospheric* CO_2 *concentration by 2100, and that each extra* ppm *will increase global mean temperatures in 2100 by a little less than* 0.01 °C. These conversion factors vary according to assumptions about the temporal trend in emissions and the future behaviour of ocean and terrestrial carbon cycles, but provide a crude tool for estimating the climatic impacts of various carbon mitigation scenarios.

Although the warming experienced since the 19th century is marked, it does not directly reflect the total amount of CO_2 released as a result of human activities. Only a fraction of this total is ultimately added to the atmospheric CO_2 stock because of re-absorption by the oceans and the land surface. An estimate of the contemporary (1990s) fast carbon cycle is illustrated in Figure 1.10 (The Royal Society 2001). In this figure, the carbon flows from fossil-fuel emissions to the atmosphere, and the net carbon flows to ocean and land are known with relatively high confidence (see below). A simple balance equation requires that, despite ongoing tropical deforestation, there is a net terrestrial carbon sink of 1.5 PgC yr^{-1}. The partitioning of the net terrestrial sink between human activities (primarily a source) and 'natural' carbon sinks is less certain, as is the partition between tropical and temperate regions. The partition between tropical and temperate regions is derived from studies of the atmospheric distribution of CO_2 (Prentice *et al.* 2001). The biggest uncer-

tainty in this budget comes from quantification of land-use-change emissions:
if these are overestimated, the terrestrial carbon sink is overestimated.

Currently, *ca.* 8.1 $PgC\,yr^{-1}$ are emitted as CO_2, from industrial activity
and tropical deforestation, but only 40% (3.2 $PgC\,yr^{-1}$) of this makes a net
contribution to the atmospheric build-up (Figure 1.10). It is this 40% that
contributes to the radiative forcing of the Earth's atmosphere, but to understand the future of this radiative forcing it is also essential to understand the
fate and permanence of the remaining 60%. This book focuses on the management of the land surface for carbon sequestration and emission reductions
but, before describing land surface processes in some detail, we summarize
the role played by the oceans in absorbing CO_2 from the atmosphere.

The oceans

About 50 times more carbon resides in the oceans than in the atmosphere.
Large-scale exchange between the two occurs over time-scales of hundreds
of years, but CO_2 is readily exchanged across the sea–air interface on much
shorter time-scales because of its high solubility and chemical reactivity in
water. On an annual basis, the oceans absorb 1.7($\pm$0.5) $PgC\,yr^{-1}$ from the
atmosphere (Prentice *et al.* 2001). In spite of uncertainty in a number of processes, the precision in this estimate is relatively high, reflecting consistency
between model outputs, values derived from measurements of atmospheric O_2
and $\delta^{13}C$, and scaled-up *in situ* measurements (Sabine *et al.* 1999; Orr *et al.*
2001; Prentice *et al.* 2001).

The transfer of CO_2 into or out of the oceans occurs naturally, mediated by
both physical and biological processes. Molecular diffusion across the sea–air
interface can occur in either direction, the net flux depending on the difference
in the partial pressure of CO_2 in each medium ($pCO_{2\,air}$ and $pCO_{2\,sea}$). The
rate of this transfer into water is modelled as a function of wind speed, but
depends on sea temperature, salinity and pH.

Once in solution, 99% of the CO_2 reacts chemically with water to produce
bicarbonate and carbonate ions, leaving 1% in the original dissolved, non-
ionic form of CO_2. The carbon may then be the subject of further chemical
reactions or be absorbed into biomass by phytoplankton. Photosynthesis in
the oceans produces particulate organic carbon that sinks to significant depth.
Most of this exported carbon ultimately returns to the surface by way of the
underlying oceanic circulation, outgassed as CO_2, usually a large distance
from its source. The effect of this 'biological pump' mechanism is large: the
atmospheric concentration of CO_2 would be 200 ppm higher in its absence
(Maier-Reimer *et al.* 1996). A second biological process occurs at the same
time, whereby marine organisms, supplied with carbon by phytoplankton,
fix carbonate ions by synthesizing calcium carbonate shells, which then sink,
thus removing carbonate from the surface waters and reducing their alkalinity.
This process tends to increase $pCO_{2\,sea}$ and acts in opposition to the main
biological pump effect. The ratio between these two processes determines the
overall effect of biological activity on surface ocean $pCO_{2\,sea}$ and hence the
natural air-sea exchange rate of CO_2.

The absorption of anthropogenic CO_2 is a purely physical process and is considered to be superimposed upon the biological pump systems that are ultimately controlled by the supply of nutrients from deep water (Falkowski 1994). Uptake of CO_2 from the atmosphere occurs by enhancing natural exchange processes: a higher $pCO_{2\,air}$ leads to an increased mean atmosphere–ocean concentration gradient, and hence to increased oceanic sink activity and reduced source activity. The spatial pattern of oceanic circulation creates geographically separated upwellings of 'old' deep water, rich in organic carbon that may have been out of contact with the atmosphere for many years. The air–sea exchange of CO_2 reaches a physico-chemical equilibrium quickly relative to the slow tempo of oceanic circulation, and hence the long-term rate of net CO_2 absorption is ultimately limited by the rate at which oceanic circulation brings currents of deep water to the surface.

The future uptake potential of CO_2 by the oceans is likely to be controlled by a number of factors. The principal constraint is chemical: as atmospheric CO_2 concentration increases, the ratio of bicarbonate to carbonate ions also increases. This reduced availability of carbonate ions impairs the capacity for dissolved CO_2 to dissociate ionically, and hence reduces the capacity for CO_2 to dissolve from the air into the water in the first place. This effect is significant and places heavy constraints on absorption at higher atmospheric CO_2 concentrations. In addition, the velocity of oceanic circulation places an upper limit on the net rate of CO_2 absorption and the reduced solubility of CO_2 in water at higher temperatures will still further reduce transfer to the oceans. Overall, models indicate that the annual atmosphere–ocean flux of CO_2 will become larger over the 21st century, reaching 4.5–$6.7\,\mathrm{PgC\,yr^{-1}}$ by the end of the century, but that the rate of increase will slow, particularly after the first 30–50 years.

The terrestrial biosphere

As both the atmospheric stock and ocean sink of CO_2 are well determined (but the land-use-change source less so), a simple balance equation requires that there is a terrestrial carbon sink of *ca.* $3.2\,\mathrm{PgC\,yr^{-1}}$, as illustrated in Figure 1.10. Attempts to measure the terrestrial carbon sink directly are hampered by the spatial heterogeneity of carbon-transfer processes in the terrestrial biosphere. Given their spatial extent, biomass and productivity, forests are prime candidates for the location of the major portion of this carbon sink (Malhi *et al.* 1999; Malhi & Grace 2000). This seems to be confirmed by field observations. Extensive inventories of forest biomass in temperate and boreal regions suggest that there has been a substantial increase in the carbon stock in northern forest biomass, of the order of $0.6\,\mathrm{Pg\,yr^{-1}}$. Such extensive inventories are not available in most tropical forest regions, but a compilation of results from forest plots in old-growth forests shows that these forests are increasing in biomass, resulting in a land carbon sink of $0.85 \pm 0.25\,\mathrm{PgC\,yr^{-1}}$ (Phillips *et al.* 1998, 2002). The forest inventory estimates do not include changes in soil and litter carbon. When forest productivity and biomass are increasing, it is likely that soil and litter carbon reserves are also increasing, in total by an amount similar to the increase in reserves in living biomass if soil and biomass residence times are similar. This suggests a total sink of *ca.* 1.5 PgC yr^{-1} in tropical forests (Malhi *et al.* 1999), and 1.2 Pg yr^{-1} in temperate forests, implying that forests account for most of the terrestrial carbon sink (2.7 PgC yr^{-1} out of 3.2 PgC yr^{-1}), although it is possible that savannahs and grasslands also play a part.

What may be causing this terrestrial sink? A number of processes are likely to be responsible, each with their own regional pattern. Firstly, there is the *recovery of forests on abandoned agricultural lands.* This is a major factor in Europe and North America, and the change of age structure within forests appears to be a more important factor than the expansion of forest area. Another likely factor is CO_2 *fertilization*, where the rising atmospheric concentrations of CO_2 are stimulating plant photosynthesis, with consequences for the amount of carbon stored in plant biomass, litter and soil-organic carbon. Results from over 100 recent experiments in which young trees have been grown exposed to doubled atmospheric CO_2 concentrations have demonstrated an increase in tree growth of 10–70% (Norby *et al.* 1999; Idso 1999). A key uncertainty is the extent to which the fertilization effect is limited by availability of other nutrients such as nitrogen and phosphorus. It has been suggested that plants may respond by investing a greater proportion of their extra carbon into the production of roots and root exudates to increase their nutrient supply (Lloyd *et al.* 2002). These high CO_2 effects may affect all forest ecosystems, but they may be particularly important in tropical regions where productivity is intrinsically high. Increased atmospheric CO_2 also results in an *enhanced water-use efficiency*, which may lengthen the growing season of plants in seasonally dry regions. Finally, human activities have resulted in an *enhanced global nitrogen cycle*, through the release of nitrogen oxides during fossil-fuel and biomass combustion and the release of ammonia through fertilizer use, farming and industry (Galloway *et al.* 1995). There is evidence that nitrogen deposition is enhancing forest growth in temperate regions (Nadelhoffer *et al.* 1999; Oren *et al.* 2001); this effect is less important in boreal and tropical regions which are further from the nitrogen sources and, in the case of tropical regions, constrained by lack of phosphorus (Tanner *et al.* 1998).

Whatever the causes of the carbon accumulation in forest regions, there is also great interannual variability in the carbon balance. This is apparent both from ecophysiological models of forest processes, and from studies of the spatial distribution of atmospheric CO_2, which indicate that tropical regions are the primary driver for much of this interannual variability. Figure 1.11 shows a time-series of the net carbon balance of tropical land regions, as derived from an atmospheric study (which includes land-use-change effects), and from a biosphere model (which does not include land-use change). Tropical regions become a net carbon source during El Niño years because dry conditions in much of Amazonia and tropical Asia result in greater fire incidence (both anthropogenic and natural) and a drought-induced reduction in photosynthesis.

On a longer time-scale, it is likely that the terrestrial carbon sink will diminish in magnitude as the CO_2 fertilization effect decreases in magnitude

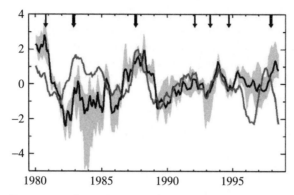

Figure 1.11. Time-series (solid black line) of the carbon balance of tropical land regions (20° N to 20° S), inferred from an inversion at global atmospheric CO_2 concentrations with an estimate of uncertainty (grey shading). The dark-grey line shows the carbon balance inferred from a biogeochemical model, which does not include deforestation. The tropics tend to be a major source of carbon in El Niño years, which are indicated by arrows. Most of the interannual variation in the terrestrial carbon balance is localized in the tropics (from Bousquet *et al.* 2000).

and structural factors limit the amount of new carbon that can be stored in forest biomass. What the most important limiting factors will be and when they will become important is still unknown. Furthermore, it is possible that climatic warming will enhance plant respiration and the decomposition of soil organic matter, leading to natural ecosystems becoming net sources of carbon and accelerating climate change. Measurements of CO_2 fluxes suggest that in tundras and high latitude boreal forests, where climatic warming is greatest, the enhanced carbon sink in biomass is being offset by the release of soil carbon caused by the thawing of biomass (Goulden *et al.* 1998; Oechel *et al.* 1993, 2000). There is currently little evidence of a similar effect (net loss of soil carbon) in tropical regions, although some climate-biosphere simulations suggest that the warming and drying of eastern Amazonia may result in a dieback of forest and a major release of carbon to the atmosphere (Cox *et al.* 2000).

Implications for ecology and biodiversity

The biosphere is not like to be a purely passive sink for carbon: the changes contributing to the terrestrial carbon sink are likely to be causing profound changes in the ecological balance of ecosystems, with consequences for ecosystem function and species diversity. Laboratory studies show that responsiveness to high CO_2 varies between species (Norby *et al.* 1999); for example, at the most basic level, the CO_2 response is much higher in plants with a C3 photosynthetic mechanism (all trees, nearly all plants of cold climates, and most temperate crops including wheat and rice) than it is in those with a C4 mechanism (tropical and many temperate grasses, some desert shrubs and some important tropical crops including maize, sorghum and sugar cane). This has the potential to alter the competitive balance between trees and grasslands. Certain functional groups such as pioneers or lianas may also benefit disproportionately. There have been only a few systematic field studies that have looked for long-term trends in forest composition. For example, in the RAINFOR project (Malhi *et al.* 2002), field researchers are re-censusing old-growth forest plots across the Amazon basin to look for evidence of shifts in forest biomass and composition.

The future

In the short term at least, anthropogenic CO_2 emissions are set to accelerate. The evidence that this will affect climate is now almost unequivocal. Learning how to minimize these emissions and deal with their consequences is likely to be one of the great challenges of the 21st century. A variety of strategies will need to be adopted, including shifting to renewable energy sources, increasing carbon use efficiency, and possibly sequestering CO_2 in deep sediments or the deep ocean (IPCC Working Group III 2001).

One of the most immediate options, and the one that is the focus of this book, is the option of locking up carbon in the terrestrial biosphere. Biosphere management options could include:

- the prevention of deforestation;

- the reduction of carbon loss from forests by changing harvesting regimes, converting from conventional to reduced-impact logging, and controlling other disturbances such as fire and pest outbreaks;

- reforestation/afforestation of abandoned or degraded lands;

- sequestration in agricultural soils through change in tilling practices; and

- the increased use of biofuels to replace fossil-fuel combustion.

How much potential does the biosphere-management option have?

We noted above that by the end of 2000 *ca.* 190 PgC had been released from the biosphere by human activity. Thus, if *all* agricultural and degraded lands were reverted back to original vegetation cover (an extremely unlikely scenario), a similar amount of carbon would be sequestered.

Slightly more realistically, the IPCC Third Assessment Report (Kauppi *et al.* 2001) confirms previous estimates (Brown *et al.* 1996) that the potential avoidance and removal of carbon emissions that could be achieved through the implementation of an aggressive programme of changing forestry practices over the next 50 years is *ca.* 60–87 PgC. About 80% of this amount could be achieved in the tropics. Changes in agricultural practices could result in a further carbon sink of 20–30 Pg over the same period (Cole *et al.* 1996), resulting in a maximum land-management carbon sink of 80–120 Pg, and a mean annual sink of *ca.* 2 PgC yr^{-1}. Figure 1.12 shows how this potential sink is distributed between various activities.

It is important to emphasize that here we are discussing an *additional, deliberately planned land-carbon sink* that would complement the 'natural'

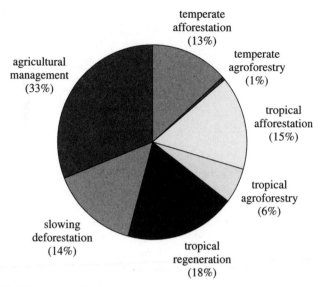

Figure 1.12. The potential of various land-management activities to mitigate global emissions of CO_2 by increasing the carbon-sink potential of forestry and agriculture or reducing emissions at source (reducing deforestation). Estimates provided by the IPCC suggest that a maximum mitigation of 100 PgC could be achieved between 2000 and 2050. (Reproduced from The Royal Society (2001).)

sink mentioned previously. The two sinks are sometimes confused in discussion. For example, although the natural carbon sink may reduce with climatic warming and possibly become a net source, intact, well-managed forests will almost always contain more carbon than degraded forests or agricultural lands. Therefore, improved carbon-focused forest management will almost always result in net carbon sequestration.

How does this land-management sink potential compare with expected carbon emissions over the 21st century? The IPCC 'business as usual' scenario suggests that that *ca.* 1400 PgC would be emitted by fossil-fuel combustion and land-use change over the 21st century. More detailed recent emissions scenarios suggest that, without conscious environment-based decision making, emissions will total between 1800 PgC (scenario A2, a regionalized world) and 2100 PgC (scenario A1F, a fossil-fuel-intensive globalized world) over the 21st century (Nakicenovic *et al.* 2000). With more environmentally focused policies, total emissions are expected to vary between 800 and 1100 PgC. Whatever the details of the scenario, it is clear that even an extensive land carbon-sink programme could only offset a fraction of likely anthropogenic carbon emissions over the coming century. Fossil-fuel emissions alone (not considering any further emissions from ongoing tropical deforestation) over the 21st century may exceed by 5–10 times even the maximum possible human-induced forest-carbon sink. Using the simplistic conversion factor outlined above (3 PgC emissions = 1 ppm atmospheric CO_2 = 0.01 °C temperature rise), *a managed land-use sink of* 100 PgC *over the 21st century would reduce projected* CO_2 *concentrations in 2100 by ca.* 33 ppm, *and reduce the projected*

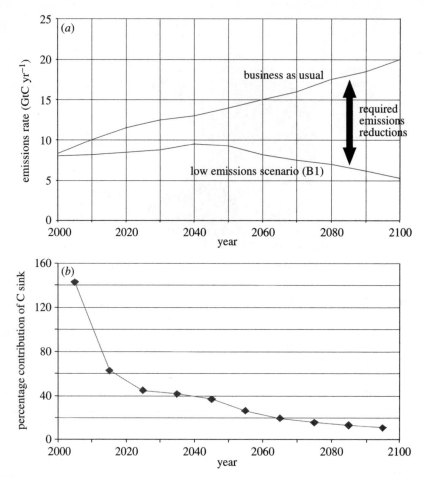

Figure 1.13. (*a*) A 'business as usual' carbon emissions scenario (IS92a) and a low-emissions scenario for the 21st century (IPCC 2001). (*b*) The percentage contribution that a human-induced land carbon sink of 1.5 PgC yr^{-1} could make towards a move from the 'business-as-usual' pathway to a low-emissions pathway.

global mean temperature increase by 0.3 °C: a modest but significant effect. Using a similar calculation for historical CO_2 emissions, Prentice *et al.* (2001) estimated that a complete reversion of agriculture to forest would reduce atmospheric CO_2 concentrations by 40 ppm, a comparable figure.

Absorbing carbon in trees clearly cannot 'solve' the global warming problem on its own. Where forest-carbon absorption can be effective, however, is in being a significant component in a package of CO_2 mitigation strategies, and providing an immediate carbon sink while other mitigation technologies are developed. Carbon absorbed early in the century has a greater effect on reducing end-of-century temperatures than carbon absorbed late in the century. The immediate potential of forestry is illustrated in Figure 1.13. Suppose that a global carbon emissions goal for the 21st century is to move our emissions pathway from the IPCC 'business-as-usual' scenario (IS92a) to a low-emissions scenario (SRES scenario B1), as illustrated in Figure 1.13*a*. The required carbon offset is the difference between these two emissions curves. Now let us suppose that an ambitious forest-carbon-sink programme can be implemented immediately, aiming to absorb 75 PgC by 2050, at a uniform rate of 1.5 PgC yr^{-1}. Figure 1.13*b* illustrates the proportional contribution that such a carbon sink could make to the required total carbon offset. *For the next decade, such a land carbon sink would on its own be sufficient to move us onto the low-emissions pathway, and for the subsequent two decades it could provide about half of the required carbon offsets.* Thus even a less ambitious carbon offset programme could play a significant role over the next few decades. As the century progresses and the magnitude of the required carbon reductions increases, the relative potential of forest-carbon sinks declines. A forest-carbon offset programme implemented in 2050 would only be able to produce between 10 and 30% of the required offsets. Thus, to be relevant, a forest-carbon sequestration programme has to absorb most of its carbon within the next few decades. Tropical ecosystems have the highest productivities, and are therefore likely to be the most effective sinks at this short time-scale.

In conclusion, the managed absorption of carbon in forests has the potential to play a significant role in any carbon-emissions-reduction strategy over the next few decades. Such a strategy can be viewed as partly undoing the negative effects of previous centuries of forest clearance, both in climatic and biological terms. The relative potential contribution of a forest-carbon sink declines later in the century, and therefore forest-carbon absorption cannot be viewed as a long-term solution to the global warming problem. It can only be a useful stopgap. As a stopgap, however, it is essential that carbon sinks are not allowed to divert resources and attention from required developments and changes in technology, energy use, and energy supply, the only developments that can provide a long-term solution to the great carbon disruption.

Acknowledgements

Y.M. acknowledges the support of a Royal Society University Research Fellowship, and P.M. acknowledges support of the UK Natural Environment Research Council.

References

Amthor, J. S. & Baldocchi, D. D. 2001 Terrestrial higher-plant respiration and net primary production. In *Terrestrial global productivity* (ed. J. Roy, H. A. Mooney & B. Saugier), pp. 33–52. Academic.

Berner, R. A. 1997 Paleoclimate: the rise of plants and their effect on weathering and atmospheric CO_2. *Science* **276**, 544–546.

Bickle, M. J. 1994 The role of metamorphic decarbonation reactions in returning strontium to the silicate sediment mass. *Nature* **367**, 699–704.

Bousquet, P., Peylin, P., Ciais, P., Le Quere, C., Friedlingstein, P. & Tans, P. P. 2000 Regional changes in carbon dioxide fluxes of land and oceans since 1980. *Science* **290**, 1342–1346.

Brown, S., Sathaye, J., Cannell, M. & Kauppi, P. E. 1996 Management of forests for mitigation of greenhouse gas emissions. In *IPCC climate change 1995: impacts, adaptations and mitigation of climate change* (ed. R. T. Watson, R. H. Zinyowera, R. H. Moss & D. J. Dokken), pp. 773–797. Cambridge University Press.

Cole, C. V. *et al.* 1996 Agricultural options for mitigation of greenhouse gas emissions. In *IPCC climate change 1995: impacts, adaptations and mitigation of climate change* (ed. R. T. Watson, R. H. Zinyowera, R. H. Moss & D. J. Dokken), pp. 745–771. Cambridge University Press.

Cox, P. M., Betts, R. A., Jones, C. D., Spall, S. A. & Totterdell, I. J. 2000 Acceleration of global warming due to carbon-cycle feedbacks in a coupled climate model. *Nature* **408**, 184–187.

Crutzen, P. J. 2002 The geology of mankind. *Nature* **415**, 23.

DeFries, R. S., Field, C. B., Fung, I., Collatz, G. J. & Bounoua, L. 1999 Combining satellite data and biogeochemical models to estimate global effects of human-induced land cover change on carbon emissions and primary productivity. *Global Biogeochem. Cycles* **13**, 803–815.

Dixon, R. K., Brown, S., Houghton, R. A., Solomon, A. M., Trexler, M. C. & Wisniewski, J. 1994 Carbon pools and flux of global forest ecosystems. *Science* **263**, 185–190.

Etheridge, D. M., Steele, L. P., Langenfelds, R. L., Francey, R. J., Barnola, J. M. & Morgan, V. I. 1996 Natural and anthropogenic changes in atmospheric CO_2 over the last 1000 years from air in Antarctic ice and firn. *J. Geophys. Res. Atmos.* **101**, 4115–4128.

Falkowski, P. G. 1994 The role of phytoplankton photosynthesis in global biogeochemical cycles. *Photosynth. Res.* **39**, 235–258.

Fearnside, P. M. 2000 Global warming and tropical land-use change: greenhouse gas emissions from biomass burning, decomposition and soils in forest conversion, shifting cultivation and secondary vegetation. *Climatic Change* **46**, 115–158.

Fischer, H., Wahlen. M., Smith. J., Mastroianni, D. & Deck, B. 1999 Ice core records of atmospheric CO_2 around the last three glacial terminations. *Science* **283**, 1712–1714.

Galloway, J. N., Schlesinger, W. H., Levy, H., Michaels, A. & Schnoor, J. L. 1995 Nitrogen-fixation: anthropogenic enhancement, environmental response. *Global Biogeochem. Cycles* **9**, 235–252.

Goldewijk, K. K. 2001 Estimating global land use change over the past 300 years: the HYDE database. *Global Biogeochem. Cycles* **15**, 417–433.

Goulden, M. L. (and 11 others) 1998 Sensitivity of boreal forest carbon balance to soil thaw. *Science* **279**, 214–217.

Houghton, R. A. 1996 Terrestrial sources and sinks of carbon inferred from terrestrial data. *Tellus* B **48**, 420–432.

Houghton, R. A. 1999 The annual net flux of carbon to the atmosphere from changes in land use 1850–1990. *Tellus* B **51**, 298–313.

Houghton, R. A., Skole, D. L., Nobre, C. A., Hackler, J. L., Lawrence, K. T. & Chomentowski, W. H. 2000 Annual fluxes or carbon from deforestation and regrowth in the Brazilian Amazon. *Nature* **403**, 301–304.

Idso, S. B. 1999 The long-term response of trees to atmospheric CO_2 enrichment. *Glob. Change Biol.* **5**, 493–495.

IPCC 2001 *Climate change 2001: the scientific basis. Contribution of Working Group I to the Third Assessment Report of the International Panel on Climate Change.* (ed. J. T. Houghton, Y. Ding, D. J. Griggs, M. Noguer, P. J. van der Linden, X. Dai, K. Maskell & C. A. Johnson). Cambridge University Press.

Kauppi, P. (and 15 others) 2001 Technological and economic potential of options to enhance, maintain, and manage biological carbon reservoirs and geo-engineering. In *Climate Change 2001: mitigation*, pp. 302–343. Cambridge University Press.

Keeling, C. D. & Whorf, T. P. 2000 Atmospheric CO_2 records from sites in the SiO air sampling network. In *Trends: a compendium of data on global change.* Annual Report. Carbon Dioxide Information Analysis Center, Oak Ridge National Laboratory, TN, US Department of Energy.

Lloyd, J., Bird, M. I., Veenendaal, E. & Kruijt, B. 2002 Should phosphorus availability be constraining moist tropical forest responses to increasing CO_2 concentrations? In *Global biogeochemical cycles in the climate system* (ed. E. D. Schulze, S. P. Harrison, M. Heimann, E. A. Holland, J. Lloyd, I. C. Prentice & D. Schimel). Academic.

Lorius, C. & Oeschger, H. 1994 Palaeo-perspectives: reducing uncertainties in global change. *Ambio* **23**, 30–36.

Maier-Reimer, E., Mikolajewicz, U. & Winguth, A. 1996 Future ocean uptake of CO_2: interaction between ocean-circulation and biology. *Climate Dynam.* **12**, 711–721.

Malhi, Y. (and 25 others) 2002 An international network to monitor the structure and dynamics of Amazonian forests (RAINFOR). *J. Vegetat. Sci.* **13**, 439–450.

Malhi, Y. & Grace, J. 2000 Tropical forests and atmospheric carbon dioxide. *Trends Ecol. Evol.* **15**, 332–337.

Malhi, Y., Baldocchi. D. D. & Jarvis. P. G. 1999 The carbon balance of tropical, temperate and boreal forests. *Plant Cell Environ.* **22**, 715–740.

Marland, G., Boden, T. A. & Andres, R. J. 2001 Global, regional, and national annual CO_2 emissions from fossil-fuel burning, cement production, and gas flaring 1751–1998. In *Trends: a compendium of data on global change.* Carbon Dioxide Information Analysis Center, Oak Ridge National Laboratory, TN, US Department of Energy.

Nadelhoffer, K. J., Emmett, B. A., Gundersen, P., Kjonaas, O. J., Koopmans, C. J., Schleppi, P., Tietema, A. & Wright, R. F. 1999 Nitrogen deposition makes a minor contribution to carbon sequestration in temperate forests. *Nature* **398**, 145–148.

Nakicenovic, N. (and 28 others) 2000 *IPCC Special Report on emissions scenarios.* Cambridge University Press.

Nepstad, D. C. (and 11 others) 1999 Large-scale impoverishment of Amazonian forests by logging and fire. *Nature* **398**, 505–508.

Norby, R. J., Wullschleger, S. D., Gunderson, C. A., Johnson, D. W. & Ceulemans, R. 1999 Tree responses to rising CO_2 in field experiments: implications for the future forest. *Plant Cell Environ.* **22**, 683–714.

Oechel, W. C., Hastings, S. J., Vourlitis, G., Jenkins, M., Richers, G. & Grulke, N. 1993 Recent change of arctic tundra ecosystems from a net carbon-dioxide sink to a source. *Nature* **361**, 520–523.

Oechel, W. C., Vourlitis, G. L., Hastings, S. J., Zulueta, R. C., Hinzman, L. & Kane, D. 2000 Acclimation of ecosystem CO_2 exchange in the Alaskan Arctic in response to decadal climate warming. *Nature* **406**, 978–981.

Oren, R. (and 10 others) 2001 Soil fertility limits carbon sequestration by forest ecosystems in a CO_2-enriched atmosphere. *Nature* **411**, 469–472.

Orr, J. C. (and 12 others) 2001 Estimates of anthropogenic carbon uptake from four three-dimensional global ocean models. *Global Biogeochem. Cycles* **15**, 43–60.

Pagani, M., Arthur, M. A. & Freeman, K. H. 1999 Miocene evolution of atmospheric carbon dioxide. *Paleoceanography* **14**, 273–292.

Pauly, D. & Christensen, V. 1995 Primary production required to sustain global fisheries. *Nature* **374**, 255–257.

Pearson, P. N. & Palmer, M. R. 1999 Middle Eocene seawater pH and atmospheric carbon dioxide concentrations. *Science* **284**, 1824–1826.

Pearson, P. N. & Palmer, M. R. 2000 Atmospheric carbon dioxide concentrations over the past 60 million years. *Nature* **406**, 695–699.

Perlin, J. 1989 A forest journey: the role of wood in the development of civilization. Cambridge, MA: Harvard University Press.

Petit, J. R. (and 18 others) 1999 Climate and atmospheric history of the past 420 000 years from the Vostok ice core, Antarctica. *Nature* **399**, 429–436.

Phillips, O. L. (and 10 others) 1998 Changes in the carbon balance of tropical forests: evidence from long-term plots. *Science* **282**, 439–442.

Phillips, O. L. (and 13 others) 2002 Changes in the biomass of tropical forests: evaluating potential biases. *Ecolog. Applic.* **12**, 576–587.

Prentice, I. C. *et al.* 2001 The carbon cycle and atmospheric carbon dioxide. In *Climate change 2001: the scientific basis* (ed. IPCC), pp. 183–237. Cambridge University Press.

Ramankutty, N. & Foley, J. A. 1999 Estimating historical changes in global land cover: croplands from 1700 to 1992. *Global Biogeochem. Cycles* **13**, 997–1027.

Roy, J., Suagier, B. & Mooney, H. A. 2001 *Terrestrial global productivity.* San Diego, CA: Academic.

Sabine, C. L., Key, R. M., Johnson, K. M., Millero, F. J., Poisson, A., Sarmiento, J. L., Wallace, D. W. R. & Winn, C. D. 1999 Anthropogenic CO_2 inventory of the Indian Ocean. *Global Biogeochem. Cycles* **13**, 179–198.

Schlesinger, W. H. 1990 Evidence from chronosequence studies for a low carbon-storage potential of soils. *Nature* **348**, 233–234.

Shackleton, N. J. 2000 The 100 000-year ice-age cycle identified and found to lag temperature, carbon dioxide, and orbital eccentricity. *Science* **289**, 1897–1902.

Steininger, M. K., Tucker, C. J., Townshend, J. R. G., Killeen, T. J., Desch, A., Bell, V. & Ersts, P. 2001 Tropical deforestation in the Bolivian Amazon. *Environ. Conserv.* **28**, 127–134.

Tanner, E. V. J., Vitousek, P. M. & Cuevas, E. 1998 Experimental investigation of nutrient limitation of forest growth on wet tropical mountains. *Ecology* **79**, 10–22.

The Royal Society 2001 The role of land carbon sinks in mitigating global climate change. Policy Document 10/01, pp. 1–27.

Vitousek, P. M., Aber, J. D., Howarth, R. W., Likens, G. E., Matson, P. A., Schindler, D. W., Schlesinger, W. H. & Tilman, D. G. 1997 Human alteration of the global nitrogen cycle: sources and consequences. *Ecol. Appl.* **7**, 737–750.

Whitmore, T. M., Turner II, B. L., Johnson, D. L., Kates, R. W. & Gottschang, T. R. 1990 Long-term population change. In *The Earth as transformed by human action* (ed. B. L. Turner II, W. C. Clark, R. W. Kates, J. F. Richards, J. T. Mathews & W. B. Meyer), pp. 25–39. Cambridge University Press.

Williams, M. 1990 Forests. In *The Earth as transformed by human action* (ed. B. L. Turner II, W. C. Clark, R. W. Kates, J. F. Richards, J. T. Mathews & W. B. Meyer), pp. 179–201. Cambridge University Press.

Williams, S. N., Schaefer, S. J., Calvache, M. L. & Lopez, D. 1992 Global carbon dioxide emission to the atmosphere by volcanoes. *Geochim. Cosmochim. Acta* **56**, 1765–1770.

Chapter 2

Changes in the use and management of forests for abating carbon emissions: issues and challenges under the Kyoto Protocol

SANDRA BROWN, IAN R. SWINGLAND, ROBIN HANBURY-TENISON, GHILLEAN T. PRANCE AND NORMAN MYERS

Introduction

The global carbon cycle is recognized as one of the major biogeochemical cycles because of its role in regulating the concentration of carbon dioxide (CO_2), the most important greenhouse gas (GHG), in the atmosphere. Forests play an important role in the global carbon cycle because they store large quantities of carbon in vegetation and soil, exchange carbon with the atmosphere through photosynthesis and respiration, are sources of atmospheric carbon when they are disturbed by human or natural causes (e.g. use of poor harvesting practices, cleared and burned for conversion to non-forest uses, wildfires, etc.), and become atmospheric carbon sinks (i.e. net transfer of CO_2 from the atmosphere to the land) during land abandonment and regrowth after disturbance (Brown *et al.* 1996). Humans have the potential through changes in forest land use and management to alter the magnitude of forest-carbon stocks and the direction of forest-carbon fluxes, and thus alter their role in the carbon cycle.

The recognition that land-use change and forestry (LUCF) activities could be both sources and sinks of carbon led to their inclusion in the Kyoto Protocol. There are several articles in the Protocol that make provisions, in relation to a country's reduction target, for net changes in GHG emissions by sources and removals by sinks on the land resulting from direct human-induced activities. Article 3.3 is limited to afforestation, reforestation and deforestation since the base year of 1990. Article 3.4 provides for additional human-induced activities such as forest management, cropland management, grazing land management, and revegetation since 1990. Article 6, or Joint Implementation, allows for emission-allowance trading between developed countries. Emission reduction units can result from projects aimed at reducing emissions by sources or enhancing sinks of GHGs in any sector of the economy, providing that any emission reduction units from a project are additional to any that would otherwise occur. Similarly, Article 12, or the Clean Development Mechanism (CDM), allows for emission-offset trading between developed and developing countries, while at the same time assisting developing countries achieve sustainable development. Emission reductions resulting from such project activities shall be real, measurable, long-term benefits related to mitigation of climate change, and additional to any that would occur without the project.

A recent decision on the CDM limited the LUCF activities to afforestation and reforestation (UNFCCC 2001), although as we will discuss in this chapter, a large opportunity is lost without inclusion of projects that are designed to avoid deforestation and improve the sustainability of agriculture in developing countries (see also Chapter 4). This decision to limit LUCF activities under the CDM is mainly a result of the controversy that has arisen over the use of biological means to absorb or reduce carbon emissions (often referred to as carbon sinks). Carbon sinks as used in this context refers to direct human-induced changes in how forests and agricultural lands are used and managed; it does not refer to enhancing carbon storage that might occur due to increases in atmospheric CO_2 or increased nitrogen deposition, for example. Objections to carbon sinks are based primarily on two arguments. First, sinks may allow developed nations to delay or avoid technological adjustments to reduce their reliance on fossil fuels. And, second, technical and operational difficulties would reduce the value of sinks, allowing for inflated claims of carbon offsets.

The goals of this chapter are to present the key component of the Kyoto Protocol with respect to emissions-reduction targets and what impact these targets may have on reducing the threat of climate change; the potential to mitigate carbon emissions by changes in the use and management of forests; the technical and scientific issues surrounding LUCF projects and how through experience gained by implementing pilot projects these are being addressed; and the ancillary benefits and technology transfer from such projects. The focus of our chapter is on the potential of LUCF activities under the CDM, as this is where most of the controversy exists, yet it is also where most pilot projects exist and where most experience has been gained.

The Kyoto Protocol targets

In 1997, the Third Conference of the Parties (COP-3) to the United Nations Framework Convention on Climate Change (UNFCCC) met in Kyoto, Japan, and produced a document (the Kyoto Protocol) of appropriate actions for strengthening the commitments by developed countries to reduce their emission of GHGs. This Protocol included commitments by 38 developed countries to reduce their annual emissions of GHGs for the period 2008–2012 by an average of 5.2% below emissions in the baseline year of 1990. (The US pulled out of the Kyoto Protocol in 2001.) In 1990, those countries emitted 3.87 GtC (gigatonnes of carbon) (Marland *et al.* 2000). Emissions from the rest of the world in 1990 were 2.22 GtC (Marland *et al.* 2000). Thus the Kyoto Protocol

would require a reduction of *ca.* 0.2 GtC yr^{-1} during the five-year commitment period, or a total of 1 GtC. However, deforestation, mainly in the tropics, accounted for an additional 1.6 GtC yr^{-1} or *ca.* 25% of the total fossil-fuel
emissions (Bolin & Sukumar 2000).

It is widely accepted that a reduction in carbon emissions of 1 Gt will
have very little impact on projected climate change. To have a significant
impact, reductions over the next few decades have to be much greater (Arnell
et al. 2002). For example, to stabilize concentrations of CO_2 at 550 ppm by
2150, a stated policy of the European Union (in comparison with current levels of *ca.* 370 ppm; Keeling & Whorf 2000), carbon emissions will need to be
reduced by *ca.* 136 Gt during the next 50 years from a business-as-usual scenario (IPCC IS92a emission scenario). To ensure that the world is on the path
for stabilization at 550 ppm, carbon emissions would need to be reduced by
ca. 8 Gt during the first Kyoto commitment period (see Arnell *et al.* (2002)
and data from Nakicenovic *et al.* (2000)). Recent estimates have projected
costs of emissions reduction but do not indicate that adjustments of the order
of 8 GtC are achievable in the relevant time-frame, solely through technological means (Blok *et al.* 2001). Whether or not the Kyoto Protocol is ratified, it
is evident to us that to have a meaningful impact on climate change, *all* available mechanisms for reducing atmospheric concentrations of CO_2 will have to
be used.

The potential to mitigate carbon emissions by LUCF activities

Land-use change and forestry activities can mitigate carbon emissions by:

- emission avoidance through conserving existing carbon stocks on the
  land (e.g. avoiding deforestation, changing harvesting regimes, converting
  from conventional to reduced-impact logging);

- carbon sequestration or expanding the storage of carbon in forest ecosystems by increasing the area and/or carbon density of forests (e.g. by
  protecting secondary and other degraded forests to allow them to regenerate, restoring native forests through assisted and natural regeneration,
  establishing plantations on non-forested lands, and increasing the tree
  cover on agricultural or pasture lands); and

- substitute sustainably grown wood for energy intensive and cement-based
  products (e.g. biofuels, construction materials) (Myers & Goreau 1991;
  Brown *et al.* 1996; Kauppi & Sedjo 2001).

Several projects that include such LUCF activities just described have been
developed in the pilot phase of 'activities implemented jointly' (AIJ), established under the Berlin Mandate in 1995 (Trexler *et al.* 1999).

Most of the land-use and forestry practices described above that mitigate
GHG emissions make good social, economic and ecological sense even in the
absence of climate-change considerations (Brown *et al.* 1996). Land-use and

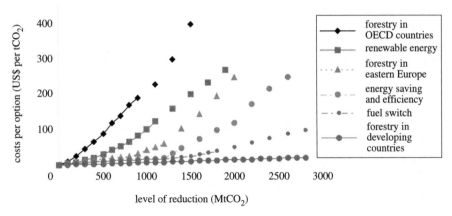

Figure 2.1. Indicative curves of costs (US$ per tCO_2) of emission reduction or carbon sequestration by level of total reduction. (From Kauppi & Sedjo 2001.)

forestry activities for mitigation are often criticized because of the impression that GHG mitigation is the main goal of the project. Instead, LUCF activities can meet the more conventional objectives for managing forests such as: sustainable forest development; industrial wood and fuel production; traditional forest uses; protection of soil, water and biodiversity; recreation; rehabilitation of damaged lands, etc. The carbon conserved and sequestered from managing for these objectives will be an added benefit.

Because photosynthesis has been shown to increase at high CO_2 concentrations, it is assumed that plants will take up more CO_2 in an enriched carbon dioxide atmosphere of the future (CO_2-fertilization effect). Thus, using LUCF activities to mitigate carbon emissions may result in carbon gains that are due, in part, to the CO_2-fertilization effect. However, the Kyoto Protocol is explicit in saying that carbon credits can only accrue from direct human-induced changes in the use and management of the land and the carbon credits must be measurable, transparent, and verifiable. In fact, the IPCC special report 'Land use, land-use change, and forestry' (Watson *et al.* 2000) goes to great lengths in proposing how forestry activities could be measured to factor out the CO_2-fertilization effect. Recent research results suggest that, at least for a young pine forest in North Carolina, some initial stimulation in carbon fixation occurred when exposed to about twice the present atmospheric CO_2 concentrations but, after three years, soil-nutrient limitations caused the gain to diminish (Oren *et al.* 2001). If indeed such a CO_2-fertilization effect is small or even non-existent, as suggested in the article by Oren *et al.* (2001), then this makes the argument for additional forestry projects designed to abate carbon emissions even more compelling.

The IPCC Third Assessment Report (Kauppi & Sedjo 2001) confirms previous estimates (Brown *et al.* 1996) that the potential avoidance and removal of carbon emissions that could be achieved through the implementation of an aggressive program of changing forestry practices on *ca.* 700 million hectares over the next 50 years is *ca.* 60–87 Gt, equivalent to *ca.* 12–15% of the 'business-as-usual' fossil-fuel emissions (IPCC IS92a scenario) over the same period (see also Chapter 4). The Third Assessment Report also confirmed that activities in tropical forest lands are the lowest cost GHG mitigation strategy. As total reduction levels increase, tropical forestry's cost advantage over forestry in OECD countries, renewable energy, energy efficiency and fuel switching becomes increasingly significant (Figure 2.1). Such cost-effective measures in developing countries are more likely to encourage developed countries to invest in such projects without major disruptions to their economies.

A recent update of the IPCC assessment of the amount of carbon emissions that could be prevented from entering the atmosphere through reducing deforestation in the tropics resulted in an estimate of 157 MtC yr^{-1} (Niles *et al.*, Chapter 4 this book), compared with the 120–350 MtC yr^{-1} reported in Brown *et al.* (1996). The Niles *et al.* study included 46 tropical countries whereas that by Brown *et al.* (1996) included 52 tropical countries. In both studies, the rates of avoided deforestation were based on a study by Trexler & Haugan (1995). Niles *et al.* (Chapter 4 this book) further modified the rates reported by Trexler & Haugan in light of more recent assessments of tropical deforestation (FAO 2001). Niles estimated that *ca.* 1.4 Mha yr^{-1} of forests could be practically protected from deforestation or *ca.* 10% of the current deforestation rates as reported by the FAO (2001). This rate of protection from deforestation is about half that used in the study by Brown *et al.* (1996).

Deforestation is generally accomplished by burning considerable quantities of biomass. Biomass burning converts the nitrogen content in the biomass to nitrous oxide, another potent GHG and one that has a greater warming potential than CO_2. Preventing deforestation therefore also avoids considerable nitrous oxide emissions, the quantity of which is not well known (Houghton *et al.* 1997).

It has also recently been shown that many mature tropical forests continue to sequester carbon from the atmosphere. Several studies in the Amazon indicate a sink strength of the order of 1 tC ha^{-1} yr^{-1} or less (Phillips *et al.* 1998; Bolin & Sukumar 2000; Malhi & Grace 2000). Although it is not clear what the mechanism is for this sink and whether it is anthropogenic or not, conserving tropical forests under threat of destruction both avoids GHG emissions and sequesters additional carbon (Niles 2000; Chambers *et al.* 2001).

Although there is potential to avoid carbon emissions through changes in forest harvesting (e.g. conventional to reduced-impact logging), the magnitude of these potential savings has not been estimated to date. According to the Food and Agriculture Organization's recent assessment of tropical forests (FAO 2001), *ca.* 11.5 Mha of tropical forests were harvested per year during the 1990s. Based on an analysis of logging practices in Papua New Guinea and Indonesia, implementation of reduced-impact logging over conventional logging would avoid *ca.* 1.6–2.1 tC ha^{-1} yr^{-1} (S. Brown 2000, unpublished analysis). Assuming similar savings if reduced-impact logging was adopted globally in the tropics, a first approximation of the carbon emissions avoided would equal up to *ca.* 20 Mt yr^{-1}. However, reduced-impact logging results in less timber being produced per unit area, which might cause an increase in the area under logging to maintain timber output and thus the amount of carbon emissions avoided would be smaller.

During the Kyoto commitment period of 2008–2012, establishing new forests (regeneration, agroforestry and plantations) and slowing tropical deforestation could avoid and sequester *ca.* 990 MtC (210 Mt for establishing new forests (from Brown *et al.* 1996) and 783 Mt for slowing deforestation (Niles *et al.*, Chapter 4 this book)) or nearly all of the 1 GtC target for the first commitment period. However, the carbon mitigation potential described here is just that, and achieving these potentials would require a significant global 'will' as well as considerable capacity and resources to implement such projects. Technological change by developed countries must account for the largest proportion of emissions reduction; thus there is no escape from technological change through carbon sinks; there is no 'loophole'.

Technical and scientific issues surrounding LUCF activities

Objections have been raised to carbon sinks on the grounds of 'permanence', 'additionality', 'leakage', measurement, verification and lack of technology transfer. There is nothing unique about carbon sinks in respect to permanence, additionality, leakage, measurement, verification, or technology transfer. Means exist, or can be devised relying on existing principles and technology, to deal with all of these concerns with respect to carbon sinks, as we discuss below. Further details about measuring, monitoring and verification of carbon benefits are presented in Chapter 7, and will not be discussed further here.

There are many LUCF projects in various stages of design and implementation around the world, ranging from forest protection, changes in forest management, forestation (afforestation, reforestation and restoration), and community forestry and agroforestry (Brown *et al.* 2000). Most of the forestation projects are in non-tropical countries and most of the other project types are in tropical countries. Much experience has been gained to date by these projects in advancing the field in permanence, carbon monitoring, without-project baseline development, and leakage prevention. The focus in this section is on how these issues are being addressed in CDM-type pilot projects where these issues are viewed as being the most challenging.

Permanence/duration of projects

The life spans of forests (except those planted for wood products) are measured in centuries and extend beyond any currently advanced target period for reduction of atmospheric CO_2 and far beyond the life of any alternative technology-based installation. Recent research has demonstrated that tropical forests continue to sequester CO_2 throughout their life (Chambers *et al.* 2001). Projects that continue to store or sequester carbon for the selected target period or beyond are 'permanent' for all relevant purposes.

Concerns about permanence of biological sinks emerge because of the risk that the stored carbon could be released back to the atmosphere by natural (e.g. fires, disease outbreaks, hurricanes) or anthropogenic events (e.g. the non-enforcement of contracts, non-compliance with guarantees, expropriation, uncertain property rights, policy changes, land tenure, market risks). Of recent concern is the potential impact of future climate change on forest-carbon budgets, with models predicting that climate warming will enhance soil and plant respiration, thus reducing a forest's sink capacity. However, a recent review of this issue concluded that there is considerable uncertainty in these projections (The Royal Society 2001). For example, the models used to make the predictions are based on: business-as-usual CO_2 emission scenarios with no consideration for mitigation of emissions, the assumption of a pristine terrestrial biosphere, a relation between temperature and soil respiration that has recently been challenged by new findings, and no allowance for changes in the way humans manage the terrestrial biosphere.

Several practical approaches have been proposed for dealing with the problem that carbon stored in biological systems may be released to the atmosphere. One is to acknowledge that carbon sinks are a temporary means for abating emissions of GHGs and to assess the economic and environmental benefits of temporary storage (Chomitz 2000). The economic and environmental reasons include postponing climate change, buying time for developing and discovering alternative technologies to abate emissions, buying time for capital stock turnover, offering limited periods which are capable of being insured and, providing a means for host countries (who may be unwilling to lock up their lands in carbon projects forever) to preserve sovereignty and the opportunity to follow other future development pathways (Chomitz 2000; Marland *et al.* 2001).

Proposals have been made that basically view forestry projects as providing a service from nature that can be 'rented' (Ministry of the Environment, Government of Colombia 2000; Marland *et al.* 2001). The traditional system of a rental contract for limited-term use of an asset is ideally suited for the transfer of carbon credits where permanence is neither guaranteed nor wanted (Marland *et al.* 2001). The renter (or purchaser such as an entity in an Annex 1 country) can benefit from the limited-term carbon credits, while the seller retains long-term discretion over the resource. Under these proposals, at the end of the rental period the renter would have to replace the credits by renting new credits, purchase permanent credits, or incur a debit. When the credits expire, the land would be released from any further obligations; or the owner might decide to extend the project for another time period and be free to renegotiate.

Additionality and baselines

There is a concern that many carbon-sink projects would have happened anyway for commercial or political reasons other than the climate-change obligations and therefore add nothing to the effort to reduce global warming. In other words, there is no real reduction in emissions below business as usual, or

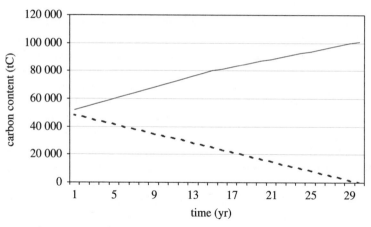

Figure 2.2. An example of a without-project or business-as-usual baseline (dashed line) and a with-project scenario (solid line). The carbon offsets would be the difference between the with- and without-project cases. This example represents a project that protects *ca.* 1000 ha of secondary forest from further degradation and deforestation over a 30-year period.

no additionality, as required by the language of the climate agreements. While additionality assessments for a given mitigation project have different components and are based on multiple sources of information, most additionality problems apply equally to projects in the energy or forestry sectors (Chomitz 2000).

Not all forestry projects are alike when it comes to showing additionality (Chomitz 2000). For example, projects that have direct financial benefits and involve practices that are well understood may be adopted regardless of concerns for carbon credits. An example of this is industrial-scale exotic-tree plantations for pulpwood or sawtimber. Although these plantations could sequester large amounts of carbon, the financial returns are high enough that they might have been implemented regardless of climate change (business as usual). Tree plantation projects for timber products could have serious difficulties in showing additionality, particularly as the area of industrial plantations in developing countries has grown at *ca.* 4 Mha yr^{-1} over the past 10 years or so (Brown 2000). On the other hand, forestry projects that have little to no monetary benefits and yet impose ongoing costs on a developer are unlikely to be undertaken spontaneously and thus are likely to meet the additionality criterion (Chomitz 2000). Examples of this situation include forest protection from logging, forest restoration on degraded lands, reforestation for watershed protection and plantations in remote areas where tree growth rates are slow.

Once additionality has been demonstrated, a baseline or a projection of the 'business-as-usual' carbon emissions or storage needs to be developed for all mitigation projects. The difference between the carbon emissions or removals of the baseline for without-project activities and the carbon emissions or removals for with-project activities represents the carbon value. Figure 2.2 provides an example of a project baseline without-project carbon stocks and with-project carbon stocks. It represents a project that protects *ca.* 1000 ha of secondary forest from further degradation and deforestation over a 30-year period. By protecting the forest, it is allowed to rebuild carbon stocks as well as avoid emissions from the deforestation. By the end of this example project, *ca.* 100 ktC may be generated from avoided emissions and sequestration.

Baselines can be established by projecting past trends and current situations to calculate the amount of carbon stored or emitted based on the conventional pattern of land use and forestry. Comparable baselines are used in planning virtually all infrastructure and long-term capital investments such as power plants. Other methods include benchmarking models, similar to those used in industry, and those of minimum performance benchmarks (Brown 1998).

Changes in land use are not random phenomena, but rather are predictable, based on some combination of biophysical factors, presence of transportation networks, access to markets, and agroclimatic suitability (Kaimowitz & Angelsen 1998; Chomitz 2000). An array of tools including remote-sensing data, spatial land-use change models, forest growth models and field measurements is already being used to develop relatively simple, yet credible, baselines by project type and region.

Leakage

Leakage is defined as the unanticipated decrease or increase in GHG benefits outside of a project's accounting boundary, as a result of the project activities. Potential leakage results from two effects: market effects, when project activities change supply and demand equilibrium; and activity shifting, when the activity causing carbon emissions in the project area is displaced outside a project's boundary. Identification and quantification of leakage remains one of the most challenging technical issues related to the development of carbon projects. This has been the subject of many studies, and it appears to be equally problematic for both land-use and energy projects (Chomitz 2000; Schlamadinger & Marland 2000). The mere presence of the potential for leakage does not make a project unattractive; instead strategies need to be developed to either mitigate it and/or account for it. Further discussion and a framework for addressing leakage in forestry projects are presented in Chapter 8 and in Brown (1998) and will not be discussed further here.

Experience to date has been limited to a few projects, and hindered by the lack of data, and short time-frames since project inception. Qualitative methods may need to be developed further, together with efforts to generate more-accurate data at the right level of definition (Aukland *et al.* 2003).

Ancillary benefits and technology transfer

Forest-based carbon projects can provide numerous additional environmental and socio-economic benefits to host countries and local communities (Chomitz & Kumari 1998; Frumhoff *et al.* 1998; Klooster & Masera 2000). Carbon-sink projects can provide the capital needed to help countries meet multiple national and local sustainable development objectives: technology transfer, expansion of national parks, alleviation of poverty among the rural poor and increased country capacity to adapt to and thus reduce vulnerability to climate change.

Environmental co-benefits from forest projects include conservation of existing, or restoration of, biodiversity, protection of habitat and protection of soil and water resources. Protection of water resources results in improved water-flow regimes and water quality, which in turn reduce siltation and flood risk, which in turn protects downstream water users, fisheries, coastal coral reefs and hydroelectric facilities (Chomitz & Kumari 1998). Most projects involving improvements in forest management provide substantial environmental and socio-economic benefits for the local owners (Klooster & Masera 2000). For example, in Michoacan, Mexico, a community-owned logging operation in the common-property forested (ejido) land provides rural development benefits (e.g. community stores, library, public transportation, recreational facility and agriculture extension) and employment for a majority of the communities' male population, while at the same time careful logging and reforestation activities increases the coverage and quality of the community forest and increases its carbon stocks. The average long-term increase in carbon stocks was *ca.* 1.8 Mt, yet the community (and others like it in Mexico) receives no financial compensation for the global benefits of these activities (Klooster & Masera 2000).

Establishment of fuel-wood plantations can reduce impacts on native woodlands, especially in arid regions (Kanowski *et al.* 1992), and thus may help to slow the pace of desertification. However, if exotic forest plantations are used to replace native ecosystems such as grasslands or woodlands, biodiversity would be reduced. Such projects should be disallowed except in situations where plantations of non-native species are all that will grow on severely degraded lands, and serve as a 'nursery' for regeneration of native species (Lugo *et al.* 1993).

One of the concerns about allowing forestry projects in the CDM revolves around the assertion that the transfer of emission-reducing technology to developing countries may be reduced. The fear is that carbon sinks will provide a substitute for, or disincentive to, transfer of clean energy technology to developing countries. However, the benefits of technology transfer will depend on the nature of the technology. For example, small-scale, locally replicable technology is likely to diffuse faster and have greater benefits to employment and poverty alleviation than the importation of large-scale sophisticated technology (Chomitz 2000). There are many forestry-related technologies, such as tree selection, nursery management, improved silvicultural practices, improved forest management and harvesting technologies, biodiversity conservation, wildlife management, etc., that lend themselves to local adoption and diffusion to the rural poor. Projects that incorporate alternative provision of fuel would also transfer biofuel or small-scale electrification technologies. Projects that incorporate improved agricultural practices to address the loss of agricultural land would transfer improved crop production technologies.

Conclusions

Recent international effort regarding global warming has focused on the Kyoto Protocol. In that context, controversy has arisen over the use of biological means to absorb or reduce emissions of CO_2 (often referred to as carbon 'sinks'). Objections to carbon sinks are based primarily on two arguments. First, sinks may allow developed nations to delay or avoid technological adjustments: the 'loophole' argument. Second, technical and operational difficulties would reduce the value of sinks, allowing for inflated claims of carbon offsets: the 'floodgates' argument. We conclude that neither argument bears scrutiny.

The atmosphere does not distinguish between emissions and removals. In order to achieve any significant change in atmospheric concentrations of GHG, both emissions reductions and emissions removals can be effective and, as we discussed here, both are needed. Carbon sinks, unlike most mitigation strategies, offer opportunities both to reduce CO_2 emissions through avoiding further deforestation and improving forest management and to remove atmospheric CO_2 through establishment of new forests on marginal lands or protection of secondary forests. As carbon-sink strategies can be implemented relatively quickly because little new technology is needed, they readily lend themselves to local adoption and diffusion to the rural poor.

The Third Assessment Report of the IPCC concluded that biological sinks can make an important, albeit limited, contribution to the transition to a lower emissions environment, and can do so at significantly lower cost than other mitigation techniques. This is the case regardless of whether or not the Kyoto Protocol is ratified. Well-designed forestry projects can, in addition, provide significant environmental and socio-economic benefits to host countries and local communities, particularly in the tropics. There is no meaningful distinction between carbon sinks and other mitigation techniques in so far as difficulty of regulation is concerned. A regulatory framework for such projects can be implemented relying on existing principles and techniques. A well-designed regulatory framework, including adhesion to international agreements on bio-diversity, desertification, wetlands, and indigenous peoples' rights, would strengthen sustainable development, while at the same time enhancing efforts to address climate change.

Acknowledgements

We thank many of our colleagues for providing helpful comments and insights during the preparation of this chapter: in particular, Naomi Pena, Eric Bettelheim, John Kadyszewski, Alan Bernstein, Chris Aldridge, and two anonymous referees.

References

Arnell, N. W., Cannell, M. G. R., Hulme, M., Mitchell, J. F. B., Kovats, S., Nicholls, R. J., Parry, M. L., Livermore, M. T. J. & White, A. 2002 The consequence of CO_2 stabilisation for the impacts of climate change. *Climatic Change* **53**, 413–446.

Aukland, L., Moura Costa, P. & Brown, S. 2003 A conceptual framework and its application for addressing leakage on avoided deforestation projects. *Climatic Policy.* (In the press.)

Blok, K., de Jager, D. & Hendriks, C. 2001 Economic evaluation of sectoral emission reduction objectives for climate change: summary report for policy makers. Joint publication by ECOFYS Energy and Environment, The Netherlands, AEA Technology, UK and National Technical University of Athens, Greece. (Available at http://europa.eu.int/comm/environment/enveco/climate_change/sectoral_objectives.htm.)

Bolin, B. & Sukumar, R. 2000 Global perspective. In *Land use, land-use change and forestry. Special Report of the IPCC* (ed. R. T. Watson, I. R. Noble, B. Bolin, N. H. Ravindranath, D. J. Verardo & D. J. Dokken), pp. 23–51. Cambridge University Press.

Brown, P. 1998 *Climate, biodiversity, and forests: issues and opportunities emerging from the Kyoto Protocol.* Washington, DC: World Resources Institute.

Brown, C. 2000 The global outlook for future wood supply from forest plantations. Working paper no. GFPOS/WP/03. Food and Agriculture Organization, Rome.

Brown, S., Sathaye, J., Cannell, M. & Kauppi, P. 1996 Management of forests for mitigation of greenhouse gas emissions. In *Climate change 1995. Impacts, adaptations and mitigation of climate change: scientific-technical analyses. Contribution of Working Group II to the Second Assessment Report of the Intergovernmental Panel on Climate Change* (ed. R. T. Watson, M. C. Zinyowera & R. H. Moss), ch. 24. Cambridge University Press.

Brown, S., Masera, O. & Sathaye, J. 2000 Project-based activities. In *Land use, land-use change and forestry; special report to the intergovernmental panel on climate change* (ed. R. T. Watson, I. R. Noble, B. Bolin, N. H. Ravindranath, D. J. Verardo & D. J. Dokken), pp. 283–338. Cambridge University Press.

Chambers, J. Q., Higuchi, N., Tribuzy, E. S. & Trumbore, S. E. 2001 Carbon sink for a century. *Nature* **410**, 429.

Chomitz, K. M. 2000 Evaluating carbon offsets from forestry and energy projects: how do they compare? Report, Development Research Group, World Bank, Washington, DC.

Chomitz, K. M. & Kumari, K. 1998 The domestic benefits of tropical forests: a critical review emphasizing hydrological functions. World Bank Policy Research Working Paper no. WPS1601.

FAO 2001 Global forest resources assessment 2000, main report. FAO Forestry Paper 140. Food and Agriculture Organization. (Available at www.fao.org/forestry/fo/fra/index.jsp.)

Frumhoff, P. C., Goetze, D. C. & Hardner, J. H. 1998 Linking solutions to climate change and biodiversity loss through the Kyoto Protocol's clean development mechanism. Report. Union of Concerned Scientists, Cambridge, MA.

Houghton, J. T., Meira Filho, L. G., Lim, B., Treanton, K., Mamaty, I., Bonduki, Y., Griggs, D. J. & Callander, B. A. 1997 Revised 1996 Guidelines for National Greenhouse Gas Inventories. Reference Manual. Joint publication by IPCC/OECD/IEA.

Kaimowitz, D. & Angelsen, A. 1998 *Economic models of tropical deforestation: a review.* Bogor, Indonesia: Center for International Forestry Research.

Kanowski, P. J., Savill, P. S., Adlard, P. G., Burley, J., Evans, J., Palmer, J. R. & Wood, P. J. 1992 Plantation forestry. In *Managing the world's forests* (ed. N. P. Sharma), pp. 375–401. Dubuque, IA: Kendall-Hunt.

Kauppi, P. & Sedjo, R. 2001 Technical and economic potential of options to enhance, maintain and manage biological carbon reservoirs and geo-engineering. In *Climate change 2001: mitigation. Contribution of Working Group III to the Third Assessment Report of the IPCC* (ed. B. Metz, O. Davidson, R. Swart & J. Pan), pp. 301–344. Cambridge University Press.

Keeling, C. D. & Whorf, T. P. 2000 Atmospheric CO_2 concentrations: Mauna Loa Observatory, Hawaii, 1958–1999. Report no. NDP-001, Carbon Dioxide Information Center, Oak Ridge National Laboratory, Oak Ridge, TN, USA. (Available at http://cdiac.esd.ornl.gov/ndps/ndp001.html.)

Klooster, D. & Masera, O. R. 2000 Community forest management in Mexico: making carbon sequestration a by-product of sustainable rural development. *Glob. Environ. Change* **10**, 259–272.

Lugo, A. E., Parotta, J. A. & Brown, S. 1993 Loss in species caused by tropical deforestation and their recovery through management. *Ambio* **22**, 106–109.

Malhi, Y. & Grace, J. 2000 Tropical forests and atmospheric carbon dioxide. *Trends Ecol. Evol.* **15**, 332–337.

Marland, G., Boden, T. & Andres, R. J. 2000 Global, regional, and national CO_2 emission estimates from fossil fuel burning, cement production, and gas flaring 1751–1997. Report no. NDP-030, Carbon Dioxide Information Center, Oak Ridge National Laboratory, Oak Ridge, TN. (Available from http://cdiac.esd.ornl.gov/ndps/ndp030.html.)

Marland, G., Fruit, K. & Sedjo, R. 2001 Accounting for sequestered carbon: the question of permanence. *Environ. Sci. Policy* **4**, 259–268.

Ministry of the Environment, Government of Colombia 2000 Expiring CERs, a proposal to addressing the permanence issue. In United Nations Framework Convention on Climate Change, report no. UNFCCC/SBSTA/2000/MISC.8, pp. 23–26. (Available at www.unfccc.de.)

Myers, N. & Goreau, T. J. 1991 Tropical forests and the greenhouse effect: a management response. *Climatic Change* **19**, 215–225.

Nakicenovic, N. (and 27 others) 2000 *Emission scenarios. A Special Report of Working Group III of the Intergovernmental Panel on Climate Change* (ed. N. Nakicenovic & R. Swart). Cambridge University Press.

Niles, J. 2000 The additional benefits of reducing carbon emissions from tropical deforestation. Morrison Institute for Population and Resource Studies, Working Paper no. 0084. Stanford University, Stanford, CA.

Oren, R. (and 10 others) 2001 Soil fertility limits carbon sequestration by forest ecosystems in a CO_2-enriched atmosphere. *Nature* **411**, 469–472.

Phillips, O. L. (and 10 others) 1998 Changes in the carbon balance of tropical forests: evidence from long-term plots. *Science* **282**, 439–442.

Schlamadinger, B. & Marland, G. 2000 Land use and global climate change: forests, land management and the Kyoto Protocol. Report, Pew Center on Global Climate Change, Washington, DC, USA.

The Royal Society 2001 The role of land carbon sinks in mitigating global climate change. Policy document no. 10/01. (Available at www.royalsoc.ac.uk/files/statfiles/document-150.pdf.)

Trexler, M. & Haugen, C. 1995 *Keeping it green: tropical forestry opportunities for mitigating climate change.* Washington, DC: World Resources Institute.

Trexler, M., Kosloff, L. & Gibbons, R. 1999 Overview of forestry and land-use projects pursued under the pilot. In *The UN framework convention on climate change activities implemented jointly (AIJ) pilot: experience and lessons learned* (ed. R. K. Dixon), pp. 121–166. Kluwer.

UNFCCC 2001 United Nations Framework Convention on Climate Change agenda items 4 and 7. In *Proc. Conference of the Parties, 6th Session, Part 2, Bonn, 16–27 July 2001*. (Available at www.climnet.org/cop7/FCCCCP2001L.7.pdf.)

Watson, R. T., Noble, I. R., Bolin, B., Ravindranath, N. H., Verardo, D. J. & Dokken, D. J. (eds) 2000 *Land use, land-use change, and forestry: a special report to the Intergovernmental Panel on Climate Change*. Cambridge University Press.

Chapter 3

An overview of a free-market approach to climate change and conservation

Richard L. Sandor, Eric C. Bettelheim and Ian R. Swingland

Introduction

The last decade of the 20th century witnessed the convergence of environmental protection initiatives and financial markets. Market-based mechanisms such as emissions trading have become widely accepted as a cost-effective method for achieving environmental improvements.

Historical precedent seems to indicate that the evolutionary nature of markets follows a concise seven-stage process. The evolution of environmental markets is undergoing a process similar to that experienced by other established or 'mature' markets. Examples can be drawn from the equity, commodity and fixed-income markets. More recently, the seven-stage process can be observed in the emergence of sulphur dioxide trading under the Acid Rain Programme in the US.

As societies move towards a carbon-constrained world, greenhouse-gas-emissions (GHG-emissions) trading is gaining acceptance by the private sector and governments as a cost-effective way to reduce the risk that human-induced climate change is causing. Therefore, we are witnessing the same evolutionary process in the case of carbon dioxide (CO_2) emissions.

The benefits of using market mechanisms such as emissions trading can also be seen in the field of conservation. Carbon sinks such as forests can play a major role in the protection and enhancement of habitats, thus contributing to overall environmental gains in the form of improved water quality and biodiversity preservation (Walsh 1999).

In the near term we can expect that the convergence of environment and finance will take the form of a greater interrelationship between a corporation's financial performance and its environmental management, as well as increased use of market-based mechanisms to address such issues as water quality and fisheries.

The emergence of emissions trading

The past decade has seen the convergence of environmental and financial markets in the form of the 'commoditization' of natural resources such as air and water. These resources have traditionally been treated as having a 'zero' price, which encouraged over consumption and contributed to the problem sometimes referred to by economists as 'the tragedy of the commons.'

The principle behind the market-based approach is to treat the environment as a truly scarce resource by establishing limits on its use. The use of a property-like instrument—such as emissions allowances and offsets—provides a mechanism that can ensure efficient use of the resource and yields a price in a market that was previously not available. The price of tradeable emission rights signals the value society places on use of the environment and denotes the financial reward paid to reduce those emissions. Importantly, these rewards are received by those who own the property rights in the resource and therefore are most likely to manage it efficiently. Certainty as to ownership, and legal title, is fundamental both to the success of the market and to ensuring that the value of the resource is realized by those entitled to it. This not only avoids the 'tragedy of the commons', but also liberates new capital that can be dedicated to environmental improvement (see De Soto 2000).

Emissions trading has its intellectual roots in a seminal article by Nobel Laureate Ronald Coase, entitled 'The problem of social cost' (Coase 1960). Coase argued that assigning property rights to public goods will yield a socially efficient use of resources, even when externalities are present. Once rights are assigned, parties can negotiate—given perfect information and low transaction costs—through the market to achieve an optimal usage of common property resources. The assignment of rights and the means by which they can transferred are the function of property laws and market regulations. Once these are present, together with agreed terms of trade, the market can operate freely, allowing buyers and sellers to adjust their needs as best suits their individual requirements.

These market-based mechanisms represent a movement away from highly prescriptive environmental policies that are thought to impose higher compliance costs compared with more flexible regulations. It is widely believed that traditional 'command and control' regulations fail to exploit the least-cost opportunities to cut pollution, and do little to reward innovative pollution avoidance and reduction efforts. The goal of market-based regulation is to reduce the cost of achieving a given pollution-reduction target or, equivalently, to realize larger pollution reductions at the same cost. The cap-and-trade emissions-trading approach exploits differences in pollution-mitigation costs faced by different emission sources. Trading uses a price signal and profit motive to encourage the sources that can cut pollution most cost effectively to take advantage of their comparative advantage and make more of the overall pollution cut. The goal is to help society find and move along the least-cost pollution-reduction supply curve. From a political economy perspective, by lowering the unit price of cutting pollution, emissions trading is thought to increase the quantity of pollution reduction the public is willing and able to purchase. In addition to the transparency and accountability features of trading systems, improved affordability of environmental protection is one of the central reasons emissions trading is gaining greater acceptance.

Historical evolution of markets

In order to better understand the current state of environmental markets, it is useful to examine the historical development of other 'mature' markets. The history of markets indicates that their evolutionary path follows a concise seven-stage process. Examples can be drawn from the equity, commodity and fixed-income markets (Sandor 1992). More recently, the seven-stage process can be witnessed in the emergence of sulphur dioxide trading under the Acid Rain Programme in the US.

To understand how markets can evolve, we present a seven-stage process that helps describe the many forces that accrue over time and sometimes develop into more sophisticated and efficient markets. The steps can be characterized as follows:

1 The occurrence of a major structural change that creates a demand for capital.

2 The creation of uniform standards for a commodity or security.

3 The development of a legal instrument that provides evidence of ownership.

4 The development of informal spot markets (for immediate delivery) and forward markets (non-standardized agreements for future delivery) in commodities and securities where 'receipts' of ownership are traded.

5 The emergence of securities and commodities exchanges.

6 The creation of organized futures markets (standardized contracts for future delivery on organized exchanges) and options markets (rights but not guarantees for future delivery) in commodities and securities.

7 The proliferation of over-the-counter markets and deconstruction of traded instruments.

Within this framework, we present some historical examples of the market-evolution pattern for equities, commodities and fixed-income securities, and we consider its application to environmental markets.

Examples of the seven-stage process

In 1492, the 'discovery' of America (from the European perspective) created a tremendous structural change. The Age of Discovery demanded a great amount of financial capital, as business activity expanded in both the New World and between Europe and Asia. An important byproduct of this era was the formation of the Dutch East India Company. This was a critical innovation, which led to the acceptance of the limited liability corporation. Before that, there were 'partnerships' that raised capital, but it was the limited liability corporation and the development of transferable equity shares that provided a standard instrument and the evidence of ownership. Its use ultimately led to trading on a number of regional exchanges in and around Amsterdam, followed in the 16th century by the development of futures and options trading on these shares.

In the case of agricultural commodities, the removal of restrictions on grain imports into England and the Crimean War acted as the structural changes, stimulating grain production in the US, which became a large exporter of agricultural goods. Growth in demand for grain continued as the US population reached 35 million by the end of the Civil War. Capital was needed to finance the storage and shipment of grain from the Midwest to the major population centres in the East Coast. At that time, there was unorganized trading in physical sacks of grain, which had to be inspected on an individual basis. The creation of the Chicago Board of Trade in 1848 ushered in grain standards and grading procedures, an innovation that preceded the creation of government standards by 50 years. Ultimately, a tradeable legal instrument called the 'warehouse receipt' emerged, which provided evidence of ownership and facilitated both capital raising and ownership transfer. The birth of futures trading in 1865 was followed by options trading at a later stage.

A more modern example of the market evolution pattern is the fixed-income market for mortgage-backed securities. The post-World War II economic boom in the US created a great demand for housing in California, which had to be financed by institutions in the eastern part of the country. Although standardized mortgages guaranteed by the Federal Housing Authority (FHA) and the Veterans Administration (VA) assured capital flows into the sector, it was a highly inefficient market. Mortgages were sold on an individual basis or in small packages and the buyer had to have individual documentation for each loan. The 'credit crunch' of 1966 and 1969 and the uncertainty surrounding the timely payment of the principal and interest during foreclosures gave rise to the formation of the Government National Mortgage Association (GNMA). This enabled the 'bundling' of small loans into securities to be collateralized by the FHA/VA and backed by the US government. It provided an efficient and homogeneous evidence of ownership and conveyance vehicle, which ultimately evolved into spot and forward markets, primarily among Wall Street dealers and mortgage bankers. This informal arrangement served the function of an exchange until the world's first interest-rate futures contract—based on the GNMA mortgage-backed instrument—was launched at the Chicago Board of Trade in 1975. From that date, financial futures secured acceptance and ultimately, in the 1980s, so did collateralized mortgages.

Therefore, looking at equities, physical commodities and fixed-income instruments, and examining their development from the 16th to the 20th century, indicates that they all follow the pattern of market evolution we have outlined. We are now on the verge of a whole new field of tradeable products in the form of environmental contracts and derivatives (Sandor 1999).

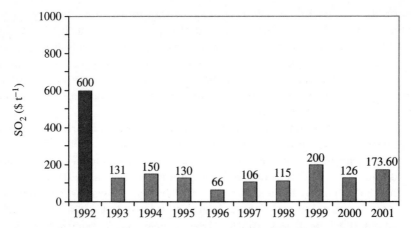

Figure 3.1. SO$_2$: price forecast and auction results. (The figure of $600 for 1992 is the median forecast from Hahn & May (1994). Auction prices from the Chicago Board of Trade and USEPA (1999).)

The example from the SO$_2$ market in the US is particularly informative. A latent demand for this market in abating sulphur gases resulted from a significant increase in the burning of high-sulphur coal by electric utilities in order to satisfy the demand for electricity. Increased pollution in the form of sulphuric emissions accompanied the increased output of electricity. Generated in more densely populated sections of the US, this pollution resulted in large increases in respiratory problems for affected populations. In addition, acidification damaged rivers, streams and forests. Latent demand became effective demand as public concern over human health and environmental problems motivated legislators to pass the Clean Air Act Amendments (CAAA) of 1990.

As the examples below show, the CAAA simultaneously performed three functions:

1 It standardized an environmental commodity (a legally authorized allowance to emit 1 tonne of sulphur dioxide).

2 It produced the 'evidence of ownership' necessary for financial instruments.

3 It established the infrastructure to efficiently transfer title.

The system has been highly successful and has achieved more reductions than the law requires at costs that are an order of magnitude lower than the highest forecasts. There has not been an incident of non-compliance in almost seven years of the programme's existence. Studies by the General Accounting Office and non-governmental organizations put the annual costs of the programme at $1–2 billion, while the health benefits have been estimated to range from $12 billion per year to $40 billion per year, according to a US Environmental Protection Agency (USEPA) report. Compliance flexibility and trading have lowered compliance costs more than 75% compared with initial forecasts.

Figure 3.1 shows the average forecast compared with actual allowances prices at the annual USEPA auction over the course of the acid-rain programme. Prior to enactment of the CAAA, industry studies forecast compliance costs as high as $1800 per tonne of SO_2 reduction, with most forecasts in the $300–1000 per tonne range. In reality, allowances, or emission permits, currently sell for less than $200 per tonne and have averaged *ca.* $130 at the annual EPA auctions held at the Chicago Board of Trade over the programme's life. Motivated by the ability of a company to 'bank' excess allowances, reductions in excess of what is required by law have been achieved.

There has also been steady growth in the trading of allowances, from 700 000 tonnes in 1995 to *ca.* 12 million tonnes in 2001. The market has now reached a value of *ca.* $2 billion each year for registered trades. Environmental Financial Products estimates that, in addition, there may be $2 billion a year in derivatives such as options, forwards and other unregistered trades.

The programme works because acid rain is a regional problem and multiple sources contribute to the problem. It relies on a fixed environmental goal—an emissions limit, or cap. Direct monitoring of emissions is used both to verify that the cap is achieved and to insure the value of the tradeable allowances. The relevant variable to be measured is the total loading of SO_2 emissions in the atmosphere, not emissions from an individual source. Violations of SO_2 air-quality standards will prevent a company from buying allowances. The emission-monitoring protocols are clearly established by law. Differences in mitigation costs across sources contribute to costs savings.

Cap-and-trade emissions-trading systems are successful from both an environmental and economic viewpoint because they provide industry with the flexibility in method, location and timing of emission reductions. The entrepreneurial skills of industry are harnessed for pollution reduction. The system provides direct financial incentives for least-cost solutions and technological innovation to reduce emissions. All of these characteristics of a successful emissions-trading programme may be applied to GHGs.

The emergence of an international emissions-trading market for GHGs

The evolution of environmental markets undergoes a process similar to that experienced by other established or 'mature' markets. We believe there is a case for extending what we have learned in the SO_2 cap-and-trade programme to other areas, mainly global warming.

It might be useful to frame this discussion in light of what the eminent economist Joseph Schumpeter called the three phases of the inventive process: invention, innovation and imitation (Schumpeter 1942). The first is the creation of the idea. The second is innovation, which is the commercialization of the idea. The third is the diffusion or replication and the widespread use of the idea. Economists and business leaders have long been concerned with the process of invention and innovation. Although the primary areas of attention have been in the industrial arts, students of technological change would probably agree that non-patentable creative activity in the economic and financial markets has spawned significant social benefits. Simple examples of financial innovations that have had immeasurable impact include the development of double-entry bookkeeping and the limited liability corporation. These may indeed rank with industrial inventions such as the steam engine, or even the semiconductor.[1]

With the success of the sulphur-trading programme and other environmental markets, such as the market mechanisms established under the Montreal Protocol to deal with ozone-depleting substances, trading in GHGs represents the replication or imitation phase. Emissions trading is a market-based option that has been proven in solving other pollution problems. It should be applied to limiting emissions of CO_2, methane and other heat-trapping GHGs. Emissions trading has become a more widely accepted approach to the climate-change issue and it also might help provide incentives to support efforts to enhance biodiversity conservation.

The scientific community still debates whether the potential warming of the planet is natural or human induced. Nonetheless, there is a general consensus that the rapid increase in the atmospheric concentrations of GHGs introduces the risk of fundamental and costly changes in the Earth's climate system. While the exact nature, timing and magnitude of the expected climatic changes cannot be predicted with certainty, the nature of the risks includes more severe drought/precipitation cycles, longer and more extreme heat waves, spread of tropical diseases, damage to vegetation and agricultural systems due to comparatively rapid climate shifts, and threats to coastlines and coastal properties due to higher sea levels and storm surges.

In the United Nations Framework Convention on Climate Change (UNFCCC), ratified by most of the nations of the world, industrialized countries agreed 'to aim to reduce' GHG emissions to 1990 levels by the year 2000. At the Third Conference of the Parties to the UNFCCC (COP-3), the Parties agreed to the Kyoto Protocol. Broad acceptance of trading was reflected in its text. The central goal of the Kyoto Protocol is to slow the human contribution to increased atmospheric concentrations of CO_2. The Protocol specifies quantified emission limits for developed countries, as well as the further articulation of the economic mechanisms of emissions trading, Joint Implementation and the Clean Development Mechanism (CDM), and the role of carbon sequestration or 'sinks'.[2]

Benefits for conservation

The Kyoto Protocol's goal of slowing the pace of rapid climate change would, on its own, provide an enormous service towards the preservation of biolog-

---

[1] Economics Nobel prize winner Kenneth Arrow made this observation in the 1970s in Chicago.

[2] During the Sixth Conference of the Parties (COP-6) second meetings in Bonn in July 2001, the Parties to the Convention (excluding the US) agreed to allow reforestation projects under the CDM, to develop some simplified CDM procedures and to allow some credits for sequestration resulting from reforestation as well as from forest and soil management in developed countries.

ical diversity. More directly, Kyoto acknowledged that carbon sinks, such as forests and soils, act to capture and store atmospheric CO_2. An immediate opportunity to provide financial support for conservation can arise from a GHG-emissions-trading system. This emerging market can be harnessed to help finance reforestation and encourage improvement in agricultural soil quality and agricultural watersheds. To the extent that the Kyoto Protocol can be implemented in ways that provide financial support for these efforts, protection and expansion of habitats that support biological diversity will be enhanced.

The presence of an emissions-trading market will introduce a clear financial value for GHG emissions released or captured. A new and visible price will be associated with the carbon-mitigation environmental service produced by expanded forest stocks and increased soil sinks. New and expanded forests and soils sinks can earn a direct cash award in the carbon-mitigation market. This opportunity to profit in the emissions-trading market (by selling emission credits to those entities who find it less costly to outsource part of their emission-mitigation commitment) provides a new source of funding for activities that will also protect biological species. This is an indirect market in support of biodiversity, but a potentially powerful one nevertheless (Walsh 1999).

Traditional approaches to habitat protection, national parks and other limited-use areas are often resented, particularly in areas with substantial population growth and limited alternative sources of income. By excluding local people and limiting or preventing their use of the resources, these methods encourage illegal activities, including poaching and logging, stimulate costly and often destructive internal migration and encourage the misuse of resources. These negative externalities are avoided and positive externalities achieved when the value of the environmental services of the area are fully realized and that value is received by local people. Where, for example, the value of growing forests exceeds their value as sources of timber or fuel, they are protected with the concomitant effects of preserving watersheds, wildlife habitat, biodiversity and amenity. This not only provides additional income, but it also encourages sustainable use of the resource and employment. New opportunities for sustainable harvest of natural products, ecotourism and horticulture arise or are enhanced. Local people thereby become stakeholders in their environment rather than trespassers on it (see Schumpeter (1942) and Chapter 12).

The potential for emissions-trading solutions can be extended to agriculture and forestry. Taking US agriculture as an example, farmers can offer a highly effective system for capturing or 'sequestering' carbon from the atmosphere. A major means of sequestering more carbon in cropland is through best-management practices. The most effective and readily available methods for increasing the amount of carbon stored in soils is a set of activities referred to as 'conservation systems'. Most important among these are the various forms of conservation tillage. Crop roots and stalks are left in place, thus reducing soil venting (and carbon release) effects of conventional tilling practices. Low- and no-till practices lead to a substantial increase in the amount of carbon built up and stored in soils (Sandor & Skees 1999).

Conservation-tillage practices also provide a wide range of terrestrial and aquatic habitat benefits, ranging from less erosion and less herbicide and water run-off compared with fields where conventional plowing is done. In addition to improving local water habitat, the prospect of basin-wide improvements in water quality can help reduce large-scale regional problems. In the case of developing countries, by increasing the carbon content of soil and providing increased crop yields, conservation-tillage practices may help to avoid pressure to convert forests to croplands.

If managed properly, participation in the international carbon market could soften farm-income cycles by taking land out of crop production and putting it into conservation when relative prices favour carbon sequestration over food production. Leading scientists expect that climate change brought about by increased GHGs may bring more extreme draughts and floods. Thus farmers and foresters cannot only sell a new 'crop' in the international environmental service market, they can also help solve a problem that threatens their own livelihood.

The emerging market for GHG-emission reductions

Markets for GHG-emissions trading are emerging around the world despite uncertainties regarding the Kyoto Protocol and the likelihood of an international regime created by the United Nations. However, these emerging markets, and an international market linking them, are still in their infancy. The standards or protocols for monitoring, verification, legal contracts, trade documentation and eligibility of offsets are not yet in place. There are no organized exchanges or clear market prices. Each transaction is different, leading to high transactions costs. In short, the commodity, and the trading of it, are now moving through the seven-stage process (Sandor & LeBlanc 2002).

Nonetheless, the amount of activity related to GHG-emissions trading is significant. Table 3.1 indicates some of the initiatives undertaken by international agencies, such as The World Bank Carbon Fund and the research and support activities of the United Nations and European umbrella organizations, as well as programmes and proposals of national governments and emerging groups of national trading partners.

Natural trading partnerships are developing. The evolutionary process of market development also mirrors the history of international political cooperation. International agreements tend to grow from small beginnings—the European Coal and Steel Community has evolved to the Common Market and, now, the European Monetary Union. In the case of carbon trading, a group of countries is beginning to coalesce into what we call a 'plurilateral' trading regime, involving a system of conventions and regulations evolving first among a small group of countries. In the context of the Kyoto Protocol negotiations, these include the Umbrella Group, consisting of the US and countries that sided with it in supporting unrestricted use of trading mechanisms and sinks and the countries of the EU, which took an opposite stance on trading issues. However, the EU released a proposal at the end of October 2001 to establish an emissions-trading programme to start in 2005.

Table 3.1. *Government and multilateral GHG-emissions-trading initiatives*

International agency initiatives	Emerging plurilateral trading groups	National GHG-emissions trading and CDM/JI programmes or proposals
World Bank Carbon Fund	*Umbrella Group*	UK
UNCTAD Global Policy Forum	Japan	Denmark
OECD Workshops & Research	US	EU
International Energy Agency	Canada	Germany
UNEP	Australia	Norway
UNDP	New Zealand	Netherlands
UNIDO	Iceland	US
European Commission	Norway	Canada
Nordic Council	Russia	New Zealand
	Ukraine	Russia
	EU	Ireland
	North America	Slovakia
	US	32 host countries with CDM/AIJ offices or projects, including Costa Rica, Brazil and Central America
	Mexico	
	Canada	
	Baltic countries	

At the national-governmental level, the UK launched an emissions-trading system for GHGs in early 2002, developed by the government and a consortium of businesses known as the Emissions Trading Group. The British government has also indicated that it will attempt to merge this initiative into the pilot EU programme with as little friction as possible.

Efforts are also under way in the Netherlands, where the government plans to launch a CO_2-trading system by 2004–2005, and in Germany, where a public–private task force is preparing a proposal for a trading system design. In Japan, a working group comprised of members of the public and private sector has been meeting to discuss setting up an emissions-trading market. Denmark launched the first national domestic GHG-emissions-trading market, but it was limited to the power sector.

Bipartisan support to take domestic action is gaining momentum in the US Congress. Senators McCain (Republican, Arizona) and Lieberman (Democrat, Connecticut) recently announced support for an economy-wide cap-and-trade system for GHGs. Legislators have advanced proposals for registries for carbon sequestered in biomass and soil. Discussions at recent hearings before the Senate Commerce and Environment and Public Works Committees indicate the interest of numerous Senators in implementing measures to reduce US GHG emissions, including implementing a cap-and-trade system for the utility sector. The Senate Foreign Relations Committee passed a unanimous resolution in the middle of 2001 calling on President Bush to return to the bargaining table to either revise the Kyoto Protocol or negotiate a new binding international agreement. Governments of New Jersey and New Hampshire and others have made specific commitments to reduce GHG emissions.

Table 3.2. *Examples of local and private GHG-emissions-trading initiatives*

Provincial, state and local-government efforts	Private corporations and exchanges	Examples of private transactions
US Oregon New Jersey California New Hampshire Wyoming Midwestern states NE states and Canada *Australia* New South Wales (NSW) Western Australia *Brazil* Amapá Amazonas Paraná *Canada* PERT (Ontario) GERT (British Columbia) British Columbia Alberta *International* International Council of Local Environmental Initiatives	internal trading: BP, Shell, Pemex corporate emissions targets: Alcan, Pechiney, DuPont, OntarioPower Generation, TransAlta, Suncor Energy, Alcoa Chicago Climate Exchange Dutch Electricity Board/FACE Foundation Edison Electric Institute/Utilitree Hancock Natural Resources Group registries: Cantor Fitzgerald (www.CO2e.com), Natsource/Arthur Andersen, Environmental Resources Trust Pew Center on Global Climate Change World Resources Institute International Climate Change Partnership International Petroleum Exchange Winnipeg Commodity Exchange Chicago Board of Trade Paris Bourse Dexia International Emissions Trading Association World Business Council for Sustainable Development (WBCSD)	Nuon–GSF SFM–Salish and Kootenai Tribes OPG–PetroSource Environmental Financial–Costa Rica Ontario Power–ZAPCO BP–The Nature Conservancy (TNC) Arizona Public Service–Niagara Mohawk Suncor–Niagara Mohawk Sumitomo–United Energy Systems (Russia) Pacific Power Australia–NSW Tesco–Uganda forest Waste Management Inc.–Enron American Electric Power–TNC Central & Southwest–TNC Illinova–Environmental Synergy Consorcio Noruego–Costa Rica Toyota–NSW

Table 3.2 indicates a sampling of regional and private activities and efforts to foster GHG-emissions trading.

While some state and regional governments around the world have initiated their own emissions-trading efforts in response to climate change, the activity in the private sector is perhaps more impressive.

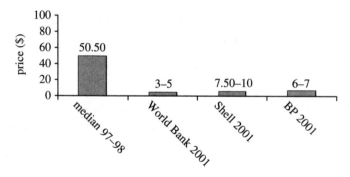

Figure 3.2. CO_2: 1997/1998 median price forecasts and 2001 actual trading prices ($ per tonne of CO_2). (Median forecasts from Charles River Associates, Wharton Econometrics, Professor Robert Stavins, Professor Richard Cooper.)

It is estimated that tens of millions of dollars have changed hands in private GHG-emissions transactions. The private sector's response is most likely based on the perception that GHG-emission limitations of some sort will emerge and will drive fundamental changes in energy systems, although uncertainties in terms of timing and precise rules remain.

Individual companies, such as BP and Royal Dutch Shell, have instituted internal trading programmes. Other companies, such as Suncor, DuPont, Ontario Power, Alcan, TransAlta, Pechiney and Alcoa have voluntarily adopted a limit on their emissions and are meeting the goal with a combination of internal reductions and external trading or offset purchases. Several other US, Canadian, European and Japanese companies have conducted pilot trades or made investments in sequestration or other offset projects. Groups of companies have sponsored offset investments—such as Edison Electric Institute in the US and the FACE Foundation in the Netherlands. The Chicago Climate Exchange, a voluntary pilot programme for trading GHGs starting in the US, includes 52 companies and organizations that have agreed to participate in the design phase of a formal emissions-trading market. Voluntary private registries or trading platforms are also being established, which will help provide the necessary market infrastructure.

The innovative market-based tool of GHG-emissions trading is now undergoing the same evolution path observed with the history of SO_2 trading. Nonetheless, some researchers predict that GHG-emissions trading will not work. They are forecasting prices of GHG reductions to meet the Kyoto Protocol targets of the order of $200 per tonne of carbon reduced, or a total of $120 billion annual cost to the US economy. If the flexibility and incentives of emissions trading are allowed, this is likely to be an order of magnitude too high, similar to the forecasts of the cost of SO_2 reductions made prior to the enactment of the CAAA. Others estimate the cost of compliance with the Kyoto Protocol reduction schedules, assuming the full use of emissions trading, closer to $20 per tonne of carbon reduced. This translates to a total annual cost in the US of $12 billion, an amount the $9 trillion US economy could easily absorb. Figure 3.2 shows the median forecast for CO_2 compared with actual trading prices during 2001.

Other emerging environmental markets

We can also see the Schumpeterian replication stage in other emerging environmental markets. Water trading and the linkages between sustainability issues and equity performance are gaining momentum.

Water scarcity caused by pollution will provide the structural change to encourage the development of market-based mechanisms for water quality improvement. A wide range of existing pollution reduction and mitigation options suggests that market instruments can be used to aid clean-up efforts to minimize some of the environmental, economic and health problems associated with water pollution.

The relationship between a corporation's financial performance and its environmental management policies is also gaining strength. The last few years have seen the development of several funds and indices, such as the Dow Jones Sustainability Index. These sustainable-investment instruments track companies based on a set of criteria that measure their pro-activity in issues ranging from environmental performance, pollution mitigation and workforce diversity.

As the performance of many of these indices has showed, sustainability and maximization of shareholder value are compatible objectives. Many corporations understand the need to manage environmental and social risk exposure. Environmental stewardship and participation in emissions-trading programmes have opened new opportunities for the creation of profit centres and increased stakeholder gains.

Conclusions

Market-based mechanisms such as emissions trading have become widely accepted as a cost-effective method for achieving environmental improvements. There is growing appreciation that market-based solutions offer a low-cost method for managing environmental risks. The convergence of environmental and capital markets may offer sizable benefits for conservation practices in agriculture and forestry worldwide. Further evidence of this convergence can be found in recent developments, such as water trading and sustainable investing, which are also inherently linked to emissions trading.

History shows that market evolution follows a seven-stage process that can be observed in equities, fixed-income securities, physical commodities and the SO_2-allowance-trading programme. The SO_2 cap-and-trade emission-reductions programme has been enormously successful. However, there was great scepticism at the start, much like the scepticism now being expressed about carbon trading. The sulphur-trading model can be successfully extended to GHGs. Although its international dimensions add complications, we have successful environmental precedents such as the effort to slow high-level ozone depletion via the Montreal Protocol. This issue is not daunting. Transactions in carbon offsets have already occurred and additional trading is under way. The carbon-trading history will not be unlike that of other environmental markets, where government regulation gives value to the commodity while the design and implementation are left to market forces, letting governments ratify the process.

A 'bottom-up' characterization of the development of a global market is demonstrated by the numerous initiatives and activities worldwide that promote emissions trading and GHG reductions, even in the absence of compelling rules or regulations. As more national governments institute laws and regulations for GHG emissions, multiple standardized trading systems are expected to develop. The final form of the market will likely be global, but it appears that it will emerge through the evolution and ultimate linking of individual efforts.

An effective and efficient market-based solution will become even more important as we move quickly towards a carbon-constrained world. Active use of market mechanisms could prove an inexpensive insurance policy against the unknown but potentially catastrophic problems that may emerge because of the rapid increase in global carbon emissions and other environmental degradation.

References

Coase, R. 1960 The problem of social cost. *J. Law Econ.* **3**, 1–44.

De Soto, H. 2000 *The mystery of capital. Why capitalism triumphs in the West and fails everywhere else.* New York: Basic Books.

Hahn, R. W. & May, C. A. 1994 The behavior of the allowance market: theory and evidence. *Electric. J.* **7**, 28–37.

Sandor, R. L. 1992 In search of trees. In *Combating global warming—study on a global system of tradeable carbon emission entitlements.* Geneva: United Nations Conference on Trade and Development.

Sandor, R. L. 1999 The role of the United States in International Environment Policy. In *Preparing America's foreign policy for the twenty-first century* (ed. D. L. Boren & E. J. Perkins), pp. 253–266. Norman, OK: University of Oklahoma Press.

Sandor, R. L. & LeBlanc, A. M. 2002 *The Chicago Climate Exchange and the future of emissions trading.* Wiley.

Sandor, R. L. & Skees, J. R. 1999 Creating a market for carbon emissions: opportunities for US farmers. In *Choices.* Ames, IA: American Agricultural Economics Association.

Schumpeter, J. A. 1942 *Capitalism, socialism and democracy.* New York. Harper and Brothers.

USEPA 1999 *Progress report on the EPA acid rain program. EPA 430-R-99-011.* US Environmental Protection Agency.

Walsh, M. J. 1999 Maximizing financial support for biodiversity in the emerging Kyoto Protocol markets. *Sci. Total Environ.* **240**, 145–146.

Chapter 4

Potential carbon mitigation and income in developing countries from changes in use and management of agricultural and forest lands

JOHN O. NILES, SANDRA BROWN, JULES PRETTY,
ANDREW S. BALL AND JOHN FAY

Introduction

The recent Third Assessment Report of the Intergovernmental Panel on Climate Change confirmed earlier findings that emissions avoidance and carbon sequestration by changes in the use and management of forests can make a meaningful, if limited, contribution to reducing atmospheric carbon dioxide (CO_2) (Brown *et al.* 1996; Kauppi & Sedjo 2001). However, forestry and land-use issues remain some of the more controversial components of the evolving global climate-change response (Niles 2002). Underlying this debate is an urgent need to estimate how reforesting degraded lands, avoiding deforestation and adopting sustainable agriculture practices in developing countries could realistically contribute to climate-change mitigation. Developing countries have no specific emission-reduction targets under current climate-change deliberations. Nevertheless, there are many opportunities for mitigating atmospheric carbon in sustainable land management. Detailed nation-by-nation global estimates of land-based mitigation in developing countries have been bypassed in recent scientific literature (Nakicenovic *et al.* 2000; Watson *et al.* 2000).

Our research addresses this science-policy shortfall by elaborating multiple land-use carbon mitigation potentials and associated incomes for 48 host nations. Here we present new analyses for reforesting degraded lands, implementing sustainable agricultural practices on existing lands and for slowing tropical deforestation.

Of the three mitigation strategies mentioned above, only reforestation appears to be eligible for financing under the most recent rules agreed to under the Kyoto Protocol (UNFCCC 2001). Notwithstanding this restriction, integrating a broad array of sustainable forestry and agriculture is likely to lead to more effective outcomes at both the project level and at larger scales (Niles & Schwarze 2001). For example, improved agriculture practices, although not eligible for financing under Kyoto, will help to enable forest restoration, as improved practices and corresponding increases in agricultural yields will stabilize land-use change and reduce competition for use of lands more suited for forest cover. Similarly, improved agriculture practices will reduce pressure on the need to clear more land, usually at the expense of forests. Sustainably managed new forests will also reduce timber and fuelwood pressures on existing natural forest, possibly avoiding deforestation. Equally, financial incentives to conserve remaining forests will effectively translate into incentives to manage both new forests and existing farmlands more sustainably. Thus, these three strategies will be more effective when done in concert. However, financing outside of the current Kyoto regime in the short term will be needed for avoiding deforestation and adopting sustainable agriculture.

Land-based opportunities to mitigate carbon emissions

Many land-based opportunities to increase carbon stocks or avoid carbon emissions exist. For forests, carbon stocks can be increased and carbon emissions avoided by:

- protecting secondary and other degraded forests to allow them to regenerate naturally;

- restoring native forests through assisted and natural regeneration;

- maintaining existing forest-carbon stocks and sink processes by avoiding deforestation;

- establishing plantations on non-forested lands; and

- managing forests sustainably to provide biomass energy.

(Trexler & Haugen 1995; Brown *et al.* 1996; Sathaye & Ravindranath 1998; Watson *et al.* 2000.) Here, we analyse the first three of these. The other two remain to be addressed by others.

On agricultural lands, carbon stocks can be increased in the soil and in woody vegetation by:

- adopting zero- or minimum-tillage practices on arable land;

- improving rangeland management;

- using green manures and cover crops;

- amending soil with straw and manures; and

- increasing the tree cover on agricultural or pasture lands with agroforestry.

(Pretty 1995; Drinkwater *et al.* 1998; Lal *et al.* 1998; Smith *et al.* 1998; Tilman 1998; Smith 1999; Petersen *et al.* 2000; Robertson *et al.* 2000; Sanchez & Jama 2000; USDA 2000; Pretty & Ball 2001; Robert *et al.* 2001; WCCA 2001.)

Methods

To assess how much carbon developing countries could prevent from entering the atmosphere (by reducing emissions) or remove from the atmosphere (by sequestration), country-specific potential areas for reforestation through natural and assisted regeneration (excluding commercial plantations), adoption of sustainable agricultural practices and avoided deforestation were estimated from a variety of sources (see below). We did not include commercial plantations in this analysis, as establishing additionality (a criteria of projects under the Kyoto Protocol) may be difficult because their area in developing countries is increasing, they produce direct financial benefits and involve practices that are well understood and may be adopted regardless of concerns for carbon (Chomitz 2000).

Data on the area and rate of adoption of forestry and agricultural practices were multiplied by estimates of the change in carbon stocks that the various land-management options produce in individual countries. Owing to data limitations, not all developing countries may yet be assessed for all types of activities. Furthermore, we did not address bio-energy, reductions in agricultural inputs, changes in soil carbon associated with averted deforestation and reforestation, or maintained sinks in protected forest.

To be consistent across mitigation options, we used low (conservative) to central estimates of carbon stock changes for any activity. This reflects that there are still relatively few studies of actual long-term carbon mitigation activities in developing countries. Some reasonable burden of proof for crediting carbon-friendly mitigation is likely to restrain reported carbon mitigation to conservative values (Sathaye *et al.* 1997). Adoption rates of various practices remain the largest source of uncertainty in our analysis. There is very little information on these estimates to conduct sensitivity analyses, so we report only central estimates here. The specifics of the analyses by mitigation option are described below.

Reforestation and regeneration

As far as mitigation in developing countries, planting trees is the only land-use option valid in the first commitment period (2008–2012). Under terms of the so-called Bonn Agreement reached during the COP-6 second meeting in July 2001, developed nations may sponsor a limited amount of reforestation and afforestation projects in developing countries. Any carbon offsets that pass various litmus tests of credibility can be used by a sponsoring developed nation to meet its so-called Kyoto commitment. Limits were placed on the overall amount of credit that any developed country could generate to reduce atmospheric carbon. Furthermore, individual projects were limited in their size, each one only able to generate 15 kt of CO_2 equivalent annually (UNFCCC 2001).

Two broad categories of projects fall under the rubric of reforestation and afforestation. Some projects rely primarily on more environmentally friendly techniques, such as assisted regeneration, agro-forestry and forest restoration, to maintain or restore the natural environment. Other projects, primarily industrial plantations, will seek to grow carbon as fast as possible. There will be a spectrum of projects within these two main camps, and the distinctions are somewhat artificial. Our results only apply to the more environmentally benign category of tree planting that includes natural regeneration, reforesting degraded lands and agro-forestry, and *not plantations*, for two primary reasons.

1   In tropical countries, plantations are already being planted at a rate of *ca.* 1.9 million hectares per year (Brown 2000). Proving that a plantation is additional (that is, that it would not have been planted in the absence of carbon incentives) will be difficult. In contrast, there is currently very little reforestation of degraded lands, agro-forestry or accelerating natural forest regeneration.

2   Just over half the tropical plantations are a result of converting a natural forest to a managed one (Brown 2000). This raises a host of environmental concerns as well as net carbon benefits and accounting issues. Therefore, our analysis proceeds from the premise that, while plantations may be beneficial in many instances, proving the inspiration and consequences for industrial plantations will be difficult and we do not estimate this potential.

To calculate this carbon-uptake potential for non-commercial plantation tree planting, we used data for areas of lands that could be reforested with natural and assisted regeneration from Trexler & Haugen (1995). They based the estimated areas on the amount of deforested land present at the time of the study that could be regenerated without significant inputs, an assessment of the forces impeding regeneration and the likelihood of influencing them, and expert opinions on a country's environmental priorities and foreseeable interest in promoting regeneration. Trexler & Haugen projected areas undergoing regeneration from 1990 to 2040 and we used the areas projected for the period 2000–2010. For China, we estimated the rate of natural reforestation in the future (384 000 hectares per year) could equal half of the annual plantation rates reported for the years 1989–1993 and 1994–1998 (Fang *et al.* 2001). Several studies were used to check the availability of land for forest restoration (FAO 1998; Nilsson & Schopfhauser 1995), as well as a nation-specific query of a USGS map (USGS 1997) of forest degradation. No constraints were found to limit these rates of forest recovery for a ten-year period.

The area undergoing regeneration was then multiplied by area-weighted estimates of the potential for carbon accumulation, rates ranging from 0.5 to 2.5 tC ha^{-1} yr^{-1} for dry tropical regions to 2.5 to 5.0 tC ha^{-1} yr^{-1} for humid tropical areas. These rates only consider carbon accumulation in vegetation; we did not include soil carbon, a factor that could elevate this range (Post & Kwon 2000). Appropriate rates were selected based on case studies or, where not possible, a country's general climatic profile. These rates of carbon uptake have been modified from those used by Trexler & Haugen, based on a variety of literature sources for general climatic zones and specific countries

Table 4.1. *Annual carbon mitigation and associated incomes via forest restoration for the years 2003–2012*

Country	Reforestation rate (1000 ha yr^{-1})	Carbon over 2003–2012 (MtC)	Net present value 2003–2012 (US$ million)
Latin America			
Bolivia	5	0.7	4.8
Brazil	750	103.1	713.7
Colombia	100	13.8	95.2
Costa Rica	10	1.4	9.5
Ecuador	50	6.9	47.6
Guatemala	25	3.4	23.8
Guyana	10	1.4	9.5
Honduras	50	6.9	47.6
Mexico	500	13.8	95.2
Nicaragua	30	4.1	28.5
Panama	10	1.4	9.5
Paraguay	20	0.6	3.8
Peru	100	13.8	95.2
Venezuela	50	6.9	47.6
subtotal	**1710**	**177.9**	**1231.4**
Africa			
Angola	20	0.6	3.8
Benin	20	0.6	3.8
Botswana	3	0.1	0.5
Burkina Faso	50	0.8	5.7
Cameroon	30	4.1	28.5
Central African Rep.	2	0.3	1.9
Chad	2	0.0	0.2
Cote d'Ivoire	50	6.9	47.6
Dem. Rep. Congo	100	13.8	95.2
Ethiopia	20	1.9	13.3
Kenya	5	0.1	1.0
Madagascar	10	1.0	6.7
Mali	5	0.1	0.6
Mozambique	60	1.7	11.4
Niger	5	0.1	0.6
Nigeria	10	1.0	6.7
Senegal	25	0.4	2.9
South Africa Sudan	100	2.8	19.0
Tanzania	100	2.8	19.0
Uganda	10	1.4	9.5
Zambia	5	0.1	1.0
Zimbabwe	50	1.4	9.5
subtotal	**682**	**41.7**	**288.3**

(Brown & Lugo 1982; Tomich *et al*. 1998; Uhl *et al*. 1988; Brown & Lugo 1990; Brown & Gaston 1995; Brown *et al*. 1995; Hughes *et al*. 1999; Silver *et al*. 2000; Fang *et al*. 2001). Rates of carbon accumulation are poorly known for most parts of the world and there is a considerable range in estimates. Due to many of the difficulties of establishing viable forest restoration (Reid

Table 4.1. (*Cont.*)

Country	Reforestation rate (1000 ha yr^{-1})	Carbon over 2003–2012 (MtC)	Net present value 2003–2012 (US$ million)
Asia			
Bangladesh	5	0.1	1.0
China	384	21.1	146.2
India	150	4.1	28.5
Indonesia	15	2.1	14.3
Laos	20	2.8	19.0
Malaysia	100	13.8	95.2
Myanmar	120	16.5	114.2
Papua New Guinea	100	13.8	95.2
Philippines	100	13.8	95.2
Thailand	50	4.8	33.3
Vietnam	25	3.4	23.8
subtotal	**1069**	**96.2**	**665.7**
grand total	**3461**	**315.8**	**2185.4**

& Rice 1997) and to account for likely monitoring and verification requirements (Sathaye *et al.* 1997), we used the lower end of the range for all countries in estimating the potential amount of carbon that could be sequestered (Table 4.1).

We assumed that if appropriate incentives develop this year or next, countries could begin reforestation programmes in 2003. Given that reforestation programmes will create cumulative carbon benefits, a timed carbon stream was calculated and then summed for the next 10 years (Table 4.1). Lands that are restored in 2003 (the beginning of our study period) will accumulate carbon for the full 10 years, while lands restored in 2012 will only accumulate carbon for that year.

The total amount of carbon that could be sequestered by reforestation to create native forests over the ten-year period is 316 million tonnes on 3.5 million hectares of land. The greatest potential exists in countries of Latin America (56% of the total), followed by Asia (30% of the total) and Africa (14% of the total).

Sustainable agricultural practices

Agricultural systems contribute to carbon emissions through several mechanisms:

- the cultivation of soils resulting in the loss of soil organic matter;

- the clearing of forests to create new cropland;

- the direct use of fossil fuels in farm operations; and

- the indirect use of embodied energy in inputs that are energy intensive to manufacture.

Table 4.2. *Carbon-sequestration rates* (tC ha^{-1} yr^{-1}) *according to four scenarios for sustainable agricultural management*

Agricultural system	Low	Medium	High	Very high
arable	0.3	0.65	1.3	3.1
rice paddy	0.1	0.1	0.1	0.1
permanent crops/agroforestry	0.4	0.6	0.6	0.8
permanent pasture	0.3	0.5	0.7	0.9

Source: adapted from Watson *et al.* (2000) and Pretty & Ball (2001).

(Reicosky *et al.* 1995; Rasmussen *et al.* 1998; Robertson *et al.* 2000; USDA 2000; Pretty & Ball 2001.)

Agriculture can also sequester carbon when organic matter accumulates in the soil, or in aboveground woody biomass used in agroforestry systems or for production of biomass for energy sources that substitute for fossil fuels. Soil organic matter, and thus carbon, can be increased to new higher equilibria with sustainable management practices. The greatest dividend comes from conversion of annual crops to agroforests, as there is a benefit from both increased soil organic carbon and the accumulation of carbon in woody biomass. Grasslands within rotations, zero-tillage (or no-till) farming, green manures and cover crops, and high amendments of straw and manures to the soil, also lead to substantial carbon sequestration.

While sustainable agricultural practices were not included in the list of carbon-mitigation techniques that could generate credits under the Kyoto Protocol, sustainable agriculture programmes will be essential for implementation of forest restoration projects. Sustainable agriculture in developing countries can lead to a decreased need for additional forest clearing, particularly those that lead to improvements in soil fertility (Sanchez & Jama 2000). For agricultural practices, we use FAO statistical data on area of arable land, permanent crops and permanent pastures for the 48 selected countries of Africa, Asia and Latin America to calculate the carbon-sequestration potential of agricultural lands. The potential area for carbon sequestration under improved sustainable agricultural practices were assessed on the basis of recent data on more than 200 sustainable agriculture projects (Pretty 1997, 1999; Pretty & Hine 2001), a range of agro-ecological zones, crop types and a range of land-area categories (Table 4.2). As the focus of this analysis is on what sustainable methods can do to increase marginal quantities of soil and aboveground carbon, we do not take account of existing stocks of carbon, but rather the incremental gain over existing stocks.

We used four scenarios derived from a hierarchy of improved sustainable agriculture practices, and are conservative in our estimates of rates of carbon accumulation (cf. Watson *et al.* 2000; Pretty & Ball 2001). For arable, this relates to:

1 arable low—zero tillage with intensive cropping;

2 arable medium—zero tillage with mixed rotations;

3   arable high—zero tillage with mixed rotations, cover crops and green
    manures, composts; and

4   arable very high—agroforestry plus cover crops and green manures, com-
    posts.

The following equation was used to calculate the potential annual carbon
sequestration, C_{seq}, through adoption of sustainable agriculture technologies
and practices,

$$C_{seq} = ((A_a - A_{ir})C_a R) + (A_{ir}C_i) + (A_{pt}C_{pt}R) + (A_{pa}C_{pa}RG_r),$$

where

A_a = area under arable crops,

A_{ir} = area under irrigated rice,

A_{pt} = area under permanent crops,

A_{pa} = area under permanent pasture area,

C_a = annual per-hectare carbon sequestration under arable,

C_i = annual per-hectare carbon sequestration under irrigated rice,

C_{pt} = annual per-hectare carbon sequestration under permanent crops,

C_{pa} = annual per-hectare carbon sequestration under permanent pasture,

R = ratio to correct for agroecological zone (varying from 0.2 to 1.0),

G_r = ratio to correct for pasture likely to be subject to improvement
    (all 0.1),

with areas measured in millions of hectares and carbon-sequestration rates
measured in tC ha^{-1} yr^{-1}.

We apply an agroecological zone factor to correct carbon sequestration for
climate, with the following multipliers: 1.0 for humid tropics; 0.8 for humid
temperate; and 0.4 for both dry temperate and dry tropical. Some countries
cross these zones, and so are allocated a factor derived from the proportion
of area in each zone.

It is estimated that some 70% of grasslands worldwide are degraded,
mainly due to overgrazing. Improved management can lead to carbon sequestration, particularly by improving root growth in grasses. Management practices include grazing control to maximize growth, fire management, soil
improvements, varietal choice, addition of nitrogen-fixing legumes and use
of permanent grasses with deep-rooting systems. We correct the data with a
grassland factor to represent the proportion of permanent grasslands likely
to be subject to these types of intervention. Most remote, upland and arid
grasslands will not be sites for significant increases in carbon sequestration.
It is assumed that technically only 10% of grasslands could be improved.

An irrigated rice factor was used to correct for the amount of irrigated rice
in each country. Irrigated rice can accumulate a maximum of 0.5 tC ha^{-1} yr^{-1}
with the use of organic matter, fertilizers and plant-residue management. We
also correct for reported area of paddy rice, as this is greater than actual

Table 4.3. *Annual carbon mitigation and associated incomes via sustainable agriculture for the years 2003–2012*

Country	Sustainable agriculture adoption rate (Mha yr^{-1})	Carbon over 2003–2012 (MtC)	net present value 2003–2012 (US$ million)
Latin America			
Bolivia	0.7	2.4	16.6
Brazil	5.1	44.8	310.4
Colombia	0.9	5.0	34.8
Costa Rica	0.1	0.5	3.2
Ecuador	0.2	1.7	11.5
Guatemala	0.1	1.4	9.8
Guyana	0.0	0.4	2.8
Honduras	0.1	1.5	10.6
Mexico	2.1	23.8	164.6
Nicaragua	0.2	2.2	15.2
Panama	0.0	0.5	3.7
Paraguay	0.5	2.3	15.6
Peru	0.6	3.1	21.6
Venezuela	0.4	3.4	23.7
subtotal	**11.0**	**93.1**	**644.1**
Africa			
Angola	1.2	2.2	15.1
Benin	0.0	1.1	7.4
Botswana	0.5	0.7	4.6
Burkina Faso	0.2	1.1	7.8
Cameroon	0.2	5.2	35.7
Central African Rep.	0.1	1.6	11.1
Chad	1.0	2.0	13.9
Cote d'Ivoire	0.4	4.6	31.7
Dem. Rep. Congo	0.5	6.4	44.2
Ethiopia	0.6	3.5	23.9
Kenya	0.5	1.8	12.1
Madagascar	0.6	1.7	11.7
Mali	0.7	2.0	14.0
Mozambique	0.9	2.0	13.5
Niger	0.3	1.7	11.8
Nigeria	1.4	9.7	66.8
Senegal	0.2	1.0	6.8
South Africa	2.0	6.3	43.8
Sudan	2.5	7.3	50.2
Tanzania	0.8	2.1	14.7
Uganda	0.2	2.4	16.9
Zambia	0.7	2.2	15.0
Zimbabwe	0.4	1.3	9.2
subtotal	**15.9**	**69.7**	**482.1**

hectares owing to double and triple cropping. Carbon-uptake rates cannot approach those of other crops, where zero tillage, cover crops, green manures, mixed rotations and agroforestry can lead to greater annual improvements in

Table 4.3. (*Cont.*)

Country	Sustainable agriculture adoption rate (Mha yr^{-1})	Carbon over 2003–2012 (MtC)	Net present value 2003–2012 (US$ million)
Asia			
Bangladesh	0.3	5.3	36.9
China	11.3	84.3	583.5
India	4.5	78.2	541.3
Indonesia	0.9	21.3	147.1
Laos	0.0	0.6	4.3
Malaysia	0.2	5.1	35.5
Myanmar	0.2	7.0	48.1
Papua New Guinea	0.0	0.5	3.1
Philippines	0.3	6.7	46.5
Thailand	0.5	13.6	94.4
Vietnam	0.2	4.6	32.1
subtotal	**18.5**	**227.3**	**1572.9**
grand total	**49.6**	**420.6**	**2910.8**

soil organic carbon. Data on the amount of irrigated rice for each country were used to reduce the arable area subject to carbon sequestration at higher rates.

In our analyses, we do not account for a potential double benefit arising when shifting agriculturalists adopt settled sustainable agriculture methods, as this is analysed in the avoided-deforestation section. However, these two scenarios are not completely separate. If some of the 300–500 million farmers practicing shifting cultivation in and around tropical forests were to adopt sustainable agriculture using regenerative methods, and so farm permanently the same piece of land, then they would be both accumulating carbon in their soils and not cutting down and burning the forest. We also do not account for other land-use conversions that could lead to carbon sequestration or carbon emissions (such as wetland conversions).

In the aggregate analysis reported here (Table 4.3), medium sequestration rates of carbon sequestration were used. For example, for arable land, uptake rates of 0.65 tC ha^{-1} yr^{-1} were used, which is considerably less than the 3.1 tC ha^{-1} yr^{-1} possible with agroforestry, cover crops and composts.

In the long term, all agricultural lands could theoretically adopt sustainable agriculture practices that lead to carbon sequestration at medium scenario rates. Based on data for adoption rates of sustainable agriculture practices in the past decade (Pretty 1997, 1999; Pretty & Hine 2001), we estimate that 20% of current agricultural lands could be under sustainable agriculture over the next 10 years. Some countries, such as Argentina and Brazil, may achieve this much sooner. These agricultural practices are expected to continue to sequester carbon for at least 20 years (Smith *et al.* 1998; Sanchez & Jama 2000; Pretty & Ball 2001; WCCA 2001; Batjes 2000).

The total increase in carbon stocks from improved agriculture is 420 million tonnes (Table 4.3). For agriculture, the greatest opportunity for increased carbon stocks occurs in Asian countries, followed by Latin American and African countries.

Avoided deforestation

Tropical deforestation causes an estimated 20% of worldwide anthropogenic carbon emissions. As such, many scientists and non-governmental actors strongly believed that any avoided emissions from protecting tropical forests should be eligible (and thus valuable) under Kyoto carbon accounting. However, measures to protect threatened tropical forests, according to the Bonn Agreement, will not be eligible carbon offsets for use in the first commitment period of the Protocol. This political decision was hotly contested, with a host of nations, groups and individuals opposed to including tropical forest conservation in the treaty and others adamantly in favour (Niles 2002).

Measures to prevent the continued deforestation in the tropics would enable and complement reforestation and sustainable agriculture in several ways. First of all, if sustainable agricultural is implemented, this will tend to decrease land pressures for converting standing forests for production. Additionally, financial incentives to conserve forests will translate into incentives for both forest restoration and sustainable agriculture. Thus, while these strategies are often referred to in discrete terms, in fact, holistic forest and land management would be a more effective way to use land practices to mitigate atmospheric carbon, while also securing a host of other secondary benefits.

For our analysis, the potential emission reductions via avoided deforestation were calculated by multiplying the most recent estimates of annual forest loss times area-weighted carbon stocks for forests in most major tropical countries (expansion of analysis by Niles (2000a) through addition of more countries). We assumed that deforestation rates would remain constant because there are no other reliable projections of probable forest loss, and on a global basis, gross deforestation has remained relatively constant for the past few years (FAO 1997, 2001). The one study making future projections did not show an appreciable change using various studies for the period 2000–2010 (Alcamo & Swart 1998). Data from the FAO (1999) were used to estimate forest loss with a few exceptions. For Brazil, the average of the FAO estimate and Brazil's National Institute for Space Research (INPE 2000) average rate for 1989–1998 was used to estimate deforestation rates. For the Philippines, the average of FAO and two estimates in Lasco & Pulhin (2000) were used.

Multiple data sources for carbon stocks were used for various areas including Africa (Brown & Gaston 1995), Asia (Brown *et al.* 1993) China (Ni 2001; Fang *et al.* 2001) and the Americas (FAO 2001), as well as specific modifications from other sources (Brown 1997; Masera *et al.* 1997; Fearnside 1997; Trexler & Haugen 1995; Houghton *et al.* 2000; Tomich *et al.* 1998; Nilsson & Schopfhauser 1995; Niles 2000a, b). For the 48 countries evaluated, we estimate total emissions from deforestation to be 1.3 GtC yr^{-1} (*ca.* 17% of worldwide carbon releases), a nation-specific calculation very close to other published estimates (Watson *et al.* 2000). There is still large uncertainty for many parameters needed to make accurate estimates of greenhouse gas emissions

from tropical deforestation. These uncertainties include gross rates of deforestation (Mathews 2001), forest degradation (Nepstad *et al.* 1999), carbon
stocks, burning efficiencies (Delmas *et al.* 1995), other gas fluxes (Alcamo
& Swart 1998) and gas fluxes on lands following deforestation (Fearnside
1997). Nevertheless, in terms of total potential carbon-emission reductions,
the greatest source of data uncertainty is in estimates of the ability of nations
to undertake durable tropical forest conservation.

To estimate the maximum amount of deforestation that could be halted, we
modified a prior study that estimated, on a decadal basis, individual countries'
abilities to slow deforestation rates (Trexler & Haugen 1995). This study's
estimates of possible avoided deforestation for the years 1995–2000 proved
too optimistic in light of the recent assessment by the FAO (2001). This may
be due to market failures for avoided carbon emissions or other ecosystem services provided by tropical forests (Kremen *et al.* 2000). Efforts to slow tropical
deforestation in recent years have mostly failed and gross tropical deforestation rates have probably risen slightly in recent years to approximately 16 million hectares (FAO 2000*a*, *b*; Mathews 2001). Furthermore, widespread forest
degradation remains poorly understood or quantified.

The Trexler & Haugen study is unique in that it has pan-tropical coverage and its conclusions were derived from country-specific information based
on surveys of land tenure, development plans, forestry experience, political
stability and other key variables. We updated several features of this seminal
study, namely carbon stocks and carbon uptake rates, rates of deforestation,
as well as other minor changes. We assumed that the ratio of forest destruction stopped would be equal across biomass variances, so that the percent
of avoided deforestation would be the percent of avoided emissions. If all
48 countries considered carried out significant efforts to stall deforestation,
we estimate a maximum of 157 million tonnes of carbon could be reduced
annually (Table 4.4). This maintenance of tropical forest ecosystems could
secure tens of millions of additional tonnes in sequestered carbon over several
decades from possibly CO_2 fertilization as well as other, yet unknown, causes
(Phillips *et al.* 1998; Malhi & Grace 2000; Niles 2000*b*; Lugo & Brown 1992).
This potential added benefit was not included in our analysis because this
ecosystem service is not the result of direct human management and CO_2
fertilization remains relatively uncertain.

Calculation of host-country benefits

The income from any potential carbon-offset trades is difficult to predict.
There is continuing uncertainty as to the fate of the Kyoto Protocol as well
as critical rules for developing country participation in forest and land-use
activities. As the rules for the Kyoto Protocol now stand, only certain types
of forest planting will be eligible for incorporation (and thus financing) in
the Protocol's framework. We estimated host-country benefits from a carbon
perspective for all three mitigation categories addressed in this chapter for
several reasons. First, the US and other countries recalcitrant to join the
Protocol may develop land-use incentives for developing countries in a parallel

Table 4.4. *Annual carbon mitigation and associated incomes via avoided deforestation for the years 2003–2012*

Country	Annual deforestation (1000 ha yr^{-1})	Deforestation halted (1000 ha yr^{-1})	Carbon over 2003–2012 (MtC)	Net present value 2003–2012 (US$ million)
Latin America				
Bolivia	581	116.2	133.6	1 018.4
Brazil	2 554	383.1	603.4	4 598.4
Colombia	262	52.4	52.4	399.3
Costa Rica	41	10.3	11.3	85.9
Ecuador	189	75.6	68.8	173.9
Guatemala	82	12.3	22.8	524.3
Guyana	9	0.5	0.6	4.3
Honduras	102	20.4	10.7	81.6
Mexico	508	50.8	38.1	290.4
Nicaragua	151	7.6	8.9	67.6
Panama	64	12.8	20.6	157.1
Paraguay	327	65.4	65.4	498.4
Peru	217	10.9	10.4	79.4
Venezuela	503	50.3	50.3	383.3
subtotal	**5 590**	**868.4**	**1 097.3**	**8 362.3**
Africa				
Angola	237	11.9	4.3	33.0
Benin	60	15.0	4.4	33.2
Botswana	71	7.1	0.5	3.5
Burkina Faso	32	3.2	0.5	4.1
Cameroon	129	12.9	14.0	106.7
Central African Rep.	128	12.8	12.8	97.5
Chad	94	9.4	2.0	15.4
Cote d'Ivoire	31	6.2	5.1	39.0
Dem. Rep. Congo	740	37.0	63.6	485.0
Ethiopia	62	3.1	0.8	6.1
Kenya	3	0.2	0.0	0.2
Madagascar	130	13.0	12.7	97.1
Mali	114	5.7	1.3	9.8
Mozambique	116	5.8	1.7	12.6
Niger	0	0.0	0.0	0.0
Nigeria	121	12.1	3.0	22.6
Senegal	50	10.0	1.6	12.2
South Africa	15	0.8	0.1	0.9
Sudan	353	35.3	11.3	86.1
Tanzania	323	64.6	14.5	110.8
Uganda	59	8.9	4.5	34.4
Zambia	264	26.4	6.2	47.3
Zimbabwe	50	6.0	0.4	2.7
subtotal	**3299**	**312.1**	**167.8**	**1278.5**

framework, and there is some suggestion that this is in the works (US State Department 2001). Second, it may be useful for future rounds of negotiations to know not only the potential to manage carbon, but also the potential for

Table 4.4. (*Cont.*)

Country	Annual deforestation (1000 ha yr^{-1})	Deforestation halted (1000 ha yr^{-1})	Carbon over 2003–2012 (MtC)	Net present value 2003–2012 (US$ million)
Asia				
Bangladesh	9	0.5	0.4	3.0
China	87	13.1	4.0	30.3
India	0	0.0	0.0	0.0
Indonesia	1 084	108.4	142.0	1 082.2
Laos	148	7.4	8.3	63.2
Malaysia	400	20.0	23.1	176.0
Myanmar	387	19.4	22.3	170.3
Papua New Guinea	133	6.7	7.4	56.8
Philippines	262	26.2	29.2	222.6
Thailand	329	49.4	45.6	347.9
Vietnam	135	13.5	17.7	134.8
subtotal	**3 029**	**267.1**	**300.5**	**2 289.9**
grand total	**11 918**	**1 447.6**	**1 565.5**	**11 930.5**

developing countries to realize economic gain if carbon is used as a currency for engaging in mitigation activities.

Early carbon-exchange and trading systems have carbon-emission-reduction credit values set between US$1–38 per tonne of carbon, though most commonly in the $2.50–$5.00 range. We used a $10 per tonne of carbon value to represent a mid-level estimate of the price of carbon reductions or sequestration. While the current prices are generally between $10 and $30 per tonne of carbon, this may be due to the speculative nature of a market for worldwide carbon management.

Should a market emerge in the coming years, it is reasonable to expect that the cost of carbon would rise by a factor of two. In 1998, the then chair of the White House Council of Economic Advisors predicted that under a global system of trading, carbon would cost $14–$23 per tonne of carbon (Yellen 1998). Because many of the carbon values that we are estimating will occur in the years before any potential commitment periods for a global change treaty, we felt $10 per tonne of carbon represented a best-guess scenario for the value of a tonne reduced or sequestered in the year 2003. Furthermore, we assumed that this price would remain fixed in absolute dollars for the period of 2003–2012 and would thus decline slowly in real terms. To compute the income derived from the activities we outlined, standard net present value (NPV) procedures based on a 3% discount rate for each of the ensuing 10 years were used to calculate the total value of the income stream for various activities over the 10 years. All values reported in the above tables are in net present 2003 dollars.

Over the next 10 years, slowing tropical deforestation offers the largest potential opportunity for mitigating carbon emissions—just short of 1.6 billion tonnes (Table 4.5). This would generate a value of about $11.9 billion over the ten-year period. The carbon-mitigating potential of adopting sus-

Table 4.5. *Summary of carbon mitigation and incomes via forest restoration, sustainable agriculture and avoided deforestation for the years 2003–2012*

Region	Forest restoration (MtC)	Sustainable agriculture (MtC)	Avoided deforestation (MtC)	Total carbon from all activities (MtC)	Total net present value, all activities (US$ million)
Latin America	177.9	93.1	1 097.3	1 368.3	10 237.8
Africa	41.7	69.7	167.8	279.2	2 048.9
Asia	96.2	227.3	300.5	624.0	4 528.5
grand total	**315.8**	**390.1**	**1 565.6**	**2 271.5**	**16 815.2**

tainable agriculture practices is almost 0.4 billion tonnes of carbon over the same period, with a value of about $2.8 billion. Natural forest restoration, the mitigation category allowed in the Kyoto Protocol, appears able to sequester just over 0.3 billion tonnes for a total value of around $2.1 billion. Looking at these countries, for which there were sufficient data, the largest total potential is in the 14 Latin America countries (60% of the total by carbon), followed by the 11 Asian countries (27%) and by the 23 African countries (12%).

These estimates of host-country income potentials do not consider that outside financial investment may or may not be available. The investment climate in many developing countries is, like everywhere in the world, full of risks. Realizing these incomes would necessitate a substantially greater investment in sustainable land uses than is currently the case. Currently, the developed world is spending less than half a billion dollars on sustainable forest management and biodiversity (Frumhoff *et al.* 1998). The United Nations has estimated that tens of billions of dollars annually are needed to adequately address deforestation and forest degradation (United Nations 1999).

Conclusions

The potential carbon-mitigation options discussed here present a practical highest limit to the amount of carbon that could be maintained in vegetation and soils or sequestered from the atmosphere with an ambitious decline in tropical deforestation and widespread implementation of carbon-friendly sustainable agriculture practices and natural forest reforestation/regeneration schemes in developing countries located in the tropical and subtropical latitudes. These estimates are not likely to represent scenarios for land management in the coming decade (cf. Black-Arbalaez *et al.* 2000) unless significant commitments to taking action to reduce the potential for climate change are made. Inertia, poverty, infrastructure, markets, institutions, competing land uses and a wide range of other factors will limit the realization of these potentials (cf. Seymour & Dubash 2000), as well as a lack of supportive national and international policy frameworks. On the other hand, our calculations take no account of the additional benefits of carbon sequestration in forest soils undergoing reforestation, increased use of biomass and reduced use of fossil-fuel inputs and reduced agricultural emissions. They also underestimate the potential carbon sequestration on sustainable agriculture with a complete package of zero tillage, green manures and agroforestry. And most important, given the recent political decisions surrounding the Kyoto Protocol, two of three categories represented here (sustainable agriculture and avoided deforestation) are not eligible for additional financing. Without markets for new behaviour and land management in developing countries, realizing these 'potentials' will almost certainly never be approached.

On balance we believe our estimates represent an upper bound for carbon mitigation in the various counties for the practices studied. More research is needed on reducing the uncertainty of, and raising the ability to meet, plausible implementation rates. In order for any of these potentials to be realized, there will need to be novel markets and effective policy mechanisms for ensuring sound implementation of land-use practices that conserve or sequester carbon. These measures will need to compensate amenable developing nations and their people for lost opportunity values that competing land uses would otherwise provide and ensure that carbon mitigation is done in an equitable and fair manner.

References

Alcamo, J. & Swart, R. 1998 Future trends of land-use emissions of major greenhouse gases. *Mitigat. Adapt. Strategies Glob. Change* **3**, 343–381.

Batjes, N. 2000 Options for increasing soil-organic matter levels in support of sustainable agriculture and carbon sequestration in West Africa: an exploratory study with special attention to three pilot sites in Senegal. In *Int. Workshop on Carbon Sequestration in Soil, Dakar, Senegal, 25–27 September 2000.*

Black-Arbalaez, T. (and 20 others) 2000 National strategy study for implementation of the CDM in Colombia: executive summary. National World Bank Strategy Studies and Ministerio del Medio Ambiente, Bogota, Colombia.

Brown, S. 1997 Estimating biomass and biomass change of tropical forests: a primer. FAO Forestry Paper no. 134. Rome: Food and Agriculture Organization.

Brown, C. 2000 The global outlook for future wood supply from forest plantations. Working Paper no. GFPOS/WP/03. Rome: Food and Agriculture Organization.

Brown, S. & Gaston, G. 1995 Use of forest inventories and geographic information systems to estimate biomass density of tropical forests: application to tropical Africa. *Environ. Monit. Assess.* **38**, 157–168.

Brown, S. & Lugo, A. E. 1982 The storage and production of organic matter in tropical forests and their role in the global carbon cycle. *Biotropica* **14**, 161–187.

Brown, S. & Lugo, A. E. 1990 Tropical secondary forests. *J. Trop. Ecol.* **6**, 1–32.

Brown, S., Iverson, L., Prasad, A. & Liu, D. 1993 Geographic distribution of carbon in biomass and soils of tropical Asian forests. *Geocarto Int.* **4**, 45–59.

Brown, S., Lenart, M. & Mo, J. 1995 Structure and organic matter dynamics of a human-impacted pine forest in a MAB reserve in subtropical China. *Biotropica* **27**, 276–289.

Brown, S., Sathaye, J., Cannell, M. & Kauppi, P. 1996 Management of forests for mitigation of greenhouse gas emissions. In *Climate change 1995: impacts, adaptations and mitigation of climate change: scientific-technical analyses* (ed. R. T. Watson, M. C. Zinyowera & R. H. Moss). Contribution of Working Group II to the

Second Assessment Report of the Intergovernmental Panel on Climate Change, pp. 773–798. Cambridge University Press.

Chomitz, K. M. 2000 *Evaluating carbon offsets from forestry and energy projects: how do they compare?* Washington, DC: Development Research Group, World Bank.

Delmas, R., Lacaux, J. & Brocard, D. 1995 Determination of biomass burning emission factors: methods and results. *Environ. Monit. Assess.* **38**, 181–204.

Drinkwater, L. E., Wagoner, P. & Sarrantonio, M. 1998 Legume-based cropping systems have reduced carbon and nitrogen losses. *Nature* **396**, 262–265.

Fang, J., Chen, A., Peng, C., Zhao, S. & Ci, L. 2001 Change in forest biomass carbon storage in China between 1949 and 1998. *Science* **292**, 2320–2322.

Fearnside, P. 1997 Greenhouse gases from deforestation in Brazilian Amazonia: net committed emissions. *Climatic Change* **35**, 321–360.

FAO 1997 *State of the world's forests: 1997.* Rome: Food and Agriculture Organization.

FAO 1998 *Asia-Pacific forestry towards 2010. Report of the Asia-Pacific forestry sector outlook study.* Rome: Food and Agriculture Organization.

FAO 1999 *State of the world's forests: 1999.* Rome: Food and Agriculture Organization.

FAO 2000a Carbon sequestration options under the Clean Development Mechanism to address land degradation. World Soil Resources Reports 92. Rome: Food and Agriculture Organization.

FAO 2000b *Global forest resources assessment 2000.* (Available at www.fao.org/forestry/fo/fra/index.jsp.)

FAO 2001 *State of the world's forests: 2001.* Rome: Food and Agriculture Organization.

Frumhoff, P., Goetz, D. & Hardner, J. 1998 *Linking solutions to climate change and biodiversity loss through the Kyoto Protocol's Clean Development Mechanism.* Cambridge, MA: Union of Concerned Scientists.

Houghton, R. A., Skole, D. A., Nobre, C. A., Hackler, J. L., Lawrence, K. T. & Chomentowski, W. H. 2000 Annual fluxes of carbon from deforestation and regrowth in the Brazilian Amazon. *Nature* **403**, 301–304.

Hughes, R. F., Kauffman, J. B. & Jaramillo, V. J. 1999 Biomass, carbon, and nutrient dynamics of secondary forests in a humid tropical region of Mexico. *Ecology* **80**, 1892–1907.

INPE 2000 *Monitoring of the Brazilian amazon forest by satellite.* Brazil: Instituto Nacional de Pesquisas Espacias.

Kauppi, P. & Sedjo, R. 2001 Technical and economic potential of options to enhance, maintain and manage biological carbon reservoirs and geo-engineering. In *Climate change 2001: mitigation* (ed. B. Metz, O. Davidson, R. Swart & J. Pan). Contribution of Working Group III to the Third Assessment Report of the IPCC. Cambridge University Press.

Kremen, C., Niles, J., Dalton, M., Daily, G., Ehrlich, P., Guillery, P. & Fay, J. 2000 Economic incentives of rain forest conservation across scales. *Science* **288**, 1828–1832.

Lal, R., Kimble, J. M., Follett, R. F. & Cole, C. V. 1998 *The potential of US cropland to sequester carbon and mitigate the greenhouse effect.* Chelsea, MI: Ann Arbor Press.

Lasco, R. D. & Pulhin, F. B. 2000 Forest land use change in the Philippines and climate change mitigation. *Mitigat. Adapt. Strategies Glob. Change* **5**, 81–97.

Lugo, A. E. & Brown, S. 1992 Tropical forests as sinks of atmospheric carbon. *Forest Ecol. Manag.* **54**, 239–256.

Malhi, Y. & Grace, J. 2000 Tropical forests and atmospheric carbon dioxide. *Trends Ecol. Evol.* **15**, 332–337.

Masera, O. R., Ordonez, M. J. & Dirzo, R. 1997 Carbon emissions from Mexican forests: current situation and long-term scenarios. *Climatic Change* **35**, 265–295.

Mathews, E. 2001 *Understanding the FRA: forest briefing no. 1.* Washington, DC: World Resources Institute.

Nakicenovic, N. (and 27 others) 2000 *Special report on emission scenarios.* A Special Report of Working Group III of the Intergovernmental Panel on Climate Change. Cambridge University Press.

Nepstad, D. (and 11 others) 1999 Large-scale impoverishment of Amazonian forest by logging fire. *Nature* **398**, 505–508.

Ni, J. 2001 Carbon storage in terrestrial ecosystems of China: estimates at different spatial resolutions and their responses to climate change. *Climatic Change* **49**, 339–358.

Niles, J. 2000*a* Preliminary estimate for 25 nations of the potential for forest conservation in the Clean Development Mechanism. Unpublished report, Stanford University, Stanford, CA.

Niles, J. 2000*b* The additional benefits of reducing carbon emissions from tropical deforestation. Morrison Institute for Population and Resource Studies, Working Paper Series, No. 0084. Stanford University, Stanford, CA.

Niles, J. 2002 Tropical forests and climate change. In *Climate change policy: a survey* (ed. S. H. Schneider, A. Rosencranz & J. O. Niles), pp. 337–371. Washington, DC: Island Press.

Niles, J. & Schwarze, R. 2001 The value of careful carbon accounting. *Climatic Change* **49**, 371–376.

Nilsson, S. & Schopfhauser, W. 1995 The carbon sequestration potential of a global afforestation program. *Climatic Change* **30**, 267–293.

Petersen, C., Drinkwater, L. E. & Wagoner, P. 2000 *The Rodale Institute's farming systems trial. The first 15 years.* Kutztown, PA: Rodale Institute.

Phillips, O. (and 10 others) 1998 Changes in the carbon balance of tropical forests: evidence from long-term plots. *Science* **282**, 439–442.

Post, W. & Kwon, K. 2000 Soil carbon sequestration and land-use change: processes and potential. *Glob. Change Biol.* **6**, 317–327.

Pretty, J. N. 1995 *Regenerating agriculture: policies and practice for sustainability and self-reliance.* London: Earthscan.

Pretty, J. N. 1997 The sustainable intensification of agriculture. *Nat. Resources Forum* **21**, 247–256.

Pretty, J. N. 1999 Can sustainable agriculture feed Africa? *Environ. Dev. Sustain.* **1**, 253–274.

Pretty, J. & Ball, A. 2001 Agricultural influences on carbon emissions and sequestration: a review of evidence and the emerging trading options. Occasional Paper 2001-03, Centre for Environment and Society, University of Essex.

Pretty, J. & Hine, R. 2001 Reducing poverty with sustainable agriculture. Final Report of Research Project. University of Essex, Colchester. (Available at www2.essex.ac.uk/ces.)

Rasmussen, P. E., Goulding, K. W. T., Brown, J. R., Grace, P. R., Janzen, H. H. & Körschens, M. 1998 Long term agroecosystem experiments: assessing agricultural sustainability and global change. *Science* **282**, 893–896.

Reicosky, D. C., Kemper, W. D., Langdale, G. W., Douglas, C. L. & Rasmussen, P. E. 1995 Soil organic matter changes resulting from tillage and biomass production. *J. Soil Water Conserv.* **50**, 253–261.

Reid, J. & Rice, R. 1997 Assessing natural forest management as a tool for tropical forest conservation. *Ambio* **26** 382–386.

Robert, M., Antoine, J. & Nachtergaele, F. 2001 *Carbon sequestration in soils. Proposals for land management in arid areas of the tropics.* Rome: AGLL, FAO.

Robertson, G. P., Paul, E. A. & Harwood, R. R. 2000 Greenhouse gases intensive agriculture: contributions of individual gases to radiative warming of the atmosphere. *Science* **289**, 1922.

Sanchez, P. A. & Jama, B. A. 2000 Soil fertility replenishment takes off in east Southern Africa. In *Int. Symp. on Balanced Nutrient Management Systems for the Moist Savanna and Humid Forest Zones of Africa, Cotonou, Benin, 9 October 2000.*

Sathaye, J. & Ravindranath, N. H. 1998 Climate change mitigation in the energy and forestry sectors of developing countries. *A. Rev. Energy Environ.* **23**, 387–437.

Sathaye, J., Makundi, B., Goldberg, D., Andrasko, K. & Sanchez, A. 1997 Sustainable forest management for climate change mitigation: monitoring and verification of greenhouse gases. *Mitigat. Adapt. Strategies Glob. Change* **2**, 87–339.

Seymour, F. & Dubash, N. 2000 *The right conditions: the World Bank, structural adjustment and forest policy.* Washington, DC: World Resources Institute.

Silver, W. L., Ostertag, R. & Lugo, A. E. 2000 The potential for carbon sequestration through reforestation of abandoned tropical pastural and agricultural lands. *Restor. Ecol.* **8**, 394–407.

Smith, K. A. 1999 After Kyoto protocol: can scientists make a useful contribution? *Soil Use Manag.* **15**, 71–75.

Smith, P., Powlson, D. S., Glendenning, M. J. & Smith, J. U. 1998 Preliminary estimates of the potential for carbon mitigation in European soils through no-till farming. *Glob. Change Biol.* **4**, 679–685.

Tilman, D. 1998 The greening of the green revolution. *Nature* **396**, 211–212.

Tomich, T., Noordwijk, M., Budidarsono, S., Gillison, A., Trikurniati, K., Murdyaso, D., Stolle, F. & Fagi, A. 1998 *Alternatives to slash-and-burn in Indonesia: summary report and synthesis of phase II.* Bogor, Indonesia: ASB-Indonesia and CRIFC.

Trexler, M. & Haugen, C. 1995 *Keeping it green: tropical forestry opportunities for mitigating climate change.* Washington, DC: World Resources Institute and Environmental Protection Agency.

Uhl, C., Buschbacher, R. & Serrao, E. A. S. 1988 Abandoned pastures in eastern Amazonia I. Patterns of plant succession. *J. Ecol.* **76**, 663–681.

United Nations 1999 Matters left pending on the need for financial resources: Secretary General's Report, United Nations Commission on Sustainable Development, Intergovernmental Forum on Forests. Third Session, 3–14 May 1999. Document E/CN.17/IFF/1999/4.

UNFCCC 2001 (United Nations Framework Convention on Climate Change) *Review of the implementation of commitments and of other provisions of the Convention.* Decision FCCC/CP/2001/L.7. (Available at www.unfccc.int/resource/docs/cop6secpart/l07.pdf.)

USDA 2000 (US Department of Agriculture) *Growing carbon: a new crop that helps agricultural producers and the climate too.* Washington, DC: Natural Resources Conservation Service.

USGS 1997 (US Geological Survey) *The global ecosystem land cover characterization.* (Available at http://edcdaac.usgs.gov/glcc/glcc.html.)

US State Department 2001 Remarks to The Royal Institute of International Affairs Conference, Dr. Harlan L. Watson, Senior Climate Negotiator and Special Representative, US Department of State. (Available at www.state.gov/g/oes/climate/ index.cfm?docid=5273.)

Watson, R. T., Noble, I. R., Bolin, B., Ravindranath, N. H., Verardo, D. J. & Dokken, D. J. (eds) 2000 *Land use, land-use change and forestry.* Special report to the Intergovernmental Panel on Climate Change. Cambridge University Press.

WCCA 2001 *Conservation agriculture: a worldwide challenge. World Congress on Conservation Agriculture, Madrid.* Rome: Food and Agriculture Organization.

Yellen, J. 1998 Testimony before the House Commerce Subcommittee on energy and power. (Available at www.state.gov/www/policy_remarks/1998/980519_yellen_ climate.html.)

Chapter 5

The role of multilateral institutions

AGNES KISS, GONZALO CASTRO AND KENNETH NEWCOMBE

Why are The World Bank and other multilateral development banks becoming involved in carbon markets?

The World Bank and other multilateral development banks (MDBs) are international organizations whose mission is to alleviate poverty by supporting and spurring economic development. In the past few decades, environmental and other aspects of sustainability have become important explicit development goals. This is reflected, for example, in the mission statement of The World Bank: 'to fight poverty with passion and professionalism... to help people help themselves and their environment, with lasting results'.

MDBs function mainly by lending money to developing country governments on concessional terms and by providing technical assistance to help their clients identify and implement needed policy and institutional reforms, investments and projects. Sometimes funds are provided on a grant basis, such as grants from the Global Environment Facility (GEF) implemented by The World Bank or other GEF-implementing agencies. GEF funds may be given to government institutions or to non-government organizations (NGOs), through the 'medium-sized-grant' window, which provides grants up to $1 million to NGOs, corporations, etc. Eligible recipients under this window include private-sector corporations in principle, although the recipients of these funds to date have mainly been non-profit NGOs. One member of The World Bank Group, the International Finance Corporation (IFC), provides financing directly to the private sector as a means of catalysing investment in developing countries.

Environmental issues have been on the agenda of the MDBs for several decades, with an emphasis on reducing and mitigating the potential negative environmental (and social) impacts of the development activities they finance. In recent years, this 'safeguard' approach has been complemented by efforts to 'mainstream' environment in development programmes, based on a growing appreciation of the direct linkage between good environmental management, sustainable economic development and long-term poverty alleviation.

Most recently, MDBs have begun to assume a major role in protecting 'global public goods,' including the global environment. Most developing country governments have committed themselves to the objectives of a variety of international environmental treaties and conventions. Presently, the greatest focus is on the United Nations Framework Convention on Climate Change (UNFCCC), the Convention on Biological Diversity (CBD) and the Convention to Combat Desertification (CCD). The MDBs have a responsibility to support their clients in fulfilling these commitments and have developed policies and operational programmes for this purpose. The GEF was established in 1989 as a mechanism for channelling financial and technical assistance to developing countries to help them participate in the worldwide effort to preserve global environmental values. The funds are provided by the 150-plus GEF member governments. The World Bank serves as the Trustee of the GEF Trust Fund and as one of its three Implementing Agencies (together with the United Nations Development Programme (UNDP) and the United Nations Environment Programme (UNEP)).

Given their core mission of poverty alleviation through economic development, MDBs have a strong interest in the potential of the emerging global carbon market as a new tool to yield economic development benefits, particularly for the poor in developing countries. In this context, standing ('sequestered') carbon is seen as a potentially marketable new product from the rural landscape. It is a growing market with great potential, and one in which developing countries may have a significant comparative advantage.

The Kyoto Protocol of the UNFCCC provides an opening for global resource transfers through two market-based mechanisms that enable financial transactions between industrialized and developing countries for the purchase of greenhouse-gas-emissions (GHG-emissions) reductions:

1 *Article 6* provides for the 'Joint Implementation' (JI) of projects by industrialized countries, including those with economies in transition. It allows an entity in one such country to finance or purchase 'emissions-reduction units' (ERUs) from a project in another industrialized country. Eligible projects include, for example, emissions reductions in energy, industry and transport sector activities, as well as carbon sequestration through land-use change, agriculture and forestry activities.

2 *Article 12* provides for the 'Clean Development Mechanism' (CDM), under which an entity in an industrialized country may purchase 'Certified Emissions Reductions' (CERs) from a project in a developing country, or 'removal units' (RMUs) if the project concerns carbon sequestration (long-term removal from the atmosphere) through afforestation and reforestation activities. The CDM has two purposes: to assist developing countries achieve sustainable development through the transfer of cleaner technologies or sustainable forestry and agro-forestry practices, and financial resources for specific projects; and simultaneously to contribute to the reduction of global carbon emissions.

Under the right circumstances, developing countries may have a comparative advantage to supply the 'product' of emissions reductions/sequestration (or 'carbon' for short) to the global market. Experience from The World Bank's Prototype Carbon Fund (PCF) shows that environmentally credible emissions reductions can be achieved in developing countries in the range of \$3–\$5 per ton of carbon dioxide (CO_2) equivalent, compared with a marginal abatement cost of \$10–\$15 per ton of CO_2 equivalent in most countries within the Organisation for Economic Co-operation and Development (OECD). However, without substantial assistance with project development and government legal and institutional capacity building, only a small part of this potential will be realized over the next decade.

By engaging in the emerging carbon market, developing countries can obtain financial benefits in the short term. They will also contribute to the reduction of atmospheric GHGs, and thus to the mitigation of climate change in the longer term. This in itself is a significant development benefit given that many developing countries are extremely vulnerable to the expected impacts of climate change, including sea-level rise, decreased rainfall in already arid regions, expansion of certain vector-borne diseases, etc. Similarly, there is the potential for considerable synergy between the carbon market and biodiversity conservation. Biodiversity is an important economic asset of many developing countries and of their rural populations in particular, and much of that biodiversity occurs in natural ecosystems that also serve as significant carbon stores.

Targeting rural poverty: carbon sequestration as a sustainable natural-resource use

The livelihoods of rural people are highly dependent upon the value that they can extract from the ecosystem, particularly from renewable natural resources such as soil, grasslands, forests, wildlife and fish. Usually these resources are extracted and consumed, either directly or as marketed products. With the continuing growth of rural populations in many parts of the world, these already tenuous consumption-based livelihoods are increasingly threatened. More and more, demand exceeds supply and extraction rates exceed regeneration rates, leading to unsustainable 'mining' of these theoretically renewable resources.

As a result, 'sustainable use' of natural resources has become a Holy Grail of the development community—much sought after but highly elusive. Despite countless initiatives, however, there are few convincing examples of ecologically sustainable consumptive use of natural resources anywhere in the world. Even in the classic case of extractive reserves in Brazil, often cited as a model, many of the rubber trees are dying due to over tapping and newcomers are undermining the livelihoods of the original indigenous rubber-tappers.

Uses that do not require extraction and actual consumption of the resources in question are therefore of particular interest from a sustainability standpoint. 'Ecotourism' has become a very popular model for generating income through non-consumptive use of wildlife and the natural habitats they live in. The concept behind ecotourism is that visitors are willing to pay to see wildlife and/or local communities in their natural and traditional environments, thereby providing a direct incentive to preserve those environments. In many cases, ecotourism is part of a 'multiple-use' approach, which does not preclude other uses of these resources. For example a protected area reserved for tourism may be surrounded by a 'buffer zone', where hunting or tree cutting are allowed, or these activities may be permitted only for certain species or outside the main tourist season.

As a basis for economic development, however, ecotourism has some important limitations. Many natural areas that are critical for poverty alleviation and/or biodiversity do not lend themselves to tourism due to difficult access, insecurity, endemic diseases or other constraints. To be truly environmentally friendly, tourism must also be on a relatively small scale, which limits the economic returns and the number of people who can benefit from it. The solution of 'low-volume, high-price' tourism works only where there is an exceptional attraction, such as the mountain gorillas of central Africa and the giant pandas of Sichuan Province in China. A limited number of 'luxury operators' can follow this model in areas such as the East African savannah or prime coral reefs, but their success is undermined if too many 'high-volume' outfits operate in the same area. Tourism is a highly competitive field that requires more up-front and ongoing investment in time, capital, training and marketing than its proponents and prospective beneficiaries may be prepared for. There is also a significant issue of 'leakage,' in that a substantial portion of tourism revenues never reaches the destination country, much less the local rural community.

Overall, while there are many more or less successful 'community-based tourism enterprises' around the world (which do provide some incentive for conservation), there are very few places where tourism alone currently represents a viable economic alternative to extractive uses or to conversion of natural areas to other uses. A limited number of external or local entrepreneurs may profit substantially, and a larger number of people may derive some income (e.g. through employment or sale of crafts), but the majority of the local rural community continue to earn their livelihood primarily through some form of farming. Most funding for biodiversity conservation and rural economic development in and around important natural habitats still comes from multilateral and bilateral donors and international conservation organizations, not self-financing tourism operations.

A global carbon market represents an important potential for another form of non-extractive non-consumptive use. Like ecotourism, it can give direct value to standing trees and unplowed grasslands. In addition, relatively intact natural forests and grasslands combine significant carbon storage with retaining biodiversity that is essential to the welfare of the rural poor, as sources of food (including famine reserves), medicines, building materials, etc. As in the case of ecotourism, the key question is whether or not the income generated can be sufficient, and sufficiently well distributed, to make standing forest or rangeland an economically viable land-use alternative in the eyes of the ultimate land users. In many cases the solution will be a multiple-use approach, where a package of environmentally friendly and sustainable land uses compete successfully with more destructive ones. Such a package will usually include agriculture, which remains the economic base of rural communities, but agricultural practices will emphasize compatibility with the additional land uses as well as sustainability and higher incomes.

World Bank activities relating to biodiversity and carbon

The World Bank has been supporting projects to conserve natural ecosystems since the 1970s, with substantial growth in both volume and breadth in the 1990s. Between 1990 and 1999, The World Bank supported 226 biodiversity projects in 85 countries, with a combined total value of $2.7 billion. The World Bank supports biodiversity objectives through four main windows: loans from the International Bank for Reconstruction and Development (IBRD), concessional loans from the International Development Association (IDA), GEF grants and grants made available to Brazil through the World-Bank-administered Rainforest Trust Fund, which is funded by the G-7 countries. In addition, most projects attract co-financing from bilateral agencies and government counterparts.

The World Bank's biodiversity portfolio is linked to the objectives of The World Bank's Environment Strategy through its contribution to enhancing rural livelihoods. There is a broad understanding that the maintenance of biodiversity (broadly defined to include the conservation of functioning ecological systems) is a necessary ingredient to achieve sustainable poverty alleviation in rural landscapes. The nature of The World Bank's biodiversity portfolio provides important opportunities and entry points to link carbon sequestration and biodiversity. Preserving natural habitats is an essential element of biodiversity conservation, and the same habitats (primarily forests, grasslands and wetlands) play an important role in absorbing and sequestering carbon. The World Bank and its clients are and will be exploring many such 'win–win' opportunities.

The World Bank's biodiversity portfolio initially focused largely on Protected Areas (PAs). While PAs are still considered important conservation tools, the portfolio has evolved and expanded over the past decade and increasingly emphasizes sustainable natural-resources management in the context of ecological sustainability, direct participation of local communities and indigenous people in the benefits of conservation, and the development of markets for environmental services. New projects also tend to emphasize ecosystem approaches in which biodiversity is addressed holistically within PAs, in their surrounding areas and in the productive landscapes that are an integral part of any given ecosystem. They also emphasize local-level priority setting, planning, action and monitoring to ensure that both local and global objectives are addressed. This 'integrated ecosystem management approach' also represents the newest Operational Programme of the GEF (Operational Programme 12), and is an explicit priority of the CBD.

The development of markets for environmental services provides a vital prospect for ensuring environmental management in the long term, with less dependence on short-term unreliable external funding. Projects of this kind are designed to capture the economic value that natural ecosystems provide to society, by establishing mechanisms to enable financial transactions between the providers and consumers of these services. The simplest and most familiar example of a market for environmental services involves the 'water-capture' function of forests upstream of water plants or supply systems. Recognizing the importance of these forests for ensuring a predictable flow of clean water, the water utility pays for the 'water-capture' service to an institution (either government or private) that applies the payment to maintain the forests intact. To be sustainable, the water utility normally recovers the cost of the payments from its customers.

The Catskills watershed in New York state is a well-known example, in which the city of New York has paid for land purchases, concessions and maintenance in order to maintain its famously clean water supply, thus avoiding the need to billions of dollars in a water-treatment plant (see Chichilnisky & Heal 1998). In Colombia and in Ecuador, water user groups and municipal authorities are paying for water-capture services, sometimes by purchasing substantial areas of the watersheds and placing them under conservation. In fact, in Colombia, power companies must by law pay a percentage of their revenues to regional corporations that are responsible for watershed management (although it is not clear whether these funds are then actually used for watershed management). In El Salvador, municipalities downstream of El Impossible National Park have agreed to make a financial contribution to park management as payment for watershed services (for further information on these Latin America examples, see World Bank Group (2000)). In the West Cape Province of South Africa, the 'Working for Water' programme receives a budgetary allocation from the water Ministry and from a water tax on plantations to conserve water by clearing the watershed of invasive plant species that evapotranspire at much higher rates than the native *fynbos* vegetation. Further information on initiatives to create markets and generate payment for environmental services can be found at the website of the Katoomba Group (www.katoombagroup.com).

More sophisticated approaches seek to capture not just one environmental service (such as water capture), but the multiple benefits generated by natural ecosystems. This requires innovative approaches and the development of markets for services that traditionally have not entered financial markets or national accounts and thus have been considered 'free'. It also creates opportunities for synergy between resources available for reducing atmospheric GHGs (such as the CER market) and those available for conservation of biodiversity (such as the GEF and the substantial funding provided each year by governments, multilateral and bilateral donors, and international and national conservation organizations).

Costa Rica is currently implementing one such project with the support of The World Bank. Under Costa Rica's 'Ecomarkets' project, landowners in rural areas receive a payment (provided for in Costa Rica's forestry law) for conserving and managing forests that provide four key services: water capture, biodiversity protection, scenic beauty and carbon sequestration. The payment is currently set at $40.00 per hectare per year. Initially, these payments were financed through a tax on gasoline. The Ecomarkets project aims at developing a true market in which consumers of these four environmental services pay for them through a government intermediary (FONAFIFO). As in the examples above, the water-capture function will be paid by a recovery mechanism from water utilities. It is envisioned that the tourism industry will contribute a share of the total payments, given that this industry benefits directly from the scenic beauty of intact forests. The global environmental services of biodiversity conservation and carbon sequestration will be paid through instruments that serve as 'proxy consumers' for the international community. The innovative aspect of this project is that the various benefits are all generated from the same hectare of land, thus creating the opportunity to develop and draw synergistically upon multiple consumers for multiple environmental services. This diversification increases the chances of achieving financial sustainability and being economically competitive with alternative land uses that could otherwise involve clearing the forest. Similar projects are currently under development in El Salvador, Guatemala and Ecuador.

World Bank activities relating to developing carbon markets: the PCF

The existence of a global market for stored (sequestered) carbon does not necessarily translate to improved income or other benefits for the rural poor. A positive development outcome depends on how the market is structured and how it operates, at international, national and local levels. Key factors include investors' reactions to economic and political risks, rules governing ownership of the assets and institutional systems for distributing benefits and mitigating any negative impacts.

In April 2000, with shareholding from 17 private corporations and six governments, The World Bank began implementation of the PCF (for further details, see PCF 2001). Its objective is to help spur the development of a global carbon market and to 'learn by doing' how to use carbon purchase transactions to achieve environmentally credible and cost-effective emissions reductions benefiting developing countries and economies in transition. Through the PCF, The World Bank has pioneered JI and CDM transactions ahead of all other market players. The fund has helped to buy down entry barriers for private investment and to encourage and assist developing-country governments to open their marketplaces for carbon-purchase transactions. PCF transactions have served to benchmark the processes of achieving high-quality emissions reductions across a range of energy-sector technologies and some forestry applications.

The World Bank is well suited to playing this catalytic role. First, it has the international credibility and 'convening power' to attract substantial 'buy in' (including financial contributions) from both governments and the private sector. It also has access and influence at the highest levels of government in its borrowing member countries, which is important to reduce both real and perceived political and other risks to investors. Furthermore, The World Bank is recognized to have some of the most comprehensive and stringent environmental and social 'safeguard policies' of all multilateral and bilateral development institutions.

The PCF has three primary strategic objectives:

1 To show how project-based GHG-emissions-reduction transactions can promote and contribute to sustainable development and lower the cost of compliance with the Kyoto Protocol.

2 To provide the Parties to the UNFCCC, the private sector and other interested parties with an opportunity to learn by doing in the development of policies, rules and business processes for the achievement of emission reductions under JI and the CDM.

3 To demonstrate how The World Bank can work in partnership with the public and private sector to mobilize new resources for its borrowing member countries while addressing global environmental problems through market-based mechanisms.

The PCF contributors (participants) currently include six governments (Canada, Finland, Japan, the Netherlands, Norway, Sweden) and 17 corporations, and its assets total *ca.* $145 million. These funds will be used to purchase CERs, guided by the provisions of the Kyoto Protocol. The PCF serves as a mechanism to spread risk and responsibilities. Rather than making individual investments and deals, participants invest collectively and receive a pro rata share of the emissions reductions, verified and certified in accordance with carbon-purchase agreements reached with the respective project sponsors in developing countries. The World Bank is actively engaged in assisting the participants and project sponsors to define and negotiate these agreements and in building the local capacity to implement them.

To date, the PCF has focused mainly on projects involving renewable energy and energy efficiency, as these are the best-accepted mechanisms for reducing GHG emissions. Presently, the scope for carbon-offset projects in developing countries involving 'land use, land-use change and forestry' (LULUCF) is limited by the provisions of the Kyoto Protocol. During the first commitment period (2008–2012), the Bonn Agreement allows industrialized countries to sponsor only a limited amount of reforestation and afforestation projects in developing countries, and does not allow for any JI or CDM projects involving carbon sequestration through improved agricultural practices or protecting/maintaining existing forests or other natural vegetation (see Chapter 4).

However, the relation between land-use changes and carbon emissions represents an important area as far as The World Bank is concerned, because of the potential to involve and benefit developing countries whose economies and populations are primarily rural. The PCF has therefore taken a leadership role in pioneering initiatives involving LULUCF, two examples of which are described below.

1 In Romania, the PCF is supporting afforestation of 6728 hectares of degraded land in the southwest and southeast of the Romanian Plain and the ecological reconstruction of part of the Lower Danube floodplain, using invasive local tree and non-timber species that will be planted

to increase biodiversity across the production landscape. Part of an island in the Danube is being reforested as a conservation area under a green-corridor programme already in place, and a biodiversity monitoring plan will be included in the design. Planting began in spring 2002.

2　In Brazil, the Plantar project involves creation of both CERs and carbon sinks. The CERs arise from charcoal production (from sustainably harvested eucalyptus) displacing coal/coke in pig-iron reduction, and in reducing methane in carbonization. In addition to creation of a carbon sink of 23 000 hectares, the native cerrado forest ecosystem will be restored both on a 470 hectare parcel of pasture land and in the 4600 hectares of reserve land required to be set aside under Minas Gerais law (20% of plantation area) whenever plantations are being established. In this project, benefits are 'bundled' with the GHG benefits, as the entire forest production landscape is integrated with restoration forestry as a conservation management landscape.

A particular effort is made to ensure that these projects restore/protect natural forests and yield biodiversity benefits, as well as CERs, going beyond the provisions of the Kyoto Protocol. This represents a good example of how The World Bank is using the PCF to bring environmental and social protections and global public goods into the carbon market, in keeping with its mandate and mission.

The PCF has primarily an energy-sector focus and can only spend up to 10% of its assets in LULUCF activities. Therefore, The World Bank is in the process of launching a 'Biocarbon Fund' and a Community Development Carbon Fund (CDCF), which will pioneer environmentally and socially credible carbon-asset creation across a range of common and replicable land-use and forestry initiatives. One of the key objectives of these funds will be to use carbon markets to achieve convergence between the CBC, CCD and the UNFCCC. The CDCF will also aim to demonstrate how transaction costs for small-scale projects that benefit rural populations can be reduced, making them competitive with larger-scale operations on the basis of dollars per ton of carbon. Each fund will have a 'for-credit' and a 'not-for-credit' window, with differentiated mandates from different shareholders. The 'for-credit' window will deal with afforestation/reforestation under the CDM during the first commitment period of the Kyoto Protocol. An 'over the horizon' window will deliver carbon-sequestration credits from activities that are not yet creditable under the Kyoto Protocol, but that offer high environmental, biodiversity and development benefits. It is anticipated that these new funds will support both projects involving creating or enhancing carbon sinks, and projects to prevent or reduce the release of carbon that is already fixed in the form of forests, other vegetation and organic material in soils. They will also support research and development on methods for establishing baselines and other key elements of implementing LULUCF carbon projects.

Challenges of capturing carbon markets for sustainable development

While there is clearly enormous potential for capturing the financial and other benefits of the emerging global carbon market to support the objectives of sustainable development, the process of doing so is far from simple. There are a number of obstacles to be overcome. As noted above, The World Bank has mobilized resources for the PCF as a mechanism to address some of these problems, both by creating favourable market conditions and by facilitating pilot projects that provide an opportunity for 'learning by doing'.

One important challenge is that the governments and citizens of developing countries do not yet recognize or perceive carbon markets as a viable and potentially significant source of resources for their own development objectives. The World Bank and other MDBs (among others) will need to help raise awareness at all levels about the concept and the mechanisms, including it in dialogue concerning energy and land-use sectors. The success of PCF and other projects will be one of the most important demonstrations.

Once the awareness and interest have been generated, there is the additional challenge of ensuring the existence of an attractive investment climate. The global carbon market is, and will continue to be, primarily a private-sector affair, and the private sector is interested in secure investments and guaranteed results. Issues such as political instability, fiscal mismanagement or opaqueness, weak judicial systems and a general lack of accountability in public service can all play a negative role in undermining potential investors' interest in engaging in some developing countries. Investors are also likely to be concerned about 'reputational risks' should they (knowingly or inadvertently) become associated with a project that has negative environmental or social impacts, such as displacing indigenous populations or vulnerable minorities. The World Bank and other MDBs are actively engaged in assisting borrowing member countries to address such issues, but the rate of progress is not sufficiently rapid to overcome these limitations in the short term. In order to attract private-sector carbon investment, it may be necessary to create 'islands' of reduced risk, that is, relatively self-contained projects where these factors can be investigated, identified and mitigated. Subsidization can be another option, particularly in a pilot phase, with The World Bank or other partners 'buying down' investors' risks either through grants or concessional loans or by providing risk guarantees.

The Environmentally and Socially Sustainable Development family within The World Bank is particularly interested in the contribution that the emerging market in carbon-offset credits can make to sustainable rural development, particularly in the area of community-based natural-resource management efforts. Many communities in developing countries will, however, need assistance to position themselves and develop the organizational and other faculties to take advantage of this opportunity. In fact, without careful planning, the exploitation of carbon-market opportunities may have negative impacts on the rural poor. Whenever an asset increases in value, the poorest and politically least-empowered sectors of the population risk losing any access to or control over it (see Chapter 16).

In most industrialized countries, the majority of land, including forest land, is either privately owned or in the public domain and under the management of national or local government agencies (including the semi-sovereign Native American reservations in North America). By contrast, in many developing countries (particularly in Africa and southern Asia), a substantial proportion of land is held in some form of communal ownership, usually based on traditional rights that have been more or less recognized or formalized through the modern legal system. Formalized examples include the Maasai group ranches in Kenya, village leases in Tanzania and community conservancies in southern Africa. In many cases, these communal landholders are among the poorest sectors of society and are also both a principle source and the main victims of deforestation. As such, they are obvious targets to benefit from the significant financial assets—linked to forest protection and re-afforestation—that are now becoming available in the form of international carbon-offset credits.

Communal ownership of land and land-based natural resources, on the other hand, present special challenges for the use of market-based mechanisms such as carbon-offset credits. These challenges can translate into higher barriers and risks for 'carbon investors', who may therefore prefer to work with private or state landowners rather than take on the uncertainties of working in community-based settings. The challenge therefore is to lower these barriers and risks, thereby enabling communal landholders to position and prepare themselves to become competitive in this market.

Key issues to be addressed include the need for:

- the ability to enter into legally binding contracts and agreement;

- effective mechanisms for making and enforcing decisions;

- transparent and acceptable mechanisms for distribution and use of the financial proceeds;

- monitoring and accountability; and

- provisions to compensate or otherwise accommodate individuals who may suffer negative impacts of group decisions.

A particular challenge in mobilizing carbon markets at the community level is the disjunction between the short-term needs of the people and the longer-term nature of the carbon 'product'. Poor rural communities in developing countries are typically faced with difficulties in meeting basic daily needs such as food, clothing, medicine, transportation and school fees. In order for a land use to be considered desirable, or even viable, it must generate direct benefits of food or income in the short term. Carbon sequestration, however, is a long-term process whose value is delivered over a period of decades. For example, Sustainable Forest Management recently paid the Confederated Salish and Kootenai Tribes $50 000 for the rights to 47 974 tons of CO_2 equivalent to be sequestered over a period of 80 years, through the reforestation of 100 hectares of fire-destroyed high-altitude pinelands on their reservation in Montana. As part of the agreement, carbon storage on the site is to be maintained for 100 years (the tribes will own the rights for the last 20 years).

In order to bridge the gap between short-term needs and long-term production, some form of 'front-loading' of payments is needed. The same challenge arises in other forms of payment for environmental services. For example, in Costa Rica, landholders commit themselves to continuing forest protection and management for a period of 20 years, but they receive the full payment for this service in the first five years. Similarly, one IFC-financed sustainable forest-management project buys the future value of forest products 'up front'. Such front-loading inevitably creates a risk that the landholders may not continue to live up to commitments once the payments have been completed, and weak judicial systems in many developing countries mean that investors may have little recourse should their partners renege on their agreements. Therefore, the question will arise as to whether the market value of the sequestered carbon is sufficient to allow payments that are high enough to compete with alternative land uses (such as clearing a forest for agriculture), both initially and over a long period of time. There is clearly a need to develop and demonstrate innovative financing instruments to overcome this dilemma.

One important role for The World Bank and other MDBs is to assist developing country governments in overcoming the policies that constrain the emergence of functional carbon markets. Examples include energy or other price subsidies that reduce incentives for energy efficiency, a lack of legislation/judicial instruments enabling individuals or communities to enter into contractual business relationships, land-use policies that require people to clear land (deforestation) in order to claim it, forest-sector policies that require concessionaires to actively engage in logging or lose the concession, and land-tenure and natural-resource policies that prevent rural communities from controlling or capturing the benefits from land/resources other than conventional crops or livestock.

References

Chichilnisky, G. & Heal, G. M. 1998 Economic returns from the biosphere. *Nature* **391**, 629–630.

PCF 2001 *Annual report*. Washington, DC: Prototype Carbon Fund. (Available at www.prototypecarbonfund.org.)

World Bank Group 2000 *Environmental economics and indicators: paying for systems of environmental payment services*. Washington, DC: World Bank Group (http://lnweb18.worldbank.org/ESSD/essdext.nsf/44DocByUnid/3BCC183DF3 93834685256B500063D718?Opendocument).

Chapter 6

Electricity generation: options for reduction in carbon emissions

H. W. WHITTINGTON

Introduction

Industrialization and economic development require an ample supply of electricity at an affordable price. The relationship between energy supply and economic well-being is well-established and, although the causality is a matter for debate, it is true that the most successful economies use the most electrical energy.

Originally, electricity was derived from the burning of fossil fuels: these were abundant, cheap and were available in most parts of the world. The technology to exploit these primary energy resources was widely available and operated reliably. The only significant input from a renewable resource was that from hydroelectricity, which presently accounts for around one-fifth of global electricity production. However, hydropower is available only to those countries with suitable hydrology and topology.

As evidence mounts for change in global climate, an assessment of ways in which to reduce the contribution to this effect from electricity production must be undertaken. The electricity supply industry is currently responsible for *ca.* 30% of the UK's total carbon dioxide (CO_2) emissions (the rest is divided approximately equally between transport and commercial/residential premises) (DEFRA 2002). Between 1990 and 1998, CO_2 emissions from power stations were reduced by 7.5%, mainly by closing old, inefficient, coal-burning plant and installing more-efficient gas-burning technology. However, recently the levels have been rising: in the last year (DEFRA 2002) there was a 2.5% increase on the base year of 1990. This has occurred as a result of the policy of decommissioning nuclear power stations (which emit no CO_2) and replacing them with fossil-fuelled, mainly gas-burning, plant. This trend is predicted to continue both in the UK and in continental Europe.

In addition to CO_2, power stations emit annually an estimated 2 534 000 t of SO_2 (71% of the national total) and 718 000 t of NO_x (26% of the national total).

Table 6.1. *How CO_2 emissions from UK power stations reduced in the early 1990s, but have begun to increase as nuclear plants are shut down and replaced by gas-fired generation*

	1990	1998	1999	2000
MtC	54.1	40.6	38.8	42.0
% reduction		−25.0	−4.4	+8.3

Source: (DEFRA 2002).

Options for reduction in gaseous emissions

With the global dominance of fossil fuels and the widespread availability of suitable technology to generate electricity, such fuels will be used for the foreseeable future. Several options present themselves for reducing gaseous emissions from fossil-fuelled power stations.

Switching to different fossil fuel for reduced emissions

Low-sulphur coal, sourced from different parts of the world, reduces SO_2 production. Using gas instead of coal also reduces emissions: CO_2 output is halved and SO_2 falls to almost zero because of the superior efficiency of gas power stations, up to 53% as opposed to 35% for coal (IEE 1994). Gas is especially efficient when used in combined-cycle technology, where the hot exhaust gases from a gas turbine are used to produce steam, which then powers a steam turbine. A major proportion of the reduction in carbon emissions in UK since 1990 (DEFRA 2002) has been as a result of the switch from coal to gas for electricity generation (DTI 2001), as is shown in Table 6.1.

Fuel switching to nuclear power

Despite public concerns over waste disposal and uncertainties over economics, fuel switching to nuclear power currently remains the largest, proven, carbon-free generation option, accounting, in the USA and UK, for around one-fifth and one-quarter, respectively, of electricity produced annually.

Uranium is a far more effective fuel per kilogram than other fuel. One tonne of uranium produces the equivalent amount of electricity as 16 000 t of coal and 80 000 barrels of oil. Spent fuel is transferred to a storage facility next to the reactor to allow the radioactive level and heat to decrease. Waste fuel is stored in pools of water and the fuel is held there for about six months. The spent fuel from the reactor still contains ^{235}U, so it can be recycled. Reprocessing the spent fuel produces uranium, plutonium and waste.

Safe disposal/storage of waste from the nuclear fuel cycle presents a challenge. Three categories exist, depending on the level of radioactivity. Low-level waste is created at all stages of the nuclear fuel cycle: intermediate waste is produced by the reactor operation and recycling of materials; high-level waste is spent fuel containing fission products from the recycling process.

There appear to be three alternative routes for nuclear power in the future:

1 A complete phase-out of nuclear power. For this to be successful, alternative plans must be made for electricity generation in the short term.

2 A continued growth of nuclear power for the foreseeable future, at its present rate. This is unlikely for the reasons of public concern, stated above.

3 A progressive reduction followed by return to current levels if alternative generating methods have not been successful. This allows alternative methods of power generation to be introduced in the short term, to be abandoned if they fail. However, there is a danger that the capability to design and build nuclear plant may have been lost in the interim.

Even if the decision to build new nuclear plant were to be taken, in order to create a level playing field, it is argued that the environmental costs of generating electricity from fossil fuels would have to be reflected in the prices consumers were charged. Electricity supply companies might be obliged to enter long-term contracts to purchase a set proportion of their power from different sources, so that generators, whether gas or nuclear, have the incentive to build base-load stations.

The existing planning procedures and regulatory approvals system are viewed by many as cumbersome and overly lengthy. Some streamlining would be necessary to ensure new nuclear reactors could be built effectively and efficiently. However, overarching all these considerations is the question of the radioactive waste disposal—arguably the thorniest problem the nuclear industry has to overcome. It is necessary for the Government to set an overall policy before there is any realistic chance of future nuclear expansion.

Remove harmful emissions from flue gases

In flue-gas desulphurization, SO_2 is washed out of the flue gas using limestone slurry, producing gypsum as a byproduct (IEE 1994). This technique can reduce the SO_2 content of flue gas by up to 90%, but, since it results in an efficiency reduction of the plant, CO_2 output is increased.

Improve technology of combustion processes to reduce emissions

A typical process is gasification, where the hot coal reacts with oxygen and steam to form a gas made up mainly of hydrogen and carbon monoxide, which can then be burnt to drive a gas turbine coupled to a generator. To improve the overall efficiency, the heat from the gasification process and from the gas-turbine exhaust is used to produce steam to drive a steam turbine. The combined process is called an 'integrated gasification combined cycle'.

Make use of waste heat to improve efficiency

The exhaust heat can also be used to heat water that can be used to heat homes or offices in a combined heat and power (CHP) plant. Efficiencies of up

Table 6.2. *A comparison of typical cost (or estimates, where there are no costs available) and the annual potential for CO_2 reduction of different methods of electricity generation*

Technology	Cost (pence kWh^{-1})	Carbon abatement potential in 2050 (MtC yr^{-1})
end-use efficiency	low	65
photovoltaic	10–16	N/A
onshore wind	1.5–2.5	5
offshore wind	2.0–3.0	>20
energy crops	2.5–4.0	10
wave	3.0–6.0	>20
nuclear	3.0–4.0	>20
gas turbine[a]	2.0–2.3	—
coal[b]	3.0–3.5	—

[a]Combined-cycle gas turbine: combination of gas turbine and steam turbine.
[b]Integrated-gasification combined cycle: combination of gasification of coal and combined-cycle gas turbine.

to 80% are possible (IEE 1994) if there is a need for the heat. Ideal locations for CHP tend to be hospitals and schools, where there is a large demand for electricity and heat. CHP is the most cost-effective option to generate and reduce emissions. The UK Government has set a target of 10 GW of CHP by 2010, which, it is claimed, at 15% of the current electricity market, would secure £3 billion of new investment into the UK economy, £600 million in annual energy savings for UK businesses and one-fifth of the Government's 20% carbon reduction target (EA 2002) by 2010.

Exploitation of renewable energy

Around 23% of global electricity production is presently renewable in nature: it is large-scale hydroelectric development. Other sources of renewable energy include wind (both onshore and offshore), solar panels, biomass and wave and tidal energy.

Biomass includes energy from waste, landfill gas, sewage gas, agricultural or forestry residues and fast growing energy crops. Solar energy can also be used in both passive and active heating systems in addition to the direct generation of electricity. Cost estimates and potential for carbon reduction for some renewables compared with the best fossil-fuelled plant are given in Table 6.2. An impression of the potential for reduction in CO_2 offered by the different technologies follows (PIU 2002).

Declared net capacity

Declared net capacity (DNC) is a scaling factor given to renewable sources of electricity generation to account for the fact that the machine nameplate output cannot be guaranteed. The DNC represents that proportion of generation

Table 6.3. *DNC capacity of renewable sources*

Energy source	Declared net capacity
hydroelectricity	1.0
waste	1.0
biomass	1.0
wind	0.43
tidal	0.33
wave	0.33
solar	0.17

Source: House of Lords (1999)

capacity which can be regarded as always available. Table 6.3 shows values of DNC for the most abundant renewables.

Wind energy

The Earth's winds are created as a result of the heating of the planet's surface by the Sun, setting up pressure gradients balanced by the Coriolis force set up by the Earth's rotation. These winds are modified by thermodynamic and frictional forces at the Earth's surface.

Environmental impact can be gauged by considering a typical large wind-energy installation of, say, 300 MW. This would save *ca.* 20 Mt of CO_2 over its 20-year lifetime (IEE 1994) but the 300 or so wind turbines, especially in such a large group, cause a visual impact on the surrounding environment.

As a result, the planning authority and developer must work together to decide how best to install the turbines in an area. Of particular importance are size, colour and number of turbines. In practice, the total raw wind-energy potential must be reduced to a feasible level by:

- excluding areas which are environmentally sensitive (this means excluding building wind-energy farms in areas of landscape importance, e.g. in national scenic areas, green belt and areas of archaeological interest and in areas of nature conservancy importance, including special protection areas and national and local nature reserves); and

- allowing for 'accessibility', defined by three factors: clustering and proximity, build rate and restrictions of the electricity network.

Some idea of just how this affects the raw potential can be obtained using an example, namely, the potential Scottish on-shore wind resource, which is 11.5 GW (Scottish Executive 2001a, b). In practice, allowances have to be made that reduce this figure considerably. Features such as national environmental and cultural designations and local environmental regulation remove around two-thirds of the land area available for wind turbines (Scottish Executive 2001a, b). Recently, the Ministry of Defence has indicated that it would not generally favour wind farms in certain low-flying areas and this accounts for a further quarter of the country. Local transmission-system limitations which could cause bottlenecks reduce the resource still further, as do public acceptability of the turbines. All of these translate the 11.5 GW resource to 3 GW (Scottish Executive 2001*a, b*) of practical resource (this may be compared with the total of all generation plant in Scotland, which presently stands at *ca.* 10 GW (EA 2002)).

Practical build rate

Build rate is defined as the generation capacity installed per year. Currently, the maximum historical build rate in the UK is 105 MW per annum in 1992/1993. Two years later the European wind industry managed 400 MW per annum. The prediction is that the European build rate will double to 800 MW per annum but a realistic UK build rate would be a doubling of the present rate to 210 MW per annum because of the complex nature of the UK terrain compared with that in Europe. Network issues may also limited wind energy development.

A modern aerogenerator is rated *ca.* 1 MW: this suggests 3000 new aerogenerators in Scotland. As a visual-amenity comparison, there are *ca.* 12 000 large steel transmission towers (pylons) in the entire UK. Currently, a typical wind farm is *ca.* 35 units, so *ca.* 85 new sites would have to be developed.

Typical installation characteristics

For a 1 MW unit-size of wind turbine, typical capital costs would be approximately £800 kW^{-1} and annual operation and maintenance costs of approximately £300 kW^{-1}. The farm would have, on average, a turbine density of 15 turbines per square kilometre and would be designed to operate on an average mean wind speed of greater than 7 m s^{-1}. Buffer zones would be included: 100 m around woodland, 400 m around settlements and 6 km around airports.

Municipal solid-waste combustion

Technology

Currently, in the UK, 80% of household waste is dumped in landfill sites (EA 2002). This is regarded as a short-term solution as suitable sites become full and costs increase. There is much controversy over the categorization of waste-to-energy plants, with some planners feeling that the technology should not fall into the category of renewable. Such plants are fed from local waste, which is reduced to small amounts of disposable sterile waste for integration with combined heat and power schemes and recycling policies.

Installation characteristics

The capital costs (Carlin 1996) for a combustion plant are just over £4000 kW^{-1}, with annual costs of £325 kW^{-1}. For example, a 25 MW plant would require an initial outlay of around £100M with annual running costs of £12.25M. One tonne of waste generates 475 kWh, so a 25 MW plant would consume *ca.* 350 000 t of waste each year, which, at the current landfill tax of £7 t^{-1} for waste, would cost £2.45M.

Using energy from waste combustion to provide both electricity and heat is possible through the use of CHP plants, where most of the energy released through combustion is captured. This leads to an increase in the efficiency of the plant and therefore reduces pollution. In order to make full use of its heat output, any plant must be situated close to the area where the heat will be required. This means that the use of heat in towns requires a CHP plant near to the residential area, to reduce heat losses and the cost of distribution systems. If the area using the heat also supplies the waste for combustion (such as in hospitals or farms) then the entire system is much more self supporting. Many different types of waste can be used for combustion, such as waste from domestic and commercial properties. Municipal solid waste includes:

- scrap tyres, burnt whole or as pellets;

- straw, burnt as bales or chopped up and blown into a furnace;

- poultry litter; and

- industrial wood waste.

Regulations for waste combustion depend entirely on the type of fuel used. Local authority air-pollution-control authorization and a waste-management licence may be required or, in the case of plants where wastes are discharged into sewers or controlled waters, the local sewerage authority or River Purification Authority must also be consulted. A plant can meet all requirements for air pollution but still emit odours and as a result, close proximity to housing may not be welcomed by the residents. Emission levels are regulated on a local scale by the Local Authority Air Pollution Control authorization.

Anaerobic digestion

Anaerobic digestion produces biogas, a gaseous mixture with high methane content. Using biogas for heating and/or electricity generation displaces fossil fuels and thus is beneficial to the environment. However, methane is a strong greenhouse gas (GHG) and only through combustion can it be converted to the less harmful CO_2. Although CO_2 and methane are both damaging to the environment, the production of methane is already present at most sewage treatment works, so it can be argued that the introduction of anaerobic digestion as a means of electricity generation would not have an adverse effect on the environment, as it would merely capture an untapped resource. Sewage treatment authorities have tightened the controls on disposal of sludge such as pumping into the sea, which increases the waste available for energy production. This indicated that there should be a logical push for anaerobic-digestion-based electricity generation. The visual impact of a digestion plant is not likely to be large, as most installations will be at municipal sewage works. The digesters can be as much as 15 m high but can be partly buried to reduce the visual impact and also reduce the energy demand for the digestion process due to the heat insulation benefits. A gas flare is required to dispose of excess gas.

An anaerobic-digestion plant requires a waste-management licence under the Environmental Protection Act 1990, covering areas such as acceptance, handling and storage of wastes, operation and monitoring of flare stacks and gas-cleaning equipment, odour control, handling, storage and use or disposal of digestate and monitoring of pathogens.

Landfill gas

Landfill gas, a mixture of CO_2 and CH_4, is formed under anaerobic conditions where organic waste is broken down by micro-organisms (Ewall 2000). With a calorific value half that of natural gas, landfill gas is collected in gas wells when a small pressure is applied. Once a scheme is commissioned, gas production starts within two years of when the anaerobic conditions have been placed on a landfill site. Production reaches its maximum around five years after commissioning and starts to decline after 15 years.

The methane is used in gas turbines (with a typical efficiency of 26%) and dual-fuel engines (with a typical efficiency of 42%) (Ewall 2000). Landfill gas is an established and proven technology, with over 165 schemes in England and Wales with a DNC of 340 MW.

The regulations for landfill gas generation require planning permission for use of the land and a waste management licence. This licence covers the operational aspects of the site during its active life but also may include the decommissioning of the site for restoration to its original condition after the landfilling has stopped. The waste regulation authority is responsible for monitoring a site once it has closed.

Hydroelectric power

Technology

Hydroelectric power uses precipitation (rain and snow) to drive a generator, producing electricity. Hydroelectric-power plants are categorized into three basic groups.

1 *High head:* the most common type, where water is stored behind a dam to provide a flow of water which is set according to the needs of the network.

2 *Low head:* uses head heights from a few metres to the natural flow rate of the river controlled by low dams, weirs and channels. Low-head plants (sometimes termed 'run-of-river') have no capacity for storing water, so power is controlled by the seasonal flow of the river.

3 *Pumped storage:* operates both as a conventional high-head plant and as an energy store, by absorbing electricity by pumping water to an upper reservoir. Depending on the ratio of pumped-storage energy to natural catchment run-off, this type of station may be a net energy producer,

an energy-neutral store or an absorber of energy. However, even as a net absorber of energy, it represents a valuable resource to the system planner and to the system operator. Because of the ability to change from pumping to generating, a pumped storage station appears, to the system operator, the same as a conventional power station of roughly twice the pumped storage installed capacity. For example, if a 100 MW station switches from pumping to generating, it appears to the system operator as a generator of 200 MW (100 MW from generation plus 100 MW from the pumping load, which has now disappeared), neglecting inefficiencies in pumping and generation. The planner also benefits, since the ability to switch the mode of operation means that a new power station of slightly less than twice the rating of the pumped storage station does not have to be built.

Resource

Hydroelectricity accounts for at least 50% of national electricity production in 63 countries and at least 90% in 23 countries (Baird 1993a). About 10 countries obtain essentially all their commercial electricity from hydro, including Norway, several African nations, Bhutan and Paraguay. There is ca. 700 GW of hydro capacity in operation worldwide, generating 2600 TWh per annum (ca. 19% of the world's electricity production). About half of this capacity and generation is in Europe and North America, but the proportion is declining as Asia and Latin America commission large amounts of new hydro capacity. Hydropower also plays an important role in reducing emissions of GHGs, by an estimated 10%, through displacement of thermal generation. Small, mini- and micro-hydro plants (usually defined as plants less than 10 MW, 2 MW and 100 kW, respectively) play a key role in many countries, often being the mainstay of rural electrification. An estimated 300 million people in China, for example, depend on small hydro. Only ca. 18% of the world's technically feasible hydro potential and 28% of the economic potential have been developed so far. Around 6400 TWh per annum economic potential therefore remains to be exploited (equivalent to ca. 1800 GW). Only 7% of the economic potential has been developed in Africa, 19% in South America, 19% in the Russian Federation, 20% in Asia, and 40% in Oceania. However, 61% have been developed in North and Central America and 65% in Europe (excluding the Russian Federation).

It is estimated that development of half of the world's remaining economically feasible hydro potential could reduce GHG emissions (1990 estimates) by 13%, with an even greater impact on SO_2 emissions. There has, however, recently been growing organized opposition to large-scale water-resources development projects, some of which incorporate hydro schemes. Hydropower's positive benefits are well known and have to be set against the negative impacts. Most of the UK's resource is located in Scotland, where ca. 1.1 GW is presently installed (Scottish Executive 2001a, b). An estimated further 1 GW is technically feasible, mainly as small-scale schemes but the economics case is often difficult to make.

Tidal energy

Technology

Tidal energy (Baird 1993*b*) makes use of the bulk movement of the oceans, twice per day. Two generic types of tidal energy device exist:

1 *Barrage:* a barrier, constructed across the path of the tide when flowing, holds the tide back to create a hydraulic head between the two sides. When the tide ebbs, the same technique is used, giving four generating periods per day. Barriers are expensive and projects usually need an additional use for the barrier to be successful, e.g. as a causeway for road transport.

2 *Tidal mills:* these are similar to an underwater wind turbine; as with wind, both axial flow and the cross flow rotor are available. Power cables are run back to the mainland to connect back to the grid. Tidal mills are still relatively small generators, in the 10 kW range. Several countries are active in tidal technology, including the UK, Japan, Russia and Australia; currently the UK has only conducted trials on tidal mills and has no installed capacity. The Department of Trade and Industry has predicted that, between 2005 and 2010, 322 MW will be installed in the UK.

Over the past three decades the feasibility of using ocean tides to generate electric power has been investigated at many sites throughout the world. Results suggest that the potential for economic development is small.

Resource

Of the *ca.* 22 000 TWh per year dissipated by the tides, 200 TWh is now considered economically recoverable and less than 0.6 TWh is produced by existing plants. By far the largest tidal plant in service is Rance (France), with a capacity of 240 MW and an annual output exceeding 500 GWh. Others include the 20 MW Annapolis plant in Canada, several small units in China with total capacity of *ca.* 5 MW and a 400 kW experimental unit near Murmansk in Russia. In the UK, the maximum practical rated capacity is 16 GW at *ca.* 5% load factor, which translates to *ca.* 40 TWh annual production: 25% of this is in the Pentland Firth (Scotland).

Worldwide, the following five areas account for well over half of the potentially developable energy (Baird 1993*b*):

1 the headwaters of the Bay of Fundy (Canada);

2 the Severn estuary (United Kingdom);

3 the Gulf of St Malo (France);

4 the Southeast coast of China; and

5 Russian coasts bordering the White Sea and Sea of Okhotsk.

Other potentially feasible sites include the Mersey estuary and smaller sites bordering the Irish Sea and Bristol Channel (United Kingdom), the Gulf of Kachch (India), the west coast of Korea, the northwest coast of Australia, Cook Inlet (Alaska) and the Gulf of San José (Argentina).

At the moment the tidal industry is not yet an established renewable energy source, but it will grow rapidly if the interested countries produce positive trial reports. Scotland has two promising areas for tidal stream: the Pentland Firth in northeast Scotland and the Mull of Galloway in southwest Scotland.

An alternative to building a barrage is to install tidal mills in the tidal flow. These are similar to windmills and have the advantage that they do not require the damming of an estuary. Around the UK, the resource is estimated to be 0.4 GW with an annual output of *ca.* 2 TWh (Scottish Executive 2001*a, b*).

Wave energy

Energy from incident waves, especially in the North Atlantic approaches, offers a considerable renewable resource (Whittington & Jordan 1983). Devices to extract this energy can be split into the following three categories:

1 *Shoreline devices:* typical examples are the oscillating water column (OWC), tapered channel device (TAPCHAN) and the Pendular. The OWC is a vertical column positioned in the water, which uses the wave height to change the air pressure in the column to drive a gas turbine to generate electricity. The TAPCHAN uses a tapered channel to increase wave height to overflow and flood a raised lagoon, which stores water to release through a water turbine, generating electricity. The Pendular is a box open to the sea with one end hinged to hydraulic pumps, generating electricity when the front flap flips back and forth with the waves.

2 *Nearshore devices:* these are designed to operate in moderate depths of *ca.* 20 m located around the ends of harbour walls; a typical example is the OSPREY, which combines wave and wind for its generating resources.

3 *Offshore devices:* used in waters more than 40 m in depth; typical examples are the Swedish Hosepump, McCabe Wave Pump, the Danish Wave Piston Floating Pump, and the Edinburgh Duck (to be replaced by the Sloped IPS Buoy).

The UK has a practicable resource (Scottish Executive 2001*a, b*) of *ca.* 3 GW, which could deliver 8 TWh each year.

Geothermal energy

Geothermal energy (Boyle 1998) is renewable heat energy from deep in the Earth: different variants exist, namely, hot dry rock, magma and geopressured geothermal energy.

Heat is brought to the near-surface by thermal conduction and by intrusion into the Earth's crust of molten magma originating from great depth. Ground water is heated to form hydrothermal resources—naturally occurring hot water and steam. The use of hydrothermal energy is economic today at a number of high-grade sites. Hydrothermal resources are tapped by existing well-drilling and energy-conversion technology to generate electricity or to produce hot water for direct use. Earth's energy is used by geothermal heat pumps.

For generation of electricity, hot water, at temperatures ranging from *ca.* 150 °C to more than 400 °C, is brought from the underground reservoir to the surface through production wells, and is flashed to steam in special vessels by release of pressure. The steam is separated from the liquid and fed to a turbine engine, which drives a generator.

If the reservoir is to be used for direct-heat application, the geothermal water is usually fed to a heat exchanger before being injected back into the Earth. Heated domestic water from the output side of the heat exchanger is used for home heating, greenhouse heating, vegetable drying and a wide variety of other uses.

Development of geothermal energy has a net positive impact on the environment compared with development of fossil-fuelled plant. Geothermal power has sulphur-emissions rates that average only a few per cent of those from fossil-fuel alternatives. The newest generation of geothermal power plants emits only 0.2% of carbon (as CO_2) per MWh of electricity generated compared with the cleanest fossil-fuel plant (Boyle 1998).

Solar energy

Solar water heating

In Britain, each square metre of a south-facing roof can receive up to 1000 kWh of solar radiation during a year. Roofs represent an energy source for both space heating and hot water by using solar collectors to capture some of this solar radiation. As a consequence, there is a reduction in the consumption of fossil fuels.

In Britain it is possible to use the Sun to provide most of an average family's hot water requirements from about May to September and to obtain some 'pre-heating' of the cold water supply during the other months. In principle it is possible to scale-up the size of a solar water heater to provide central heating, in general it is not cost effective. However, a solar water heater can be used in a preheating arrangement if the hot water produced is not used elsewhere. Hot water is normally produced by heating the cold mains water to the required temperature with a gas- or oil-fired boiler or an immersion heater. By slightly modifying the conventional heating system, solar collectors may be introduced.

Photovoltaics

Solar cells convert energy from the Sun directly into electricity by what is known as the photovoltaic effect. Conversion efficiencies are over 24% and power levels from a few milliwatts to tens of kilowatts (Archer 2001). Photovoltaics is a growing industry, serving a wide range of terrestrial applications.

Passive solar architecture

The Sun can meet the entire annual space-heating needs of buildings in sunnier parts of the world. However, in much cloudier and colder climates, the Sun can still make a very useful contribution. It may seem surprising, but solar energy can actually save more units of energy needed for space-heating the further a building is away from the Equator. This is partly because ordinary windows can capture more solar energy from low-angle sun-rays, and partly because ambient temperatures tend to drop relatively more rapidly than the solar supply available. Low temperatures generate a demand for heat, even in July if you live in some northern parts of Europe. Thus, a house in Shetland, if appropriately designed, can save more fuel than the same house located in Cornwall; or one in Norway more than one in the south of France.

Biomass

Photosynthesis by green plants converts large amounts of sunlight into energy-rich biological material called biomass, for example, trees, crop and forest residues. Products derived from biomass, such as grains, wood, sugar and alcohol, may be used as fuel. Coal, oil and gas are products of photosynthesis from millions of years ago. Firewood is also widely used: this is the product of more recent and present day photosynthesis (Ewall 2000).

The world's total energy use is *ca.* 10% of the biomass stored annually. The world's stored biomass energy (90% of this in trees) is as large as the proven fossil-fuel reserves. The total fossil-fuel store equals *ca.* 100 years of photosynthesis. The amount of carbon stored in biomass is equal to the amount of atmospheric carbon in the form of CO_2 and to the amount of CO_2 in the oceans' surface layer; this is important for the cycling of extra CO_2 produced from burning fossil fuels.

About 13% of the world's primary energy comes from biomass (equivalent to 25 million barrels of oil per day) and is used in the rural areas of less-developed countries.

Wood fuel

Wood-fuel-fired power stations (Ewall 2000) are likely to become increasingly popular as the Government's emphasis on the development of renewable energy sources increases. Wood is not perceived to be an environmentally friendly fuel, as its burning produces CO_2. However, this fuel is regarded as 'CO_2 neutral' because the carbon released during burning is only that which was absorbed during tree growth; thus, the gas is simply recycled. The scale of a wood-fuel-fired power plant depends on a number of factors:

- location with regards to inhabited areas;

- size of available area;

- capacities of the local area electricity-supply network;

- size of the available wood resource; and

- extent of local transport infrastructure.

Wood fuel is less dense than coal, so the storage space required will be greater. The efficiency of electricity generation from wood can be increased through gasification, where the solid fuel is converted into a combustible gas by thermal processing. For example, in Scotland there are over 920 000 hectares of woodland and forest, accounting for *ca.* 12% of the land area. The Government promotes the management of these woodlands for multipurpose forestry, including environmental conservation, access and wood production. Estimations of the amounts of wood required to produce 1 MW of power generation run at between 350 hectares for the 'high-efficiency gasification' technique and 630 hectares for the standard approach, running at 20% efficiency. It is estimated that a 6 MW power station will generate up to 50 traffic movements per day in total, through delivery lorries and staff. This means that local road access must already be well established or will require improvement.

Network issues

If there is no change in current trends, the replacement of coal and nuclear power stations seems likely to be with gas-fired plant in the short term. It is to be hoped that a more sustainable solution will emerge in the longer term.

The majority of renewable resources is located in isolated areas of the country where demand is low and, at present, the electricity network could not transmit this energy to high demand areas (Scottish Executive 2001a, b).

In addition, the statistical nature of renewable resource availability means that new operation and control algorithms will have to be researched. Presently, the penetration of stochastic renewable energy into the grid will probably be limited to *ca.* 20% (House of Commons 2002) for operational reasons, independent of the size of the resource or the prevailing economics. In future, the target must be to move towards a network that can accommodate a range of generating sources: a mixed-fuel economy. The exact balance cannot be specified at present with any confidence.

Conclusions

The provision of a realistically priced and reliable supply of electricity which has due regard to environmental targets is a complex task. New technologies will make a contribution, but only after the relevant economic analysis. Fiscal instruments are increasingly being used to encourage the industry to adopt specific solutions: these must be accompanied by the necessary regulatory changes to give market steers to developers. However, at this stage it would be unwise to attempt to pick a winner from the list of contenders. Those responsible for balancing environmental imperatives with security of supply must be aware of the complicated interaction between these two features and economics.

Renewable energy, at first sight, offers an attractive option for electricity production with reduced GHG production. However, effective management of all prospective renewable-energy installations will need, above all, a technical assessment of the range of exploitation strategies; for example, a comparison may be made between local production of, say, hydrogen and the more traditional transmission of electricity. Such resources will have to compete with others in any national, or grid, system and detailed economic analysis to determine the approach to deployment which best fits the trading regime into which the energy will be sold. Consideration will also be necessary to determine how best to control the introduction of this radically new resource such that it does not attract punitive cost overheads before the technology reaches commercial maturity.

In terms of the different renewable options available, wind energy can be seen as a short-to-medium-term replacement as thermal plant closes. However, for wind energy to be successful, the network will have to be modified to absorb additional renewable capacity, but it has a massive potential for generating electricity that cannot be ignored.

Globally, hydroelectricity is currently the largest developed source of renewable electricity, but future large-scale projects will probably be limited to the less-developed world: the best schemes in the developed countries have already been exploited. Wave and tidal can be looked as medium- to long-term generators of electricity, as their respective industries are not as mature as competing renewable resources.

Municipal solid-waste combustion and landfill-gas technologies can be seen as a short-term generation solution. The waste is located near to the high demand areas where the network can cope with the extra capacity. Agriculture and forestry waste can be seen as a means of generating electricity for rural areas, which depend on imports from high generation areas.

Despite all that has been said above, nuclear power is proven and could take its place in any future generation portfolio. Unfortunately, there exists suspicion and mistrust of the technology, mainly surrounding waste management and radioactivity release. Unless this is overcome, the lack of confidence engendered by this public mistrust may result in few, if any, new nuclear power stations being built.

References

Archer, M. 2001 Turning point? Energy policy at the crossroads. In *Proc. 5th British Energy Seminar, London and Edinburgh, October–November 2001*, pp. 5–8. British Energy Plc.

Baird, S. 1993a Hydroelectric power. Fact sheet. The International Council for Local Environment Initiatives. (Available at www.iclei.org/efacts/hydroele.htm.)

Baird, S. 1993b Tidal Energy. Fact sheet. The International Council for Local Environment Initiatives. (Available at www.iclei.org/efacts/tidal.htm.)

Boyle, G. (ed.) 1998 *Renewable energy: power for a sustainable future*, pp. 380–383. Oxford University Press/Open University Press.

Carlin, J. 1996 Trends in municipal solid waste generation. In *Renewable energy annual 1996*. Energy Information Administration document DOE/EIA-0603(96),

Office of Coal, Nuclear, Electric and Alternate Fuels, US Department of Energy, Washington, DC.

DEFRA 2002 Atmospheric emissions estimates 1970–2000. In *Digest of environmental statistics*. Department for Environment, Food and Rural Affairs (Available at www.defra.gov.uk/environment/statistics/des/help.htm.)

DTI 2001 *UK energy in brief*, p. 17. Government Statistical Service Publication. Department of Trade and Industry. (Available at www.dti.gov.uk/EPA/eib/index.htm.)

EA 2002 The UK electricity industry and the environment 2000. Review. London: The Electricity Association. (Available at www.electricity.org.uk/inds_fr.html.)

Ewall, M. 2000 *Primer on landfill gas as green energy*. Part 4, Pennsylvania Environmental Network series on Green Energy. (Available at www.penweb.org/issues/energy/green4.html.)

House of Commons 2002 DTI Select Committee Report HC 364-I. London: HMSO.

House of Lords 1999 Electricity from renewables: European communities. House of Lords 12th report, HL 78-I, para. 173. (Available at www.parliament.the-stationery-office.co.uk/pa/ld199899/ldselect/ldeucom/78/7805.htm.)

IEE 1994 *The environmental effects of electricity generation*, pp. 12–14. IEE factfile. London: The Public Affairs Board, Institution of Electrical Engineers.

PIU 2002 *The energy review*. London: Performance and Innovation Unit, Cabinet Office.

Scottish Executive 2001*a Scotland's Renewable Resource 2001*, vol. I: *The analysis*. Scottish Executive Document no. 2850/GR/02, Issue D.

Scottish Executive 2001*b Scotland's Renewable Resource 2001*, vol. II: *Context*. Scottish Executive Document no. 2850/GR/03, Issue B.

Whittington, H. W. & Jordan, J. R. 1983 Operation and control of a 2 GW wave energy scheme. *Proc. Inst. Elect. Engrs* A **130**, 340–348.

Chapter 7

Measuring, monitoring and verification of carbon benefits for forest-based projects

SANDRA BROWN

Introduction

Many forest-based projects have been developed and are currently under various stages of implementation. Much experience has been gained from these projects with respect to measuring, monitoring, and accounting for the carbon benefits derived from them. Focusing on carbon simplifies project development because the problem is reduced to calculating the net differences between carbon stocks for the 'with-project' and the 'without-project' conditions (also referred to as the business-as-usual baseline) on the same piece of land over a specified time period. The challenge is to identify which carbon stocks need to be quantified in the project, to measure them accurately to a known, and often predetermined, level of precision, and to monitor them over the length of the project.

The focus of this chapter is on measuring, monitoring, and verifying the carbon benefits from the implementation of forest-based projects. The main goals are to:

- describe criteria and approaches for selecting which carbon pools to measure;

- describe the tools and techniques commonly available to measure and monitor these pools;

- illustrate how these tools have been applied to existing pilot projects;

- discuss other relevant measuring and monitoring issues; and

- discuss the need for project verification.

Which carbon pools to measure?

Land use and forestry projects are generally easier to quantify and monitor than national inventories, due to clearly defined boundaries for project activities, relative ease of stratification of project area, and choice of carbon pools to measure (Brown *et al.* 2000*b*). Criteria affecting the selection of carbon pools to inventory and monitor are: type of project; size of the pool, its rate of change, and its direction of change; availability of appropriate methods; cost to measure; and attainable accuracy and precision (MacDicken 1997*a*, *b*). The carbon credits from a project for all pools measured (pools 1 to n) are given by

$$\sum_{1}^{n} (\text{C in pool}_1 \text{ for with-project case} - \text{C in pool}_1 \text{ for without-project case}),$$

where the carbon pool is the product of the area of a given land use and the carbon density (carbon per unit area).

It is clear that for some carbon pools the difference will be positive, e.g. stopping deforestation or lengthening forest rotation will lead to more carbon in trees on average (with-project) than conversion of forests to agriculture or shorter rotation (without-project). For other pools, the difference could be negative, e.g. the dead-wood pool in a reduced impact logging project will be less than the dead-wood pool in a conventional logging practice. Basically, a selective or partial accounting system can be used that must include all pools expected to decrease (i.e. those pools that are smaller in the with-project case than in the without-project case) and a choice of pools expected to increase (i.e. those pools that are larger in the with-project case than in the without-project case) as a result of the project (Brown *et al.* 2000*b*). Only pools that are measured (or estimated from a measured parameter) and monitored are incorporated into the calculation of carbon benefits.

The major carbon pools in forestry projects are live biomass, dead biomass, soil, and wood products (Table 7.1). These can be further subdivided as needed, e.g. live biomass includes aboveground trees, roots, and understorey, and dead biomass can include fine litter, lying dead wood, and standing dead trees. Decisions about which pools to chose for measuring and monitoring for different types of forestry projects are also illustrated in Table 7.1. Carbon in trees should be measured for practically all of these project types as this is where most of the carbon benefits will be derived from; measurement of carbon in the understorey is recommended in cases where this is a significant component, such as in agroforests or open woodlands; dead wood should be measured in all forest-based projects, as this can be a significant pool of carbon, and must be measured in projects related to stopping or changing harvesting practices. Land-use change and forestry projects have often been targeted for criticism because it has been suggested that changes in soil-carbon pools are difficult to measure. However, for most forestry projects, soil need not be measured if it can be shown that the project will not result in a loss of soil carbon. Most projects related to forests, whether they be protection of

Table 7.1. *A decision matrix of the main carbon pools for examples of forestry projects*

	Carbon pools						
	Live biomass			Dead biomass			Wood Products
Project type	Trees	Herbaceous	Roots	Fine	Coarse	Soil	
avoid emissions							
stop deforestation	Y	M	R	M	Y	R	M
improved forest management	Y	M	R	M	Y	M	M
sequester carbon							
restore native forests	Y	M	R	Y	Y	M	N
plantations	Y	N	R	M	M	R	Y
agroforestry	Y	Y	M	N	N	R	M

This table illustrates the selection of pools to quantify and monitor. Y, yes: indicates that the change in this pool is likely to be large and should be measured. R, recommended: indicates that the change in the pool could be significant but measuring costs to achieve desired levels of precision could be high. N, no: indicates that the change is likely to be small to none and thus it is not necessary to measure this pool. M, maybe: indicates that the change in this pool may need to be measured, depending upon the forest type and/or management intensity of the project.
Source: based on Brown *et al.* (2000*b*).

threatened forests, improved management for timber harvest, forest restoration, or longer rotation plantations, will not cause soil carbon to be lost and, if anything, will cause carbon in soil to be maintained or increase.

The decision matrix presented in Table 7.1 implies that one design does not fit all projects, i.e. measuring and monitoring designs will vary by project type and the resources available to make the measurements. Regardless of the fact that one design does not fit all types of projects, the specific methods used to measure any given pool should give accurate and precise results, be based on peer-reviewed and tested methods, and be cost and time efficient.

Tools and techniques available for measuring carbon in forest-based projects

Before implementing a carbon project, experience with pilot projects has shown that an assessment of the area, including collecting as much relevant data as possible, is a time- and cost-efficient activity. Relevant information includes: a land-cover/land-use map of the project area; identification of pressures on the land and its resources; history of land use in the project area; the climate regime (particularly temperature and rainfall); soil types, topography and socio-economic activities (e.g. forestry and agricultural practices). Such information is useful to delineate relatively homogeneous forest strata (e.g. by forest type, soil type, topography, land use, etc.) for designing the measuring and monitoring sampling scheme, improving baseline projections, and developing guidelines for leakage avoidance. Preliminary sampling of the identified strata is also needed to determine their variability in carbon stocks.

This information is then used to determine the number of plots needed in each stratum to achieve desired precision levels based on sampling error.

Techniques and methods for sampling design and for accurately and precisely measuring individual carbon pools in forestry projects exist and are based on commonly accepted principles of forest inventory, soil sampling, and ecological surveys (Pinard & Putz 1996, 1997; MacDicken 1997a, b; Post et al. 1999; Winrock International 1999; Brown et al. 2000a; Hamburg 2000). For making an inventory of forest carbon, the use of fixed-area permanent plots (using a series of nested plots for uneven-aged and a single plot for even-aged forests) and tagging all trees is recommended; this approach is generally considered to be the statistically superior means for evaluating changes in forest-carbon pools. Within these plots, all the carbon pools can be measured or estimated, with the exception of wood products. Methods are well established and tested for determining the number, size, and distribution of permanent plots (i.e. sampling design) for maximizing the precision for a given monitoring cost (MacDicken 1997a).

To estimate live tree biomass, diameters of all trees are measured and converted to biomass and carbon estimates (carbon equals 50% of biomass), generally using allometric biomass regression equations. Such equations exist for practically all forests of the world; some are species specific and others are more generic in nature (see, for example, Alves et al. 1997; Brown 1997; Schroeder et al. 1997; Chambers et al. 2001; Keller et al. 2001). Sampling a sufficient number of trees to represent the size and species distribution in a forest to generate local allometric regression equations with high precision, particularly in complex tropical forests, is extremely time-consuming and costly, and generally beyond the means of most projects. From field experience, it has been shown that grouping all species, even in species-rich tropical forests, produces regression equations with high r^2 (generally greater than 0.95).

Experience to date with the development of generic regression equations, for both tropical and temperate forests, has shown that measurements of diameter at breast height, as is typical for trees, explains more than 95% of the variation in tree biomass even in highly species rich tropical forests. Thus the need to develop species-specific equations is not warranted (see, for example, Brown 1997; Chambers et al. 2001; Keller et al. 2001). However, in many forests, particularly in the tropics, unique plant forms occur such as species of palms and early colonizers. In these cases it is recommended that local regression equations be developed (in two pilot projects in the tropics, local regression equations were developed for *Cecropia* spp. (early colonizers) and several species of palms (Delaney et al. 2000; S. Brown & M. Delaney 2001, unpublished report)). For palms, it has been shown that height is the key independent variable for explaining variations in biomass, rather than diameter-at-breast-height (DBH).

The advantage of using generic regression equations, stratified by, for example, ecological zones or species group (broadleaf or conifer), is that they tend to be based on a large number of trees (Brown 1997) and span a wider range of diameters; this increases the accuracy and precision of the equations. It is very important that the database for regressions equations contains large diameter trees, as these tend to account for more than 30% of the aboveground biomass in mature tropical forests (Brown & Lugo 1992; Pinard & Putz 1996). A disadvantage is that the generic equations may not accurately reflect the true biomass of the trees in the project. However, field measurements, e.g. diameter and height relationships of the larger trees, or destructive harvest of two or three representative large trees performed at the beginning of a project, can be used to check the validity of the generic equations. For plantation projects, developing or acquiring local biomass regression equations is less problematic, as much work has been done on plantation species (Lugo 1997).

Dead wood, both lying and standing, is an important carbon pool in forests and one that should be measured in many forestry projects (Table 7.1). Dead wood is generally divided into coarse and fine, with the breakpoint set at 10 cm diameter (Harmon & Sexton 1996). Although coarse dead wood, including standing and lying, is often a significant component of forest ecosystems, often accounting for 10–20% of the aboveground biomass in mature forests (e.g. Harmon *et al.* 1993; Delaney *et al.* 1998), it tends to be ignored in many forest-carbon budgets. Methods have been developed for this component and have been tested in many forest types and generally require no more effort than measuring live trees (Harmon & Sexton 1996; Brown 2002).

Total root biomass is another important carbon pool and can represent up to 40% of total biomass (Cairns *et al.* 1997). However, quantifying this pool can be expensive and no practical standard field techniques yet exist (Körner 1994; Kurz *et al.* 1996; Cairns *et al.* 1997). A recent literature review by Cairns *et al.* (1997) included more than 160 studies covering tropical, temperate, and boreal forests that reported both root biomass and aboveground biomass. The mean root-to-shoot ratio (R/S) based on these studies was 0.26, with a range of 0.18 (lower 25% quartile) to 0.30 (upper 75% quartile). The R/S did not vary significantly with latitudinal zone (tropical, temperate and boreal), soil texture (fine, medium and coarse), or tree type (angiosperm and gymnosperm). Further analyses of the data produced a significant regression equation of root biomass density versus aboveground biomass density when all data were pooled (r^2 of 0.83). Such a regression equation is useful for estimating root biomass from aboveground biomass in a cost-efficient way.

The ability to measure soil-carbon pools is a source of contention in forestry projects as mentioned above; however, as for vegetation, there is a well established set of methods and documentation for measuring soil-carbon pools (Post *et al.* 1999). Measuring change in soil carbon over relatively short time periods is more problematic but, as shown in Table 7.1, this pool need not be measured in most projects. In cases where changes in soil carbon are included, rates of soil oxidation under different land uses are available in the literature (e.g. those summarized in the land-use and forestry sector of the *IPCC guidelines for national greenhouse gas inventories*; Houghton *et al.* 1997).

The long-term effectiveness of carbon storage in wood products depends on the uses of wood produced through project activities. In projects that reduce output of harvested wood by preventing logging or by improved forest management (and deforestation if some of the wood cut during deforestation entered the wood-products market), the change in the wood-products pool would be negative because the production for the with-project case would be less than for the without-project case. This negative change in the wood-product pool would reduce some of the carbon benefits from the project and this would have to be accounted for. In plantation projects, wood that goes into long- to medium-term products (e.g. sawtimber for housing, particle board, paper) represents an additional carbon storage. Several methods exist for accounting for the storage of long-lived wood products (Winjum *et al.* 1998). Recently, an IPCC Expert group for the Land Use and Forestry sector of the Guide- lines for GHG inventories (Houghton *et al.* 1997) completed a report that describes and evaluates the approaches available for estimating carbon emis- sions or removals for forest harvesting and wood products (Brown *et al.* 1999; Lim *et al.* 1999).

Tools and techniques for ongoing project monitoring

Monitoring relates to the ongoing measurement of carbon pools and for com- pliance of the project's activities. For ongoing carbon monitoring, permanent sample plots are generally considered as the statistically superior and cost- and time-efficient means for evaluating changes in carbon stocks (MacDicken 1997*a*). Not all of the initial carbon pools need be measured at every interval in some projects; the judicious selection of some pools could serve as indica- tors that the project is following the expected trajectory. The frequency and intensity of monitoring depends to a large extent on the nature of the project. Those projects designed to avoid emissions through averting deforestation or logging need primarily to establish that no trees are removed or clearings made over the course of the project (monitoring for compliance) and that the amount of carbon is remaining constant or increasing (monitoring for carbon). In projects designed to sequester carbon, e.g. in forest restoration or through establishment of new forests, changes in all carbon stocks being claimed need to be remeasured periodically. This can be readily accomplished by the remeasurement of marked trees in permanent plots and remeasuring the other components with the methods described above.

Remote-sensing technology may be useful for monitoring forestry projects, although to date it has hardly been used. Interpretation of satellite imagery has been used mostly for producing land-use maps of project areas and for estimating rates of land-use change or deforestation in the project formulation phase. However, remote-sensing technology has potential for monitoring com- pliance of forest protection projects and trends in plantation or agroforestry establishment at the subnational to national scales. Monitoring of improved forest management or secondary forests, particularly in the tropics, is difficult with the current suite of satellites, but future development and launching of new satellites may overcome this problem.

Not all remotely-sensed monitoring activities need to use data from satel- lites. Because forestry projects have well-defined boundaries and are relatively small in area (several thousand to hundreds of thousand hectares), remotely-

Figure 7.1. 3D digital image (colour image converted to black and white) of a forest transect in the Noel Kempff Climate Action Project, captured by the dual-camera videography system. (Reproduced with permission from Dana Slaymaker (Winrock International).)

sensed data from low-flying airplanes can be used for monitoring. A promising advance in this area couples dual-camera digital videos (wide-angle and zoom) with a pulse laser profiler, data recorders, and differential GPSs (geographical-positioning systems) mounted on a single engine plane (D. Slaymaker 2000, personal communication; EPRI 2001). Transects can be flown over project areas at any desired density. Computer interpretation of the digital imagery collected by this system is able to produce three-dimensional (3D) images (Figure 7.1) from which measures of crown diameter and tree height (from the pulse laser) for individual trees are made. Correlations between crown diameter and DBH are then used to estimate tree diameter for all trees within 'plots' and these DBH estimates are then used to estimate biomass and carbon using the standard regression equations described above. For one forest stratum in the Noel Kempff Project in Bolivia (mixed liana forest, see below for more details of this project), ground measurements gave a mean carbon content in the aboveground trees of 89.6 tC ha^{-1} with a 95% confidence interval of 7.8 tC ha^{-1}, and videography measurements gave a mean of 87.7 tC ha^{-1} with a 95% confidence interval of 5.4 tC ha^{-1} or, in other words, the same value as from the ground measurements but with higher precision (EPRI 2001).

Pilot project experience

In this section I present the results of two pilot projects that have different designs for measuring and monitoring the carbon benefits. I present the results of the first set of field measurements in the project areas to establish the initial carbon stocks. Further discussion of the without-project baseline for the Noel Kempff Project is given in Brown *et al.* (2000*a*).

The Noel Kempff Climate Action Project, Bolivia

In 1996, the government of Bolivia, the Bolivian organization Fundación Amigos de la Naturaleza (FAN), American Electric Power and The Nature Conservancy (TNC) designed a forest-based joint implementation pilot project to allow for the expansion of Noel Kempff Mercado National Park. Pacifi-Corp and British Petroleum America (now BP Amoco) joined the project in 1997. The duration of this $9.5 million project is 30 years. This project, located in northeastern Bolivia in the department of Santa Cruz, is the largest pilot forestry project to date to be implemented in terms of its area (*ca.* 634 000 hectares), funds invested and projected carbon offsets. Further details of this project are given in Brown *et al.* (2000*a*).

The project obtains carbon benefits from two main activities:

1 averted logging where removal of commercial timber and the associated damage to unharvested trees has been halted; and

2 averted conversion of forested lands to agricultural uses where loss of carbon in forest biomass and soil has been halted.

Inventory of carbon pools

The project design for measuring the carbon pools is based on the methodology and protocols in MacDicken (1997*a*). The carbon inventory of the area was based on data collected from a network of permanent plots, located using a differential GPS (DGPS). A total of 625 plots was established across the project area with the number of plots sampled in a given strata based on the variance of an initial sample of plots in each strata, the area of the strata, and the desired precision level (±10%) with 95% confidence (Table 7.2). A fixed area, nested plot design was used (4 m radius plot for trees with DBH of greater than or equal to 5–20 cm, and 14 m radius for trees with DBH

Table 7.2. *Estimates of carbon stocks* (tC ha^{-1}) *and total carbon content in the forests of the Noel Kempff Climate Action Project*

S (no. of plots)	A	AG	P	SD	LD	U	L	BG	S	M
tall evergreen (171)	226 827	129	0.5	4.1	11.0	2.0	3.6	25.8	26.9	203
liana (131)	95 564	56	0.5	2.3	4.7	3.8	4.0	11.1	39.9	122
tall flooded (64)	99 316	132	1.1	3.2	11.3	1.9	3.1	26.4	44.8	224
short flooded (35)	49 625	112	0.2	3.0	9.6	2.1	2.9	22.3	55.5	207
mixed liana (218)	159 471	90	1.5	4.4	7.7	2.6	4.3	17.9	24.4	152
burned (6)	3 483	57	0.2	1.6	4.9	0.9	4.2	11.4	36.0	116
total area	643 286									
weighted mean		106.7	0.8	3.6	9.1	2.4	3.7	21.3	33.3	181
total carbon content (Mt)	114.9									
95% CI, % of mean	4.2									

S, strata; A, area in ha; AG, aboveground woody; P, palm; SD, standing dead; LD, lying dead; U, understorey; L, litter; BG, below ground; S, soil; M, mean; CI, confidence interval. *Source:* from Delaney *et al.* (2000).

$\geqslant 20$ cm) and the following components were measured in each plot: all trees with DBH $\geqslant 5$ cm, understorey, fine litter, standing and lying dead wood,[1] and soil to 30 cm depth (Table 7.2). Tree biomass was estimated from a general biomass regression equation for moist tropical trees (Brown 1997); the validity of this equation was confirmed with the destructive harvest of two large-diameter trees. Biomass regression equations for early colonizing tree species and palms were developed by destructive harvesting of a sample of individuals of such species. Root biomass was estimated from root-to-shoot ratios given in Cairns *et al.* (1997).

The total amount of carbon in the project area was *ca.* 115 MtC, most of which was in aboveground biomass of trees (60%), followed by soil to 30 cm depth (18%), roots (12%) and dead wood (7%); the understorey and fine litter accounted for *ca.* 3% of the total. The 95% confidence interval of the total carbon stock was ±4%, based on sampling error only; regression and measurement error were not included. Inclusion of the error due to regression and measurement is likely to increase the total error to no more than double, as the sampling error has been shown to be the largest source of total error (up to 80% or more) in measuring carbon stocks (Phillips *et al.* 2000).

From this pilot project, encompassing several strata of complex tropical forests, the measurement of carbon stocks can be accomplished with a high degree of precision: the key is to establish the required number of plots to reach the targeted precision levels ahead of time and to install the required number of plots.

---

[1] In the original inventory in 1997, lying dead wood was not measured; a subset of 55 plots were measured in 1999 and a ratio of lying dead wood to live dead wood was calculated and used to estimate the quantity of lying dead wood in the unmeasured plots.

Future monitoring

For the averted deforestation component, very little additional carbon monitoring is planned, because it is expected that the change in the carbon content of the existing forest will grow little over this time. The key component of this activity is to ensure that the forest is not being cleared: it is planned to monitor this remotely with this digital dual-camera videography technology described above.

For the averted logging component, the monitoring plans call for five-year interval remeasurement of a set of paired plots (about 100 paired plots) in a nearby proxy concession that was established to measure the amount of dead biomass produced during the felling of a tree and associated activities such as yarding and skidding, as well as the rate of regrowth after harvesting and without harvesting. The remeasurements will be used to determine any delayed mortality and determine any differences in carbon accumulation rates between logged and unlogged plots. These data will be used to revise the carbon benefits as necessary. After two remeasurement times, the plans call for the establishment of an additional set of paired plots in another harvested block to determine whether logging practices are changing over time. Research is underway to adapt the videography system to monitor this impact.

The Guaraqueçaba Climate Action Project, Brazil

The Guaraqueçaba Climate Action Project (GCAP), located in the Atlantic forest in Paraná, Brazil, is being developed by Central and South West Services (now AEP), TNC and SPVS. The project area is located within the Guaraqueçaba Environment Protection Area (APA), a Federal Reserve of 775 000 hectares. The existing project area of *ca.* 4500 hectares has *ca.* 15% of the lands in pasture, 20% of the land in young to very young secondary forests and 65% of the land in late secondary forests; all these forests have been disturbed or cleared in the past. The project involves the purchase of water-buffalo ranches with plans to protect all remaining forests, reforest some of the pasture lands with native species, allow the remaining pasture to regenerate naturally, and allow regrowth in the secondary forests over a 40-year life.

The carbon benefits of this project result from emissions avoidance (protection from deforestation) and carbon sequestration (reforestation and natural regeneration of areas with pasture, enrichment planting and recovery of successional forests areas). In the absence of the project, it is expected that the lowland forests would continue to be cleared and degraded and upland forests would continue to be degraded. With the project, lands that were threatened with deforestation are being protected and degraded lands reforested.

Inventory of carbon pools

The approach taken for this project is generally the same as that described above for the Noel Kempff Project. Using a combination of remote-sensing data and on-the-ground measurements, the project area has been classified into four forest (based on disturbance and successional stage) and three non-

Table 7.3. *Estimates of the carbon stocks* (tC ha^{-1}) *and total carbon content for the forest strata of the Guaraqueçaba Climate Action Project, Brazil*

Strata	Mature altered $n = 69$	Medium/ advanced $n = 46$	Young $n = 13$	Very young $n = 12$
area (ha)	763.0	2269.6	583.9	363.8
mean	153.5	113.5	96.5	40.3
min	73.6	65.1	41.1	5.7
max	398.7	197.4	203.7	73.2
variance	2638.6	952.4	2280.7	414.7
standard error	6.2	4.6	13.2	5.9
CV (%)	34	27	50	51

Content includes trees, roots, understorey, dead wood and litter, but excludes soils. Mean (tC ha^{-1} ±95% CI) 111.9±6.8; total (tC) 445 464; 95% CI (% of mean) 6.1. CV, coefficient of variation.
Source: S. Brown & M. Delaney (2000, unpublished report).

forest (based on presence/absence of shrubs) strata upon which the carbon benefits from this project will be estimated. The total number of plots established in the initial inventory was 168, a number based on initial field measurements in each strata as described above for the Noel Kempff Project. Using criteria described above, the main carbon pools included in this project were live trees to a minimum diameter of 2.5 cm, dead wood, roots, and soil (to 30 cm depth), litter and understorey in the younger forest strata.

For the initial inventory, the total carbon pool (excluding soil) in the forest strata is estimated to be *ca.* 446 000 tC with a precision level of 6% of the mean at 95% confidence (Table 7.3). The overall weighted mean carbon content of forests is 112 tC ha^{-1} (Table 7.3), 78% of which is in the live aboveground woody biomass, 13% of which is in roots, 7% of which is in dead wood, and *ca.* 2% of which is in litter and understorey combined (S. Brown & M. Delaney 2000, unpublished report). Litter and understorey were not measured in the altered mature forest, as it was assumed to be an insignificant component and not worth the time and cost to measure (even in the advanced/medium stratum, litter and understorey represented less than 2% of the total vegetation pool).

Soil carbon (in the top 30 cm) was measured in the two young forest strata only because these are the only strata likely to produce measurable changes in soil-carbon content over the project life, and a baseline value needed to be established. The total carbon in the soil of these two strata is 59 377 t with a 95% confidence interval of 13% of the mean. Establishment of additional plots in these two young strata is planned for 2002, to decrease the variation in the vegetation and soil-carbon pools.

Future monitoring

The carbon content of the pasture/shrub formations has been estimated to develop the baseline carbon content. As these formations are restored with native tree species and undergo succession, permanent plots will be established in them and remeasured at five-year intervals over the length of the project. The number of plots to be established will be based on the variance of the lowland advanced to medium successional forests as this will be the target forest and its variance will likely reflect the variance of the restored forest.

As significant carbon benefits are expected from the protection of the forests from further degradation, the plots established during the initial inventory will be remeasured at 5-year intervals during the length of the project. As these are permanent plots with tagged trees and mapped dead wood, the changes in carbon stocks will be able to be measured directly; this will result in smaller errors.

Other measuring and monitoring issues

Future monitoring tools

Although the above projects call for ongoing monitoring of carbon stocks, and at present it is planned that this will be done by revisiting the permanent plots, new technological advances are likely to produce systems that can monitor carbon stocks remotely, after some initial calibration. The dual-camera videography system described above is one such advance that is showing high promise for accomplishing this task (EPRI 2001).

Data quality and archiving

To develop a reliable baseline and a measurement and monitoring plan for both the initial and future measurements of carbon-offset projects, steps must be taken to control errors in sampling and analysis. To accomplish this and to ensure the quality and credibility of the estimates of the quantities of carbon sequestered and/or retained, a quality assurance and quality control (QA/QC) plan is necessary as part of any project's protocol. This plan should include formal procedures to verify methods used to collect field data and the techniques to enter and analyse data. A set of standard operating procedures (SOPs) for all aspects of the field and laboratory activities should be part of the project's documents. To ensure continuity it is also important that all data collected use the same procedures during the project life and are archived using acceptable standards by all partners involved in the project. Adhering to these procedures will ensure that in the event that there is a change in personnel among participating organizations, or if any of the people involved are questioned about any aspect of the project, all will be well informed.

Carbon-offset projects of the type described here are still in their infancy, and must hold up to the scrutiny of the scientific community as well as outside organizations who will ultimately verify the carbon-offsets resulting from project activities. The QA/QC plan must be part of the project's set of documents to be available for review and inspection. The QA/QC plan and SOPs should be updated as necessary when new field equipment or procedures become available.

Because of the relatively long-term nature of these projects, data archiving (maintenance and storage) will be an important component of the work. Original field sheets, laboratory analysis, data analyses, reports, models, assumptions, etc., should all be kept in their original form as well as in some form of electronic media and all of these should be kept in a dedicated and safe place, preferably in more than one place. When storing data in an electronic form one has to keep in mind the rapid pace at which software and hardware are changing; all data should be stored in a form that is likely to be retrievable as new software is developed. What form the data needs to be stored in needs to be investigated further.

Verification

Verification of projects is akin to auditing in the financial world and offers a way to provide credibility and transparency of a project's claims to concerned entities such as regulatory bodies, investors, etc. Internal verification could be accomplished by implementation of the QA/QC plan as described above. External or third-party verification could be based on an assessment of the project's compliance with a set of defined eligibility criteria. A single set of internationally accepted eligibility criteria would facilitate direct comparisons of projects, while a variety of such criteria may result in projects and their carbon benefits of differing quality (Moura Costa *et al.* 2000).

Verification activities may include:

- evaluation of the project in relation to eligibility criteria based on requirements of international protocols (e.g the Kyoto Protocol);

- review of project's documentation for estimating the carbon benefits (e.g. procedures, methodologies, analyses, reports);

- inspection or calibration of measurement and analytical tools and methods;

- repeat sampling and measurements of carbon stocks;

- assessment of the quality and comprehensiveness of the data used in calculating the project baseline and offsets and therefore the confidence in the final claims;

- assessment of risks associated with the project and the carbon benefits; and

- the presence or absence of non-greenhouse gas externalities such as environmental and social impacts (Trines 1998; Moura Costa *et al.* 2000; Brown *et al.* 2000*b*).

To date there has been little experience with third-party verification of carbon benefit claims of projects (Moura Costa *et al.* 2000). The lack of policy guidelines related to verifying the design and implementation of projects results in a range of methods and approaches being used, leading to discrepancies between claims of different projects. This in turn leads to uncertainty, and thus raises concerns about the use of forestry projects for abating carbon emissions. To improve this situation and lead to the implementation of consistently credible projects, international agreement is needed in relation to protocols used for: determining additionality, baselines and leakage; estimating uncertainty and measurement error; accounting and calculating carbon benefits; determining precision levels required for quantification of carbon benefits; and determining time-frames over which projects are implemented (Moura Costa *et al.* 2000). Finally, international policy makers must establish an accreditation body to certify and oversee project verification.

References

Alves, D. S., Soares, J. V., Amaral, S., Mello, E. M. K., Almeida, S. A. S., Fernandes da Silva, O. & Silveira, A. M. 1997 Biomass of primary and secondary vegetation in Rondonia, western Brazilian Amazon. *Global Change Biol.* **3**, 451–462.

Brown, S. 1997 Estimating biomass and biomass change of tropical forests: a primer. FAO Forestry Paper no. 134, Rome.

Brown, S. 2002 Measuring carbon in forests: current status and future challenges. *Env. Pollut.* **116**, 363–372.

Brown, S. & Lugo, A. E. 1992 Aboveground biomass estimates for tropical moist forests of the Brazilian Amazon. *Interciencia* **17**, 8–18.

Brown, S., Lim, B. & Schlamadinger, B. 1999 Evaluating approaches for estimating net emissions of carbon dioxide from forest harvesting and wood products. IPCC/OECD/IEA Programme on National Greenhouse Gas Inventories, Paris.

Brown, S., Burnham, M., Delaney, M., Vaca, R., Powell, M. & Moreno, A. 2000*a* Issues and challenges for forest-based carbon-offset projects: a case study of the Noel Kempff Climate Action Project in Bolivia. *Mitigat. Adapt. Strategies Global Change* **5**, 99–121.

Brown, S., Masera, O. & Sathaye, J. 2000*b* Project-based activities. In *Land use, land-use change, and forestry: special report to the Intergovernmental Panel on Climate Change* (ed. R. Watson, I. Noble & D. Verardo), ch. 5, pp. 283–338. Cambridge University Press.

Cairns, M. A., Brown, S., Helmer, E. H. & Baumgardner, G. A. 1997 Root biomass allocation in the world's upland forests. *Oecologia* **111**, 1–11.

Chambers, J. Q., Higuchi, N., Araujo, T. M. & Santos, J. C. 2001 Tree damage, allometric relationships, and above-ground net primary production. *For. Ecol. Manag.* **152**, 73–84.

Delaney, M., Brown, S., Lugo, A. E., Torres-Lezama, A. & Bello Quintero, N. 1998 The quantity and turnover of dead wood in permanent forest plots in six life zones of Venezuela. *Biotropica* **30**, 2–11.

Delaney, M., Brown, S. & Powell, M. 2000 1999 Carbon-Offset Report for the Noel Kempff Climate Action Project. Report to The Nature Conservancy, Winrock International, Arlington, VA.

EPRI 2001 Final report on assessing dual camera videography and 3-D terrain reconstruction as tools to estimate carbon sequestering in forests. EPRI, Palo Alto, CA and American Electric Power, Columbus, OH.

Hamburg, S. P. 2000 Simple rules for measuring changes in ecosystem carbon in forestry-offset projects. *Mitigat. Adapt. Strategies Global Change* **5**, 25–37.

Harmon, M. E. & Sexton, J. 1996 Guidelines for measurements of woody detritus in forest ecosystems. US LTER Publication no. 20. US LTER Network Office, University of Washington, Seattle, WA.

Harmon, M. E., Brown, S. & Gower, S. T. 1993 Consequences of tree mortality to the global carbon cycle. In *Carbon Cycling in Boreal and Subarctic Ecosystems, Biospheric Response and Feedbacks to Global Climate Change, Proc. Symp. USEPA, Corvallis, OR* (ed. T. S. Vinson & T. P. Kolchugina), pp. 167–176.

Houghton, J. T., Meira Filho, L. G., Lim, B., Treanton, K., Mamaty, I., Bonduki, Y., Griggs, D. J. & Callander, B. A. 1997 *Revised 1996 Guidelines for National Greenhouse Gas Inventories*. Paris: IPCC/OECD/IEA.

Keller, M., Palace, M. & Hurtt, G. 2001 Biomass estimation in the Tapajos National Forests, Brazil examination of sampling and allometric uncertainties. *For. Ecol. Manag.* **154**, 371–382.

Körner, C. 1994 Biomass fractionation in plants: a reconsideration of definitions based on plant functions. In *A whole plant perspective on carbon–nitrogen interactions* (ed. J. Roy & E. Garnier), pp. 173–185. The Hague: SPB Academic.

Kurz, W. A., Beukema, S. J. & Apps, M. J. 1996 Estimation of root biomass and dynamics for the carbon budget model of the Canadian forest sector. *Can. J. For. Res.* **26**, 1973–1979.

Lim, B., Brown, S. & Schlamadinger, B. 1999 Carbon accounting for forest harvesting and wood products: a review and evaluation of possible approaches. *Environ. Sci. Policy* **2**, 207–216.

Lugo, A. E. 1997 *Rendimiento y aspectos silviculturales de plantaciones maderas en America Latina*. Serie Forestal no. 9, Oficina Regional de la FAO para America Latina y el Caribe, Santiago, Chile.

MacDicken, K. 1997*a* A guide to monitoring carbon storage in forestry and agroforestry projects. Winrock International, Arlington, VA.

MacDicken, K. 1997*b* Project specific monitoring and verification: state of the art and challenges. *Mitigat. Adapt. Strategies Global Change* **2**, 27–38.

Moura Costa, P., Stuart, M., Pinard, M. & Phillips, G. 2000 Elements of a certification system for forestry-based carbon offset projects. *Mitigat. Adapt. Strategies Global Change* **5**, 39–50.

Phillips, D. L., Brown, S. L., Schroeder, P. E. & Birdsey, R. A. 2000 Toward error analysis of large-scale forest carbon budgets. *Global Ecol. Biogeogr.* **9**, 305–313.

Pinard, M. A. & Putz, F. E. 1996 Retaining forest biomass by reduced impact logging damage. *Biotropica* **28**, 278–295.

Pinard, M. & Putz, F. 1997 Monitoring carbon sequestration benefits associated with reduced-impact logging project in Malaysia. *Mitigat. Adapt. Strategies Global Change* **2**, 203–215.

Post, W. M., Izaurralde, R. C., Mann, L. K. & Bliss, N. 1999 Monitoring and verification of soil organic carbon sequestration. In *Proc. Symp. Carbon Sequestration in Soils Science, Monitoring and Beyond, 3–5 December* (ed. N. J. Rosenberg, R. C. Izaurralde & E. L. Malone), pp. 41–66. Columbus, OH: Batelle Press.

Schroeder, P., Brown, S., Mo, J., Birdsey, R. & Cieszewski, C. 1997 Biomass estimation for temperate broadleaf forests of the US using inventory data. *For. Sci.* **43**, 424–434.

Trines, E. 1998 SGS's carbon offset verification service. *Commonw. For. Rev.* **77**, 209–213.

Winjum, J. K., Brown, S. & Schlamadinger, B. 1998 Forest harvests and wood products: sources and sinks of atmospheric carbon dioxide. *For. Sci.* **44**, 272–284.

Winrock International 1999 Field tests of carbon monitoring methods in forestry projects. Forest Carbon Monitoring Program, Winrock International, Arlington, VA.

Chapter 8

Understanding and managing leakage in forest-based greenhouse-gas-mitigation projects

Reimund Schwarze, John O. Niles and Jacob Olander

Introduction

Projects that increase forest cover or decrease deforestation can help reduce atmospheric carbon dioxide (CO_2). This principle underpins the inclusion of certain land use, land-use change and forestry (LULUCF) activities in both the United Nations Framework Convention on Climate Change (UNFCCC) and the Kyoto Protocol. Concerns have been expressed, however, that LULUCF projects may only produce greenhouse-gas (GHG) benefits that are illusory due to a phenomenon known as 'leakage'.

The most frequently cited example of leakage is an LULUCF forest protection project to reduce GHG emissions. The leakage concern is that forest protection could cause deforestation to move from the protected forest to a nearby forest, with no net GHG benefit. Although this example pertains to the LULUCF sector, project activities in virtually all sectors of GHG mitigation (energy, transportation, etc.) have the potential to cause leakage. As such, leakage constitutes a key challenge for policymakers and project developers to address in forthcoming climate-change policy formulation.

Leakage would not be of great concern if every country measured every GHG flux in its borders. Any unintended consequences (leakage) of a climate-change project or policy in one area would be registered in another area's GHG accounting system. But under the principle of 'common but differentiated responsibilities' (Article 3 of the UNFCCC), developed nations under the Kyoto Protocol assume binding limits on their GHG emissions, while developing countries do not. This differentiated approach inevitably creates the risk of leakage, since the world is increasingly economically interconnected; changes in economic activity and prices reverberate locally and around the world. Without comprehensive monitoring, emissions *reductions* by a project in one area may be measured, while project-induced emissions *increases* outside project boundaries may not be measured.

Table 8.1. *Types of leakage*

causes	project
	policy
effects	positive
	negative
mechanisms	activity shifting
	market effects
	life-cycle effects
	ecological
scales	local
	regional
	national
	global
sectors	energy (fossil fuels)
	LULUCF (biomass)

This chapter analyses leakage in the LULUCF sector since, rightly or wrongly, leakage risk is perceived as more severe for this sector than for energy, transport or industry. Our analysis emphasizes, but is not limited to, the use of LULUCF projects in the Kyoto Protocol's Clean Development Mechanism (CDM). Effectively managing leakage will also be necessary for projects and policies that evolve independent of, or parallel to, the Kyoto Protocol.[1]

What is leakage?

The Special Report on LULUCF by the Intergovernmental Panel on Climate Change (IPCC) defines land-use leakage as '...the indirect impact that a targeted land use, land-use change and forestry activity in a certain place at a certain time has on carbon storage at another place or time' (IPCC 2000, § 2.3.5.2, p. 71). In another section of this report, the IPCC defines leakage as the 'unanticipated decrease or increase in GHG benefits outside of the project's accounting boundary... as a result of the project activities' (IPCC 2000, § 5.3.3, p. 246). Various types of leakage are listed in Table 8.1.

Causes: projects or policies

Although leakage is often thought of primarily as a project-based concern, unintended GHG fluxes can occur with the adoption of regulations or policies. The Kyoto Protocol, as currently interpreted, could push certain commercial forestry operations to relocate to developing countries, where they would be unencumbered by GHG liabilities (Niesten *et al.* 2001). The same concern also affects energy-intensive industries (Smith 1998).

---

[1]As may be the case if the US remains opposed to the treaty and forges other GHG partnerships.

Effects: positive or negative

Leakage is often considered undesirable or bad; in the case of GHG fluxes, 'bad' means more emissions or less sequestration. In this chapter, this type of leakage is called *negative leakage* and would ideally be avoided. There are also situations where unintentional outcomes may be *positive* (more emission reductions, more sequestration). For example, emissions-reducing activities may be adopted voluntarily outside project boundaries, as has apparently been the case with reduced-impact logging (RIL) techniques in a carbon-offset project sponsored by the New England Power Company in Sabah, Malaysia (UtiliTree 2000).

Mechanisms

Unintended GHG fluxes arise through two principal avenues (IPCC 2000; Brown *et al.* 1997; Vine *et al.* 1999):

1 *Activity shifting*   A project or policy can displace an activity or change the likelihood of an activity outside the project's boundaries. One example of negative activity-shifting leakage would be a plantation project that displaces farmers and leads them to clear adjacent forests.

2 *Market effects*   A project or policy can alter supply, demand and the equilibrium price of goods or services, causing an increase/decrease in emitting activities elsewhere. For example, if a large forest-conservation project reduces the local timber supply so that demand is unmet, this may increase prices and pressures on forests elsewhere.

In economic terms, market-driven leakage is mediated by a change in the price of goods, whereas activity shifting is when human or other capital changes location. Importantly, these two leakage types may, in some cases, be inversely related (notably in the case of forest conservation). If a project displaces people and activities to adjacent areas, market leakage may diminish. This is because activity-shifting leakage moves economic activity, while market leakage occurs through net changes in production for a given regional distribution of activities.

Two other types of leakage bear mentioning:

1 *Life-cycle emissions shifting*   Mitigation activities increase emissions in upstream or downstream activities, for instance, a forest-conservation project leads to increased road traffic from tourists or a reforestation project increases the operation of machinery, creating fossil-fuel emissions.

2 *Ecological leakage*   Ecological leakage is a change in GHG fluxes mediated by ecosystem-level changes in surrounding areas. In an example of positive ecological leakage, stopping deforestation can prevent carbon emissions in forests *adjacent* to the intended protected forests. An exam-

ple of negative ecological leakage would occur if a carbon plantation introduces a pathogen to surrounding forests, leading to their decline and a net carbon release to the atmosphere. The magnitude of ecological leakage compared with other types of leakage has not been studied.

Scale: local to global

Leakage can manifest itself at various scales. If a project or policy alters local prices or behaviours, then local markets and activities may be changed. Though it is unlikely that any single project would significantly alter world timber or crop prices, the sum total of many similar individual projects might conceivably impact global markets. Similarly, ecological impacts of avoiding deforestation from any single project will not likely alter global circulation patterns. However, numerous projects to stop deforestation could theoretically serve to maintain historical global circulation patterns (McGuffie *et al.* 1995).

Sectors: fossil fuel or biomass

Leakage can occur in all sectors of the economy where GHG mitigation is conducted. For the sake of convenience, one can divide the economy into two sectors: parts of the economy that produce primarily fossil-fuel emissions (energy, transport, industry); and parts that produce emissions from some form of biomass (vegetation, forests, soils, etc.). LULUCF projects are often perceived as being particularly leakage prone. Energy projects, however, also face risks of activity shifting and market leakage that will need to be considered at the policy and project levels.

Globally, it has been argued that the Kyoto Protocol may drive some energy-intensive industries to relocate to developing countries (Babiker 2001). Unencumbered by the constraints and costs of GHG-emissions limits, this form of international leakage could undermine the apparent reductions. At the project level, clean-energy projects may displace capital stock or change relative prices of fuels and cause leakage of emissions. A climate-change-mitigation project that builds relatively clean-burning natural gas plants (an existing market trend in many countries) could increase the price of natural gas in this area. This, in turn, could drive other investments to use coal or oil for new generating capacity, negating some, but not necessarily all, of the GHG benefits of the gas plant.

Estimates of market leakage for forestry activities (see Table 8.3) are generally higher than market leakage estimates in the energy sector of 10–20% (summarized in Murray *et al.* (2002), p. 3). Other studies, however, set energy-sector market leakage at a comparable level. For example, Felder & Rutherford (1993) derive leakage rates of up to 45% for the energy sector.

Leakage and forestry projects

Several types of forestry projects can mitigate GHG accumulation in the atmosphere, and each may be subject to different kinds and degrees of leakage. For the sake of simplicity, we divide LULUCF projects into two broad categories in our analyses:[1]

1 Projects that avoid CO_2 emissions by avoiding deforestation or reducing forest degradation (*'conservation'* projects). Included in this broad category would be a wide range of activities, from outright conservation to RIL and improved forest and fire management.

2 Projects that increase carbon sequestration, removing atmospheric CO_2 by growing trees on previously forested areas (*reforestation*) or areas that have not historically supported trees (*afforestation*).

For each of these broad project types, we will examine the kinds of leakage that might occur. Our results from a review of the literature on the *types of leakage* for these broad project types are summarized in Table 8.2. Where possible, we also discuss the *magnitude* of potential leakage. Our review of the scale of concern is hampered by the fact that most LULUCF projects have not been operational long enough to allow detailed examination. The Noel Kempff Mercado Climate Action Project in Bolivia is the project with the most comprehensive leakage analysis thus far (Winrock International 2002). What modelling has been done has been primarily on market effects of large-scale carbon sequestration or forest set-aside programmes (see Table 8.3).

Conservation projects

Land use and land-use change projects may reduce emissions from forests by avoiding deforestation or through the introduction of management practices that lead to increased carbon storage in forests (for example, by increasing rotation length and reducing harvest intensity). Avoided deforestation and proactive forest management have been specifically excluded as eligible project types under the Kyoto Protocol's CDM for the first commitment period (UNFCCC 2001). Comprehensive efforts to curb global warming will eventually need to promote these tools, since deforestation and forest degradation, mostly in the developing world, constitute some 20–25% of global GHG emissions (Schimel *et al.* 1996).

Deforestation results from a mix of economic, social and political causes that vary from site to site. In general, the primary *proximate causes* of deforestation in the tropics are logging and conversion to agriculture or grazing (Rowe *et al.* 1992). These activities span a spectrum from subsistence agricultural to production of globally traded commodities (e.g. vegetable oil, wood pulp, cacao, rice, etc.). Behind the proximate deforestation causes are *driving forces* such as policies, attitudes and institutions that influence production and consumption (Turner *et al.* 1993). Deforestation is often a complex process influenced by cultures, markets, government policies, property rights and

---

[1] We do not discuss projects that use biomass to substitute for fossil-fuel-intensive products or processes (e.g. biofuels) as a separate category. Emissions reductions from displaced fossil-fuel emissions pertain essentially to the energy sector, while biomass plantations as a source of supply can be considered under reforestation and afforestation.

Table 8.2. *Leakage and forest projects in developing countries*

Type of activity	Drivers of leakage[a]	Leakage mechanisms	Leakage scale	Effects[b]
project type: conservation[c]				
replace or prevent subsistence agriculture	subsistence needs (+ or −)	activity shift ecological market	local local local	−/N/+ + −/N/+
replace or prevent commercial agriculture	cash crop markets (−)	activity shift ecological market	local/global local local/global	−/N/+ + −/N/+
stop commercial logging	timber markets (−)	activity shift ecological market	local/global local local	− + −
stop forest-products harvest for local needs	subsistence needs (−)	activity shift ecological market	local local local	− + −
RIL, enhanced forest management	technology transfer (+)	activity shift ecological market	local local local/global	+ + N
project type: reforestation and afforestation[d]				
ecosystem restoration	resource and land availability (+ or −)	activity shift ecological market	local local local	+/N/− + +/N/−
small-scale reforestation for local needs	land availability (−), timber supply (+)	activity shift ecological market	local local local	N/− + N
commercial plantations	timber markets (+ or −), land availability (−)	activity shift ecological market	local local local/global	+/N/− +/N/− +/N/−

[a]Considering only socioeconomic drivers of leakage, not ecological leakage drivers. A plus sign refers to a driving factor for positive leakage and a minus sign refers to a driver of negative leakage.
[b]Positive (+), negative (−) or neutral (N).
[c]Excluded from the CDM for the first commitment period (2008–2012) of the Kyoto Protocol in negotiations as of November 2001.
[d]Allowed in the CDM, with limitations.

local politics. Deforestation is often driven by rural poverty and basic needs such as food, shelter and fuel. Effective leakage-control measures will need to address both the proximate causes (land-use changes) and underlying forces (poverty, land tenure, etc.) of deforestation on a case-by-case basis.

The magnitude of *activity-shifting leakage* will vary greatly across conservation projects. If neighbouring forested lands are easily accessible and the

Table 8.3. *Magnitude of LULUCF market leakage*

CDM activity	Study	Method	Period (yr)	Leakage potential	Driving factors
plantations	(1)	top-down	100	50%	increased timber supply, adverse changes in age classes of trees and forest management intensity
plantations	(2)	top-down	50	100%	rising agricultural land rents
plantations	(3)	top-down	50	regionally high, but no global impact	increased timber supply
plantations	(4)	top-down	50	non-negligible	increased timber supply
averted deforestation	(5)	top-down	125	little or no perceivable impact	intensification of existing forest management and additional plantations in subtropics
RIL	(6)	bottom-up	1	60%	maximum leakage potential based on a complete substitution of decreased timber production

The studies referred to in the table are labelled as follows: (1) Sohngen & Sedjo (2000); (2) Alig *et al.* (1997); (3) Perez-Garcia (1994); (4) Kadekodi & Ravindranath (1997); (5) Sohngen *et al.* (1999); (6) Brown *et al.* (1997).

displaced activity is mobile, activity-shifting leakage is likely. Where forested land is not readily available (in regions where land use is already consolidated) or where capital or labour are not mobile, the risk of activity-shifting leakage may be quite low. Projects that improve forest management rather than eliminate forest harvest altogether will be far less vulnerable to activity-shifting leakage. When new GHG-friendly ideas or technologies are economically competitive, projects may cause positive leakage. For instance, if RIL is more profitable for timber companies than traditional techniques, positive activity-shifting leakage could easily occur as RIL disseminates beyond the project boundary.

The risks of *market leakage* will depend on the nature of the market and the scale of any project. While a single conservation project is unlikely to affect global markets, it may affect local markets. In most cases, leakage risk will be less than 100%. For every forest protected, it is unlikely that there will be an equal expansion in production into other forest areas. Factors such as intensification, product substitution and reuse are likely to replace some of the displaced output.

Little analytical work has been conducted on the magnitude of possible leakage from individual forestry projects. Most modelling has evaluated market effects of global scale carbon sequestration, and only two studies specifically address forest conservation (see Table 8.3).

In terms of leakage, conservation projects that eliminate logging activities could constrain supply and lead to increased demand for wood from new sources. Sohngen *et al.* (1999) studied the effect of an increased worldwide timber demand on harvesting rates in inaccessible northern forests such as Siberia and in tropical South-American and African rainforests. Their study suggests that higher timber prices would produce a stronger response in harvesting northern inaccessible forests than it does in additional logging in the tropics, despite similar characteristics (low productivity, long rotation periods). Moreover, they show that an increasing timber price will more likely lead to an intensification of forest management in existing temperate zone forests (e.g. shorter rotation periods) or to the new establishment of plantations in emerging subtropical regions (i.e. South and Central America, Africa and the Asia Pacific region). The latter results from a greater harvest productivity in temperate zones and subtropical plantations compared with logging of inaccessible tropical forests. These results illustrate the enormous complexity of estimating leakage. Projects that stop deforestation caused by logging can reduce timber supply, raise prices and lead to more logging in temperate forests (negative leakage). Or they can cause more plantations to be established (possibly positive leakage). Interestingly, the former scenario is not a leakage problem, since it displaces emissions to where they would be accounted, e.g. within Annex I boundaries.

Climate-change-mitigation projects that minimize harm from logging operations (RIL techniques) could be assumed to result in no or little market leakage, since RIL essentially seeks to maintain a given timber output but with less damage. Conversely, Brown *et al.* (1997) derived a considerable leakage potential of RIL techniques based on data of a carbon-offset project in Sabah, Malaysia. This project caused leakage because on one-third of the project area timber production *initially* decreased by *ca.* 50 m^3 ha^{-1} relative to conventional logging. The total timber shortfall was set at 22 050 m^3. They calculated the *maximum* leakage potential by estimating the additional area that must be logged to make up for this deficit. Assuming that RIL techniques would be used to compensate this shortfall, they arrived at an off-site carbon emission of 23 112 tC (tonnes of carbon), equal to 60% of the annual gross carbon benefits of the project (38 700 tC). This maximum figure is useful in demonstrating a simple means of quantifying potential leakage. The true leakage effect of this project will most likely be smaller, since *over time* RIL should increase timber output compared with conventional logging by sustaining less damage to young trees.

Reforestation and afforestation

Tree-planting projects run the gamut from diversified community-based agro-forestry systems that meet local needs, to restoration of degraded grazing land to large-scale commercial monocultures that supply global markets. Without adequate empirical data, it is difficult to say whether certain types of sequestration project may be more or less leakage prone. In general, small-scale reforestation/afforestation projects focused on environmental restoration and local community needs should have more positive leakage profiles than large-scale commercial plantations, mainly because they aim to minimize the drivers and scale of potential leakage.

If carried out on currently productive land, reforestation or afforestation may cause *activity-shifting leakage* as displaced people migrate to other forest areas. Displacement of local communities from lands has been a frequently cited concern, especially in the case of large-scale commercial reforestation projects (World Rainforest Movement 1999; Sawyer 1993). In Honduras, for example, thousands of small farmers and ranchers were reportedly displaced from the north coast valleys to make way for the establishment of oil-palm cooperatives (CFAN 2001). While oil-palm plantations would most probably *not* be considered forestry under the Kyoto Protocol, this case demonstrates the enormous displacement potential of large-scale mono-component land-use change projects.

As a rule, activity-shifting leakage will depend on whether reforestation engages or displaces landowners. If reforestation is an alternative or complementary land use for existing landowners, and economic benefits are comparable to non-forest alternatives, then the risk of negative activity-shifting leakage will likely be low. Projects that yield valuable environmental services may lead to additional carbon and other benefits, outside the project boundary (e.g. positive leakage). One example would be an agroforestry project that improves water quality and enhances agricultural production, leading to additional communities practicing agroforestry.

Market leakage from reforestation/afforestation projects can potentially be either positive or negative. In certain circumstances, however, reforestation/afforestation projects will be virtually free of market-leakage risk. This would be the case for projects that serve exclusively to sequester and store carbon for the long term and/or produce other environmental services, such as restoration projects for watershed protection or biodiversity conservation, *on previously degraded lands*. If a reforestation/afforestation project generates products that are substitutes for others that come exclusively from natural forest sources (e.g. firewood for local use), this should tend to produce positive market-based leakage by creating a new supply of locally available resources.

Large-scale timber plantations may be particularly prone to market leakage. They could depress timber prices by increasing supply, which in turn could reduce the incentive to establish new timber plantations elsewhere. This could lead to either positive leakage (if the 'foregone' plantations would have replaced carbon-rich native forests) or negative leakage (if the 'foregone' plantations would have taken place on degraded lands with a lower carbon content). Equally plausible, timber plantations might reduce timber prices and lessen harvesting on other natural forests. Whether market forces will lead to a decline in forest harvesting (positive leakage) or the abandonment of plantations (negative leakage) will depend on local market conditions and circumstances. Reforestation/afforestation projects also may lead to negative market leakage if they reduce agricultural or livestock output or increase agricultural land rents.

Although still relatively limited, virtually all research on the amount of leakage has been done on market leakage from commercial plantations projects. The most advanced study in this field, carried out by Sedjo & Sohngen (2000), is based on modelling a high additional input of 50 Mha of carbon plantations established over a 30-year period. This is roughly equivalent to a doubling in the current rate of plantation establishment.[1] The general result of this model is that potential leakage from this programme could be considerable. This study suggests that 50 Mha of new carbon plantations would decrease sequestration outside the new forests by *ca.* 50%. This effect is largely due to accompanying adverse changes in age classes of trees and increased management intensity rather than a diminished incentive to establish new plantations.[2]

An even more drastic result was derived by Alig *et al.* (1997). They found a leakage rate for carbon-sequestration projects exceeding 100% following a 4.9 Mha afforestation programme in the US. Their result is driven by an increase in agricultural land rents that results in a more than one-to-one conversion rate of forestry to agriculture. Afforested lands in this study were not required to remain in forestry (i.e. permanent set-asides) but also exposed to economic pressures from increased agricultural land and output prices.

The Cintrafor Global Trade Model (CGTM) (Perez-Garcia 1994) resembles Alig *et al.*'s work in some respects, but analyses the impacts of a US tree-planting programme on the forest sector using an economic model of *world* forest-products markets. This study examines impacts of a large tree-planting programme in the southern US on the forested land base in the US's north and west regions, as well as Canada (*regional effects*), and on US forest-products trade with countries around the Pacific Rim and with European markets (*global effects*). The local effects in this study are found to be significant, but there is almost no perceivable global impact from this tree-planting programme due to existing trade links.

Kadekodi & Ravindranath (1997) show in a separate study that a nationwide teak tree-planting programme in India, while tripling the output value of forest products and reversing the forest-product trade in favour of India, would also reduce global teak prices. Leakage results from this programme since the global price decline would cause *existing* teak planters to face a smaller return on their investments.

---

[1] The current worldwide rate of newly established of plantations is 1.6 Mha yr^{-1} according to FAO (1998). If simply extrapolated, it is equal to 48 Mha over a 30-year period.

[2] The 50 Mha impulse of this study would reduce land areas in commercial (i.e. 'non-carbon') plantations only by 0.2–7.8 Mha (less than 15%).

Table 8.4. *Project-level options for managing leakage*

Projects	Project-specific approaches				Standardized approaches	
	Site selection	Multi-component project	Leakage contracts	Off-site monitoring	Discounting	Aggregate baselines
Noel Kempff, Bolivia	—	✓	✓	✓	—	—
Rio Bravo, Belize	—	✓	—	✓	—	—
CARE, Guatemala	—	✓	—	—	—	—
Krkonose, Czech Rep.	✓	—	—	—	—	—
Ecoland, Costa Rica	✓	—	✓	—	—	—
Costa Rican National Parks	—	✓	—	—	✓	✓
Scolel Te, Mexico	—	✓	—	✓	—	—
RIL/Sabah, Malaysia	—	—	✓	—	—	—

Sources: Compiled from Noel Kempff Technical Operating Protocols (1999), Brown *et al.* (1997) (Rio Bravo, CARE, Krkonose), Trexler *et al.* (1999) (Ecoland), Chacon *et al.* (1998) (Costa Rican National Parks) and email communications with Richard Tipper (Scolel Te) and Francis Putz (RIL/Sabah).

Options for responding to leakage: project-level response and policies

Leakage is a potentially significant risk for project activities. But, as well-designed pilot projects around the world have demonstrated, leakage is not insurmountable. We divide the tools used to reduce and manage negative leakage in LULUCF projects into *project-level approaches* and *macro-level approaches*.

Project-level options for managing leakage

At the project level, the two main categories for addressing leakage are *project-specific approaches* and *standardized approaches*. Project-specific approaches address case-by-case local circumstances such as fuelwood scarcity or ecosystem characteristics. Standardized approaches are broad measures applied across classes of projects to compensate for leakage. For example, a standardized 'leakage discount' may apply to carbon offsets generated in forest-conservation projects reflecting average leakage rates for this class of projects.

Approaches at the project level taken in various projects to date are summarized in Table 8.4 and then discussed individually.

Project-specific approaches

Site selection. At the project level, sound leakage management begins during the design of a project. Projects should be structured to maximize positive leakage (increased sequestration, reduced emissions) and minimize negative leakage (decreased sequestration, increased emissions). An obvious way to do this is for project developers to carefully seek out and consult communities with sincere interest in enhancing management of their forestlands. Thoughtful site selection might also entail locating a project in an area with few or no competing uses (such as degraded lands) or limited access (such as remote forests threatened with new logging roads) to minimize the risk of displacing people or causing negative market leakage. An example of a careful site selection is the *Krkonose* reforestation project in the Czech Republic, where the project developer chose an isolated location with virtually no risk of encroachment or displacement (Brown *et al.* 1997). Another example is the *Ecoland* forest-conservation project in Costa Rica, where virtually no forest was left standing outside the project area, making activity-shifting leakage improbable (Trexler *et al.* 1999, p. 147).

Multi-component projects. Projects should create incentives for local people to maintain the project and its GHG benefits by providing a range of socioeconomic benefits (CIFOR 2000). Multi-component projects may help realize this and avoid leakage by integrating measures to meet local needs and provide sustainable access to resources (timber, fuelwood, cropland, etc.). For example, project developers of the *Noel Kempff Mercado* forest-conservation project in Bolivia control leakage with demand-management activities. These mitigation activities include agroforestry to provide sustainable sources of wood, employment opportunities and equipment-retirement schemes (Noel Kempff Climate Action Project 1999). Similarly, the *CARE Guatemala project* increased fuelwood supply and agricultural productivity by providing trees through tree nurseries (Brown *et al.* 1997). These components minimize negative activity shifting and negative market leakage (less pressure on the original forest), while encouraging additional positive ecological leakage. Other advantages to multi-component design include possible enhanced profitability, increased local employment, numerous ecological positive feedbacks and overall higher likelihood of community support and success (Niles & Schwarze 2000).

Leakage contracts. The *Noel Kempff Mercado Climate Action Project* forest-conservation project in Bolivia uses contracts that prohibit leakage. The logging concessionaires bought out by the project signed contracts committing them to technical assistance and training in sustainable forest-management practices for their remaining concessions (supporting positive activity-shifting leakage). To decrease activity shifting, concessionaires also agreed not to use money received from the project to purchase new concessions and to abandon logging equipment on site (Noel Kempff Climate Action Project 1999). To monitor possible activity shifting by loggers, the *Noel Kempff Mercado Climate Action Project* is scheduled to follow the investments and actions of timber concessionaires who were displaced by the project. Other contractual approaches might require (and possibly compensate) farmers to plant trees or use more efficient cooking stoves. It is likely that enforcement of leakage contracts will be easier with a smaller number of stakeholders.

Monitoring. All types of climate-mitigation projects and policies should monitor leakage to a degree commensurate with the risk and possible scale of leakage. Since project design will not always be able to prevent leakage altogether, careful monitoring and measurement can provide the basis for adjusting GHG benefits accordingly.

There are several ways to monitor for potential leakage. This may involve *expanding the geographic scale of monitoring* beyond project boundaries to capture regional effects through a combination of remote sensing and sample plots in non-project areas. This method has been explored in the *Scolel Te Project* in Mexico (Tipper & de Jong 1998). Although expanding the boundaries for monitoring may capture activity-shifting and market-leakage effects, it is often difficult to isolate impacts of project leakage from other exogenous factors that affect markets and land use (e.g. demographics, access, policies, markets for agricultural products or a host of other factors). The definition of boundaries for monitoring and the interpretation of results thus represent a special challenge.

The scope of monitoring may also be expanded to examine *market linkages* beyond the immediate project vicinity. Project managers can try to track effects of a project on the supply, price and sources for timber or agricultural products. However, markets are hard to model and are notoriously difficult to predict, even under the best of circumstances. Analysing markets for timber, crops or livestock in many developing countries is complicated by the predominance of the informal sector and the lack of accurate and current data.

Another approach, proposed by Brown *et al.* (1997), is to track *selected indicators* rather than monitoring leakage directly. The use of indicators can alert monitoring agents as to the risk of leakage. This approach emphasizes key indicators of demand driving baseline land-use change. If demand for timber, fuelwood or farmland is left unmet due to a project, this would signal a risk of leakage. This, in turn, could trigger a burden of proof for project management of no leakage (or any other type of so-called 'seller liability') similar to the traffic-light approach for non-compliance (Wiser & Goldberg 1999). The indicator approach has the advantage of being relatively straightforward and transparent. Key indicators may be defined beforehand and can be objectively evaluated over time. Such an approach is likely to be more qualitative than quantitative. It remains a challenge to measure precisely how a decreased supply of farmland or forest products translate into carbon leakage.

Though laborious, tracking *activities of resource users* affected by project activities may be an effective means for capturing activity-shifting leakage. Activity shifting will often be easier monitored at the local level (although, for example, some logging companies could migrate to other countries) and it may be more tractable at the project scale. A variety of social and economic assessment methods, including surveys, follow-up interviews and review of land transactions, can be used to estimate activity-shifting leakage. As previously mentioned, the *Noel Kempff Mercado Climate Action Project* follows investments and actions of timber concessionaires displaced by the project.

Standardized approaches

Discounting.   If leakage is effectively monitored and calculated, then GHG benefits from a project may be adjusted accordingly. If projects monitor leakage in detail, any discount can be based on the specific outcomes of project implementation and monitoring. As previously illustrated, however, monitoring and calculating all possible leakage effects will be practically impossible. In order to address leakage from a practical standpoint and to simplify leakage accounting, standard coefficients could be used to adjust the GHG-benefit estimates of projects. Some observers (Lee 1997) have suggested applying a standardized discount to LULUCF projects. These adjustment coefficients will vary for different project types and different national or regional circumstances (IPCC 2000, p. 314). Case studies (IPCC 2000, § 5.3.3.2, p. 264) indicate that certain broad landscape characteristics could be used to establish these varying leakage discounts. For example, a plantation project on severely degraded lands with few alternative uses and no occupants will almost certainly be less prone to leakage than a plantation carried out on productive lands with many users and/or occupants. Establishing appropriate adjustment coefficient(s) to cover diverse leakage risks merits further research, but ultimately will require policy decisions that balance the needs for accuracy and workability.

Project eligibility criteria.   A drastic form of 'discounting' would be to rule out projects that are perceived to be particularly leakage prone. For example, if forest-conservation projects in developing countries are set non-eligible for CDM projects (as under the current Article-12 ruling of COP-6*bis*), potential carbon credits from these activities are effectively discounted at a rate of 100%. Given that leakage will mostly be project specific and can be addressed through careful project design, removing whole suites of objects would risk eliminating projects that yield positive GHG benefits and net local benefits. A favourable alternative approach would be to grant projects with appealing leakage profiles a streamlined approval and monitoring process similar to the preferential treatment of small-scale renewables and energy-efficiency CDM projects decided at COP-6*bis* (UNFCCC 2001).

Aggregate baselines.   Another way of expanding a project's accounting boundary is to use aggregate baselines. This technique would entail developing national, regional or sectoral baselines on land-use change and management. Experience with standardized baselines, however, has shown that calculating national or sector-type baselines brings in tertiary and other indirect effects that can overwhelm any attempt at project-caused calculations (Trexler 1999, p. 46). This problem is further aggravated by the fact that land-use change data for most developing countries are very incomplete. For

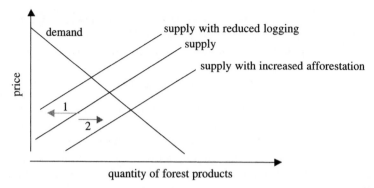

Figure 8.1. Market effects of LULUCF projects. (Arrow 1 denotes reduced logging of virgin forests. Arrow 2 denotes increased afforestation of abandoned land.)

example, deforestation-rate estimations can typically vary greatly for the same country according to different sources and methods (Mathews 2001). Aggregate baselines are also rejected by many developing countries on the grounds that such national procedures could be a 'back-door' way to coerce developing countries into a regime of quantified emission-reduction targets.

Macro-level options for reducing and managing leakage

At the macro level, we identify two major proposals that can minimize LULUCF leakage. First, a ceiling or cap can be placed on the volume of forestry projects for climate-change mitigation. This approach serves to minimize the perceived scale of leakage risks. The second option is a balanced portfolio approach. It aims to offset, or balance, market-leakage effects by combining reforestation/afforestation and avoided deforestation projects at the policy level.

The 1% ceiling on CDM sinks

The resumed session of the Sixth Conference of the Parties, Part 2 (COP-6*bis*), limited the number of credits developed countries may gain via CDM forestry projects. During the first commitment period (2008–2012), developed countries may only use CDM forestry projects to meet 1% of their respective 1990 emissions per year, for each of the five years in the first commitment period (UNFCCC 2001). Furthermore, at COP-6*bis*, a decision was taken to restrict the type of forest projects to those that involve reforestation and afforestation ('sinks') and limited the size of individual projects. Although these restrictions were not set primarily to address the risk of leakage, limiting the scope and number of projects may effectively keep in check the impact of projects on local and/or global timber markets, respectively.

The COP-6*bis* ceiling will probably not have a great impact, as it appears to have been set above the threshold likely to be reached by CDM reforestation and afforestation projects. These results are discussed in a separate paper (Vrolijk & Niles 2002).

A balanced LULUCF portfolio

Plantations may have opposite effects on local or global timber markets compared with forest conservation projects (see Figure 8.1). Reduced logging of natural forests decreases the supply of forest products (price increase) and accelerated planting of trees increases the supply (price decrease). Some authors (e.g. Chomitz 2000, p. 7) have argued that these counteracting forces could lead to a leakage-neutralizing situation, where market effects of halting deforestation offset opposite market effects of plantations and/or reforestation. While there is no empirical evidence to support this notion, basic economic rational suggests this possibility may have some merit. The possibility of such 'counteracting' forces makes an argument for trying to 'balance' the ratio of these projects. This would imply that the recent decision by policymakers to exclude forest conservation from forest projects in developing countries could exacerbate leakage. Thus the CDM executive board will not have this policy tool at its disposal, at least in the first commitment period.

Such a balanced-portfolio approach, while useful to some degree, assumes a similarity in market effects of tree planting and tree protection that may not exist. First, industrial plantations operate on different time-scales compared with forest-conservation projects. It can take ten years or more for plantations to increase the wood supply, whereas projects that stop logging reduce timber supplies in the short term and decades into the future. Interestingly, a relative symmetry could be achieved if avoided deforestation was allowed in the second commitment period when new timber plantations will start being harvested. Second, harvest intensities vary greatly among (high-yielding) industrial plantations and (low-yielding) logging of tropical forests. There is also substantial variability within similar project types across regions and ecosystems (IPCC 2000, ch. 5). A balanced portfolio approach would need to take these differences into account, something not practical on a simple per-project basis. Finally, logging is only one factor behind tropical deforestation, so carbon conserved through forest protection may only be loosely related to its effects on timber markets. The 'balancing' approach therefore seems more promising at the project level, as discussed in the paragraph entitled 'Multi-component projects' on p. 145.

Conclusions and recommendations

Unintended consequences arise in virtually every type of activity. Climate-change mitigation and sustainable development are no different. Discrete projects or policies may cause impacts that extend over a broad scale, through complex and dynamic causes and effects.

Devising solutions and rules for leakage is hampered by a dearth of substantial quantitative studies. There are no long-term peer-reviewed evaluations of climate-change mitigation leakage for actual projects. Until more studies are conducted, leakage is a legitimate concern in terms of its magnitude, although results from studies are highly variable. They also may not turn out to resemble real leakage rates that eventually are measured. There is no evidence that forestry as a sector is more prone to leakage than other sectors, such as energy or transportation (although there are some indications for this belief). Nor is there concrete evidence that any one type of forestry project is more or less susceptible to leakage than others (although there are reasons to suspect that plantations may be particularly prone to market leakage).

Leakage will probably be most determined by project-specific activities, not broad categorical groupings. *Together, these findings suggest that all climate mitigation projects—plantations, transportation, forest conservation and energy—should monitor for and address leakage at the project level.* There is no apparent and compelling reason to shun any one type of climate-change mitigation based solely on leakage.

Notwithstanding the lack of data, modelling scenarios, case studies and general observations can provide insight into preventing negative leakage and fostering positive leakage. Projects should try to maintain the same long-term output of products (or substitutes) of baseline activities to account for market leakage. Multi-faceted projects may have advantages in terms of minimizing negative leakage and maximizing positive leakage. Integrated projects that use reforestation, plantations *and* forest-conservation programmes seem well suited to create sustained, diverse economies that will not cause severe market disruptions or unwanted migration or displacement. Project diversity should also extend to non-forestry dimensions, such as clean energy, reliable transportation and other aspects. Other instruments, such as wise site selection and leakage contracts, may also help prevent negative leakage and bad projects.

At regional, national or global scales, leakage can also be addressed with complementary project types. There is some evidence, for example, that reforestation programmes and forest-protection programmes could have balancing influences on the global timber market. However, important asymmetries between growing new forests and not cutting down old ones must be addressed (timing of impacts, per-area timber effects) for the value of multiple project activities to scale up.

Ensuring the integrity of climate-change policies will also entail measuring leakage when it does occur. Monitoring will allow appropriate adjustments to be made to the amount of carbon offsets claimed by a project. Yet measuring leakage with a high degree of precision will often be costly and inconclusive. The boundaries defined, the mechanisms posited and the assumptions employed will all be subject to contradicting opinions. It is not so much a problem of not having ways to map and measure leakage—a host of economists, sociologists, geographers and foresters can develop plausible approaches for each project—the problem lies precisely in this variety, and the resulting variety of possible outcomes.

Several approaches are available for managing leakage that does occur in an affordable and sufficiently accurate manner. First, monitoring beyond the project boundaries for selected indicators of leakage is one practical solution. Second, discount factors may be applied in the short term. They should be conservative (i.e. high) as the CDM market becomes operational, and can be refined as the market matures and further information becomes available. Well-reasoned discount coefficients will be different for different regions, project types and/or markets. For activity shifting, this discount might be based on the likelihood of engaging local people. For markets, elasticities of demand and supply will be useful parameters for estimating leakage (cf. Chomitz 2000, pp. 8, 9). Projects that have an appealing leakage profile—those that minimize negative undesirable unintended consequences while promoting positive ones—could also be granted a preferential treatment in the process of approval and monitoring to reward efforts in project design.

It is also worth recalling that many projects will potentially have positive spillover effects. Positive activity-shifting leakage (e.g. broader adoption of project technologies), market leakage (e.g. reduced pressure on natural forests as timber sources) and ecological leakage (ecosystem stabilization) may end up on par with negative leakage. These positive and unaccounted GHG benefits may also 'buffer' against negative leakage that is not captured by monitoring.

Acknowledgements

The authors recognize the generous contributions of information and comments on earlier drafts of this chapter by Brent Sohngen, Duane Lakich-Muelller, John Perez-Garcia, Richard Tipper, Paige Brown, Bill Stanley and Eric Firstenberg. The opinions expressed, and any possible errors, are of course solely our responsibility.

This chapter was written under contract with The Nature Conservancy and was made possible through support provided by The Nature Conservancy and the Office of Procurement, US Agency for International Development, under the terms of Award LAG-A-00-00-00019-00. The opinions expressed herein are those of the authors and do not necessarily reflect the views of the US Agency for International Development.

References

Alig, R., Adams, D., McCarl, B., Callaway, J. M. & Winnett, S. 1997 Assessing effects of mitigation strategies for global climate change with an intertemporal model of the US forest and agricultural sectors. *Environ. Resource Econ.* **9**, 269–274.

Babiker, M. H. 2001 Subglobal climate-change actions and carbon leakage: the implications of international capital flows. *Energy Econ.* **23**, 121–139.

Brown, P., Cabarele, B. & Livernash, R. 1997 *Carbon counts: estimating climate mitigation in forest projects.* Washington, DC: World Resource Institute.

CFAN 2001 *Forestry issues. Deforestation: tropical forests in decline.* Quebec: CIDA Forestry Advisers Network. (Available at www.rcfa-cfan.org/english/issues.12.html.)

Chacon, C., Castro, R. & Mack, S. 1998 *Pilot-phase Joint Implementation projects in Costa Rica. A case study.* Washington, DC: Center for International Environmental Law. (Available at www.ciel.org/Publications/CDMCaseStudy.pdf.)

Chomitz, K. M. 2000 *Evaluating carbon offsets from forestry and energy projects: how do they compare?* World Bank Paper 2357. Washington, DC: World Bank. (Available at http://econ.worldbank.org/docs/1111.pdf.)

CIFOR 2000 *Capturing the value of forest carbon for local livelihoods.* Policy Brief from a workshop organized by the Center for International Forestry Research (CIFOR) and the University of Maryland at Como, Italy, February 2000 (distributed at COP-5).

FAO 1998 *Global fibre supply model.* Rome: Food and Agriculture Organization of the United Nations.

Felder, S. & Rutherford, T. 1993 Unilateral CO_2 reductions and carbon leakage: the consequences of international trade in oil and basic materials. *J. Environ. Econ. Mngmt* **25**, 161–176.

IPCC 2000 *Land use, land-use change and forestry* (ed. R. T. Watson, I. R. Noble, B. Bolin, N. H. Ravindranath, D. J. Verado & D. J. Dokken), ch. 5. Geneva: Intergovernmental Panel on Climate Change. (Available at www.grida.no/climate/ipcc/land_use/index.htm.)

Kadekodi, G. P. & Ravindranath, N. H. 1997 Macro-economic analysis of forestry options on carbon sequestration in India. *Ecol. Econ.* **23**, 201–223.

Lee, R. 1997 *Understanding concerns about Joint Implementaiton.* Oak Ridge, TN: Joint Institute for Energy and Environment/Oak Ridge National Laboratories.

McGuffie, K., Henderson-Sellers, A., Zhang, H., Turbridge, T. B. & Pitman, A. J. 1995 Global sensitivity to tropical deforestation. *Global Planet. Change* **10**, 97–128.

Mathews, E. 2001 *Understanding the FRA 2000.* Forest Briefing No. 1. Washington, DC: World Resources Institute. (Available at www.wri.org/wri/pdf/fra2000.pdf.)

Niesten, E., Hardner, J. & Gullison, R. E. 2001 *Inter-annex carbon leakage related to forestry.* Paper prepared for the Union of Concerned Scientists, February 2001.

Niles, J. O. & Schwarze, R. 2000 Long-term forest sector emission reductions and Article 12. In *Proc. IEA Bioenergy Task 25 Workshop: Bioenergy for Mitigation of CO_2 Emissions, Gatlinburg, TN* (ed. K. A. Robertson & B. Schlamadinger), pp. 145–155.

Noel Kempff Climate Action Project 1999 *Technical operating protocols.* Morrilton, AR: Winrock International.

Perez-Garcia, J. 1994 *An analysis of proposed domestic climate warming mitigation program impacts on international forest products markets.* CINTRAFOR Working Paper 50. (Available at www.cintrafor.org.)

Rowe, R., Sharma, N. P. & Browder, J. 1992 Deforestation: problems, causes and concerns. In *Managing the World's Forests: Looking for Balance Between Conservation and Development* (ed. N. P. Sharma), pp. 33–45. Dubuque, IA: Kendall/Hunt.

Sawyer, J. 1993 *Plantations in the tropics: environmental concerns.* Gland: IUCN/UNEP/WWF.

Schimel, D., Alves, D., Enting, I., Heimann, M., Joos, F., Raynaud, D. & Wigley, T. 1996 Radiative forcing of climate change. In *Climate change 1995: the science of climate change* (ed. J. T. Houghton, L. G. Meira Filho, B. A. Callander, N. Harris, A. Kattenberg & K. Maskell), pp. 65–132. Cambridge University Press.

Sedjo, R. & Sohngen, B. 2000 *Forestry sequestration of CO_2 and markets for timber.* Washington, DC: RFF.

Smith, C. 1993 Carbon leakage: an empirical assessment using a global econometric model. In *International competitiveness and environmental policies* (ed. T. Barker & J. Kohler), pp. 143–169. Northampton, MA: Edward Elgar Publishing, Inc.

Sohngen, B., Mendelsohn, R. & Sedjo, R. 1999 Forest management, conservation, and global timber markets. *Am. J. Agricultural Econ.* **81**, 1–13.

Tipper, R. & de Jong, B. H. 1998 Quantification and regulation of carbon offsets from forestry: comparison of alternative methodologies, with special reference to Chiapas, Mexico. *Commonwealth Forestry Rev.* **77**, 219–228.

Trexler, M., Koshoff, L. H. & Gibbons, R. L. 1999 Forestry and land-use change in the AIJ Pilot Phase: the evolution of issues and methods to address them. In *The UN Framework Convention on Climate Change Activities Implemented Jointly (AIJ) Pilot: lessons learned and applications to future market-based mechanisms to reduce GHG emissions* (ed. R. Dixon), pp. 121–165. Dordrecht: Kluwer.

Turner, B. L., Moss, R. H. & Skole, D. L. (eds) 1993 Relating land use and global land-cover change: a proposal for an IGBP–HDP core project. Report from the IGBP-HDP Working Group on land use/land-cover change. Joint publication of the International Geosphere–Biosphere Programme (Report No. 24) and the Human Dimensions of Global Environmental Change Programme (Report No. 5). Stockholm: Royal Swedish Academy of Science.

UNFCCC 2001 *Decision 5/CP.6. Implementation of the Buenos Aires plan of action.* Bonn: United Nations Framework Convention on Climate Change. (Available at www.unfccc.de.)

UtiliTree 2000 *Reduced impact logging of natural forests in Malaysia.* Washington, DC: Edison Electric Institute.

Vine, E., Sathaye, J. & Makundi, W. 1999 *Guidelines for the monitoring, evaluation, reporting, verification and certification of forestry projects for climate change mitigation.* Berkeley, CA: Lawrence Berkeley National Laboratory.

Vrolijk, C. & Niles, J. O. 2002 *The scale of land use, land-use change and forestry (LULUCF) in developing countries for climate mitigation.* Arlington, VA: The Nature Conservancy. (Available in English and Spanish at http://nature.org/initiatives/climatechange/docs/.)

Winrock International 2002 *2001 interim report on leakage and baselines for the Noel Kempff Climate Action Project.* Washington, DC: Winrock International.

Wiser, G. & Goldberg, D. 1999 *The compliance fund. A new tool for achieving compliance under the Kyoto Protocol.* Washington, DC: Center for International Environmental Law. (Available at www.ciel.org/Publications/ComplianceFund.pdf.)

World Rainforest Movement 1999 *Tree plantations: impacts and struggles.* Montevideo: World Rainforest Movement.

Part 2

ENVIRONMENTAL SERVICES

Chapter 9

The influence of land-use change and landscape dynamics on the climate system: relevance to climate-change policy beyond the radiative effect of greenhouse gases

ROGER A. PIELKE SR, GREGG MARLAND, RICHARD A. BETTS,
THOMAS N. CHASE, JOSEPH L. EASTMAN, JOHN O. NILES,
DEV DUTTA S. NIYOGI AND STEVEN W. RUNNING

Introduction

Policy-related quantification of human influences on climate has focused largely on changes in atmospheric composition. However, a large body of work has demonstrated that land-cover change provides an additional major forcing of climate, through changes in the physical properties of the land surface. The global radiative forcing by surface albedo change may be comparable with that due to anthropogenic aerosols, solar variation and several of the greenhouse gases. Moreover, in regions of intensive human-caused land-use change such as North America, Europe and southeast Asia, the local radiative-forcing change caused by surface albedo may actually be greater than that due to all the well-mixed anthropogenic greenhouse gases together (IPCC 2001).

Surface albedo change can be compared with greenhouse-gas emissions through the concept of radiative forcing (Betts 2000), but changes in vegetation cover can also modify the surface heat fluxes directly. This cannot be quantified in terms of radiative forcing, so a full quantification of land-use impacts on climate requires a new approach. Furthermore, as well as influencing local long-term weather conditions, regional-scale land-cover change can impact on the global climate system through teleconnections (Avissar 1995; Pielke 2001a; Claussen 2003). Remote changes in different locations may be of opposing sign, so spatial averaging may under represent the true global significance of the land-use effects.

These aspects of human influence on climate are not currently accounted for under the Kyoto Protocol. One reason for this may be the difficulty in

Table 9.1. *Tropical forest extent and loss (rainforest and moist deciduous forest ecosystems)*

Country	Rainforest extent in 1990 (kha)	Decrease 1981–1990 (%)	Moist deciduous forest extent in 1990 (kha)	Decrease 1981–1990 (%)
Brazil	291 597	6	197 082	16
Indonesia	93 827	20	3 366	20
Dem. Rep. Congo (Zaire)	60 437	12	45 209	12
Columbia	47 455	6	4 101	38
Peru	40 358	6	12 299	6
Papua New Guinea	29 323	6	705	6
Venezuela	19 602	14	15 465	36
Malaysia	16 339	36	0	0
Myanmar	12 094	24	10 427	28
Guyana	11 671	0	5 078	6
Suriname	9 042	0	5 726	4
India	8 246	12	7 042	10
Cameroon	8 021	8	9 892	12
French Guiana	7 993	0	3	0
Congo	7 667	4	12 198	4
Ecuador	7 150	34	1 669	34
Lao People's Dem. Rep.	3 960	18	4 542	18
Philippines	3 728	62	1 413	54
Thailand	3 082	66	5 232	54
Vietnam	2 894	28	3 382	28
Guatemala	2 542	32	731	0
Mexico	2 441	20	11 110	30
Belize	1 741	0	238	0
Cambodia	1 689	20	3 610	20
Gabon	1 155	12	17 080	12
Central African Republic	616	14	28 357	8
Cuba	114	18	1 247	18
Bolivia	0	0	35 582	22

Source: World Resources Institute (1994), adapted from O'Brien (2001).

objectively comparing the effects of different local land-surface changes with each other and with the effects of changing atmospheric composition. However, the neglect of land-use effects will lead to inaccurate quantification of contributions to climate change, with the danger that some actions may give unintended and counterproductive results. It is therefore important that possible metrics for land-use effects are explored. Here we discuss some approaches to this problem.

Historical land-use change

A documentation of global patterns of land-use change from 1700 to 2000 is presented in Klein Goldewijk (2001). Klein Goldewijk reports on worldwide

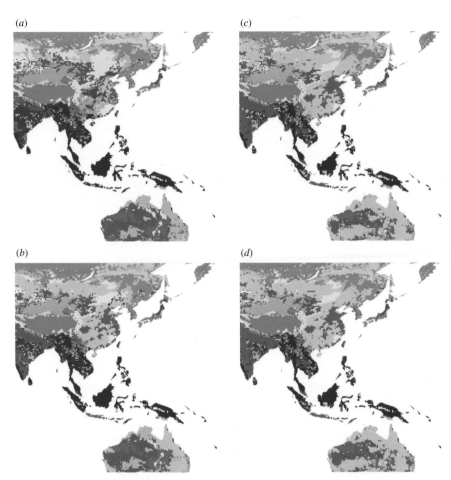

Figure 9.1. Examples of land-use change from (*a*) 1700, (*b*) 1900, (*c*) 1970 and (*d*) 1990. The human-disturbed landscape includes intensive cropland (red) and marginal cropland used for grazing (pink). Other landscape includes, for example, tropical evergreen and deciduous forest (dark green), savannah (light green), grassland and steppe (yellow), open shrubland (maroon), temperate deciduous forest (blue), temperate needleleaf evergreen forest (light yellow) and hot desert (orange). Of particular importance in this chapter is the expansion of the cropland and grazed land between 1700 and 1900. (Reproduced with permission from Klein Goldewijk (2001).)

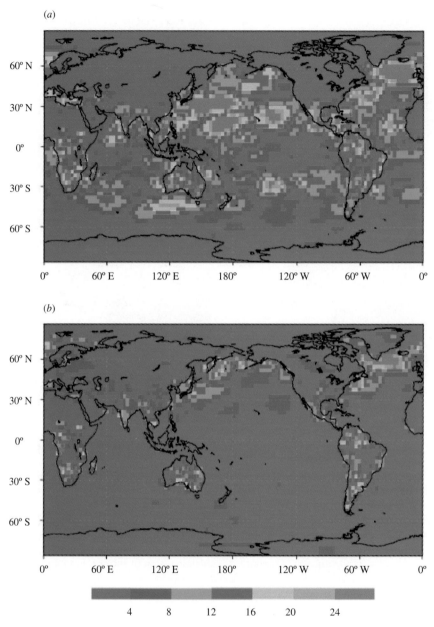

Figure 9.2. The 10-year average absolute-value change in surface latent turbulent heat flux in $W\,m^{-2}$ worldwide as a result of the land-use changes: (*a*) January, (*b*) July. (Adapted from Chase *et al.* (2000).)

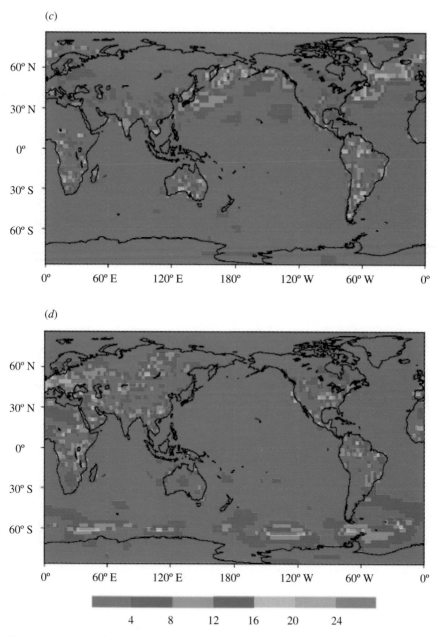

Figure 9.2. (*Cont.*) The 10-year average absolute-value change in sensible turbulent heat flux in W m^{-2} worldwide as a result of land-use changes: (*c*) January, (*d*) July. (Adapted from Chase *et al.* (2000).)

(a)

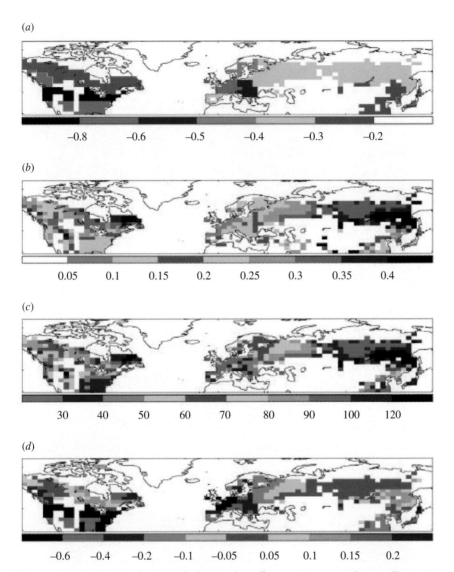

(b)

(c)

(d)

Figure 9.3. Radiative forcing of climate by afforestation, considering illustrative 1 ha plantations in the temperate and boreal forest zones. Calculations apply to the time at the end of one forestry rotation period, relative to the start of the rotation period with plantation areas unforested. (a) Global mean longwave radiative forcing due to CO_2 removal through sequestration ($nW\ m^{-2}\ ha^{-1}$). (b) Global mean shortwave radiative forcing due to albedo reduction ($nW\ m^{-2}\ ha^{-1}$). (c) Carbon emissions that would give the same magnitude of radiative forcing as the albedo reduction ($tC\ ha^{-1}$). (d) Net radiative forcing due to afforestation, found by summing (a) and (b) ($nW\ m^{-2}\ ha^{-1}$). Positive forcing implies a warming influence; where (d) shows positive values, afforestation would warm climate rather than cooling it, as would be expected by considering carbon sequestration alone (Betts 2000).

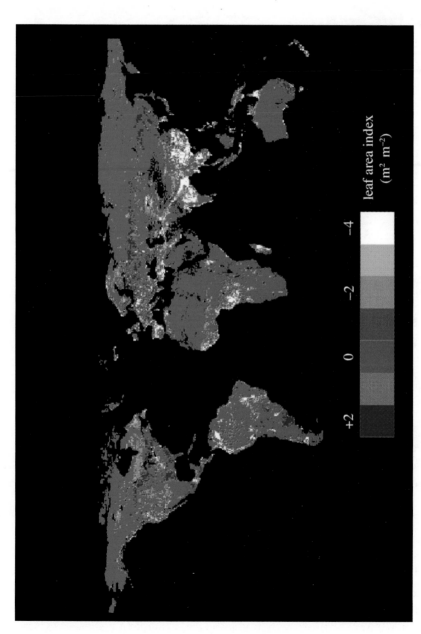

Figure 9.4. Effect of land-use changes on plant-canopy density (potential/actual). Scale 0.5 latitude × 0.5 longitude.

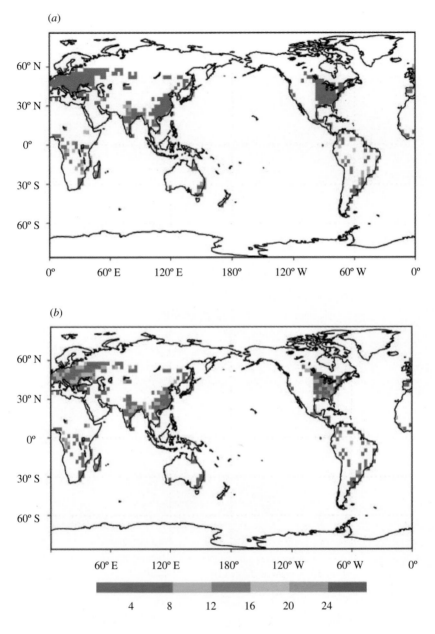

Figure 9.5. The 10-year average absolute-value change in surface latent turbulent heat flux in W m^{-2} at the locations where land-use change occurred: (*a*) January. (*b*) July. (Adapted from Chase *et al.* (2000).)

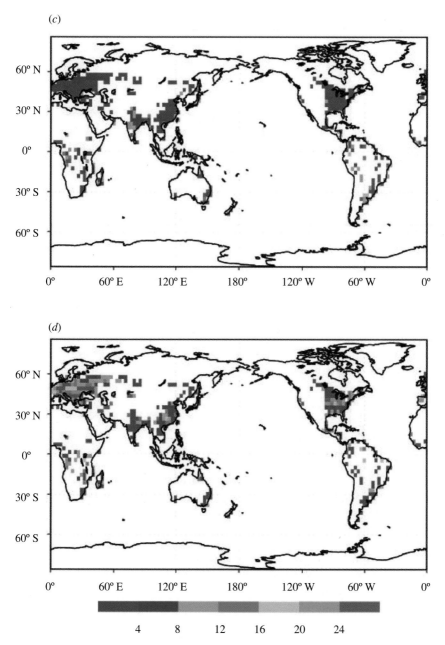

Figure 9.5. (*Cont.*) The 10-year average absolute-value change in surface sensible heat flux in W m^{-2} at the locations where land-use change occurred: (*c*) January; (*d*) July. (Adapted from Chase *et al.* (2000).)

changes of land to crops of 136, 412 and 658 Mha in the periods 1700–1799, 1800–1899 and 1900–1990, respectively. Conversion to pasture was 418, 1013 and 1496 Mha in these three time periods. Figure 9.1 illustrates these changes, including an acceleration of tropical deforestation during the 20th century. O'Brien (2000) also documents land-use change for recent years (Table 9.1).

Apart from their role as reservoirs, sinks, and sources of carbon, tropical forests provide numerous additional 'ecosystem services'. Many of these ecosystem services directly or indirectly influence climate. The climate-related ecosystem services that tropical forests provide include the maintenance of elevated soil moisture and surface air humidity, reduced sunlight penetration, weaker near-surface winds and the inhibition of anaerobic soil conditions. Such an environment maintains the productivity of tropical ecosystems (Betts 1999) and has helped sustain the rich biodiversity of tropical forests.

Impacts of land-cover change on climate

The significant role of the land within the climate system should not be surprising. As discussed by Wu & Newell (1998) for El Niño events, warming of a relatively small area in the tropical eastern and central Pacific Ocean has global climate consequences. This occurs because tropical cumulonimbus clouds occur in this region during an El Niño event, and not during average ocean conditions. These deep cumulus clouds permit the export of heat, moisture and kinetic energy to higher latitudes that do not normally receive such tropical export. Wu & Newell concluded that the long persistence, the spatial coherence of the ocean warming and its large magnitude are the reasons for this major role of El Niño events within the Earth's climate system.

Tropical land-use change has been shown in Chase *et al.* (1996, 2000), and summarized in Claussen (2003), to have an effect on the climate system similar to that from an El Niño event. Since thunderstorms preferentially form over land (Lyons 1999), the role of the tropical land surface should be expected to have a greater effect on global climate than implied by its per cent areal coverage of the Earth's surface alone. General circulation model (GCM) simulations by Chase *et al.* (2000) indicated that regional landscape change can result in alterations to surface fluxes elsewhere in the world through nonlinear feedbacks within the atmosphere's global circulation (Figure 9.2).

The alteration of tropical landscapes, primarily the conversion of forests to agriculture or pasture, changes the partitioning of solar insolation into its sensible and latent turbulent heat forms. Less transpiration associated with the agricultural and pasture regions results in less thunderstorm activity over this landscape. Lawton *et al.* (2001), for example, illustrates, for Costa Rica, the significant regional effects that tropical deforestation has on the ecological environment of adjacent mountains. The longitudinal distribution of thunderstorms in the tropics is also changed.

Unlike an El Niño, however, where the system changes back to 'average' and La Niña conditions (over time, we have learned to identify the global impacts of the different situations), land-use change is often permanent, so its global effects are not as obvious. Further, the atmospheric feedback due to similar land-use changes are variable, depending on the geographical domain or the existing land use (Niyogi 2000; Niyogi *et al.* 2002).

Deliberate land-use change (afforestation or reforestation) has been accepted as a mechanism to remove carbon dioxide (CO_2) from the atmosphere and sequester carbon in trees and soils. However, as discussed by Betts (2000) and Pielke (2001*b*), this activity may have other effects in terms of the radiative forcing in the atmosphere. For example, in regions subject to significant snow cover, afforestation would result in a lower surface albedo and hence a positive radiative forcing, resulting in a net warming effect despite the removal of CO_2 from the atmosphere (Figure 9.3). Similarly, increases in the surface fluxes of water vapour could result in positive radiative forcing.

The biogeochemical effect of enhanced CO_2 and trace-gas concentration, and of aerosol deposition (such as nitrogen), on landscape dynamics has also not been adequately considered. For example, Jenkinson *et al.* (1991) demonstrated a significant positive feedback where soils released carbon to the atmosphere under warming conditions. More recently, Lenton (2000), using a simple box model, and Cox *et al.* (2000), using GCM-sensitivity experiments, showed that biogeochemical feedbacks in conjunction with an increased CO_2 radiative warming produced an amplified regional and global-warming response. Eastman *et al.* (2001*a, b*) used a regional climate model in a sensitivity study and suggested a cooler daytime and warmer nighttime in the central Great Plains in response to greater plant growth in a doubled-CO_2 atmosphere.

Niyogi *et al.* (2003) used a coupled process-based model to show that the carbon-assimilation potential for each of the GCM land-use categories (comprising both C3 and C4 photosynthesis pathways) is sensitive to the soil-moisture availability. The presence of drought and hydrological feedbacks associated with land-use change locally or through teleconnections, therefore, has a direct impact on the source/sink capabilities of the terrestrial ecosystem.

These studies illustrate the significant role that biogeochemistry has within the climate system. This feedback, along with other climate forcings and feedbacks (Pielke 2001*b*), makes climate prediction on time-scales of years and longer a particularly difficult problem.

Quantifying land-use forcing of climate

As is evident in this book, carbon has become the currency used to assess the human intervention in the Earth's climate system. Impacts on climate are compared in terms of radiative forcing, which can be considered as perturbations to the Earth's radiation budget prior to feedbacks from the rest of the climate system. The concept of global-warming potential (GWP), where

$$\mathrm{GWP} = \frac{\int_0^{\mathrm{TH}} a_x x(t)\, \mathrm{d}t}{\int_0^{\mathrm{TH}} a_r r(t)\, \mathrm{d}t}, \tag{9.1}$$

has been adopted to convert other atmospheric constituents into their equivalent in terms of CO_2 atmospheric radiative forcing (IPCC 2001). Here, 'TH' is the time period over which the calculation is considered, a_x is the radiative efficiency due to a unit change in atmospheric abundance of the substance x (i.e. $W\,m^{-2}\,kg^{-1}$) and $x(t)$ is the time-dependent decay of the abundance from an instantaneous release of the substance. The denominator is the same expression, but for the reference substance r, defined to be CO_2.

The effects of land-surface albedo change can be quantified in terms of radiative forcing (Hansen *et al.* 1997; Betts 2001), and this has been used in attempts to compare the global significance of historical land-use change with that of other drivers of climate change (IPCC 2001). Betts (2000) suggested that radiative-forcing calculations could be used to translate albedo changes into equivalent carbon emissions (Figure 9.3); this could be useful for quantifying land-use changes in regions where the main impact is on surface albedo, such as areas subject to significant snow cover. However, in other regions, changes in other land-surface properties may not exert a radiative forcing, but still significantly influence climate. For example, the partitioning of available energy into latent and sensible heat fluxes exerts a direct impact on near-surface air temperature, so a change in this partitioning should be considered a climate forcing. Radiative forcing, and hence GWP, are therefore not able to represent the full impact of land-cover change in all regions. Some new means of quantifying land-use forcing is therefore required.

Separation of the components of the surface-energy budget could provide a possible starting point, with the surface-heat energy being separated into

$$Q_N + Q_H + Q_{LE} + Q_G = 0, \tag{9.2}$$

where

$$Q_N = Q_S(1 - A) + Q_{LW}^{\downarrow} - Q_{LW}^{\uparrow}. \tag{9.3}$$

Here, Q_N is the net radiative flux, Q_H is the turbulent sensible heat flux, Q_{LE} is the turbulent latent heat flux (evaporation/transpiration), Q_G is the heat flux into the Earth's surface, Q_S is the solar irradiance, A is the surface albedo, $Q_{LW}^{\downarrow}$ is the downward atmospheric irradiance and $Q_{LW}^{\uparrow}$ is the upward surface irradiance. The magnitude of these fluxes can be expressed in units of watts per square metre or joules per unit of time (for example, a globally averaged value of $1\,W\,m^{-2}$ is equal to $1.61 \times 10^{23}\,J$ per decade, with $1\,W = 1\,J\,s^{-1}$). One measure of land-cover change forcing of climate could be the perturbation to one of the components of the surface-energy balance equation (9.2) prior to feedbacks from the rest of the climate system.

In the past, climate-change metrics have been concerned with globally averaged responses, as exemplified in the GWP. However, as discussed previously in this chapter, global-scale climate changes can also occur due to land-use change, where Q_H and Q_{LE} are changed regionally but there is no change in the global average value. This occurred in the situation described by Chase *et al.* (1996, 2000), where there was no significant global-averaged change in these quantities (Figure 9.2). Figure 9.4 illustrates the anthropogenically caused change in leaf area index (see Nemani *et al.* 1996), which were used in the Chase *et al.* studies. It was the spatial redistribution of the Q_H and Q_{LE} pattern that resulted in the global climate change. Globally averaged climate change may therefore bear no well-defined relation to the real changes experienced in any region and these regional changes, which can be of any sign, are what impact on people and will stimulate mitigation strategies to be applied. Therefore, we identify a need for a surface 'regional climate-change potential' (RCCP), which addresses this deficiency. The RCCP would be defined to quantify where a direct human-caused change (either positive or negative) alters any of the individual terms in (9.2). These changes could be scaled by the surface area of the Earth to place them in a global context.

To provide a land-use-forcing term free of feedbacks, as in the case of radiative forcing, a land-surface scheme could be used to calculate perturbations to the surface-energy budget excluding feedbacks from the atmosphere. However, assessing the true global significance of these feedbacks is not trivial, since atmospheric circulation changes could give rise to remote climate changes that do not relate linearly to the perturbation in the region of land-use change (e.g. Gedney & Valdes 2000). To illustrate this point, the model results from Chase *et al.* (2000) presented in Figure 9.2 show the 10-year average absolute-value differences in the surface-energy flux for January and July (i.e. Q_{LE} and Q_H from (9.2)) between the climate with the current landscape and the climate with potential landscape that should exist under current atmospheric conditions without human intervention. Figure 9.5 presents the 10-year average value difference in the surface-energy flux between the two experiments for just the locations where the human-caused landscape change was prescribed in the model.

The 10-year average changes for the locations where only the land cover was altered were 5.3 and 4.7 W m^{-2} in January and 8.8 and 6.7 W m^{-2} in July for surface sensible heat flux and latent heat flux, respectively. The globally weighted changes in the sum of the absolute values of the surface sensible and latent heat flux changes for Figure 9.5 were 0.7 W m^{-2} in January and 1.08 W m^{-2} in July. With teleconnections changes also included (Figure 9.2), however, the globally averaged changes in the surface fluxes were significantly larger, with values of 9.47 W m^{-2} in January and 8.90 W m^{-2} in July. These results clearly demonstrate that regional landscape change can result in alterations to surface fluxes elsewhere in the world through nonlinear feedbacks within the atmosphere's global circulation. If the other terms in the surface-heat budget (9.2) were included, the magnitude of the differences (i.e. the RCCP) would presumably be even larger.

A potential based purely on surface-flux perturbations would not be analogous to GWP, because the latter is an index requiring an expression in terms of the abundance of atmospheric constituents. Direct comparison of land-cover change effects with greenhouse-gas emissions therefore remains a challenge. One possibility might be to dispense with quantification in terms of forcings and compare anthropogenic influences by modelling whole-system responses to individual causes of climate change. For example, Claussen (2003) compared biogeophysical and biogeochemical effects of land-cover change in terms of the overall climate change (as opposed to the forcing). A number of simulations were performed with an intermediate-complexity Earth system model, in each run altering a small part of the land surface and simulating its effects on global mean temperature (through changes in surface properties and carbon exchange). However, as stated above, global mean temperature changes may conceal important local and regional changes, so applications of this type of modelling approach again require a global quantification of absolute regional changes.

Conclusions

Atmospheric and ocean circulation patterns and their subsequent involvement within the planet's climate are dynamic, variable and difficult to predict. This limits the ability to predict the impact of land-use change and landscape dynamics on climate patterns. As a result, manipulating land-surface conditions for the purpose of carbon sequestration under the Kyoto Protocol could have a variety of unanticipated impacts on global and regional climate. The Kyoto Protocol uses only the GWPs of the regulated greenhouse-gas molecules listed in its Annex A as its mitigation currency. A more complete indication of human contributions to climate change will require the climatic influences of land-surface conditions and other processes to be factored into climate-change-mitigation strategies. Many of these processes will have strong regional effects that are not represented in a globally averaged metric. The currency of global and regional human-caused changes in terms of a regional climate change potential could offer a new metric useful for developing a more inclusive protocol. This concept would also implicitly provide a way to monitor potential local-scale environmental changes that could influence biodiversity.

Acknowledgements

The work reported in this chapter is a direct result of a meeting held on 18–23 October 2001 at the Aspen Global Change Institute entitled 'Forest management and global change: near-term decisions and long-term outcomes'. John Katzenberger's leadership in organizing this meeting is gratefully acknowledged. The work of R.A.B. forms part of the Climate Prediction Programme of the UK Department of the Environment, Food & Rural Affairs (contract no. PECD 7/12/37). Other support for this work was provided by NASA grants NAG8-1511 and NAG5-11370, and NSF LTER grant DEB 96-32852. We are very thankful to Naomi Peña for her recommendation to submit this chapter. Dallas Staley completed her standard excellent editorial preparation of this contribution.

References

Avissar, R. 1995 Recent advances in the representation of land-atmosphere interactions in general circulation models. *Rev. Geophys.* **33**, 1005–1010.

Betts, R. A. 1999 Self-beneficial effects of vegetation on climate in an Ocean–Atmosphere General Circulation Model. *Geophys. Res. Lett.* **26**, 1457–1460.

Betts, R. A. 2000 Offset of the potential carbon sink from boreal forestation by decreases in surface albedo. *Nature* **408**, 187–189.

Betts, R. A. 2001 Biogeophysical impacts of land use on present-day climate: near-surface temperature and radiative forcing. *Atmospheric Sci. Lett.* (DOI: 10.1006/asle.2001.0023.)

Chase, T. N., Pielke Sr, R. A., Kittel, T. G. F., Nemani, R. R. & Running, S. W. 1996 The sensitivity of a general circulation model to global changes in leaf area index. *J. Geophys. Res.* **101**, 7393–7408.

Chase, T. N., Pielke Sr, R. A., Kittel, T. G. F., Nemani, R. R. & Running, S. W. 2000 Simulated impacts of historical land cover changes on global climate in northern winter. *Climate Dynam.* **16**, 93–105.

Claussen, M. (ed.) 2003 Does landsurface matter in climate and weather? In *Vegetation, water, humans and the climate: a new perspective on an interactive system*, part A. A synthesis of the IGBP Core Project, Biospheric Aspects of the Hydrological Cycle. Springer. (In the press.)

Cox, P. M., Betts, R. A., Jones, C. D., Spall, S. A. & Totterdell, I. J. 2000 Acceleration of global warming due to carbon-cycle feedbacks in a coupled climate model. *Nature* **408**, 184–187.

Eastman, J. L., Coughenour, M. B. & Pielke Sr, R. A. 2001 The effects of CO_2 and landscape change using a coupled plant and meteorological model. *Global Change Biol.* **7**, 797–815.

Eastman, J. L., Coughenour, M. B. & Pielke Sr, R. A. 2001 Does grazing affect regional climate. *J. Hydrometeorol.* **2**, 243–253.

Gedney, N. & Valdes, P. J. 2000 The effect of Amazonian deforestation on the Northern Hemisphere circulation and climate. *Geophys. Res. Lett.* **27**, 3053–3056.

Hansen, J., Sato, M., Lacis, A. & Ruedy, R. 1997 The missing climate forcing. *Phil. Trans. R. Soc. Lond.* B **352**, 231–240.

IPCC 2001 *Climate change 2001: the scientific basis.* Cambridge University Press.

Jenkinson, D. S., Adams, D. E. & Wild, A. 1991 Model estimates of CO_2 emissions from soil in response to global warming. *Nature* **351**, 304–306.

Klein Goldewijk, K. 2001 Estimating global land use change over the past 300 years: the HYDE database. *Global Biogeochem. Cycles* **15**, 417–433.

Lawton, R. O., Nair, U. S., Pielke Sr, R. A. & Welch, R. M. 2001 Climatic impact of tropical lowland deforestation on nearby montane cloud forests. *Science* **294**, 584–587.

Lenton, T. M. 2000 Land and ocean carbon cycle feedback effects on global warming in a simple Earth system model. *Tellus* B **52**, 1159–1188.

Lyons, W. A. 1999 Lightning. In *Storms, hazard and disaster series* (ed. R. A. Pielke Sr & R. A. Pielke Jr), pp. 60–79. New York: Routledge.

Nemani, R. R., Running, S. W., Pielke, R. A. & Chase, T. N. 1996 Global vegetation cover changes from coarse resolution satellite data. *J. Geophys. Res.* **101**, 7157–7162.

Niyogi, D. S. 2000 Biosphere–atmosphere interactions coupled with carbon dioxide and soil moisture changes. PhD thesis, Department of Marine, Earth and Atmospheric Science, North Carolina State University.

Niyogi, D. S., Xue, Y.-K. & Raman, S. 2002 Hydrological feedback in a land–atmosphere coupling: comparison of a tropical and a midlatitudinal regime. *J. Hydrometeorol.* **3**, 39–56.

Niyogi, D. S., Xue. Y.-K. & Raman, S. 2003 Direct and interactive feedbacks of atmospheric carbon dioxide changes on terrestrial ecosystem response as a function of soil moisture availability. *J. Hydrometeorol.* (In the press.)

O'Brien, K. L. 2000 Upscaling tropical deforestation: implications for climate change. *Climatic Change* **44**, 311–329.

Pielke Sr, R. A. 2001*a* Influence of the spatial distribution of vegetation and soils on the prediction of cumulus convective rainfall. *Rev. Geophys.* **39**, 151–177.

Pielke Sr, R. A. 2001*b* Earth system modeling—an integrated assessment tool for environmental studies. In *Present and future of modeling global environmental change: toward integrated modeling* (ed. T. Matsuno & H. Kida), pp. 311–337. Tokyo: Terra Scientific.

World Resources Institute 1994 *World resources 1994–1995: a guide to the global environment.* Oxford University Press.

Wu, Z.-X. & Newell, R. E. 1998 Influence of sea surface temperature of air temperature in the tropic. *Climate Dynam.* **14**, 275–290.

Chapter 10

Economic, biological and policy constraints on the adoption of carbon farming in temperate regions

ALAN RENWICK, ANDREW S. BALL AND JULES N. PRETTY

Introduction

We begin with an analysis of the estimates of the potential capacity for agriculture to sequester carbon. The necessary land-use and management practices are then considered, followed by a discussion of the limitations in our understanding of the biological processes leading to soil-carbon sequestration and the techniques currently being developed to address this. We then consider the economics of soil sequestration. First, the difficulties in measuring the costs and benefits associated with carbon sequestration are considered. Policy implications are then discussed with particular reference to how existing agricultural policies (such as the EU's set-aside policy) may be adapted to promote carbon sequestration. Available empirical evidence on the marginal cost of carbon sequestration in agriculture is presented and this is compared with the likely value of carbon permits. Estimates of the potential financial benefits to agriculture are considered and finally conclusions are drawn as to the future positive role of temperate agriculture in carbon sequestration.

The role of agricultural land use in carbon sequestration in temperate regions

Pretty & Ball (2001) surveyed the results of long-term agricultural experiments in both Europe and North America and concluded that soil organic matter and soil carbon are lost during intensive cultivation, typically showing exponential decline after the first cultivation of virgin soils but with continuing steady loss over many years. Antle & McCarl (2002) note that when undisturbed soil is brought into cultivation the result is a loss of between 20 and 50% of soil carbon over a period of around 50 years, with the amount varying by soil type, agricultural practices and other site-specific conditions.

The Australian Greenhouse Office (AGO 2000) estimates that 80% of Australian mineral soils contain less than 80 tC ha^{-1}, representing a loss of half the soil carbon originally present in the top 20 cm of the soil profile.

The key to agriculture's contribution to mitigating climate change is that soil organic matter and soil carbon can be increased to new higher equilibria with sustainable management practices. Therefore, in most cultivated soils there is the potential to rebuild the soil-carbon stock. However, the biological processes that are ultimately responsible for the additional soil-carbon sequestration, either as recalcitrant soil-organic-matter fractions with a half life measured in hundreds of years (Puget *et al.* 2000), or as a result of increased microbial biomass resulting in increased carbon which may become tied into a decomposing cycle (Ball 1997), have yet to be fully elucidated. However, rapid advances in the field of soil microbiology are being made since the advent of techniques based on the extraction, amplification using polymerase chain reaction and examination of DNA directly from the soil without culturing, and these will lead to a greater understanding of critical soil processes. An additional advantage of storing carbon in soils is that it is less at risk from loss through wildfire and pest outbreaks than aboveground biomass or forestry. This is perhaps more important in the US and Australia, where fire is more prevalent than in Europe.

The potential role of agriculture is substantial. For example, Kern (see Lal *et al.* 1998 and references therein) estimates that US agricultural soils hold 7 Gt of carbon. It is estimated that the US has the potential to sequester between 75 and 208 Mt of carbon equivalence per year (Lal *et al.* 1998). On average this represents 8% of US emissions of greenhouse gas (GHG) or 24% of the US reduction commitment under the Kyoto Protocol. In Australia conservative estimates of potential sequestration are of between 3.5 and 5 MtC yr^{-1} over a 20-year period for the 50 Mha of arable land and 13–15 MtC yr^{-1} for the 425 Mha of rangelands (AGO 2000). In Canada it is estimated that 736 MtC could be sequestered over the next 20 years (ASCCC 1999).

The Royal Society (2001) published figures, derived from the IPCC, which suggest that globally a total of between 1.53 and 2.47 PgC yr^{-1} could be sequestered between 2000 and 2050. Using the mid-point of these annual estimates they suggest that a total of 100 PgC could be sequestered during this period, of which just under 50% could come from temperate soils. Nonetheless, there is considerable uncertainty about the actual potential for soil sequestration, let alone whether the needed international cooperation could be attained to achieve this level of sequestration. In addition The Royal Society estimates that the required reduction in carbon in the atmosphere will be a total of 1000 PgC by 2100 and 400 by 2050. They therefore argue that the land sinks and forestry can only provide a part of the required reduction.

The potential role for agriculture in helping achieve targets such as those set under the Kyoto agreement does vary between locations. For example, The Royal Society notes that, for the UK, the possibilities of mitigation through land (0.006–0.008 PgC yr^{-1}, equivalent to 4–6% of 1990 carbon dioxide (CO_2) emissions) is proportionally less than for Europe as a whole, as land area is small in relation to emissions. This disparity in the potential for soils to act

Table 10.1. *Sources and sinks in temperate agricultural systems*

	Sources	Sinks
transformations	croplands from wetlands	set-aside (to grassland or woodland)
	croplands from grasslands	
	croplands from natural ecosystems	
production	lower residue yield (inorganic fertilizer inputs)	higher residue yield
	change to crop types with lower biomass	change to crop types with higher biomass
	lower lignin content	higher lignin content
	longer fallow	shorter fallow
soil conservation	intensive till	no or minimum till
	residue straw sales	incorporation
	stubble burning	cover crops (inter-row with perennials)
		control of soil water
other	liming	animal manure or sewage sludge

Sources: Taken from NRDC (2000) and Watson *et al.* (2000).

as sinks will mean those countries where options are limited (such as the UK and Japan) may be disadvantaged compared with those countries where there is greater potential (the US, Russia, Canada, Australia). If soil sinks are accepted, then the latter countries may use them to offset emissions in place of actual reductions in emissions (which may be more costly to industry). This could alter the international competitiveness of energy-intensive products.

A key point is that agricultural soils provide a short-term solution for reducing greenhouse gases. This is because they are finite in scale and require no technological change to make them operational. Therefore, it may be reasoned that their greatest use lies in an immediate focus on carbon sequestration while effective and efficient renewable energy sources that do not emit GHGs are developed.

Losses of soil carbon occur in agricultural soils primarily due to intensive crop-production systems following conversion of natural perennial vegetation. The factors that have most influence on soil-carbon levels are the amount and quality of the input of plant residues to the soil and the climate (temperature and rainfall). Soil properties (such as clay content) also affect soil-carbon levels. Table 10.1 highlights how the sink capacity of soils can be improved and the areas where there is still potential for agriculture to act as a source of CO_2. Soil sequestration can be achieved by changing land use, for example from cropping to set-aside, or management practices such as conservation tillage.

Evidence from Europe (reviewed in Smith *et al.* (2000)) suggests that woodland regeneration can lead to accumulation of 3.3 tC ha^{-1} yr^{-1} and short-rotation coppicing to 6.62 tC ha^{-1} yr^{-1}. It is also shown that other prac-

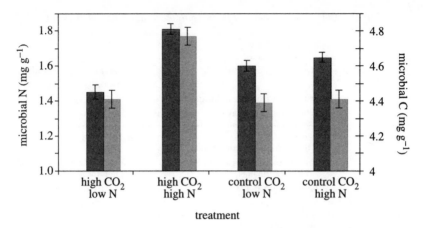

Figure 10.1. Microbial C (light grey bar) and N (dark grey bar) of control soil (360 ppm) and soil collected exposed to elevated atmospheric CO_2 (ambient plus 200 ppm CO_2) exposed to high and low N fertilization rates (350 kg ha^{-1} yr^{-1}, respectively) at Arizona free air–CO_2 enrichment site in September 1998. Standard errors are shown. (From Porteous *et al.* (2003).)

tices, such as zero till and the inclusion of grassland in rotations, can lead to substantial carbon sequestration. Pretty & Ball (2001) cite many studies that found accumulation of organic matter under integrated systems. In Australia (AGO 2000) it is argued that, because of the sheer scale of agricultural systems (45–50 Mha of land are either under pasture, cropped continuously or rotated through a crop–pasture sequence), even small changes in sequestration per hectare could lead to large increases in sequestered carbon.

The changes considered in Table 10.1 range from simple management practices to complete land-use changes. One of the most discussed changes in management practices is the move to zero- or minimum-till techniques. 'Conservation tillage', 'no-till' or 'zero-till' systems maintain a permanent or semi-permanent organic cover on the soil, comprising either a growing crop or dead organic matter. The function is to protect the soil from the action of sun, rain and wind and to feed soil biota. Decomposition of the additional dead organic matter by the soil microflora will stimulate the activity and diversity of the microflora, resulting in increased stabilization of the dead organic matter in the forms of humic substances. However, increased microbial activity and microbial biomass also lead to increased respiration rates and therefore increased release of CO_2 by soils. Current research in the area of soil biology is aimed at understanding the effects on soil microbial biomass, diversity and activity of changes in both climate and land-management changes, leading to predictive models which will be essential if the potential of soils for carbon sequestration under systems such as zero till under future climate change are to be realized. Understanding the role of microbial diversity and activity in the sequestration of carbon may lead to the developments of land-management practices, developed on the basis of empirical data, which can increase the carbon sequestration potential of soils.

Table 10.2. *Species richness and Shannon–Weiner diversity index (H') value for soil collected in Arizona, calculated from BIOLOG and DGGE profiles*

CO_2 treatment	N application	BIOLOG Species richness	BIOLOG Diversity (H')	DGGE Species richness	DGGE diversity (H')
ambient	low	31	1.490	30	1.32
ambient	high	31	1.496	30	1.31
elevated	low	31	1.499	28	1.30
elevated	high	31	1.502	23	1.17

Source: Porteous (2003).

Table 10.3. *Losses and gains of carbon under conventional and zero-tillage management systems in the USA*

System	Rotations	Gains or losses of carbon $(tC\ ha\ yr^{-1})$
plough	continuous maize or wheat	−0.105 to −0.460
	mixed rotations and cover crops	−0.033 to −0.065
zero till	continuous maize or soyabeans	0.330 to 0.585
	mixed rotations and cover crops	0.660 to 1.310

Sources: Data taken from Pretty & Ball (2001) (adapted from Reicosky *et al.* (1995); Langdale *et al.* (1992); and Edwards *et al.* (1988, 1992)).

For example, Figure 10.1 illustrates the interactive effects of atmospheric climate change and land-management practice on soil microbial biomass by showing the results of exposure of soil to elevated atmospheric CO_2 under both high- and low-fertilization regimes. This exposure resulted in a 20% increase in microbial C in soils exposed to elevated atmospheric CO_2 irrespective of the N concentration. Addition of high quantities of N increased the microbial biomass content of both soils. Whether this increase in microbial biomass is a permanent feature of the soils is unknown. However, evaluation of the microbial diversity of the control and fumigated soils, assessed using microbial-diversity measurements such as denaturing gradient gel electrophoresis (DGGE) and microbial-activity measurements such as BIOLOG plates, indicates that the increased microbial biomass observed is not accompanied by an increase in soil microbial diversity, but rather by either no change in the diversity indices or a decrease in microbial diversity when the DGGE results were interpreted (Table 10.2).

The potential result of such land-management changes is reduced soil erosion and improved soil organic matter and carbon content. The gains from such systems compared with conventional methods can be seen for the USA in Table 10.3. It would appear that intensive arable with zero tillage results in accumulation of 0.3–0.6 tC ha^{-1} yr^{-1} but zero tillage with mixed rotations and cover crops can accumulate carbon at a faster rate (0.66–1.33 tC ha^{-1} yr^{-1}).

It has been shown that through changes in land-use and management practices it is technically possible for agriculture to play a significant role in sequestering carbon. However, many technical studies fail to take into account the economic feasibility of such practices, as they ignore the cost and resource allocation implications of changes in land-use or management practice. The next section considers the economics of soil sequestration and also considers how a policy to encourage sequestration may be implemented.

Economic considerations

The issues raised when considering the economics of carbon sequestration and appropriate policy design are complex. This is mainly due to the existence of market failures. However, these failures are not unique to carbon and many of the issues are similar to the provision of other environmental benefits, and so parallels can therefore be drawn.

The public-good nature of the atmosphere means that there is little incentive for individuals or even nations to take actions to prevent GHG accumulation. Given this situation, it is clear that action has to come from coordinated government policy and this is the underlying rationale for the Kyoto Protocol. A price for carbon may be seen to arise from either direct government payments or governments setting limits and allowing trade, although Antle & McCarl (2002) do note that incentives may arise as a result of action by interested groups or by firms wishing to show environmental responsibility. Firms already engaging in carbon projects may be doing so in anticipation of future legislation.[1]

Opportunity costs

Antle & McCarl (2002) highlight the fact that the economic feasibility and competitiveness of soil C sequestration depend on the opportunity cost per tC, that is, the opportunity cost per hectare of changing land-use or management practices divided by the rate of soil accumulation. The key issue is whether this cost is competitive with alternative methods of reducing GHG such as forestry or emission reduction.

When considering the opportunity costs, a key factor is the spatial variability in the productivity of land. This variability means that the opportunity cost associated with changing land-use and management practices will also vary. For example, Asby & Renwick (2000) highlight the fact that the profitability of wheat production in the UK varies by £330 per hectare between the most and least profitable quartile group of cereal producers. This variability can also be seen by analysis of farmers' offer curves for placing land into set-aside voluntarily (CRER 2001). These are plotted in Figure 10.2.

---

[1]For example, the Tokyo Electric Power Company (TEPCO) has invested US$5 million in Tamar tree farms in Tasmania for 3000 ha of eucalyptus plantation, which is expected to yield TEPCO 130 kt of carbon credits. The payment amounts to $38 US per tC (Pretty & Ball 2001).

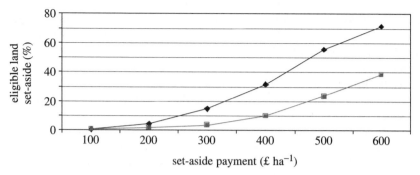

Figure 10.2. Area of arable land set-aside under different payments. Cereal price: diamonds, £70 per tonne; squares, £100 per tonne. From CRER (2001).

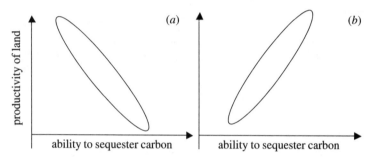

Figure 10.3. Possible relationships between land productivity and carbon sequestration.

The figure reflects producers' perceptions as to the opportunity costs of changing land use. For example, to achieve a level of set-aside of 10%, a payment of between £200 and £300 (with cereal prices of £70 per tonne) would have to be made, whereas the payment would have to be over £500 per hectare to retire 50% of eligible land.

However, as noted above, these figures reflect only the opportunity costs in terms of lost income for a change in land use. For an efficient policy the fact that land also varies in its ability to sequester carbon needs to be taken into account. The possible impact of this on the policy is highlighted in Figure 10.3. Here two hypothetical relationships between land productivity (and hence opportunity cost of land-use change) and sequestration potential are plotted. In Figure 10.3 the ellipses represent confidence intervals for the relationship between land productivity and ability to sequester carbon, such that 95% of observations can be found within them.

In Figure 10.3a an inverse relationship between the ability to sequester carbon and the productivity of land is depicted. This may be a reasonable argument based on the impact of soil organic matter on the yield potential of land.[1] Under this scenario, the most appropriate land to target for change

---

[1] The AGO argues that practices that enhance carbon are likely to have more impact on highly depleted soils.

would be the least productive land (this land would also have the lowest opportunity cost for change). This would make the opportunity cost per tonne of carbon sequestered relatively low. Figure 10.3b, on the other hand, highlights the situation where there is a positive relationship between carbon and productivity. In this case the most productive land is also that which has the most ability to sequester carbon. If this is the case, then the opportunity cost per tonne of carbon sequestered would be much higher.

Therefore, knowledge of both the productive capacity of land and its ability to sequester carbon are necessary to calculate the true opportunity cost of sequestering a tonne of carbon. However, the situation is complicated further by the fact that changes in land-use or management practices may produce other costs and benefits not directly related to carbon sequestration. These are considered in the following section.

Externalities

The benefits arising from soil sequestration are multi-dimensional in that the individual business, the wider national community and the international community all benefit. There are gains to the individual farmer because increased soil organic matter is linked to increased productivity. Wider gains to the community may be achieved, as improved soil structure can reduce pollution from agriculture (for example, from sedimentation or run-off). Finally, the mitigation of global warming provides international benefits.

It is clear that the gains to the farmer are internal and hence, as long as they have sufficient information, it is possible that they will optimize the stock of carbon for their business. However, as soil carbon is not observable, it is argued that farmers are not sufficiently aware of the quantity they have in their soil and are therefore unable to optimize soil carbon for their own benefit (Antle & McCarl 2002). In addition, as individual farmers are unlikely to take into account the national and international benefits of increased carbon in soils when operating their business, this will lead to an under-provision of soil carbon. Therefore, a policy that provides the necessary incentives to increase the level of soil carbon should move society towards a more efficient resource allocation.

An understanding of the externalities associated with increasing carbon in soils is important when considering how policy should be designed to achieve a socially optimal level of sequestration from agriculture (Pretty 1995; Pretty *et al.* 2000). McCarl & Schneider (1999a) list the possible positive and negative externalities from sequestration, shown below.

Positive externalities are as follows:

- Reduced soil erosion may result as the soil structure improves. This will lead to less sedimentation and improved water quality.

- Reduced tillage could alter soil organic matter, increasing soil water-holding capacity and leading to less irrigation water.

- Expanded conversion of agricultural lands to grasslands or forests could stimulate wildlife populations.

- Diminished use of fertilizer could alter chemical content of run-off from agricultural land with effects on quality and ecology. This would improve the situation for non-agricultural users.

- Diversion of agricultural land into energy crops may lead to technological improvements which may permit expanded electricity generation at lower cost.

Negative externalities are as follows:

- Movement of new land into forestry may have detrimental impact on the economics of forestry and lead to deforestation.

- Changes in land use may not necessarily improve the environment[1].

- Reduction in tillage in some areas may lead to an increased use of pesticides.

- If expanded carbon is equal to reduced food and fibre this may lead to higher prices and reduced exports.

The above list highlights a crucial point that introducing new land-management systems will not only provide significant greenhouse benefits but support broader objectives of ecologically sustainable development (AGO 2000). It is this link that the Australians see as an important driver for implementing activities that enhance soil carbon. It is clear though that as far as the wider environment is concerned the land use is very important. For example, the move to zero till with increased use of herbicide chemicals may improve the soil structure but may have relatively small environmental benefits in terms of improving wildlife habitats.

For an accurate measure of the opportunity cost per tonne it is clear that the externalities like those cited above need to be taken into account when calculating the costs of changing land-use or management practices. However, this does raise important questions about the valuation of environmental benefits. This is an issue that arises with many environmental payments. Unless the full benefits of environmental programmes are known, it will not be possible to design a policy that optimizes them. The impact of incorporating externalities is considered in the next subsection, where the economics of a possible method of increasing soil carbon, zero till, is examined.

The economics of zero till

In this section the economics of conservation-tillage techniques are considered. It is clear that even without payments for carbon these techniques have become increasingly popular. For example, it is estimated that around 19 Mha in the US is under various forms of conservation-tillage (not strictly zero till) and in Canada and Australia (where moisture retention is a major benefit)

---

[1]For example, there are claims that the TEPCO project discussed above is accelerating the destruction of native forests, in order to plant fast-growing eucalyptus.

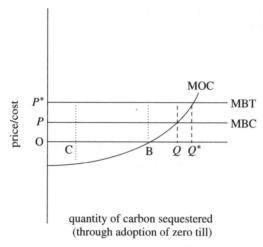

Figure 10.4. The economics of using zero till to sequester carbon.

areas are also increasing. Zero till is yet to be widely adopted in the EU. It may be assumed that those adopting conservation-tillage techniques do so because they are more profitable. If this is the case, then increased use should be possible through wider dissemination of information about the benefits through education and extension. However, other factors are important in the decision to change to low-till methods. First, as it involves a complete change in management, producers may not have the ability or confidence to adopt the methods. Second, there may be large initial capital outlays, such as for new drills and other equipment.[1] Therefore, businesses that are capital constrained may not be able to invest in this new technology. Third, it has been argued that though on average zero-till techniques may be more profitable they do result in greater year-on-year variability in returns and hence risk (ASCCC 1999).[2] The first constraint may be overcome to a certain extent by education and extension efforts. It is possible that the capital constraints may be overcome by one-off grants, or some form of conversion payments could be made for a specified period. The question of risk is one that is preoccupying policy makers in Europe and the US, and the answer may lie in some form of crop or revenue insurance.

Figure 10.4 highlights some of the issues surrounding the adoption of conservation techniques such as zero till (but can be generalized to represent all land use changes). In the figure, MOC represents the marginal opportunity cost for the farm of adopting these techniques. It is drawn as a rising function because clearly not all land is equally suitable for zero-till techniques.

---

[1]For example, in Australia drills can cost around $AU150 000. In addition one farmer made the point that due to the differences between the summer and winter planting conditions they might actually require two different types of drill (Batterham 2001, personal communication).

[2]Whether zero till leads to greater variability is contested. However, it may be argued that if producers perceive it as more risky, then they may not adopt the technique.

For example, in the UK it is estimated that around 80% of cereal land (38% of arable land) is suitable (Smith *et al.* 2000). It has been argued that some farmers will profit from conversion and hence the MOC is negative for at least part of its length.

The current situation may be reflected by a point such as C (Figure 10.4). Here a number of farms have converted to zero till with the subsequent increase in the amount of carbon sequestered in the soil. However, further gains for the sector could be made by increased adoption of the technique. These gains would continue up to point B, where internal gains from adoption of carbon sequestration would be maximized (this is the point where MOC is equal to zero). However, given the external benefits this is not an optimum amount for society. First if we consider the benefits of reduced global warming (represented by MBC),[1] then the quantity Q should be sequestered. However, if we include the other external benefits such as improved water quality (and with the assumption that the net benefits are positive), then the total marginal benefits can be represented by MBT. Under this situation, the optimal level of carbon sequestered by zero till is at the higher quantity of Q^*. Therefore, for society it would be beneficial to encourage the adoption of zero till for those farms where the internal economics do not justify it. This analysis suggests that significant progress (a movement towards point B) could be made through improved extension to farms. The figure also gives an insight to the public versus private debate. If a market for carbon is established and carbon has a value, this value may be represented by MBC. However, this would not lead to the optimum level for society as a whole and some form of government payment for the additional benefits may be required ($P^* - P$). These issues are discussed in more detail in the section on 'Policy considerations'. The following subsection considers further issues surrounding sequestration through agricultural practices.

Measurement costs

A major complication is that, in order to calculate the cost per tonne of carbon sequestered, accurate measurement of soil carbon is required. There are two issues: first whether the technology is really available to accurately calculate soil-carbon accumulation, and second the level of costs associated with obtaining these measurements.

A possible drawback with carbon sequestration is that the costs of obtaining accurate measures required for international acceptance may be so high as to make the whole scheme uneconomical. While general estimates have been made of the sequestration ability of soil, a large amount of uncertainty exists as to measurement. For an optimal policy to be designed it is clear that a fundamental prerequisite is that the amount of soil-carbon flux in soils can

---

[1]For simplicity, MBC and MBT are drawn as non-decreasing functions of quantity of carbon sequestered. This may be the case if agriculture is a small player in reducing emissions and hence the quantity sequestered through agriculture has little impact. The analysis is equally valid if we draw the marginal benefit curves as sloping downwards.

be monitored. According to the NRDC (2000) there are several options for measuring soil-carbon flux in a given country:

- Employing a system of towers that can sample changes in ambient CO_2 levels at a given site.

- Using soil investigations and census and topographical data for setting priorities for sampling soil-carbon flux throughout the country and modelling the results for a national estimate (subsequently ground-truth models assumptions can be assessed through site sampling).

- Implementing a large-scale expansion of soil-carbon flux sampling that would apply to most individual farms, such that individual farmers could receive rewards based on the actual level of carbon sequestered.

According to the NRDC, all these methods have their drawbacks. The first can be dismissed as too expensive, based on the scale necessary to create a national inventory. The second is flawed because existing investigations are not considered sufficiently comprehensive in spatial area, crop type and typography to provide sufficient data for reasonably accurate model-based national estimate. A convincing predictive ability to estimate carbon flux that considers the many variables of soil type, climate, management and crop type is not yet available, although under investigation. For the third approach, consideration of the logistical problems involved suggests it would not be feasible to institute comprehensive sampling of agricultural soil flux at the farm level at reasonable cost. For example, in the US the number of farms exceeds two million and, as a range of samples would have to be taken from larger farms with heterogeneous crops, practices and conditions the sampling requirements would be too great. In addition, none of the methods attempts to study the microbial activity and diversity present in the soils, but rather merely study the result of their activity.

The NRDC notes that, in the US, considerable resources have gone into developing a model-based approach supplemented by remote sensing. However, these aggregated approaches pose a problem for incentive programmes. Summary parameters based on estimates of the frequency of different practices may be difficult to disprove or prove at the level of a single farm or single hectare. Monitoring and incentives provided at a larger scale, for example by bundling farms, may offer practical difficulties if the bundled units are heterogeneous in terms of practices and conditions. If rewards are offered to individual farmers, then there is a need for verification and reporting at the level of the individual farmer, but the costs of such monitoring and verification may be prohibitive. Factoring in the effect of climate in terms of its spatial variability and also changes over time is an added complication for soil-carbon models.

In contrast to the NRDC, Sandor & Skees (1999) argue that it is not necessary to be concerned with measuring how much additional carbon is sequestered on an individual field, as there are more effective ways of monitoring and verification. They argue that wholesalers in carbon sequestering could develop, and while estimates at an individual level may be flawed, they argue that the error has typical statistical properties and that estimating many individual parcels and aggregating them into one parcel will improve the estimate considerably. However, such an approach still leaves unanswered the problem of incentives at the individual farm level.

Another issue related to measurement is raised by the AGO. Here they argue that information is not currently available about soil conservation management practices taking place. They argue that this is needed to establish a baseline from which future changes can be measured. This is particularly important if international agreement is to be reached on the use of soil as a carbon sink. In the EU such a database may be quite easily obtained, for arable land at least, through the Integrated Arable Cropping System. It could be extended to consider tillage methods as well as the current information on land use.

The analysis to date has shown that the calculation of the real opportunity costs associated with using agriculture to sequester carbon is complicated by the existence of externalities and the difficulties of measuring changes in soil carbon. However, even if these difficulties are overcome there is still a large number of issues surrounding the design of a policy to encourage carbon sequestration.

Policy considerations

Finiteness and permanence

The AGO notes that building soil-carbon levels is a slow process and that they could take decades to increase as a minimum sustained management of inputs will be needed over many years. A major issue with soil sequestration is that the quantity of carbon that can be sequestered is finite, as gains cannot be counted as a recurring annual sink. Initially they can offset emissions, but later the net gain falls towards zero as the new equilibrium is approached. However, once the sink has become saturated there is still the need to maintain to carbon in the soil. McCarl & Schneider (1999a) argue that the accumulation and storage of carbon needs to be considered when designing policy.

A major problem with sequestration through changes in management practice is that the process is easily reversible. If at some time the landowner reverts to less-friendly practices such as ploughing or tree felling, then the stored carbon will be lost. Therefore, land-based sinks cannot be considered to be permanent, unlike reductions in emissions. There is a need to ensure that the alterations are maintained.

A second issue raised by McCarl & Schneider (1999) is the need to prevent countervailing actions. Countervailing actions are important, as the adoption of emission-reduction strategies in one segment of the economy may lead to a substantial offset by actions in other parts of the economy. A prime example may be if agricultural land is converted to forestry (and if demand for forestry products does not change) there will be an increase in supply, which reduces price and therefore the returns from forestry. There may be an incentive to move existing land from forestry into agriculture. This is in addition to the fact that the potential exists for the new forestry land to revert after one rotation. McCarl & Schneider argue that there may be a case for a policy with a semi-permanent ban on deforestation and non-reversion clauses.

Property rights

The above points touch on the fundamental issue of property rights. This relates to the responsibilities of farmers with respect to carbon emissions and storage. If it is reasonable to argue that farmers had no need to consider the release of carbon from their land in the past, then the current position may be used to define the reference level for property rights. Having established a reference level, it may be valid to apply the 'polluter pays' principle to those who diminish carbon levels further and the 'provider gets' principle for those increasing the amount of carbon stored in their soil. However, the instigation of policies that apply the 'polluter pays' principle for those who continue to deplete soil-carbon levels may face stiff opposition from the farming community.

An example of the likely difficulties associated with payments for environmental improvement can be seen with the Countryside Stewardship Scheme as operated in the UK. Eligibility for this scheme is assessed on a number of criteria but one is to provide environmental gains. Now those who have already undertaken improvements at their own cost may not be able to show that joining the scheme will bring further gains and hence may not be accepted. In contrast those who have neglected their environment, or worse actively degraded it, can show the greatest benefit from joining the scheme. A parallel may be drawn with carbon sequestration. Those who have already undertaken conservation techniques may not be eligible for payments, while those who have degraded their soils will be able to show the most carbon-sequestering potential. If the scheme is not carefully designed, there may be an incentive for those producers who already practice conservation measures to plough up their land to take advantage of possible government payments (this is the perverse incentive problem considered by Wu & Babcock (1996)). It is argued that this problem may be overcome by setting a baseline year (such as 1990) and crediting those that can show they have changed practices since this period. It is argued that even if this not acceptable to the international community, an individual government could still buy and hold the credits from those who have already changed their land-use techniques.

Transaction costs

Antle *et al.* (2001) note that there are two costs associated with sequestering carbon. Firstly there is the opportunity cost of the farm and secondly there is the cost associated with implementing contracts and that involves brokerage fees, monitoring and other transaction costs. An example of the potential importance of contract costs has already been shown with the possible costs of measuring changes in carbon. Enforcement costs are likely to vary, depending on the way that sequestration is undertaken. For example, changes in land use are relatively easy to monitor, and the EU already has a system in place for arable land, which could be easily adapted for the needs of carbon sequestration. However, changes in practices (such as tillage techniques) would be harder to monitor and therefore ensuring compliance may be more expensive. These issues reflect the fact that there are likely to be problems with asymmetric information, as the producer is likely to know more than the regulator.

Antle *et al.* (2001) proceed to formally assess the relative merits of a per-hectare payment compared with a payment per tonne sequestered. (The 'per-tonne sequestered' in Antle *et al.*'s work is not assessed on a per-field basis but is estimated on the best available information about the impact of changes in land use or practices within specified regions (agroecozones).)

Detailed analysis is undertaken and, allowing for spatial heterogeneity, it is argued that a per-tonne payment is likely to be more efficient than a per-hectare payment. That is, the marginal opportunity cost of the per-hectare payment mechanism is likely to be greater than the per-tonne mechanism. This is particularly the case with high variability in land quality, because those farmers with land with a low ability to sequester carbon will enter a per-hectare payment scheme and hence the cost per tonne of carbon will be increased.

Consideration has to be given to the question of additionality. If farmers have changed or were going to change their practices anyway, then it may be considered inefficient to compensate them for doing so. This is particularly the case if changes have been undertaken that improve the profitability of the business (this can be seen with the adoption of zero till in many countries). However, it may be reasoned that payments are valid, as they reflect the true value of the practice to society. For example, if the economics of agriculture changes (due to, say, some technological advance) and zero till becomes for some reason less profitable than conventional tillage practices, the payment may keep farmers using zero till, thereby preserving the environmental gains in the longer term.

The analysis so far has concentrated on a discussion of the factors that impact on the economics of carbon sequestration and how these will influence policy design. The following section considers how policy may be enacted.

Policy implementation

Much work has concentrated on how a policy to encourage carbon sequestration should be designed (Antle & Mooney 1999; Feng *et al.* 2001; McCarl & Schneider 1999). An immediate question and one directly related to the overall theme of this book is whether the establishment of a market for carbon is the appropriate instrument or whether direct government payments are required. As mentioned above, a market could be developed if GHG emissions are controlled and trading allowed. However, as in the discussion of zero till highlighted, the existence of externalities means that a free-market approach is unlikely to lead to an optimal level of sequestration. For example, on the assumption that the externalities associated with carbon storage are positive, the market value for carbon itself (based purely on the costs or value of reducing carbon in the atmosphere) will be too low for agriculture to optimize sequestration.

If some form of direct government involvement is required, then the question clearly arises as to how this can best be undertaken. When considering the possible policy options to encourage soil sequestration it should be remembered that the government already heavily intervenes in the agricultural sector in all industrialized countries. This means that there may be some scope for altering existing policies to achieve the goals of carbon sequestration.

A key factor is that, for many countries in temperate climates, the price of agricultural products is maintained at an artificially high level. This means that alternative land-use options, such as the production of non-food crops or environmental goods, are disadvantaged. Therefore, it may be argued that the first step to encouraging practices such as carbon sequestration would be to remove these distortionary price supports. In relation to our earlier analysis this would reduce the opportunity cost to farms of adopting practices that sequester carbon. The EU has taken steps in this direction through the reduction of the level of price support offered for cereals. Though farmers are still influenced in their land-use decision by the fact that these price cuts have been compensated for by direct area-based and headage payments.

The 'greening' of agricultural policy offers a potential source of revenue to encourage sequestration. For example, in the US and EU, environmental payments are offered under a range of programmes (the Environmental Quality Incentives Program (EQIP) and the Conservation Reserve Program (CRP) in the US and the Rural Development Programme in the EU). Often these payments are made on a per-hectare basis (CRP, Environmentally Sensitive Areas, etc.) (Dobbs & Pretty 2001). These payments have been considered to be inefficient, as they do not take account of the relative opportunity cost of obtaining the specified benefits. For example, it has been argued in the US that much of the land 'retired' may not have been in production anyway (McCarl & Schneider 1999a). However, they are relatively easy to administer and police.

A European example highlights the potential for altering existing policies. At present in the EU a form of compulsory set-aside is in operation. This policy was initially implemented as a form of supply control; however, it became clear that it could also provide environmental benefits. It has been shown that specific land use on set-aside can lead to an accumulation of carbon. However, the current system in the EU was not designed with this in mind and hence is not an efficient approach for a number of reasons. First, in order to be eligible for area aid payments, farmers (with the exception of small farmers, who are exempt) are required to set-aside land. This is beneficial in that the coverage of set-aside is large; however, no account of the opportunity cost of producers is made. Economic efficiency could be improved by targeting set-aside at the high-cost producers. Alternatively, set-aside could be targeted at those who can provide the greatest level of environmental benefits (including carbon sequestration) through allowing trade and linking payment to value of output provided. A further problem with set-aside in its current form is that, in the UK at least, the vast majority of producers rotate the set-aside land around their holding (74% according to CRER 2001). Given that zero tillage is not widely practiced in the UK, this suggests that a gain can only arise if the losses from reploughing are less than the gains from setting aside the next piece of land. A final problem is that the set-aside rate has varied from year to year depending on the market situation for cereals. Again, this means that gains are lost as land is moved back and forth between intensive cropping and set-aside.

CRER (2001) proposes a more environmentally targeted scheme with farmers tendering to provide a specific set of benefits. These benefits are then weighted according to their importance. These weights could vary spatially. It is clear that such a scheme could include carbon sequestration as one potential benefit. Following Antle *et al.*'s arguments this should in theory be in the form of tC accumulated rather than just a change in land use, although in practice changes in land use may be the only viable indicator. A problem with this approach is that it does require the policymaker to have some idea of the relative value of the various environmental benefits on offer in order to determine the weights.

Bruce *et al.* (1998) consider the possible policy actions required to encourage a wide range of management practices for the US (Table 10.4). Here they argue that the options available to the government are some form of cost-share arrangement, education and training and conservation compliance.

Feng *et al.* (2001), consider how policy can be designed given that soil-carbon sequestration is potentially reversible. Their analysis is equally applicable whether payments come through government policy or through a fully functioning market for carbon credits, though their discussion is couched in terms of a functioning market that determines the price of carbon abatement. That is, the price of one unit of carbon credit is the price associated with one unit of permanent carbon reduction. They consider three policy designs, which they term 'pay as you go' (PAYG), 'variable-length contract' (VLC) and the 'carbon annuity account' (CAA).

The PAYG system applies the price of one full credit for each unit of carbon released or sequestered, with no consideration given to the permanence issue. However, while a sink owner gets rewarded a full credit when they remove one unit of carbon from the atmosphere, they will also have to pay a full credit when they release the sequestered carbon. In the VLC, the temporary carbon sequestering will be paid at a discounted rate. The rate of discount will depend on how long the carbon is kept out of the atmosphere. Under the CAA approach the generator/maintainer of the sink is paid the full carbon price and payment is made directly into an annuity account. As long as the sink remains in place, the sink operator can access the earnings of the annuity account but not the principal sum. The principal is recovered by the ongoing permit price if and when the carbon is released. If the sink remains permanently, the sink owner eventually earns all of the interest payments, the discounted present value of which equals the principal itself (the permanent permit price). All three methods have potential drawbacks but they do suggest that policy can be designed to overcome the problem of permanence.

Table 10.4. *Possible policy actions to attain changes in management practices*

Management practice	Relative carbon gain	Possible policy actions
cultivated lands		
adoption of no-till or reduced-till	M	CS ETA CC
use of winter cover crops	L	CS ETA
elimination of summer fallow	M	CS ETA
use of forages in rotations	M	CS ETA
use of manures and other organic fertilizers	M	CS ETA
set-aside lands		
establish perennial grasses	H	CS LR
soil/water conservation measures	H	CS ETA CC
establish forests	H	CS LR
restore wetlands	H	CS
pasturelands		
improved grazing methods	M	CS ETA
fertilizer applications	M	CS ETA
irrigation	M	CS

H denotes high; M, medium; L, low; CS denotes cost share (paying all or part of the costs of implementing the practice; cost could be defined to include lost income); CC, conservation compliance (requires landowner to participate in a market transaction, commodity support or other governmental programme with economic benefits); ETA, education and technical support (requires that practice be profitable); LR, land retirement (providing payments, usually annually, for land to be put into specific uses).
Source: Bruce *et al.* (1998).

The next section considers some of the, admittedly sketchy, empirical evidence on the costs of sequestering carbon in agriculture and how this relates to estimates of the value of carbon.

Estimates of the cost and returns from carbon sequestration

There have been a number of studies that have attempted to quantify the marginal opportunity cost of sequestering carbon in agriculture. A study of the work by McCarl & Schneider (1999*b*) suggested that agriculture could operate for as low as $10–$25 per tonne. A later paper by Antle & McCarl (2002) analysed a number of mainly US studies and concluded that the least-cost agriculture providers could be competitive with alternative methods such as forestry and emission reductions but that payments in excess of $50 per tonne may be required for agriculture to be a major player. Pautsch *et al.* (2001) estimate that the cost of soil sequestration through low tillage ranges from zero to $400 per tonne, depending on the quantity of carbon sequestered.

These estimates can be related to the current estimated market value of carbon to give some indication of whether agriculture would be competitive in a market situation of permits and trade. The estimates of the sequestration costs of agriculture seem high in relation to the current estimated market value of carbon. Pretty & Ball (2001) highlight that the range of prices in some pilot schemes is between $1 and $38 per tonne of carbon, though common values are in the low $2.50–$5.00 range. These values are similar to those found for tropical forestry by Pearce *et al.* (1998).

Earlier work seems to have been more optimistic about the likely value of carbon; for example, Sandor & Skees (1999) reported estimates of the value of carbon-emissions allowances ranging from $15 to $348 per tonne, though they concluded at the time that early market signals suggested a market value of carbon of between $20 and $30 per tonne. The current estimated value of carbon also seems low in relation to the potential damage that global warming will cause. It has been estimated that when worldwide losses are taken into account each tonne reduction in carbon could be worth as much as $95 (Eyre *et al.* 1997).

Pretty & Ball (2001) cite estimates produced in Comis (2001) that the potential addition to gross income in the US from carbon sequestration ranges from $100m (with low C accumulation and a price of $5 per tonne) to $4 billion (high C and $20 per tonne). Sandor & Skees (1999) suggest that carbon could increase the net farm income of the US farming community by 10% (though this is based on the high-end estimates as cited in Comis (2001)). Pretty & Ball (2001) use similar ranges for carbon accumulation and price as those considered in Comis (2001) and estimate that carbon could bring arable and grassland farmers between £18m and £147m per year in the UK. However, these are gross income figures and account needs to be taken of the cost to farmers of adopting the techniques required to sequester the carbon.

Although the estimates placed on the value of a tonne of carbon vary considerably, the evidence does increasingly point to a fairly low market value. This would suggest that, while the additional income to farmers in temperate climates would be welcome (especially in the current economic climate), it is clear that farmers are unlikely to become just 'carbon farmers'. In addition it is also clear that carbon does not offer a panacea for the problems associated with small 'family' farms that have preoccupied much of agricultural policy. The ability to sequester carbon is clearly related to farm area and hence, in absolute terms, it is likely to be the larger farms that gain the most from any payments either through the market or from government environmental policy. A larger farm may also be more likely to have areas suitable for carbon-intensive products such as coppicing. It is not clear that carbon sequestration on its own will help the smaller producers, although, once again, if it was linked to other environmental policies that encourage guardianship it might be beneficial.

There are other indirect impacts associated with carbon sequestration. For example, widespread conversion of land to non-food energy crops may reduce the supply of food and raise prices. As food is a staple commodity this will impact more on low-income households. However, as food is now a small proportion of overall expenditure, these effects may not be as significant as they would have been 20 years ago.

Conclusions

Agriculture provides significant possibilities for sequestering carbon. These arise because conventional agricultural techniques have led to a large loss of carbon from soils, and changes in tillage and management practices can replenish this carbon. But there remains uncertainty surrounding the role of soil sinks. This relates to factors such as the amount of carbon that can be sequestered, how the gain is measured and also how permanent the seques- tration will be. In addition, while there appears to be considerable potential, the actual contribution that agriculture can make depends on the economics of soil sequestration, and this is complicated by the problems with market failure due to the existence of external costs and benefits from land-use and management changes.

The key factor in determining the competitiveness of temperate agriculture in mitigating climate change is the opportunity cost per tC stored. Empirical evidence suggests that this can be as low as $10–$25 per tonne but that for the majority of agriculture it exceeds $50 per tonne. Whether this is competi- tive with alternative approaches and emission reductions depends on the final monetary value that is placed on a per-tonne reduction of carbon emission. This will emerge either from the establishment of a fully functioning mar- ket or from government payments. Estimates of the value have ranged from an optimistic $100 per tonne to a low of between $1 and $5 per tonne. The current evidence does appear to suggest a price in the lower regions of this range.

There has been considerable speculation as to the annual value of carbon to temperate agriculture. For example, it has been shown that, for the US, estimates range between £100 million and $4 billion. If we accept the low estimates of carbon it is clear that although it has the potential to contribute to farm income it is unlikely that the returns themselves will engender a widespread dash to carbon farming. However, a point that has been made repeatedly is that increases in soil organic matter and the methods adopted to achieve this are likely to lead other environmental benefits which might justify government payments. This is particularly relevant as the stated aim in many industrialized countries is a move to more sustainable forms of agriculture.

References

AGO 2000 *Greenhouse sinks and the Kyoto Protocol: an issues paper.* (Avail- able from the Australian Greenhouse Office at www.greenhouse.gov.au/pubs/ internationalsinks/sinks_paper.pdf.)

Antle, J. M. & McCarl, B. A. 2002 *The economics of carbon sequestration in agricul- tural soils.* In *International Yearbook of Environmental and Resource Economics*, vol. 6 (ed. T. Tietenberg & H. Folmerof). Cheltenham: Edward Elgar Publishing.

Antle, J. M. & Mooney, S. 1999 Economics and policy design for soil carbon seques- tration in Agriculture. Research discussion paper no. 36, October 1999, Montana State University, Bozeman, USA.

Antle, J. M., Capalbo, S. M., Mooney, S., Elliott, E. T. & Paustian, K. H. 2001 Spatial heterogeneity, contract design, and the efficiency of carbon sequestration policies for agriculture. Draft working paper, Department of Agricultural Economics and Economics, Montana State University, Bozeman, USA.

Asby, C. & Renwick, A. 2000 Economics of Cereal Production 1998/99. MAFF Special Studies in Agricultural Economics no. 48. University of Cambridge, UK.

ASCCC 1999 *Carbon sequestration and trading implications for canadian agriculture*. Agriculture Soil Conservation Council of Canada discussion paper. (Available at http://cattlefeeder.ab.ca/manure/carbonsequest.shtml.)

Ball, A. S. 1997 Microbial decomposition at elevated CO_2—effect of litter quality. *Glob. Change. Biol.* **3**, 379–386.

Bruce, J. P., Frome, M., Haites, E., Janzen, H., Lal, R. & Paustian, K. 1998 *Carbon Sequestration in Soils*. In Proc. Carbon Sequestration in Soils Workshop, Calgary, Canada, May 1998. Soil and Water Conservation Society.

Comis D. 2001 Dow Jones step aside: here comes the carbon soil market. United States Department of Agriculture, Washington, DC. (Available at www.ars.usda.gov/is/pr/2001/010221.htm.)

CRER 2001 Economic evaluation of set-aside. Report to DEFRA by the Centre for Rural Economics Research. (Available at www.defra.gov.uk/esg/economics/econeval/setaside/index.htm.)

Dobbs, T. & Pretty, J. N. 2001 The United Kingdom's experience with agri-environment stewardship schemes: lessons and issues for the United States and Europe. South Dakota State University staff paper no. 2001-1 and University of Essex Centre for Environment and Society occasional paper no. 2001-1.

Edwards, W. M., Shipitalo, M. J. & Norton, L. D. 1988 Contribution of macroporosity to infiltration into a continuous corn no-tilled watershed. *J. Contam. Hydrol.* **3**, 193–205.

Edwards, J. H., Wood, C. W., Thurlow, D. L. & Ruf, M. E. 1992 Tillage and crop rotation effects on fertility status of a Hapludult soil. *Soil Sci. Soc. Am. J.* **56**, 1577–1582.

Eyre, N., Downing, T., Hoekstra, R., Rennings, K. & Tol, R. 1997 Global warming damages: ExternE global warming sub-task. European Commission Final Report no. JOS3-CT95-002.

Feng, H., Zhao, J. & King, C. 2001 Carbon: the next big cash crop? *Choices Mag.* (June), pp. 16–19.

Lal, R., Kimble, J. M., Follet, R. F. & Cole, C. V. 1998 *The potential for US soil to sequester carbon and mitigate the greenhouse effect*. Chelsea, MI: Ann Arbor Press.

Langdale, G. W., West, L. T., Bruce, R. R., Miller, W. P. & Thomas, A. W. 1992 Restoration of eroded soils with conservation tillage. *Soil Tech* **5**, 81–90.

McCarl, B. & Schneider, U. 1999*a* US agricultural role in a greenhouse gas emission mitigation world: an economic perspective. *Rev. Agric. Econ.* **22**, 134–159.

McCarl, B. & Schneider, U. 1999*b* Curbing greenhouse gases: agriculture's role. *Choices Mag* (1), 9–12.

NRDC 2000 Agricultural soil carbon accumulation in North America: considerations for climate policy. U S Natural Resources Defense Council Paper. (Available at www.nrdc.org/globalWarming/psoil.asp?pf=-1.)

Pautsch, G. R., Kurkalova, L. A., BabcockB. & Kling, C. L. 2001 The efficiency of sequestering carbon in agricultural soils. *Contemp. Econ. Policy* **19**, 123–134.

Pearce, D. W. Day, B., Newcombe, J., Brunello, T. & Bello, T. 1998 The clean development mechanism: benefits of the CDM for developing countries. CSERGE report, University College London.

Porteous, F. (and 11 others) 2003 Elevated CO_2 and N influence on the soil microbial community. (In the press.)

Pretty, J. N. & Ball, A. 2001 Agricultural influences on carbon emissions and sequestration: a review of evidence and emerging options. Occasional paper no. 2001-03, Centre for Environment and Society, University of Essex, UK.

Pretty, J. N. 1995 *Rengenerating agriculture: policies and practice for sustainability and self-reliance.* Joint publication by Earthscan, London; National Academy Press, Washington; and ActionAid, Bangalore.

Pretty, J. N., Brett, C., Gee, D., Hine, R., Mason, C. F., Morison, J. I. L., Raven, H., Rayment, M. & van der Bijl, G. 2000 An assessment of the total external costs of UK agriculture. *Agric. Syst.* **65**, 113–136.

Puget, P., Chenu, C. & Balesdent, J. 2000 Dynamics of soil organic matter associated with particle-size fractions of water-stable aggregates. *Eur. J. Soil Science* **51**, 595–605.

Sandor, R. L. & Skees, J. 1999 Creating a market for carbon emissions. *Choices Mag.* 3rd qtr, pp. 13–17.

Smith, P., Powlson, D. S., Smith, J. U., Falloon, P. & Coleman, K. 2000 Meeting Europe's climate change commitments: quantitative estimates of the potential for carbon mitigation by agriculture. *Glob. Change Biol.* **6**, 525–539.

The Royal Society 2001 The role of land carbon sinks in mitigating global climate change. Policy document 10/01. (Available at www.royalsoc.ac.uk/files/statfiles/document-150.pdf.)

Watson, R. T., Noble, I. R., Bolin, B., Ravindranath, N. H., Verardo, D. J. & Dokken, D. J. (eds) 2000 Land use, land-use change and forestry. Intergovernmental Panel on Climate Change Special report. (Available at www.ipcc.ch.)

Wu, J. & Babcock, B. A. 1996 Contract design for the purchase of environmental goods from agriculture. *Am. J. Agric. Econ.* **78**, 935–945.

Chapter 11

The role of sustainable agriculture and renewable-resource management in reducing greenhouse-gas emissions and increasing sinks in China and India

JULES N. PRETTY, ANDREW S. BALL, LI XIAOYUN
AND N. H. RAVINDRANATH

Technical options for reducing or avoiding emissions and increasing sinks in agricultural systems

The 1997 Kyoto Protocol to the United Nations Framework Convention on Climate Change (UNFCCC) established an international policy context for the reduction of carbon emissions and increases in carbon sinks in order to address the global challenge of anthropogenic interference with the climate system. It is clear that both emission reductions and sink growth will be necessary for positive effects on mitigation of current climate-change trends (FAO 2000; Watson *et al.* 2000; IPCC 2001; The Royal Society 2001).

A source is any process or activity that releases a greenhouse gas (GHG), or aerosol or a precursor of a GHG into the atmosphere, whereas a sink is a mechanism that removes these from the atmosphere. Carbon sequestration is defined as the capture and secure storage of carbon that would otherwise be emitted to or remain in the atmosphere. Agricultural systems emit carbon through the direct use of fossil fuels in food production, the indirect use of embodied energy in inputs that are energy-intensive to manufacture, and the cultivation of soils and/or soil erosion resulting in the loss of soil organic matter. The direct effects of land use and land-use change (including forest loss) led to a net emission of 1.7 GtC yr^{-1} in the 1980s and 1.6 GtC yr^{-1} in the 1990s (Watson *et al.* 2000).

On the other hand, agriculture is also an accumulator of carbon when organic matter is accumulated in the soil, and when above-ground biomass either acts as a permanent sink or is used as an energy source that substitutes for fossil fuels and so avoids carbon emissions. We identify three mechanisms and 21 technical options (Table 11.1) by which positive actions can be taken by farmers by:

1 increasing carbon sinks in soil organic matter and above-ground biomass;

2 avoiding carbon dioxide (CO_2) or other GHG emissions from farms by reducing direct and indirect energy use; and

3 increasing renewable-energy production from biomass that either substitutes for consumption of fossil fuels or replacing inefficient burning of fuelwood or crop residues, and so avoids carbon emissions.

There is considerable scientific uncertainty over the causes, magnitudes and permanence of carbon sinks and emissions in agriculture and land use. We review available measures under these three mechanisms, and indicate where sink creation and emissions avoidance can be achieved.

Mechanism A. Increase carbon sinks in soil organic matter and above-ground biomass

Long-term agricultural experiments in Europe and North America indicate that soil organic matter (SOM) and carbon are lost during intensive cultivation, typically showing exponential decline after the first cultivation of virgin soils, but with steady loss continuing for many decades (Arrouays & Pélissier 1994; Reicosky *et al.* 1995, 1997; Rasmussen *et al.* 1998; Robert *et al.* 2001; The Royal Society 2001). Both erosion and biological oxidation remove carbon from soils. Conventional ploughing exposes soil to solar radiation, mixes residues into soil, and adds air to macropores, all leading to an increase in metabolic rate of microbial populations. The greatest losses of soil carbon and organic matter occur under intensive and continuous cereals (0.105 to -0.460 tC $ha^{-1}yr^{-1}$), and fell when mixed rotations and cover crops are cultivated (0.033 to -0.065 tC $ha^{-1}yr^{-1}$).

But SOM and soil-carbon pools can be increased with sustainable management practices. SOM has a stabilizing effect on soil structure, improves moisture retention, and protects against erosion (Fliessbach & Mäder 2000; Six *et al.* 2000). Long-term comparative studies show that organic and sustainable agricultural systems improve soil health through accumulation of organic matter and soil carbon, with accompanying increases in microbial activity, in the USA (Lockeretz *et al.* 1981; Petersen *et al.* 2000), Germany (El Titi 1999; Tebrügge 2000), the UK (Jordan & Hutcheon 1994; Smith *et al.* 1998), Switzerland (FiBL 2000), and New Zealand (Reganold *et al.* 1987, 1993). Substantial increases in SOM occur with use of legumes and manures (Drinkwater *et al.* 1998; Lal *et al.* 1998; Tilman 1998; Petersen *et al.* 2000).

Recent years have seen rapid adoption of 'conservation-tillage' and 'zero-tillage' (ZT) systems, first in the Americas, and now increasingly in Asia. In Brazil, Argentina and Paraguay, there were 26 million hectares of agriculture under ZT in 2001; up from 0.5 Mha in 1991 (Landers 1999; Petersen *et al.* 1999; Peiretti 2000; WCCA 2001). These systems of cultivation maintain a

Table 11.1. *Mechanisms and measures for increasing carbon sinks and reducing* CO_2 *and other GHG emissions in agricultural systems*

Mechanism A. Increase carbon sinks in soil organic matter and above-ground biomass

---

Replace inversion ploughing with conservation-tillage and zero-tillage systems

Adopt mixed rotations with cover crops and green manures to increase biomass additions to soil

Adopt agroforestry in cropping systems to increase above-ground standing biomass

Minimize summer fallows and periods with no ground cover to maintain soil-organic-matter stocks

Use soil conservation measures to avoid soil erosion and loss of soil organic matter

Apply composts and manures to increase soil-organic-matter stocks

Improve pasture/rangelands through grazing, vegetation and fire management both to reduce degradation and increase soil organic matter

Cultivate perennial grasses (60–80% of biomass below ground) rather than annuals (20% below ground)

Restore and protect agricultural wetlands

Convert marginal agricultural land to woodlands to increase standing biomass of carbon

---

Mechanism B. Reduce direct and indirect energy use to avoid GHG emissions (CO_2, methane and nitrous oxide)

Conserve fuel and reduce machinery use to avoid fossil-fuel consumption

Use conservation or zero tillage to reduce CO_2 emissions from soils

Adopt grass-based grazing systems to reduce methane emissions from ruminant livestock

Use composting to reduce manure methane emissions

Substitute biofuel for fossil-fuel consumption

Reduce the use of inorganic N fertilizers (as manufacture is highly energy intensive), and adopt targeted- and slow-release fertilizers

Use integrated pest management to reduce pesticide use (avoid indirect energy consumption)

Mechanism C. Increase biomass-based renewable-energy production to avoid carbon emissions

---

Cultivate annual crops for biofuel production, such as ethanol from maize and sugar cane

Cultivate annual and perennial crops, such as grasses and coppiced trees, for combustion and electricity generation, with crops replanted each cycle for continued energy production

Use biogas digesters to produce methane, so substituting for fossil-fuel sources

Use improved cookstoves to increase efficiency of biomass fuels

---

Source: Adapted from Ravindranath & Ramakrishna (1997), Lal *et al.* (1998), Watson *et al.* (2000), Robertson *et al.* (2000), Wenhua (2001) and Pretty & Ball (2001).

permanent or semi-permanent organic cover on the soil, comprising either a growing crop or dead organic matter in the form of a mulch or green manure. The function is to protect the soil physically from the action of sun, rain and wind, and to feed soil biota, thus reducing soil erosion and improving SOM and carbon content. Smith *et al.* (1998) reviewed long-term experiments comparing conventional tillage with ZT in UK and Germany, and concluded

Table 11.2. *Carbon sequestration in various land-use systems*

Land-use system	(1)	(2)
sustainable cropland management (reduced or zero-tillage, rotations, cover crops and green manures, animal manures and composts)	0.32–0.36	—
grazing land management (management of herds, wood, plants and fire)	0.53–0.80	—
rice paddies (plant residues, irrigation and inorganic/organic fertilizers)	0.5	—
agroforestry (management of trees on cropland)	0.22–0.50	3.10
forest management (forest regeneration, choice of species, fertilization, reduced degradation)	0.31–0.53	—
urban land management (tree planting, waste management)	0.30	—
conversion of arable to grassland	—	0.80
wetland restoration (conversion of drained land back to wetlands)	—	0.40
degraded land restoration (to crop, grass or forest land)	—	0.25

The period covered is 30–50 years after conversion or adoption. (1) Carbon accumulated under improved management within a land use (tC ha^{-1}yr^{-1}). (2) Carbon accumulated with land-use change (tC ha^{-1}yr^{-1}).
Source: Watson *et al.* (2000).

that, with ZT, SOM increases at 0.73% per year; and soil carbon increases at 0.39 tC ha^{-1} yr^{-1}. This compares with low estimates of net sequestration under ZT of 0.1–0.3 tC ha^{-1} yr^{-1}, and higher ones of 0.63–0.77 tC ha^{-1} yr^{-1} in Spain and Canada (Edwards *et al.* 1992; Lal *et al.* 1998), though some have found declines in soil carbon under ZT (Kätterer & Andrén 1999).

Watson *et al.* (2000) reviewed the carbon-sequestration potential of changing land-use management towards more sustainable practices, and concluded that the greatest dividend comes from conversion of arable to agroforestry arising from both increased SOM and above-ground woody biomass (Table 11.2). Biomass used for energy production additionally avoids carbon emissions if it substitutes for fossil fuels.

Carbon sequestration potential is higher in areas of humid temperate (0.1–0.5 tC ha^{-1} yr^{-1}) than in semi-arid and tropical areas (0.05–0.2 tC ha^{-1} yr^{-1}) (Lal *et al.* 1998). Palm *et al.* (2000) measured carbon stocks, losses and rates of accumulation in the tropics, and concluded that carbon accumulation rates are higher in above-ground biomass (at least 2 tC ha^{-1} yr^{-1}) than in soils (0.2–0.6 tC ha^{-1} yr^{-1}). Tree-based agroecosystems, either plantation crops (e.g. oil palm, cacao and rubber) or on smallholder farms, bring the greatest dividend, accumulating 3.0–9.3 tC ha^{-1} yr^{-1} (Sanchez *et al.* 1999). For this study, we use conservative rates of carbon accumulation under basic sustainable agricultural systems of 0.3–0.6 tC ha^{-1} yr^{-1}, rising to 0.66–1.3 tC ha^{-1} yr^{-1} with mixed rotations and cover crops, and to several tonnes per hectare when trees are intercropped in cropping and grazing systems.

Mechanism B. Reducing direct and indirect energy use to avoid carbon emissions

As an economic sector, agriculture also contributes to carbon emissions through the direct and indirect consumption of fossil fuel, and a wide range of approaches to energy accounting have been developed (Steinhart & Steinhart 1974; Leach 1976; Pimentel 1980; Dovring 1985; OECD/IEA 1992; Pretty 1995; Cormack & Metcalfe 2000). Most commonly, conventions state that direct energy represents what is immediately vulnerable to supply interruptions. With the increased use of nitrogen fertilizers, pumped irrigation and mechanical power in industrialized agricultural systems, all of which are particularly energy intensive, agriculture has become progressively less energy efficient over time. These three sources account for 90% or more of the total direct and indirect energy inputs to most farming systems. Thus low-input or organic rice in Bangladesh, China, and Latin America is 15–25 times more energy efficient than irrigated rice produced in the USA. For each tonne of cereal or vegetable from high-input systems, 3–10 GJ of energy are consumed in its production. But for each tonne of cereal or vegetable from low-input systems, only 0.5–1.0 GJ are consumed (Pretty 1995).

In this study, we are concerned with the contribution that production systems low in both direct and indirect energy use make to carbon emission avoidance. Sustainable agricultural systems that substitute goods and services derived from nature for externally-derived fertilizers, pesticides and fossil-fuels increase the energy-efficiency of food production (Pretty 1995, 1998; Pretty & Ball 2001). For example, ZT systems have an additional benefit to SOM accumulation of requiring less fossil fuel for machinery passes. Fuel use in conventional systems in the UK and Germany varies from 0.046–0.053 tC ha^{-1} yr^{-1} (Smith *et al.* 1998; Tebrügge 2000), whereas for ZT systems, it is 0.007–0.029 tC ha^{-1} yr^{-1}.

We use standard data on the energy used for various agricultural practices and inputs to calculate the avoided carbon emissions by reducing or changing these practices (Table 11.3). The amount of carbon produced per unit of energy used depends on the contributions made by non-renewable and renewable sources to the domestic energy sector in question. These vary from 24 kgC GJ^{-1} for coal, 19 kgC GJ^{-1} for oil, and 14 kgC GJ^{-1} for natural gas (DTI 2001). As the adjustments for renewable and non-renewable resources vary from country to country, we use 15 and 24 kgC GJ^{-1} as the two conversion factors.

Thus the application of 176kgN ha^{-1} (the annual average for China, where 24.4 Mt are consumed on 138 Mha) results in carbon emissions of 0.172–0.276 tC ha^{-1}, and so a substitution of legumes for these fertilizers would avoid these losses (the average for India is 73.5 kg ha MJ ha^{-1} of cropland, resulting in annual losses of 0.072–0.115 tC ha^{-1}). Eliminating one ploughing pass avoids 0.021–0.034 tC ha^{-1}, and reducing insecticide use from 5 kg active ingredient per hectare to zero would avoid 0.015–0.022 tC ha^{-1}. Hence a shift from an intensive plough-based system to a ZT system based on legumes for fertility and using no pesticides (Petersen *et al.* 1999) would save 0.23–

Table 11.3. *Energy consumed and carbon produced by various agricultural inputs and practices*

Inputs and practices	Indirect and direct energy used (MJ kg^{-1} or ha^{-1})	Carbon emitted at 0.015 kgC GJ^{-1}	Carbon emitted at 0.024 kgC GJ^{-1}
fertilizers			
nitrogen	65.3 MJ kg^{-1}	0.98 MJ kg^{-1}	1.57 MJ kg^{-1}
phosphorus	7.2 MJ kg^{-1}	0.11 MJ kg^{-1}	0.17 MJ kg^{-1}
potassium	6.4 MJ kg^{-1}	0.10 MJ kg^{-1}	0.15 MJ kg^{-1}
pesticides			
herbicides	238 MJ kg^{-1}	3.57 MJ kg^{-1}	5.71 MJ kg^{-1}
fungicides	92 MJ kg^{-1}	1.38 MJ kg^{-1}	2.21 MJ kg^{-1}
insecticides	199 MJ kg^{-1}	2.99 MJ kg^{-1}	4.48 MJ kg^{-1}
applications			
one spray per season	195 MJ ha^{-1}	2.93 MJ ha^{-1}	4.68 MJ ha^{-1}
one fertilizer pass	161 MJ ha^{-1}	2.42 MJ ha^{-1}	3.86 MJ ha^{-1}
one plough pass	1400 MJ ha^{-1}	21.00 MJ ha^{-1}	33.60 MJ ha^{-1}

0.37 tC ha^{-1} in addition to any carbon sequestered in SOM. The main contributor to avoided emissions comes from reducing nitrogen fertilizer use.

In the analyses in this chapter, the transformations in the agricultural systems analysed tend not to involve shifts from high-input (high-energy) to low-input systems. Most are contexts where farmers have little access to or income for external inputs, and so the challenge is to find the best ways to increase productivity using locally-available resources. However, 13 of the projects have seen modest declines in the use of external inputs. For fertilizers, most reductions have been of the order of 30–50 kg ha^{-1}, though in one case in southern India, more than 200 kg ha^{-1} have been saved (Fernandez 1999; Myers & Stolton 1999). Significant pesticide reductions have occurred in integrated pest management programmes in rice, particularly where aquaculture or diverse cropping patterns have been introduced (Eveleens *et al.* 1996; Zhu *et al.* 2000; Wenhua 2001).

Mechanism C. Increase biomass-based renewable-energy production to avoid carbon emissions

The third mechanism for agricultural systems to reduce net emissions and/or increase sinks is through the production of renewable energy from biomass. Biomass avoids GHG emissions by providing energy for heat and electricity generation, and for transportation fuel. The avoided carbon emissions avoided are thus equal to the fossil fuels substituted by the biomass energy (or woody fuels substituted by more efficient biomass systems and stoves) minus the carbon emitted by the biomass system. If biomass is harvested and burned, and the same area replanted or regenerated, there are no net carbon emissions over the harvest cycle. Land only used once provides a temporary benefit by avoiding fossil-fuel consumption. However, if biomass burning were substituted for energy derived from hydroelectric, wind, geothermal or nuclear sources, then it would represent a net source of carbon.

Several options are available for the production of renewable energy from biomass and for emissions avoidance:

- Cultivation of annual crops for biofuel production, such as maize and sugar cane for ethanol production.

- Cultivation of annuals and perennials, such as grasses (e.g. *Miscanthus*) and agroforestry (e.g. fast-growing coppiced willow and poplar), for combustion and electricity generation; and the use of plant products, such as crop residues (e.g. maize cobs, cereal straw, rice husks) or wastes (e.g. chicken manure) for combustion for electricity generation through small-scale gas turbines.

- Use of biogas digesters for methane production for light and heat, together with other rural-based renewable electricity generation (e.g. solar stoves and solar heating panels).

- Use of improved cookstoves to increase combustion efficiency of fuelwood, crop residues and dung for cooking.

Some of these options have become common locally in some countries, but have not yet received widespread attention for their net carbon sequestration and emissions-avoidance potential. In Brazil, ethanol derived from sugar-cane biomass is blended with fossil fuels, and led to the avoidance of 9.2 MtC yr^{-1} emissions in both 1997 and 1998, some 11% of the country's fossil-fuel CO_2 emissions (Watson *et al.* 2000). In both China and India, sugar-cane biomass is burned for electricity production (Shukla 1998).

Agroforestry represents an important option for agricultural systems, as trees sequester more carbon in woody biomass than cropping or pasture systems can do in soils. The USDA (2000) suggests that carbon sequestration under agroforestry can be higher than the IPCC estimates (see Table 11.2). Short rotation coppice (SRC) gives a double benefit through carbon sequestration and energy substitution, if the wood is burned instead of a fossil fuel. Under such coppicing, soil carbon increases by 6.6 tC ha^{-1} yr^{-1} over a 15-year rotation, and wood by 12–22 tC ha^{-1} yr^{-1}. Silvopasture systems can lead to increases in soil C of 5 tC ha^{-1} yr^{-1} over 35 years, and plant carbon of 10.1 tC ha^{-1} yr^{-1}. Smith *et al.*'s (2000) review of European experiments concluded that woodland regeneration can lead to accumulation of 3.43 tC ha^{-1} yr^{-1}, and SRC to accumulation of 6.62 tC ha^{-1} yr^{-1}.

A recent review of biomass energy options for the UK indicated that SRC can yield 10–18 t dry matter ha^{-1} yr^{-1}, equivalent to 4.0–7.2 tC ha^{-1} yr^{-1}, and *Miscanthus* can produce 12–25 tDM, equivalent to 4.8–10 tC ha^{-1} yr^{-1} (Grogan & Matthews 2001). Below-ground pools of carbon also increase by 0.1–1.6 tC ha^{-1} yr^{-1} (Hansen 1993; Grigal & Berguson 1998). A limitation on the spread of these systems comes from the cost of transportation of the wood, and the capital investment required to build the energy-generating plant (RCEP 2000; DEFRA 2001). One scenario for the EU suggests that if 10% of the agricultural land were devoted to these biofuel crops, and was combined with woodland regeneration, then this would lead to a reduction in emissions equivalent to the EU's commitment under the Kyoto Protocol (Smith *et al.* 2000; The Royal Society 2001). A study in India has shown that by dedicating 32 Mha (out of 66 Mha) of degraded land at a woody biomass productivity of $4\,t\,ha^{-1}\,yr^{-1}$ could produce biomass adequate for generating 100 TWh of electricity annually, meeting all the rural electricity needs as well as providing carbon mitigation benefit of 40 MtC annually (Ravindranath & Hall 1995).

Biomass accounts for 38% of energy use in developing countries (Sudha & Ravindranath 1999) and such use for energy generation creates no net accumulation of carbon levels in the atmosphere because the carbon released during combustion is compensated for by that absorbed during growth. Biomass energy becomes a contribution to carbon-emissions avoidance if it substitutes for fossil-fuel use or electricity derived from fossil fuels. In this chapter, we limit our assessment to the contribution made by firewood derived from agricultural systems, and not from forests (Ravindranath *et al.* 1997).

Biogas digesters to produce methane for cooking, lighting and heating have become widespread in China and India following progressive national policies to aid their adoption (Ministry of Agriculture 2000, 2001; Somashekhar *et al.* 2000; Wenhua 2001). Animal waste and plant material are added to the digester to produce methane, and the remaining sediment, which is high in organic matter, is returned to the soil. Fermentation in digesters occurs in three stages. Organic matter is hydrolysed into volatile organic acids, and those are then decomposed by bacteria into acetic acid, hydrogen and CO_2. They are then converted by methanogenic bacteria in the anaerobic part of the process to methane and CO_2 (usually in a volume ratio of 2:1). During the process, the C:N ratio needs to be *ca.* 10–20:1, and so plant materials, such as straw, are added as a carbon source, and animal wastes added as a nitrogen source.

Digesters are a net carbon sink if they substitute for fossil-fuel consumption or for inefficient wood or plant-residue combustion. In some contexts this is not the case, as digesters have been adopted precisely because remote rural households do not have access to national electricity grids. Nonetheless, if they substitute for the combustion of wood, crop residues and dung, there is still a net benefit as less is burned for the same amount of energy, leaving more remaining as standing biomass, and as the digested sediment is returned to the soil.

There are 8.48 million biogas digesters in China, up from 4.5 million in 1990, with projections for an additional million per year for 2001–2010 (Shuhong 1998; Ministry of Agriculture 2000). About 20% of these are incorporated into a variety of integrated models of production, such as the northern 4-in-1 model with biogas pit, pigsty, lavatory and greenhouse for vegetable production, and the southern models involving livestock-rearing with fruit, sugar cane, mulberry, fish and vegetables. There are, however, doubts that all these digesters are working to full efficiency. The rate of functioning has been poor, but has recently improved owing to the new Ministry of Agriculture coordinated programme, and the proportion of well-functioning units is now estimated to be 80–90%. In India, there are some 2.5 million family-sized biogas plants, constructed by the National Project on Biogas Development, plus another 500 larger community biogas systems (Ravindranath & Ramakrishna 1997; Shukla 1998; Somashekhar *et al.* 2000). Shukla (1998) estimates that, nationwide, 60% are functioning well (1.5 million units).

Depending on the size of these domestic digesters, their efficiency and productive period during the year, each can save the annual combustion of 1.5–4.0 tonnes of fuelwood, equivalent to an avoided emission of 0.75–2.0 tC per digester (Shuhong 1998; Shukla 1998; Wenhua 2001). There are added benefits from biogas systems. If straw is burned as fuel, only 10% of the energy is used. But energy use rises to 60% if the straw is used in a biogas digester. The 4-in-1 Chinese model also produces five tonnes of sediment each year, which is added to the soil. The content is typically 0.8–2% nitrogen, and 30–50% organic matter, and so receiving soils are not only improved for agricultural purposes, but their SOM and carbon content increases. The beneficial side-effects of these digester systems include improved rural sanitation, less labour required for collecting wood (especially for women), better respiratory health in kitchens, and increased per-hectare food production through soil-health improvement and extended growing periods with greenhouses in colder regions (Chen *et al.* 1990; Ravindranath & Ramakrishna 1997).

Improved cookstoves represent another important option for avoided emissions in developing countries. Cooking is the dominant energy-using activity for rural households, and also has a significant effect on the quality of life of women. In India, women spend 4.3 hours a day cooking (Ravindranath & Ramakrishna 1997). According to the Advisory Board on energy in India, 95% of rural households depends on non-commercial energy derived from agricultural and forest resources, particularly fuelwood, crop residues and dung. But unprocessed biomass fuel has a low energy density and, combined with poor efficiency of cooking devices, this means that per capita primary energy consumption in developing countries is 10.5 GJ yr^{-1} compared with 2.5 GJ yr^{-1} in industrialized countries (Ravindranath & Ramakrishna 1997).

There is a wide range of improved cookstoves available (Ravindranath & Ramakrishna 1997; Shukla 1998; Shuhong 1998). In China, improved cookstoves are used by 170 million households, up from 40 million in 1985. In India, there are 25.7 million units, up from 0.3 million in the mid-1980s. Each well-functioning stove saves 0.4–1.0 tonnes of fuelwood per year, equivalent to 0.2–0.5 tC per household. In this chapter we do not assess the additional value of renewable but non-biomass-based rural energy generation. These, though, are making important contributions, such as the 140 000 household-scale wind turbines with power production of 1.37 GJ installed in pastoral and coastal regions of China, the 332 000 solar cookers in use, each saving 500–700 kg fuelwood each year, and 11 Mm^2 of solar heaters with 38 PJ of annual energy-saving capacity (Ministry of Agriculture 2000; Wenhua 2001).

Review of best-practice sustainable-agriculture projects in China and India

In this section, we analyse net sequestration and emissions avoidance in China and India. We use a recently developed dataset on sustainable agriculture projects and initiatives to assess progress being made on mechanisms A, B and C (increasing sinks, reducing energy use, increasing renewable-energy production). China and India were selected as they have 46% of the world's population (in 2001). Annual growth of carbon emissions is 4.4% in China and 6.7% in India, and together they account for 45% of developing country emissions and 17% of global emissions (Sataye & Ravindranath 1998), though per-capita emissions compared with industrialized countries are low. Though energy consumption in the agricultural sector is low compared with other sectors, the growth in agricultural consumption of energy is increasing more rapidly (5.2–6.5% yr^{-1} in China in the 1990s) than growth in grain production (3.5% yr^{-1} in China in the 1990s) (Wenhua 2001; CED 2001; US Energy Information Network 2001a, b).

Both countries also have large amounts of agricultural land, and so have many opportunities for creating new carbon sinks. In India, there are 162 Mha of arable land, 7.9 Mha of permanent crops and 11 Mha of permanent pasture. In China, there are 100 Mha of drylands, 38 Mha of paddy rice, and 300 Mha of low and high grasslands (Wenhua 2001; FAO 2001). Consumption of inorganic nitrogen fertilizer is growing in both countries, and in 1999 was 24.4 Mt yr^{-1} in China and 11.9 Mt yr^{-1} in India (together accounting for 42% of world nitrogen consumption) (FAO 2001). As indicated earlier, nitrogen fertilizer is energy-intensive to manufacture, and this consumption of 36.3 Mt of N results in emissions of 36–57 MtC yr^{-1}. Both countries use large amounts of wood for energy production (11% of total energy in China and 30% in India) (FAO-RWEDP 2000). In India, fuelwood consumption for domestic households is 219 Mt yr^{-1}, crop residues 96 Mt yr^{-1} and 37 Mt yr^{-1} of cattle dung (Shukla 1998; Shuhong 1998; Ravindranath & Hall 1995). Finally, both countries have numerous novel examples of best practice in sustainable agriculture, and these provide the basic data for analysis of actual net carbon sinks currently being created, and their current economic value.

We define agricultural sustainability as farming that makes the best use of nature's goods and services while not damaging the environment (Altieri 1995; Conway 1997; Pretty 1998, 2002; Hinchcliffe *et al.* 1999; NRC 2000). It does this by integrating natural processes such as nutrient cycling, nitrogen fixation, soil regeneration and natural enemies of pests into food production processes. It minimizes the use of non-renewable inputs that damage the environment or harm the health of farmers and consumers. It makes productive use of the knowledge and skills of farmers, so improving their self-reliance, and seeks to make effective use of people's collective capacities to solve common resource management problems, such as in pest, watershed, irrigation, forest and credit management.

We use a University of Essex dataset to assess progress being made on increasing carbon sinks in sustainable agriculture systems (for details of research methodology, see Pretty & Hine (2000, 2001) and Pretty *et al.* (2003)). The research audited progress in developing countries, and assessed the extent to which farmers were increasing food production by using low-cost and locally available technologies and inputs. A total of 208 projects in 52 countries were analysed, comprising 45 projects in Latin America, 63 in Asia and 100 in Africa, in which 8.98 million farmers had adopted sustainable agriculture practices and technologies on 28.92 Mha, up from *ca.* 0.5 Mha in 1990. We have added initiatives on biogas and improved cookstoves for this analysis, bringing the total analysed here to 28 projects and initiatives from India, and 12 from China (see Appendix A for list).

These 40 initiatives involve 209 million farm households (180.69 million in China and 28.8 million in India), and cover 5.58 Mha (4.48 Mha in China and 0.75 Mha in India). We do not imply that these represent a comprehensive survey of all sustainable agriculture initiatives in these two countries. Rather, we are interested in what is already being achieved by a sample of best-practice, and what could be achieved if these principles were spread to a larger scale (more farmers and more hectares) with appropriate policies and institutions.

A variety of technical options is being used in these projects. Those contributing to mechanism A (increasing carbon sinks) include water harvesting in the drylands to rehabilitate degraded lands; agroforestry; adoption of certified organic farming; integration of livestock into systems, so increasing supply of animal manures; use of composts; watershed development programmes involving soil conservation; agroforestry and reforestation; and adoption of ZT systems. Those contributing to mechanism B (avoided emissions through reduced energy use) include inorganic fertilizers and pesticides; adoption of certified organic farming; more efficient use of water per kilogram of crop output through participatory irrigation management, thus reducing energy use; and mixed rotations and multiple cropping to increase biocontrol of pests and diseases. Those contributing to mechanism C (renewable-energy production) include biogas digesters and improved cookstoves.

We have no examples of programmes addressing pasture management, reduced dependency on concentrated feeds, or more efficient energy use in intensive production systems. We also do not assess the large-scale tree-planting programmes or forest-regeneration programmes in the two countries. In India, for example, 25 000 joint forest-management groups were formed in the 1990s, and these have substantially improved standing biomass and biodiversity of forests under their control (Shrestha 1997; Ravindranath *et al.* 2000). In China, four major shelterbelt systems have been planted in the 1990s, bringing increases in carbon sequestration combined with local ecological benefits. The Three North Shelterbelt stretches across 645 counties and 13 provinces, with 12.1 Mha planted in 11 years, and a further 6 Mha planned for 2001–2010. During the 1990s, 2 Mha of trees were planted in the Upper Yangste watershed, 6 Mha along the coast, and 10 Mha of farmland incorporated into rural shelterbelt networks in the plains of central China. Though many of these trees are technically in farmland rather than in forests, we do not include them in this analysis. The total carbon sequestration potential of forest regeneration depends in part on the durability of the end-use for the trees. Many *Pawlonia* grown in agroforestry systems and shelterbelts, for example, are used for furniture, representing a fairly permanent sink for carbon (Wenhua 2001).

We calculate the annual contributions being made in these projects to carbon-sink increases and emissions avoidance. Our focus is on what sustainable methods can do to increase marginal quantities of soil and above-ground carbon, and so we do not take account of existing stocks of carbon. We assessed each of the projects for their total contributions to mechanisms A, B and C, and calculated the net annual increase in carbon (Table 11.4). In the analysis, we apply an agroecological zone factor to correct soil-carbon sequestration for climate, as rates are higher in humid compared with dry zones, and generally higher in temperate than in tropical areas (Watson *et al.* 2000; Lal *et al.* 2000). However, given the longer growing season in the tropics, and greater potential for organic matter production, we correct soil sequestration rates with the following ratios: ×1.0 for humid tropical, ×0.8 for humid temperate and ×0.4 for both dry temperate and dry tropical.

Spreading best practice with appropriate policies and measures

These forty sustainable agricultural and renewable-resource-management projects are sequestering 27.3 MtC yr^{-1} (mechanism A) and avoiding 37.5 MtC yr^{-1} of emissions (mechanisms B and C), giving a total of 64.8 MtC yr^{-1}. This gives an average net gain of 11.61 tC ha^{-1} yr^{-1}, and an average per household of 0.31 tC yr^{-1}. Mechanism B gives the smallest net benefit of 12.6 ktC yr^{-1}, mainly because at the outset these were mostly low-input systems. The biogas and cookstove programmes are contributing 58% to the total, comprising 1.4 tC per household for biogas plants, and 0.14 tC for each cookstove. However, there are several important uncertainties, including the sustained effective use of energy-saving cookstoves and biogas plants, the longevity of the technologies, and the possibility that access to safe and abundant energy will simply result in increased total use of energy by participating households.

At the lowest carbon prices in trading systems in current use ($2–$5 per tonne of carbon), this implies a potential income for these projects and households of $130–$324 million yr^{-1}. This rises to $648 million yr^{-1} at medium rates ($10 per tonne of carbon), and could be $1.6 billion yr^{-1} (at $25 per tonne of carbon). The rates of sequestration in soils and above-ground biomass cannot be sustained indefinitely in agricultural systems, as inputs and losses come into balance over a 20–50 year period (Watson *et al.* 2000). Rates of gain are generally greatest soon after adoption of new management practices, and thus the benefits of biological mitigation in agricultural systems will be most pronounced in the 2–3 decades after adoption of new policies that encourage such changes in farm practice.

Table 11.4. *Summary of annual carbon sequestration and carbon emissions avoidance in 40 sustainable agriculture and renewable-resource-management projects of China and India*

Types of projects and initiatives (number)		Hectares	Households	Mechanism A (tC yr⁻¹)	Mechanism B (tC yr⁻¹)	Mechanism C (tC yr⁻¹)	Total (∑A,B,C)
zero tillage	India (1)	50 000	25 000	32 500	2 152	0	34 652
watershed development and soil conservation	China (6)	770 400	1 024 137	142 964	3 233	225	146 422
	India (15)	648 301	495 592	279 675	9 113	350	289 138
mixed sustainable agriculture and agroforestry	China (1)	3 000 000	—	15 300 000	0	0	15 300 000
	India (8)	5 120	4 678	4 730	227	0	4 957
irrigated rice and pest management	China (3)	1 070 800	1 056 680	535 400	30 970	0	566 370
	India (2)	41 500	83 230	20 750	216	0	20 966
biogas and improved cookstoves	China (2)	—	178 480 000	8 480 000	0	31 571 500	40 051 500
	India (2)	—	28 200 000	2 500 000	0	5 914 765	8 414 765
totals		5 586 121	209 369 317	27 296 019	12 573	37 486 840	64 828 770

We assume mid-range figures in kgC kg⁻¹ for fertilizers and pesticides as follows: N, 1.28; P, 0.14; K, 0.13; herbicides, 4.64; fungicides, 1.80; insecticides, 3.74. We assume there is 1 tC in sediment from each biogas digester and is applied to the soil. We assume 1.5 tC saved per well-functioning domestic biogas plant, and for both China and India assume 25% are at full-efficiency (1.5 tC saved per year) and 75% are at half efficiency (0.75 tC saved per year). We assume 0.35 tC saved per well-functioning cookstove, and for both China and India assume 33% are at full-efficiency (0.35 tC saved per year) and 67% at 10% efficiency (0.035 tC saved per year).

Sustainable agricultural management can contribute significantly to both net carbon sequestration and to increased food production, as well as make a significant impact on rural peoples' livelihoods. In the 208 projects analysed in 52 countries, average per-hectare food production increased by 73%, and there were additional beneficial side-effects through improvements in water tables (with more drinking water in dry seasons), reduced soil erosion combined with improved SOM, and increased agrobiodiversity (Pretty *et al.* 2003). However, it is important to note that there may also be critical trade-offs, with gains in carbon sequestration being offset by losses through increased energy use or emissions of trace GHGs, such as methane and nitrous oxide (Watson *et al.* 2000). For example, water harvesting can lead to increased SOM and higher cropping intensity, but can also increase annual fertilizer (and indirect energy) use. Increased productivity also increases the offtake of nutrients in food, which need to be replaced through nitrogen fixation and/or imported sources, and incorporation of rice straw into paddy soils can increase methane emissions.

The important challenge now is to develop the appropriate support at a range of levels for these sustainable agricultural and renewable-resource-management initiatives. Most of the projects analysed are relatively local in extent. The largest, though, have spread precisely because of explicit support and finance from national, sub-national and international levels. The 1990s saw considerable global progress towards the recognition of the need for policies to support sustainable agriculture (Izac 1997; Pretty *et al.* 2001; Dobbs & Pretty 2001). In a few countries, this has been translated into supportive and integrated policy frameworks. In most, however, such policies remain at the margins. A good example of an integrated programme comes from China, where the government's 1994 White Paper set out *Shengtai Nongye,* or agroecological engineering, as its approach to achieve sustainability in agriculture. Pilot projects have been established in 2000 townships and villages spread across 150 counties. Policy for these 'eco-counties' is organized through a cross-ministry partnership, which uses a variety of incentives to encourage adoption of diverse systems to replace monocultures. These include subsidies and loans, technical assistance, tax exemptions and deductions, security of land tenure, marketing services and linkages to research organizations. These eco-counties contain 12 Mha of land, and though only covering a relatively small part of China's total agricultural land, do indicate what is possible when policy is coordinated and integrated.

If domestic policies elsewhere were to support the types of sustainable agriculture in these projects that also sequester carbon and avoid emissions, then it is possible to predict some of the potential benefits. The average carbon sequestration rates are $0.19 \, \text{tC yr}^{-1} \, \text{ha}^{-1}$ in the projects in China and India (not counting the biogas and stove projects, and the large-scale agroforestry programmes). The average per household is $0.31 \, \text{tC yr}^{-1}$.

These projects currently cover 5.58 Mha (or 1.8%) out of a total of 300 Mha of arable land in the two countries. As indicated earlier, there has been extraordinary growth in sustainable agriculture in the 52 developing countries studied (up from 0.5 to 29 Mha in 10 years). If these 5.6 Mha were to grow to 20% of all arable land in China and India in a decade (to 60 Mha), then the annual carbon sequestered would be 11 MtC ha^{-1} yr^{-1}, worth \$55–\$275 million at trading prices of \$5–\$15 per tonne of carbon. Additional benefits would arise from spread of agroforestry, biogas and cookstove programmes.

These values exceed the typical investment costs of \$1.50–\$10 per tonne of carbon for agroforestry, enhanced natural resource management and sustainable agriculture projects in China and India (Sathaye & Ravindranath 1998). With appropriate investments through participatory and community-based institutions to ensure persistence of new practices, combined with appropriate policy support at all levels, it is clear that the biological mitigation potential in China and India is large. Joint implementation projects could increase the flow of new technology and investment leading to additional environmental and social benefits.

Barriers and integrated policy options

The majority of mitigation options are known to provide ancillary or co-benefits and thus opportunities for 'win–win' outcomes. However, there are many technical, financial and institutional barriers (IPCC 2001). Adoption of new technology or mitigation options is limited by small farm size, credit constraints, risk aversion, lack of access to information, and inadequate rural infrastructure and land tenure arrangements. Moreover, subsidies for inputs to agriculture, such as fertilizers, water supply and electricity and fuels distort markets for these products.

Though much can be done with existing resources, there are always transition costs in learning, in developing new or adapting old technologies, in developing collective management institutions, and in breaking free from existing patterns of thought and practice. Further issues such as lack of technical capability, lack of credibility about setting project baselines, and monitoring of carbon stocks pose new challenges. In the majority of developing countries, farmers lack access to technology and finance and have little capacity to bear risk. There is, therefore, a need to develop nationally relevant technical, institutional and financial policies to promote mitigation options, ensure that risk to small farmers is minimized, and raise crop productivity and incomes.

The findings in this study that poor rural households and communities can contribute both to their own economic welfare through adoption of sustainable agriculture and renewable-resource-management methods, and to the global environmental good through biological carbon mitigation, raise important challenges for policy makers and project managers in the agricultural, forestry, energy, water and engineering sectors. There is an urgent need for the integration of policies both across and within these sectors, so that technologies and social processes are adapted to the diverse needs of local communities across a wide variety of environments and economies.

Appendix A. List of the 40 analysed best-practice sustainable agriculture and renewable-resource-management projects and initiatives in China and India

Zero-tillage projects

1   Zero tillage of rice–wheat systems, Haryana (P. Hobbs, CIMMYT, personal communication).

Watershed development and soil conservation projects

1   Xiji County comprehensive management of watersheds, Ningxia (W. K. Zhi, personal communication).

2   National pilot watersheds programme, China (Wenhua 2001).

3   Loess plateau soil and water conservation project, China (Wenhua 2001).

4   UNDP poverty alleviation and sustainable development project, Yunnan (Y. Yunsong, personal communication).

5   Hebei Plain wheat–maize double-cropping project (L. Weili, personal communication).

6   East Gansu sustainable agricultural for effective use of rainfall resources (F. Tinglu, personal communication).

7   Rural communes comprehensive watershed development, Maharashtra (M. Alavi & R. Joshi, personal communication).

8   Rajasthan watershed development programme (Krishna 1999).

9   EZE sustainable agriculture, Bangalore (EZE, Banglalore).

10   World Neighbours dryland farming projects, India (World Neighbours).

11   ActionAid watershed projects, Karnataka, Tamil Nadu, Uttar Pradesh and Madhya Pradesh (ActionAid).

12   Aga Khan Rural Support Programme, Gujarat (Shah & Shah 1999).

13   Participative Integrated Development of Watersheds project, Karnataka (Fernandez 1999).

14   Indo-German watershed development project, Maharashtra (Lobo & Palghadmal 1999).

15   Society for People's Education and Economic Change, Tamil Nadu (Devavaram *et al*. 1999).

16   Doon Valley Integrated Watershed Development project, Uttar Pradesh (Thapliyal *et al*. 1999).

17 KRIBCHO Indo-British Rainfed Farming Project (West) (P. S. Sodhi, personal communication).

18 Women's Sangams of Deccan Development Society, Andra Pradesh (Sateesh & Pimbert 1999).

19 Karnataka watershed development projects (funded by DFID, Danida, KfW) (Ninan 1998).

20 Tamil Nadu watershed development projects (GOTN 2001).

21 National Council of Development Communication (V. K. Dubey, personal communication).

Mixed sustainable agriculture and agroforestry projects

1 Pawlonia agroforestry and intercopping programme, China (Wenhua 2001).

2 Learning by Doing cotton project, Punjab (P. Guest, personal communication).

3 M. S. Swaminathan Research Foundation integrated intensive farming systems, Tamil Nadu (V. Balaji, personal communication).

4 N. Kolar tamaraind agroforestry project, Karnataka (N. H. Ravindranath, personal communication).

5 Maikaal organic cotton project, Madhya Pradesh (Myers & Stolton 1999).

6 Non-pesticidal management, Nellore: Centre for World Solidarity (S. A. Shafiunnisa, personal communication).

7 Technology assessment through Institutional Village Linkage, Karanataka (G. K. Veeresh, personal communication).

8 Praja Abyudaya Samastha, Andra Pradesh (M. Balavardiraju, personal communication).

9 Ankapur village project, Nizamabad (V. Balasubramanian, personal communication).

Irrigated rice and pest management projects

1 Multiline rice cultivation, Yunnan (Zhu *et al.* 2000).

2 Paddy-rice aquaculture systems, China (Li Kangmin 1998; Wenhua 2001).

3 Rice-IPM national programme, China (Eveleens *et al.* 1996; Mangan & Mangan 1998).

4 Rice-IPM national programme, India (Eveleens *et al.* 1996).

5 Gujarat Participatory Irrigation Management programme (R. Parthasarathy, personal communication).

Biogas and improved cookstove projects

1 National biogas programme, China (Ministry of Agriculture 2000, 2001; Wenhua 2001).

2 National biogas programme, India (Ravindranath & Ramakrishna 1997).

3 National improved cookstoves programme, China (Shuhong 1998).

4 National improved cookstoves programme, India (Ravindranath & Ramakrishna 1997; Shukla 1998).

References

Altieri, M. 1995 *Agroecology.* Boulder, CO: Westview.

Arrouays, D. & Pélissier, P. 1994 Changes in carbon storage in temperate humic soils after forest clearing and continuous corn cropping in France. *Plant Soil* **160**, 215–223.

CED 2001 *China energy databook.* Berkeley, CA: Lawrence Berkeley National Laboratory, Energy Research Institute.

Chen, B. H., Hong, C. J., Pandey, M. R. & Smith, K. R. 1990 Indoor air pollution and its effects in developing countries. *World Health Stat. Q.* **43**, 127–138.

Conway, G. R. 1997 *The doubly green revolution.* London: Penguin.

Cormack, B. & Metcalfe, P. 2000 Energy use in organic farming systems. Terrington, UK: ADAS.

DEFRA 2001 Energy crops programme. Department of Environment, Food and Rural Affairs, London.

Devavaram, J., Arunothayam, E., Prasad, R. & Pretty, J. 1999 Watershed and community development in Tamil Nadu. In *Fertile ground: the impacts of participatory watershed management.* (ed. F. Hinchcliffe, J. Thompson, J. Pretty, I. Guijt & P. Shah). London: ITDG Publishing.

Dobbs, T. & Pretty, J. 2001 The United Kingdom's experience with agri-environment stewardship schemes: lessons and issues for the US and Europe. Staff Paper and CES Occasional Paper 2000-1, South Dakota State University, Brookings, SD, and University of Essex, UK.

Dovring, F. 1985 Energy use in US agriculture: a critique of recent research. *Energy Agricult.* **4**, 79–86.

Drinkwater, L. E., Wagoner, P. & Sarrantonio, M. 1998 Legume-based cropping systems have reduced carbon and nitrogen losses. *Nature* **396**, 262–265.

DTI 2001 Digest of United Kingdom Energy Statistics 2001. Department of Trade and Industry, London, UK.

Edwards, W. M., Shipitalo, M. J. & Norton, L. D. 1992 Contribution of macroporosity to infiltration into a continuous corn no-tilled watershed. *J. Contam. Hydrol.* **3**, 193–205.

El Titi, A. 1999 Lautenbacher Hof Abschlussbericht 1978–1994. In *Agrarforschung in Baden–Württemberg*, vol. 30. Stuttgart: Ministerium Ländlichter Raum Verlag.

Eveleens, K. G., Chisholm, R., van de Fliert, E., Kato, M., Thi Nhat, P. & Schmidt, P. 1996 The FAO Intercountry Programme for the Development and Application of IPM Control in Rice in S and SE Asia. UN Food and Agricultural Organization, Rome.

FAO 2000 Carbon sequestration options under the clean development mechanism to address land degradation. World Soil Resources Report no. 92. UN Food and Agricultural Organization and International Fund for Agricultural Development, Rome.

FAO 2001 FAOSTAT database, Food and Agriculture Organization, Rome. (Available at www.fao.org.)

FAO-RWEDP 2000 Regional study on wood energy: today and tomorrow in Asia. UN Food and Agricultural Organization, Rome.

Fernandez, A. 1999 The impact of technology adaptation on productivity and sustainability. In *Fertile ground: the impacts of participatory watershed development* (ed. F. Hinchcliffe, J. Thompson, J. Pretty, I. Guijt & P. Shah). London: ITDG Publishing.

FiBL 2000 Organic farming enhances soil fertility and biodiversity: results from a 21 year field trial. FiBL Dossier 1 (August). Research Institute of Organic Agriculture (FiBL), Zurich.

Fliessbach, A. & Mäder, P. 2000 Microbial biomass and size-density fractions differ between soils or organic and conventional agricultural systems. *Soil Biol. Biochem.* **32**, 757–768.

GOTN 2001 Watershed development. Policy note on agriculture. Government of Tamil Nadu, Chennai.

Grigal, D. F. & Berguson, W. E. 1998 Soil carbon changes with short-rotation systems. *Biomass Bioenergy* **14**, 371–377.

Grogan, P. & Matthews, R. 2001 Review of the potential for soil carbon sequestration ender bioenergy crops in the UK. MAFF report on contract NF0418. Institute of Water and Environment, Cranfield University, Silsoe, UK.

Hansen, E. A. 1993 Soil carbon sequestration beneath hybrid poplar plantations in the north central US. *Biomass Bioenergy* **5**, 431–436.

Hinchcliffe, F., Thompson, J., Pretty, J., Guijt, I. & Shah, P. (eds) 1999 *Fertile ground: the impacts of participatory watershed development.* London: ITDG Publishing.

IPCC 2001 Climate change 2001: impacts, adaptation and vulnerability. Third Assessment Report. Intergovernmental Panel on Climate Change, IPCC Secretariat, Geneva, Switzerland. (Available at www.ipcc.ch/.)

Izac, A.-M. 1997 Developing policies for soil carbon management in tropical regions. *Geoderma* **79**, 261–276.

Jordan, V. W. L. & Hutcheon, J. A. 1994 Economic viability of less-intensive farming systems designed to meet current and future policy requirements. *Aspects Appl. Biol.* **40**, 61–68.

Kangmin, L. 1998 Rice aquaculture systems in China: a case of rice-fish farming from protein crops to cash crops. In *Integrated Bio-Systems in Zero Emissions Applications. Proc. Conf. on Integrated Biosystems* (ed. E.-L. Foo & T. Della Senta). (Available from http://www.ias.unu.edu/proceedings/icibs.)

Kätterer, T. & Andrén, O. 1999 Long-term agricultural field experiments in N. Europe. *Agric. Ecosyst. Environ.* **72**, 165–179.

Krishna, A. 1999 Large-scale watershed programmes: watershed development in Rajasthan, India. In *Fertile ground: the impacts of participatory watershed development* (ed. F. Hinchcliffe, J. Thompson, J. Pretty, I. Guijt & P. Shah). London: ITDG Publishing.

Lal, R., Kimble, J. M., Follett, R. F. & Cole, C. V. 1998 *The potential of US cropland to sequester carbon and mitigate the greenhouse effect.* Chelsea, MI: Ann Arbor Press.

Lal, R., Kimble, J. M. & Stewart, B. A. (eds) 2000 *Global climate change and tropical ecosystems.* Boca Raton, FL: CRC/Lewis Press.

Landers, J. 1999 Policy and organisational dimensions of the process of transition toward sustainable intensification in Brazilian agriculture. Rural Week presentation to The World Bank, 24–26 March 1999, Washington, DC.

Leach, G. 1976 *Energy and food production.* Guildford: IPC Science & Technology Press.

Lobo, C. & Palghadmal, T. 1999 Kasare: a saga of peoples' faith. In *Fertile ground: the impacts of participatory watershed development* (ed. F. Hinchcliffe, J. Thompson, J. Pretty, I. Guijt & P. Shah). London: ITDG Publishing.

Lockeretz, W., Shearer, G. & Kohl, D. H. 1981 Organic farming in the corn belt. *Science* **211**, 540–547.

Mangan, J. & Mangan, M. S. 1998 A comparison of two IPM training strategies in China. *Agric. Human Values* **15**, 209–221.

Ministry of Agriculture 2000 China biogas. Report. Department of Science, Education and Rural Environment, Beijing.

Ministry of Agriculture 2001 Statistical data on renewable energy resources in China 1996–2000. Report. Department of Science, Education and Rural Environment, Beijing, China.

Myers, D. & Stolton, S. 1999 *Organic cotton: from field to final product.* London: ITDG Publishing.

Ninan, K. N. 1998 An assessment of European-aided watershed development projects in India. Centre for Development Research Working Paper no. 98.3, Copenhagen.

NRC 2000 *Our common journey: transition towards sustainability* (ed. Board on Sustainable Development, Policy Division, National Research Council). Washington, DC: National Academy Press.

OECD/IEA 1992 *Energy Balances of OECD Countries.* Paris: Organisation For Economic Cooperation And Development.

Palm, C. A. (and 10 others) 2000 Carbon losses and sequestration potential of alternatives to slash and burn agriculture. A report on the biology and fertility of tropical soils. Tropical Soil Biology and Fertility Programme, Nairobi.

Peiretti, R. 2000 The evolution of the no till cropping system in Argentina. In *Impact of Globalization and Information on the Rural Environment Conf., 13–15 January 2000, Harvard University, MA.*

Petersen, P., Tardin, J. M. & Marochi, F. 1999 Participatory development of non-tillage systems without herbicides for family farming. *Environ. Dev. Sustain.* **1**, 235–252.

Petersen, C., Drinkwater, L. E. & Wagoner, P. 2000 *The Rodale Institute's farming systems trial: the first 15 years.* Maxatawny, PA: Rodale Institute.

Pimentel, D. (ed.) 1980 *CRC handbook of energy utilization in agriculture.* Boca Raton, FL: CRC Press.

Pretty, J. N. 1995 *Regenerating agriculture.* London: Earthscan.

Pretty, J. N. 1998 *The living land.* London: Earthscan.

Pretty, J. N. 2002 *Agri-culture: reconnecting people, land and nature.* London: Earthscan.

Pretty, J. N. & Ball, A. 2001 Agricultural influences on emissions and sequestration of carbon and emerging trading options. CES Occasional Paper no. 2001-03, University of Essex, Colchester, UK.

Pretty, J. N. & Hine, R. 2000 The promising spread of sustainable agriculture in Asia. *Nat. Resources Forum* **24**, 107–121.

Pretty, J. N. & Hine, R. 2001 Reducing food poverty with sustainable agriculture. SAFE-World Research Project. University of Essex, Colchester, UK.

Pretty, J., Brett, C., Gee, D., Hine, R., Mason, C., Morison, J., Rayment, M., van der Bijl, G. & Dobbs, T. 2001 Policy challenges and priorities for internalising the externalities of modern agriculture. *J. Environ. Plan. Mngmt* **44**, 263–283.

Pretty, J. N., Morison, J. I. L. & Hine, R. H. 2003 Reducing food poverty by increasing agricultural sustainability in developing countries. *Agricult. Ecosystems Environ.* **95**, 217–234.

Rasmussen, P. E., Goulding, K. W. T., Brown, J. R., Grace, P. R., Janzen, H. H. & Körschens, M. 1998 Long term agroecosystem experiments. *Science* **282**, 893–896.

Ravindranath, N. H. & Hall, D. O. 1995 *Biomass energy and environment: a developing country perspective from India*. Oxford University Press.

Ravindranath, N. H. & Ramakrishna, J. 1997 Energy options for cooking in India. *Energy Policy* **25**, 63–75.

Ravindranath, N. H., Somashekhar, B. S. & Gadgil, M. 1997 Carbon flow in Indian forests. *Climatic Change* **35**, 297–320.

Ravindranath, N. H., Rao, U., Natarajan, B. & Monga, P. 2000 *Renewable energy and environment: a policy analysis for India*. New Delhi: Tata McGraw-Hill.

RCEP 2000 *Energy: the changing climate. 22nd report of the Royal Commission on Environmental Pollution*. Norwich: HMSO.

Reganold, J. P., Elliott, L. F. & Unger, Y. L. 1987 Long-term effects of organic and conventional farming on soil erosion. *Nature* **330**, 370–372.

Reganold, J. P., Palmer, A. S., Lockhart, J. C. & Macgregor, A. N. 1993 Soil quality and financial performance of biodynamic and conventional farms in New Zealand. *Science* **260**, 344–349.

Reicosky, D. C., Kemper, W. D., Langdale, G. W., Douglas, C. L. & Rasmussen, P. E. 1995 Soil organic matter changes resulting from tillage and biomass production. *J. Soil Water Conserv.* **50**, 253–261.

Reicosky, D. C., Dugas, W. A. & Torbert, H. A. 1997 Tillage-induced soil carbon dioxide loss from different cropping systems. *Soil Tillage Res.* **41**, 105–118.

Robert, M., Antoine, J. & Nachtergaele, F. 2001 Carbon sequestration in soils. Rome: Land and water development division, FAO.

Robertson, G. P., Paul, E. A. & Harwood, R. R. 2000 Greenhouse gases intensive agriculture: contributions of individual gases to radiative warming of the atmosphere. *Science* **289**, 1922.

Sanchez, P. A., Buresh, R. J. & Leakey, R. R. B. 1999 Trees, soils and food security. *Phil. Trans. R. Soc. Lond.* B **253**, 949–961.

Sataye, J. A. & Ravindranath, N. H. 1998 Climate change mitigation in the energy and forestry sectors of developing countries. *A. Rev. Energy Environ.* **23**, 387–437.

Sateesh, P. V. & Pimbert, M. P. 1999 *Reclaiming diversity, restoring livelihoods*. Women Sangams of the Deccan Development Society.

Shah, P. & Shah, M. K. 1999 Institutional strengthening for watershed development: the case of the AKRSP in India. In *Fertile ground: the impacts of participatory watershed management* (ed. F. Hinchcliffe, J. Thompson, J. Pretty, I. Guijt & P. Shah). London: ITDG Publishing.

Shrestha, K. B. 1997 Community forestry: policy, legislation and rules. Paper presented at National Workshop on Community Forestry and Rural Development, 24–26 July 1997, Lalipur, Nepal.

Shuhong, C. 1998 Biomass energy for rural development in China. In *Biomass energy: data, analysis and trends*. Paris: OECD.

Shukla, P. 1998 Implications of global and local environment policies on biomass energy demand: a long-term analysis for India. In *Biomass energy: data, analysis and trends*. Paris: OECD.

Six, J., Elliott, E. T. & Paustain, K. 2000 Soil macroaggregate turnover and microaggregate formation: a mechanism for C sequestration under no-tillage agriculture. *Soil Biol. Biochem.* **32**, 2099–2103.

Smith, P., Powlson, D. S., Glendenning, M. J. & Smith, J. U. 1998 Preliminary estimates of the potential for carbon mitigation in European soils through no-till farming. *Glob. Change Biol.* **4**, 679–685.

Smith, P., Powlson, D. S., Smith, J. U., Falloon, P. & Coleman, K. 2000 Meeting Europe's climate change commitments: quantitative estimates of the potential for carbon mitigation by agriculture. *Glob. Change Biol.* **6**, 525–539.

Somashekhar, H. I., Dasappa, S. & Ravindranath, N. H. 2000 Rural bioenergy centres based on biomass gasifiers for decentralised power generation: case study of two villages in southern India. *Energy Sustainable Development IV* (3), 55–63.

Steinhart, J. S. & Steinhart, C. E. 1974 Energy use and the US food system. *Science* **184**, 307–316.

Sudha, R. & Ravindranath, N. H. 1999 Land availability and biomass production potential in India. *Biomass Bioenergy* **16**, 207–221.

Tebrügge, F. 2000 No-tillage visions: protection of soil, water and climate. Report. Institute for Agricultural Engineering, Justus-Liebig University, Giessen, Germany.

Thapliyal, K. C., Lepcha, S. T. S. & Kumar, P. 1999 A new approach for government. In *Fertile ground: the impacts of participatory watershed management* (ed. F. Hinchcliffe, J. Thompson, J. Pretty, I. Guijt & P. Shah). London: ITDG Publishing.

The Royal Society 2001 The role of land carbon sinks in mitigating global carbon change. Policy Document 10/01.

Tilman, D. 1998 The greening of the green revolution. *Nature* **396**, 211–212.

US Energy Information Network 2001 China country analysis brief. (Available at www.eia.doe.gov.)

US Energy Information Network 2001 India: an energy sector overview. (Available at www.eia.doe.gov/emeu/cabs/india.)

USDA 2000 Growing carbon: a new crop that helps agricultural producers and the climate, too. Brocure. Natural Resources Conservation Service, Washington, DC.

Watson, R. T., Noble, I. R., Bolin, B., Ravindranath, N. H., Verardo, D. J. & Dokken, D. J. (eds) 2000 *IPCC Special Report on Land Use, Land-Use Change and Forestry. A special report of the Intergovernmental Panel on Climate Change*. IPCC Secretariat, World Meteorological Organisation, Geneva, Switzerland. (Available at www.ipcc.ch/.)

WCCA 2001 Conservation Agriculture. In *Proc. World Congress on Conservation Agriculture, 1-5 October 2001, Madrid*. Rome: FAO and Brussels: European Conservation Agriculture Federation.

Wenhua, L. 2001 *Agro-ecological engineering in China*. Man and the Biosphere (MAB) Series, vol. 26. Paris: UNESCO.

Zhu, Y. (and 14 others) 2000 Genetic diversity and disease control in rice. *Nature* **406**, 718–722.

Chapter 12

Social capital from carbon property: creating equity for indigenous people

LINDSAY S. SAUNDERS, ROBIN HANBURY-TENISON
AND IAN R. SWINGLAND

Public takings and perverse incentives

The history of natural-resource mismanagement is well documented. The forest sector is no different, with development programmes and objectives taking little notice of the needs or rights of forest communities. The marginalization of forest communities has been rapid and ongoing to the extent that many now form the core of the rural poor in the world today. The disparity relating to the recognition of rights and opportunity to gain the freedoms that underpin development has occurred through the exclusion of forest communities from development planning and programs. This exclusion has resulted in widespread failure of forest-management systems, and the loss of essential services provided by forests. For any carbon-trading system this in and of itself represents the biggest threat to the integrity of forest based carbon sinks.

Simply by definition, the world's forests have been our wildernesses, those wild places that represent the frontier of our development. Beyond this frontier lay the opportunity for expansion, settlement and 'success' for governments keen to provide economic development and the fiscal benefits, both official and unofficial, attached to these. Aid agencies stimulated economic development to bring developing nations closer to the to the norms of the West. The growing civil population also saw opportunity beyond the frontier. With increased population growth behind the frontier, citizens demanded their own space and property, resulting in outward migration beyond the frontier, bringing roads, access to markets and technologies, all of which change the relative value of *in situ* forest use relative to alternative land uses through land conversion. Finally, and mostly forgotten, there lived forest dwellers that were set apart from the development planning decisions, whose social wellbeing and capital were not considered and who ultimately faced one of the greatest social injustices within the developing world: that of being the 'problem' of forest-development management (Hall 2001).

Within the developing world the paradox is that there exist 'rich forests and poor people', to steal the title of Nancy Peluso's book (Peluso 1992). The history of tropical forests has seen the loss of rich forests, which has left the poor even poorer, highlighting the inseparability of natural resources from the social context within which they reside. Human development is inextricably linked to the environment and, as such, forest-management issues are poverty issues, as each is central to the other (Gordon *et al.* 1999).

There are an estimated 5 billion poor people in the world today, of which 3 billion live in rural areas and perhaps 50% of these are closely associated to the land and forests. The rate for forest conversion is estimated to be 7% per annum in tropical regions. It is the greatest land-use dynamic in the world, resulting in the predicted conversion of more than 120 million hectares in the period 1990–2010. The future looks bleak when the population in Asia alone will grow by two-thirds over the next two generations. The poor of Asia depend on the forest for products and services that range from protein and shelter to cultural and heritage values (Shen 1995; Saunders & Weber 1996). Despite these linkages, development programs based on forestry have proved to be less than successful in protecting these development assets. This reflects the lack of congruence between the incentives faced by Government officials, corporate entities and local communities. The role of forestry and local development is summarized by Creedy & Wurzbacjer (2001), who stated 'more than perhaps any other sector, forestry captures the inter-relationships between economic growth, environmental preservation and poverty alleviation.'

The 'development of wilderness' has brought roads to provide access to the riches available from the conversion of open-access forests and the land on which they grew. Access was also provided for the labour to work the land, where those members of society that were already represented in the political system were allowed to move into the forest land, expanding the extent of the political frontier and the constituency of those who enabled the expansion. The conversion of forests represented not only a conversion of natural forest wilderness to other land uses but also the conversion of a political wilderness to that already represented by the political manifestation of governments. These governments chose to enable the movement of those under their control rather than negotiate and recognize the rights of those already present, due to the ease with which they could do so, as well as the expected political benefits. This approach relies on centralist command and control systems, which meant that local forest dwellers were unimportant to politicians and public policy makers. People were the problem. The classic example of this is the transmigration of Javanese into the outer resource-rich islands of Indonesia, resulting in massive land conversion, forest fires and loss of ecological integrity. Most importantly, it undermined the social capital of indigenous Dayak and other communities to the point that their existence in some areas has been put at risk, resulting in ongoing social conflict.

Trees play an integral role in defining local cultures and institutions. Trees and forests were traditionally used as important indicators of rights within society. Trees were used to claim or denote land-use rights, land ownership and use of forests, while providing shade, fodder, soil protection and watershed conditions. Those who did not have access to banks and the monetary system often planted trees to create physical capital. The capital was manifest as property, as others in society were excluded from using the trees. For example, small holders in Sumatra grew cinnamon trees to provide for their children's medical and educational needs; Damar trees were used to demarcate land claims in Borneo; teak is grown in Sri Lanka as a kind of savings deposit. These forest assets have contributed to the quality of life and, in many indigenous societies, were the tools for poverty alleviation and the primary development assets (Schmidt *et al.* 1999). The notion of forest property is captured in the term 'social capital'. Hall (2001) described social capital as:

> ... networks of social relationships, norms and values that allow groups to meet their development objectives (Coleman 1990). Like physical, human, or financial capital, strengthening social capital may be viewed as a legitimate form of investment for development. Nowhere is this more so than in the case of common-pool resource management in the forest sector, where grass root organization and co-operation is so fundamental.

For carbon trading, social capital must be built if the risk of forest conversion is to be made acceptable to investors and the supervisors of carbon sinks as a global mechanism.

While recognizing the need for building social capital, we should not be blinded to the view that communal forest governance is easy, and the only solution. The presence of roads, new technology and the increase in the population has created new driving forces and incentives for the management of forests. Forces that traditional societies (and most contemporary ones) may have little experience of dealing with and which require them to make trade-offs between short-term profit-maximization from extractive use and long run sustainable use in the interests of the collective good of society. These trade-offs are no easy task within a civil society that is increasingly heterogeneous (Heinen 1996). However, donor agencies and governments alike need to accept the burden of correcting past mistakes to enable this to occur through supporting programs that define and codify property so that it is accessible to the poor and disenfranchised.

As assets, forests become obvious arenas for conflicting and diverse interests resulting in claiming, taking and use. The forests are both social and political arenas, where the interests of small holders, indigenous people, government management agencies, conservation groups (both local and international), timber companies and private organizations are brought to bear. With the development of international markets, governments or their officials, appropriate resource ownership and resource user rights from private or community interests. The taking of rights represents a redistribution of wealth to the government. Such appropriations are not only undertaken under the guise of 'protecting' the resource from the people; nor is it just a matter of governmental grasping, but it opens up opportunities for manoeuvring natural-resource exploitation and the associated financial benefits (Ascher 1999). These takings were completed by (i) invoking highly principled causes;

(ii) limiting the confiscation to the rights of marginal members of society; and (iii) reliance upon indirect methods such as increasing the cost of protecting rights or proving traditional rights (Ascher 1999). Indigenous people need to be protected from governments that attempt to apply these techniques to the capture of carbon entitlements. The appropriation of rights by government also meant that the nexus of enforcement of rights was passed back to their management agency, whose officials have no incentive for adopting the long-term view necessary for sustainable forest management. The officials within forest-management agencies usually face the prospect of being transferred every three years, so that any benefit they can acquire is limited to this time-frame through ensuring any personal opportunities attached to logging are maximized. These officials therefore have little incentive to protect the underlying resources that they are required to manage and protect.

Environmental agencies, which may be have been considered as being the appropriate agency for addressing the policy and government failures, have proved to be ineffective and weak in the forest-management arena. For example, their inability to address the land conversion in Sumatera, Indonesia, has resulted in significant regional costs arising from the burning of natural forests as the wilderness was converted into oil-palm plantations using fire. Likewise, in Sri Lanka, where sectoral Environmental Impact Assessment statements that are not site specific legitimize poor logging practices that damage waterways and important biodiversity values. In this latter example, the environmental agency's inability was further compounded by their inclusion as part of the Forestry Ministry, leading to a direct conflict of interest between the production and conservation objectives of government. Under government forestry programmes, such incentive systems are likely to result in so-called carbon-sink forests being harvested, placing a high risk on any associated carbon-sink contracts.

Non-sustainable logging represents a mismatch of social and private benefits attached to forests. While society as a whole may benefit from watershed protection, biodiversity, shelter, protein, etc., the reality is that most of these values have little direct financial contribution to the owner or the management agencies themselves. This disparity between private financial and social costs and benefits is reportedly changed by the addition of water benefits, when water users pay for watershed protection (Creedy & Wurzbacjer 2001). Carbon entitlements will add yet another value to the bundle of attributes changing the relative value of *in situ* protection and logging. However, as management agency officials will not directly benefit from this, it provides little additional benefit for *in situ* protection of state-managed forests than has been the case for the last decade or more. As such, there is no reason to believe that state-controlled *in situ* protection will in fact supply the carbon sequestration objectives. Forests under the management control of the forest owner or communal owners, such as indigenous people, will, however, have increased incentives for *in situ* protection. The effect of adding carbon values to the benefit stream of forests has been shown to increase the rotation length and, when combined with water yields, the rotation length was found to be infinite (Creedy & Wurzbacjer 2001).

New social scarcities

The notion of adding to the bundle of private rights mirrors the relative weights placed on logging benefits compared with sustained harvesting, shelter, cultural, wildlife and biodiversity values that were previously applied by indigenous communities. The concept of forest rights is very much multidimensional and more than simple tenure. A tree and a forest need to be viewed as a bundle of rights (Fortman 1985). Different parts of a tree or forest often differ in terms of who owns, inherits, can use or dispose of a tree or other forest products. The bundle of rights is only ever partly defined, as it represents the collective body of social experience and scarcity that existed or was understood by civil society, including local indigenous communities. The movement of the frontiers of development back through forest lands has developed an increased awareness of the consequences of deforestation, leading to the redefinition of social scarcities attached to the functions of forests other than the provision of financial capital from logging. The priority is therefore to search for the means to define these scarcities into policy and institutional frameworks that enable their effective management. In this sense, carbon-absorption functions, like watershed protection, are undefined. However, as items, products or services increase in value as a result of scarcity, social relations with respect to a resource alter, resulting in the redefinition of rights and therefore the manner in which people interact with the resource. Carbon rights or entitlements are new and will change the manner in which people interact with trees and forests, but this new creation should not be seen as a unique occurrence. It is simply a continuation of an evolving definition of forest- and tree-based property. Carbon absorption and carbon-emission trading will increase the range of property associated with a forest or trees. It will potentially change the private worth of a forest, but will local stakeholders have access to this property? If they are not made aware of the carbon entitlements and therefore cannot access the value derived from holding an entitlement, there will be no added incentive to protect the trees that absorb carbon.

From property comes capital

Capitalism creates wealth. However, past capitalism has resulted in a type of development apartheid, where the tools of wealth creation and development were not accessible to all and especially not to those that needed it most (De Soto 2000). Future success needs to address the issue of equitable access to the foundation on which development is derived: property.

Forest rights are rights to property and represent a social relation as well as formal or legal property that is usually codified in law within the Western economies. Property is more than 'the relationship between person and thing, it is the relationship between a person (or group) and all other persons in relation to that thing. A social relation by which a person, a group or a corporate entity can exclude others from the use of the thing' (Macpherson 1983). A carbon entitlement will create new property, a new stick to be added to the bundle of rights already associated with forests; a stick that enables one actor to exclude others from the use of the forest.

As a consequence of the continued appropriation of rights, many correctly argue for the exclusion of capitalism as it was, and still is, practised in the developing world, while others argue that it is the fundamental problem in any shape or form. There is clear evidence that capital-based development has provided the greatest contribution to social development. It was central to the survival of traditional communities worldwide. These communities developed physical capital to trade and settle disputes (Mauss 1950), to provide boundary demarcation and to obtain the necessary input for their subsistence and survival. What development-based capitalism has failed to see is the role of social capital and governance in the achievement of development objectives. As such, we need mechanisms that enable the transformation of physical capital into financial and economic capital that do not destroy the underlying natural capital. Not to achieve this is the single largest failing of capitalism as it has been applied to the forest sector. These failings have led to the exclusion of forest communities from political processes that would protect their rights to the opportunity to generate wealth by using their traditional physical capital as financial capital to generate empowerment and social well being. Carbon trading will create a new form of capital whose physical form is currently unrecognized in social and legal systems and whose financial and economic form may provide the incentive for a more inclusive forest-governance system, which recognizes and responds to past social injustices. Capitalism, like most social systems, can be good or bad. However, socially sensitive capitalism has the best record in producing the necessary conditions for empowerment and freedom.

For carbon entitlements, the issue needs to be addressed through deciding who should control the tools and assets of wealth creation. A continuation of past practices will place it in the hands of officials or the powerful; an attractive option is to place it directly with the poor and indigenous. To do so will require careful design of the carbon contracts; the international protocols of what is acceptable, socially and legally; the provision of cost-effective means for their participation; and a strong voice for the ongoing protection and validation of contract conditions. The generation of capital is not the overarching goal, but simply a means to an end. If indigenous people have access to the potential freedom created by appropriate entitlements to property, they can participate in the generation of wealth that capitalism brings about. It is through this wealth that they can achieve the necessary conditions for empowerment and development. Property should be considered not only for carbon but also ultimately for the full range of property currently restricted to the privileged stakeholders. Carbon-emission trading must allow access to carbon credits in a way that respects the social context of each development and provides equal opportunity for all legitimate stakeholders.

To condemn capitalism in a world dominated by it, through excluding the poor, the indigenous or the disenfranchised, denies their freedom and right to development choice. This denial will occur if the 'appropriate detail of property' and the associated specifications for the capital generated by this property are not developed within the carbon-emission-trading mechanism and instruments. The denial will equally apply if those who decry capitalism as an evil to be repelled are allowed to exclude indigenous people from the new opportunity for the freedoms that carbon-emission-trading mechanisms can create.

Forests are development assets with the potential for associated carbon entitlements under detailed contracting rules to broaden the bundle of forest-development assets. The addition of carbon entitlements will encourage retention of forest cover by local communities. The concept of carbon entitlements as property, along with the safeguards that should be applied to the process and definition of carbon entitlements, is central to the reversal of past trends. Options for carbon trading that emphasize creation of mechanisms for local people to have access to these assets through a process that ensures a third-party voice for those who have no access to carbon markets is essential.

The need to achieve equity of access to the formal property system for all of society is developed as a central theme for the protection of indigenous people. The inequitable treatment of the poor has seen their exclusion from the right to derive value from their forest resources in the past. While the Bonn Agreement and, subsequently, the Marrakech Accords ratify the use of reforestation as a legitimate carbon sink, operational details will need to develop the mechanisms to ensure equity of participation if the Kyoto Protocol is to be credible within the developing world. The signs are not encouraging, in that both the Bonn Agreement and Marrakech Accords have embraced and ratified a highly inequitable approach to the use of avoided deforestation. Here the powerful industrial state of Japan has been credited with the carbon-sink value of avoided deforestation of the Kurile Islands, while those with greatest need, the indigenous people of the developing world, have been excluded from using avoided deforestation as a means of generating wealth. This favours a rich nation against a poor people. Social and economic inequities are major contributors to global and national conflicts, yet world leaders continue to embrace inequity within their attempts to guide globalization and global co-ordination mechanisms. Surely, after the events of 2001, there is a need to avoid such discrimination and for the wealthy industrial nations to recognize that what may be in their short-term interests has significant long-term consequences. If an indigenous forest community can provide the same or better level of protection from forest conversion, why should they be considered less acceptable in benefiting from avoided deforestation carbon sinks than the Government of Japan, who have contributed so much more to the carbon loading of the global atmosphere?

Social capital from carbon property

The concept of property results in resource empowerment, and it is the basis of accumulating assets through the right to exclude others. However, it is more than simple ownership: it is conceptual and requires one to see beyond the asset. Property considers what an asset could be. For example, ownership of a car enables the holder of the ownership rights to sell it, yet the car itself does not change. Property creates capital entitlements that are legally enforceable (De Soto 2000). The poor are often excluded from formal property systems, opting instead for the working of the extralegal or informal property systems. They do so as the ease or cost of gaining access to the formal system is high relative to those associated with the extralegal system. For example, the landowners in Sri Lanka are often unable to sell their land rights (physical capital) in exchange for financial capital, which they could use to move to non-resource-dependent jobs in urban environments. As a consequence, many live away from families, in slums, and their land goes unused.

The effects of creating property within the overall development context has been detailed by De Soto (2000). The interesting aspect of this is that the findings of De Soto effectively mirror the recommendations made by the growing band of forestry experts that is promoting people-inclusive forest practices that see people not as the problem but as the solution. The major findings of De Soto are that creating property:

- fixes the economic value of potential assets;

- integrates dispersed information into one system;

- has the effect of making people accountable;

- makes assets fungible;

- networks people; and

- protects transactions.

The appropriation of forest rights by the government is predicated on the notion that the people are the problem, whereas they should be the solution. If carbon-entitlement property is accessible, the ownership of the entitlement will provide indigenous people with the potential to generate the wealth that is required for their empowerment. But to do so requires those that develop carbon entitlements to see a forest, not as sawlogs, but as a contributor to global climate protection, a function that is complementary to *in situ* forest protection as the preferred use, as opposed to the production and harvest of wood. The creation of property as a carbon entitlement is not only an endowment but also the right to establish a wider set of production from forests. To achieve these win–win options, it is essential that investors, governments and stakeholders adopt a pro-poor strategy in forming carbon-based property. To do so will create a development asset that is designed to bring the poor into the capital system and provide the choices previously denied.

Carbon entitlements must recognize how indigenous smallholders connect to the varied outside influences on natural resources, such as through policies, markets, laws and social changes. Carbon entitlements should not only reflect the law that specifies them but also spell-out how rights will be perceived, recognized, ignored, appropriated or contested. Local management is not divorced from the state, markets and other influences. In some situations these influences have minimal influence that enables highly autonomous management systems to operate. However, as influences such as geographic and market barriers are continuously eroded, previously autonomous management systems become integrated into the growing market and management system.

Adopting a pro-poor strategy is one important aspect of protecting the rights of indigenous people; another is the manner and form in which the entitlement is codified. The success, and failure, of capitalism is reflected in the manner in which Western nations integrate their property into one system, whereas developing countries operate with numerous overlapping and competing systems. Ascher (1999) identifies the duplicity of systems as one of the root causes of the wastage of forest resources and a persistent failing of government and policy.

Land rights

Codification of property is the means through which legitimate ownership is protected. It enables the holder of property to exclude other members of society or organizational entities, including governmental management agencies. The means by which it is codified provides a mechanism through which a major concern of some observers may be addressed. The concern is that the development of carbon property will enable those with wealth or authority, such as corporate entities or government agencies, to use their power and authority for their own benefit and not that of local communities. Within the property system in developing nations, individuals can remain anonymous and therefore their rights cannot be protected. Similarly the takers of rights can also be anonymous, so that they have nothing to lose. Unified and codified systems remove the anonymity and provide the options for sanction and accountability, which also creates the possibility of forfeiture of property for offenders, a large disincentive to participate in the taking of rights.

The linking of a physical asset to a property system makes them fungible, enabling comparison between assets and their values while systemization reduces the costs of management and administration. Most importantly, it offers the holders of rights the opportunity to split their assets into shares to be held or traded. For indigenous people this may include community rights, which communities allocate to individuals or hold communally according to traditional allocation rules that support local culture, while retaining the strengths of community resource-management systems. Carbon entitlements can be sold, in part or whole, at different points in time, to provide local communities with a sustainable flow of resources.

Fungible assets mean that owners are attached to assets, assets to addresses or locations and ownership to enforcement, converting stakeholders into a network of individually identifiable and accountable agents. Through this networking arrangement, the codification of property enables transactions to be tracked through time and space, providing all parties with greater certainty over ownership and transactions.

The creation of property or entitlements in carbon may therefore bring about a positive opportunity, provided it can be established in a manner that empowers indigenous people and addresses the perverse incentives to protect forests under the control of a governmental management agency. As a new stick in the bundle of rights there is a fundamental question as to how the newly created property will be assigned. Traditionally property was created in the extralegal or informal systems of society and then ratified or formalized in the legal system. The decision on the nature of carbon entitlements will influence the assignment. For example, in most legal systems the consideration of carbon as a mineral would place the initial assignment of entitlements with the government. If, however, it is viewed as a crop, then the assignment is most probably linked to the existing entitlements to use the land or the crop on it. It is imperative that the lack of experience with carbon management is not used as an excuse, by unscrupulous governments or their agencies, to exclude forest communities, as they too have no experience in the management of forests for carbon. Just as easily it could be argued that government management agencies have less appropriate experience, given their supervision and support for the devastation caused. To provide the correct set of incentives and create the opportunity to enable access to development opportunity, it is essential that carbon entitlements be assigned to indigenous or local communities.

Forest carbon-sinks entitlements

The following principles adapted from those of the Forest Stewardship Council are proposed as applicable for defining the process and assignment of forest-carbon-sinks entitlements. These entitlements will be eligible for the issuing of 'certificates' that will be the basis for trading of carbon. The process for trading will involve a national trading desk or register, which will be required to conform to international standards and will adopt rules that support these standards. While trades could be arranged outside the agreed standards, these would increase the risk to the buyer of carbon credits.

The recommended principles for the assignment and management of carbon entitlements include the following:

- Compliance with, and respect for, national laws and sovereignty including the enforcement of laws and protection of rights.

- Respect for the tenure, use rights and carbon entitlements to natural resources by defining long-term rights to forests, forest use and forest lands.

- The documentation of tenure, forest-use rights and carbon entitlements, along with formal legal recognition.

- The assignment of entitlements respects original forest rights irrespective of any reassignment of logging rights to the state and that any assignment does not threaten or diminish existing rights, or claimants of past rights.

- Boundaries of the territory involved and any third party ownership are specified wherever appropriate.

- The certificate will need to specify levels of sustainable use and the locales where this can occur. This specification will need to address the monitoring and supervision of these parameters.

- A full specification of the direct stakeholders who are involved in the agreement is required.

- Carbon entitlements can be assigned communally with the local community institutions holding the entitlement able to allocate or divide the entitlement (or benefits from the entitlement) according to processes they decide.

- Disputes over rights will be resolved before the issuance of carbon certificates, and that an independent non-governmental third party will assess each proposed assignment for the existence of claims over property.

- Indigenous people will control forest management on their lands unless they delegate or sell these rights.

- Any forest-management activity will not threaten directly or indirectly the rights of indigenous people.

- Appropriate mechanisms will be provided for the resolution of conflicts or claims. Any existing carbon entitlement certificate shall not be eligible for trading if any outstanding claim or conflict exists.

- An area of land or forest that has an assigned carbon-entitlement certificate will enable non-destructive use of forests while protecting ecologically sensitive areas and habitats.

- The certificates should address the issue of socio-economic infrastructure and the likely demand for this, as well as the impact that such infrastructure would have on local people and the forests covered by the contracts.

- Certificates will only be awarded to areas that use appropriate species and support heterogeneity.

- Forest conversion will be specifically prohibited (see Chapters 2 and 7).

The specification of these principles needs to apply to the international standards that are used to construct the certificate and guide the trading of certificates. At the national level there is a need to provide mechanisms that provide access to the national trading process. It is suggested that a national taskforce be convened for establishing the local interpretation of the above principles. The taskforce should comprise representatives of government institutions, the judiciary, legal-profession associations and non-government organizations that currently work with indigenous and local communities in natural resource and social issues. The taskforce would also have an *ex-officio* representative from a reputable international agency (the International Timber Organization) or non-governmental organization that would supervise and verify the interpretation of the principles and the manner in which they are applied. This would extend to a review of the issued certificates to ensure that conflicts are managed.

Participation in the processes that establish carbon trading is essential to the building of partnerships and the development of commitments to implement a forest-management regime. This participation needs to move beyond the informing and consultation steps of participation to include the following:

- Scoping of the social network and relationships to identify who matters most and to define the respective roles of all the players in terms of rights, responsibilities and rewards.

- An assessment of the capacity to participate both in terms of carbon trading but also in the wider social interrelationships that will need to develop.

- Development of a collaborative management agreement between the parties to outline commitments and details of the agreements, especially with respect to the boundaries and rights the agreement applies to rather than the simple specification of ownership.

- The national trading desk will ensure the ongoing involvement of all the parties, as this is an important determinant of success. Investors cannot enter the system with the expectation that they will not be required to maintain a presence—even if their presence is only sporadic and not full time. Like all partnerships, these will need to be maintained and nurtured.

Conclusion

The concept is simple. How can the natural capital of forests be turned into social capital without destroying the underlying natural resource. Carbon entitlements and trading is one such mechanism. The challenge is partly democratic and requires the admission of forest communities into the policy, the policy process and management of forest resources, as these people are the solution (Bass 2001a, b). Carbon entitlements provide policy makers, political decision makers and global watchdogs with an opportunity to apply new instruments that develop property. The allocation of entitlements can redress past social injustices that have depleted the social capital of forest communities. The linking of forest communities to forest governance is increasingly recognized as the only option. This should not come as a surprise, as it mirrors the experience in nearly all other resources such as land, water and houses. Carbon entitlements need to be sensitive to the needs of forest communities while providing them access to the benefits of a strong property system and the development freedoms this can provide. To do so requires a commitment by all stakeholders to support the management of forests for wider civil society. Carbon trading and property entitlements provide another chance to get this right, or at least better than in the past.

References

Ascher, W. 1999 *Why governments waste natural resources: policy failures in developing countries.* Baltimore, MD: Johns Hopkins University Press.

Bass, S. 2001a The importance of social values. In *The forests handbook: an overview of forest science* (ed. J. Evans), vol. 1, ch. 14. Blackwell Science.

Bass, S. 2001b Working with forest stakeholders. In *The forests handbook: an overview of forest science* (ed. J. Evans), vol. 2, ch. 10. Blackwell Science.

Creedy, J. & Wurzbacjer, A. D. 2001 The economic vlaue of a forested catchment with timber, water and carbon sequestration benefits. *Ecol. Econ.* **38**, 71–85.

De Soto, H. 2000 *The mystery of capital: why capitalism triumphs in the west and fails everywhere else*, p. 276. New York: Basic Books.

Fortman, L. 1985 The tree tenure factor in agroforestry with particular reference to Africa. *Agroforest. Syst.* **2**, 229–251.

Gordon, J. C., Berry, J. K. & Schmidt, R. 1999 The problem and potential solutions. In *Forests to fight poverty: creating national strategies* (ed. R. Schmidt, J. K. Berry & J. C. Gordon), ch. 9. New Haven, CT: Yale University Press.

Hall, A. L. 2001 People in tropical forests: problem or solution. In *Proc. Forest–Water–People in Humid Tropics Conf., Kuala Lumpur, 2000.* UNESCO.

Heinen, J. T. 1996 Human behavior, incentives and protected area management. *Conserv. Biol.* **10**, 681–684.

Macpherson, C. B. 1983 *Property: mainstream and critical positions.* University of Toronto Press.

Mauss, M. 1950 *The gift.* New York: Routledge Books.

Peluso, N. 1992 *Rich forests, poor people: resource control and resistance in Java.* Berkeley, CA: University of California Press.

Saunders, L. S. & Weber, J. 1996 The economic value of Bukit Baka: Bukit Raya National Park, Kalimantan, Indonesia. Report. USAID National Resources Management Program.

Schmidt, R., Berry, J. K. & Gordon, J. C. (eds) 1999 *Forests to fight poverty: creating national strategies.* New Haven, CT: Yale University Press.

Shen, S. (ed.) 1995 *Managing Asia's forests and biodiversity.* Essay collection. World Bank Group.

Chapter 13

Species survival and carbon retention in commercially exploited tropical rainforest

GHILLEAN T. PRANCE

Ecosystem services

There have been many recent attempts to place a value on areas of tropical forest. Costanza *et al.* (1997) attempted to place a value on the whole world's ecosystem and natural capital. They based their estimate on 17 different ecosystem services of 16 biomes and calculated a value of $16–$54 trillion (10^{12}) per year, with an average of $33 trillion. This compares with a global gross national product of $18 trillion. Estimates like this that fall outside the market are hard to calculate, but it is appropriate to consider this vital aspect of value of ecosystem services before looking at a few, in comparison, very minor market-driven approaches to forest conservation. The ecosystems services used by Costanza *et al.* to make their calculations included gas regulation such as carbon dioxide/oxygen (CO_2/O_2) balance, as well as climate regulation and control of greenhouse gas. We should not underestimate the value of rainforest for the services as well as for the enormous genetic resources of its biodiversity. There might be more forest standing if an accounting had been made of the value of ecosystem benefits before alteration. Purely on ecosystem service value, a non-use option is often more beneficial than the alternative use to which forest land has been put. The total economic value of ecosystems is discussed well in Pearce *et al.* (1989) and that of rainforests in Pearce (1990). In the latter, Pearce estimated that the indirect carbon credit due to a single hectare of conserved forest was $1300 in 1990. This was based on a value of $13.00 per tonne of carbon. Many aspects of nature's services are summed up in Daily (1997).

Ruitenbeek (1989) calculated the value of £5.8 million for the role of the Korup rainforest in Cameroon in supporting fisheries and in flood control. The proposed alternative land use was valued at slightly more than £3 million. Much deforestation could have been avoided if adequate cost–benefit analysis had been made prior to felling the trees. Any free-market approach to conservation must include much more than an analysis of the direct costs of, and profits from, forest products. Tropical forests must be valued for their role in carbon storage, flood control, watershed protection and many other ecosystem services.

Marketing and valuing rainforests

During the past 15 years or so there has been much effort to place value on areas of forest and to promote the extraction of non-timber forest products (NTFPs). This has been motivated by the desire to conserve the standing forest rather than replacement by alternative systems. There is not space here to review this vast literature, but good summaries are given by Ros-Tonen *et al.* (1995), Richards (1993), the FAO (1991) and Panayotou & Ashton (1993). Much interest in the market value of standing forests was generated by Peters *et al.* (1989*a*) when they calculated a net present value (NPV) of $6330 per hectare for a forest at Mishana in Peru. This was based on an annual possible income of $697.79 from the extraction of latex, fruits and a limited amount of timber. Piñedo-Vasquez *et al.* (1990*a*) and many other authors have challenged this high estimate. Some of the constraints are:

- the fluctuation of commodity prices (the fall in rubber prices since that work was done is a good example),

- the fact that most individuals and rural communities lack land tenure, and

- decisions about use of land in the region are based on both subsistence and market-oriented considerations and the calculations did not allow for subsistence needs.

This was followed up in greater detail by Piñedo-Vasquez *et al.* (1990*b*) in a study of use-values of tree species in a reserve in Peru. They found that 60.1% of tree species in their 7.5 hectare sample were used, representing 66.4% of individual trees. Their study, based on the methods of Prance *et al.* (1987) used for indigenous peoples, did not attempt to place a value on the forest, but it did place a use-value index on all trees used. Piñedo-Vasquez *et al.* (1992) compared the economic returns from extraction of NTFPs with forest conversion to swidden agriculture. They concluded that rural populations of Amazonian Peru can be expected to continue converting forested land to swidden agriculture unless alternative land uses become more attractive economically.

At the other end of the Amazon, Anderson (1988, 1990) and Anderson & Ioris (1992, 1994) studied the use of forest in the Amazon delta region. Their study at Combu Island near to Belém is an example of highly profitable living from extraction of 'hearts of palm' from açaí (*Euterpe oleracea*), cacao fruits and seeds, rubber latex and shrimp. This system works for a number of reasons:

- proximity to a large market in Belém;

- the high natural density of the palms in the ecosystem;

- the stability of the local population; and

- the high degree of forest conservation.

The average annual household income of a family in 1989–1990 was $4195, which is far greater than other Amazon communities at that time (e.g. Florschutz 1983; Schwartzman 1989). Anderson is careful to point out that the study at Combu is under highly specific favourable conditions and cannot be used to make general extrapolations on the viability of harvesting NTFPs elsewhere. The açaí market was further discussed in Smith (2001).

One reason for success at Combu is the natural density of palm trees in the estuarine ecosystem. Peters *et al.* (1989*b*) termed this type of forest, where one or few species dominate, 'oligarchic forests'. They gave several examples of these in addition to *Euterpe*-palm-dominated forests, where extraction is likely to prove economically profitable and sustainable:

- *Grias peruviana* in Amazonian Peru (sacha mangua, see Peters & Hammond (1990));

- *Myrciaria dubia* (camu camu, see Peters & Vasquez (1987)) in the floodplain;

- *Orbignya phalerata* (babassu, now *Attalea phalerata*, see Balick (1987)); and

- *Jessenia bataua* (see Balick 1986; Balick & Gershoff 1981).

Because the forests have dominant species rather than the more typical species-diverse rainforest (Gentry 1988; Prance *et al.* 1987; Valencia *et al.* 1994), they can generate viable economic returns from market-oriented extraction.

Grimes *et al.* (1994) calculated the value of three hectares of primary rainforest in the Upper Rio Napo region of Ecuador, inhabited by Quijos Quichua peoples. They separately valued trees on an individual basis for productivity rather that at the per-species level of Peters *et al.* (1989*a*). They excluded trees that were too young to produce, too tall or dangerous to climb or non-productive. This meant that only 72 out of 105 trees of harvestable species were counted. They came to NPVs of $2939 and $2721 for upland forest plots and $1257 for a floodplain alluvial plot. This was compared with NPVs of less than $500 for agriculture, $188 for timber extraction and $57–$287 for cattle ranching 30 km from a good market in that area of Ecuador.

Balick & Mendelsohn (1992) assessed the economic value of traditional medicines gathered in the rainforests of Belize. Their study suggests that the revenue from their two sample hectares was $564 and $3064, respectively. The NPV of $3327 per hectare was calculated on the basis of a 50 year rotation. Melnyk & Bell (1996) calculated the value of forest as a food resource to the Huottuja Indians of Venezuela. The monetary value of the food they could gather from the forest compared favourably with revenue received from other land uses, timber extraction and working as labourers to earn money to buy food.

Godoy *et al.* (2000) studied the use of rainforest by the Tawahlea of Honduras. They studied both consumption of food and sale of forest goods to establish a value of the forest. Their study falls at the lower end of those cited. They found the annual value of a hectare of rainforest to vary from $49–$1089. They suggested that at this low value the local people are more likely to clear forests for alternative uses.

These and many other papers show that valuing the forest and promoting the use of NTFPs has been a popular pursuit in the Neotropics. Following the assassination of Chico Mendes, leader of the rubber trappers in Acre State, Brazil has established a number of extractive reserves especially in the states of Acre, Amapá and Rondônia (see Schwartzman 1989, 1992; Allegretti 1990). In Brazil, more than 3 million hectares are now in extractive reserves (Nepstad & Schwartzman 1992). In these reserves it is permitted to extract NTFPs, but not to clear cut the majority of the forest. While they have slowed down deforestation in some places, the inhabitants have had a difficult existence with the fall in the price of rubber latex and the fluctuating price of brazil nuts on the commodity market. In order to sustain extractive reserves, they must be based on much more than two commodities. Conservation International worked on the promotion of vegetable ivory or tagua from the forests of Ecuador and Colombia as a means of income from this hotspot of biodiversity. While they sold a considerable amount of tagua (900 t) at double the previous market price, this project ran into a number of difficulties. Tagua buttons cracked after repeated washing in washing machines. It was then necessary to make buttons of sturdier shapes. Low-priced buttons from other synthetic sources also presented problems to the tagua project. The development and marketing of new NTFPs is not without its difficulties!

There have been several examples of trying to add value to NTFPs to strengthen the extraction industry. The Body Shop in the UK buys various products directly from the extractionists and can thereby pay a respectable price because this process avoids a long chain of intermediaries. Both brazil nut oil and babassu palm oil are supplied in this way. The author recently visited a cooperative in the town of Altamira in Pará State, Brazil, which is owned and run by the local people, mostly of tribal origin. Amazoncoop (see www.amazoncoop.org) processes brazil nuts in Altamira to produce the oil and sell it directly to The Body Shop. This combination of a cooperative and a direct purchaser needs to be expanded for other NTFPs in other places.

I have concentrated on examples from the Neotropics, but the promotion of NTFPs and the valuation of forests has been done in many other countries, for example, in India (Appasamy 1993; Ganesan 1993) and Sri Lanka (Gunatilake *et al.* 1993). The volume of *Economic Botany* (vol. 47) in which these papers were published is a good analysis of the economic valuation and sustainable management of NTFPs. Peluso (1992) described the rattan trade in Indonesia, which has been carried on for centuries through extraction, although in this case wild sources are over-exploited and cultivation seems a more promising of way of sustaining production (Dransfield 1988). An excellent analysis of the use of NTFPs in India is given by Tewari (1994), where, in addition to such aspects as value, more emphasis is placed on expanding local processing to add value, clarifying aspects of property rights and studying and understanding the sociological aspects of the extraction process.

Ecotourism

One way of marketing the standing forest is through ecotourism. Like extraction of products, there are successful and sustainable examples of ecotourism and ones that are damaging to the forest ecosystem. Some of the same constraints apply, especially that the market demand should not lead to over-exploitation by allowing too many people into a site. The Galapagos Islands are reaching this point. There the number of tourists and their itineraries have been well controlled, but each year their numbers are allowed to increase.

In Amazonia, especially in Peru, there are an increasing number of lodges and camps, and also boats, that carry out environmentally sensitive ecotourism. It is essential to encourage local initiatives, where the money spent benefits local peoples and not just large foreign tour operators. If this is not done, the system is unsustainable. A good guide to some of the places available in Central and South America is Castner (1990). Increasingly, guide books are available to encourage sensitive ecotourism (e.g. Pearson & Beletsky 2001). The Amazon Cooperative mentioned above runs Tataquara Lodge on the Xingu River in Brazil. A most exciting destination for the naturalist and ethnobotanist.

The impact of extraction

The examples of extraction of NTFPs cited here vary from theoretical estimates such as Peters *et al.* (1989a) to highly practical analyses of actual extraction (e.g. Godoy *et al.*). Some of these are likely to be sustainable, especially those in oligarchic forests (Peters *et al.* 1989b; Peters 1992), and others are over-exploiting the resource (Peluso 1992). It is therefore important to assess the pros and cons of allowing the marketing of rainforest or, indeed, any other ecosystem. To be viable, extraction must be sustainable and at the same time yield a viable livelihood for those people involved that outcompetes alternative land uses.

In many places, extraction has resulted in extinction or local extinction of species. This has happened in many island communities; for example, the extraction of the Saint Helena ebony (*Trochetiopsis melanoxylon*) for its wood, where only two individuals remained in the wild. In some parts of its range, quinine species (*Cinchona*) became locally extinct through over collection. In Brazil, in some areas of Amazonia, rosewood (*Aniba rosaeodora*) has been completely eliminated. The method of extraction can cause extinction. In Peru, the aguaje palm (*Mauritia flexuosa*) has an important marketable fruit. However, the fruits have often been collected by felling the female trees of this dioecious species. There are vast stands of male trees remaining, which do not produce fruit and have no means of reproduction. Even if a species is not made extinct by extraction, there can be enormous genetic erosion of its population. In an inventory made of forest in Rondônia, nearly all the mahogany trees had been extracted. Any that remained were either diseased or with twisted trunks and not the genetic material one would select for further timber production (Lisboa *et al.* 1987, 1991).

Heinzman & Reining (1988) studied the extraction of the leaves of *Chamaedora* palms for decorative purposes in Guatemala. They found a lower population density and flowering intensity in harvested areas than in areas where no harvesting took place. Padoch & de Jong (1989) found that there is a huge difference between the potential harvest from an area of forest and the actual quantities extracted. They found that, on average, only 2.5–3.5% of the potential amount of products that could be harvested are actually used. This contradicts the optimistic valuations of Peters *et al.* (1989a), but it could be a good thing because it means that resources are not over-exploited. However, when demand for a product increases, driven by the market forces, over-exploitation and non-sustainable methods of harvesting often occur.

One of the greatest difficulties of extraction is that often it is not compatible with a free-market approach. So many products have gone through a boom-and-bust cycle. When a product becomes acceptable on the market, the demand can soon exceed the sustainable supply or, alternatively, commercial pressure leads to the manufacture of synthetic substitutes (Torres & Martine 1991). A good analysis showing that extractive products are not always compatible with the market's need for standardization and continual growth by expansion is that of Homma (1989). One result of success is that it can then lead to cultivation of the species concerned. This cultivation will lead to habitat destruction rather than conservation of the species of the forest as a carbon sink.

The study by Peters & Hammond (1990) of several fruits that are extracted in the Peruvian Amazon estimated the quantity of fruits that could be taken while maintaining the population of the species. This type of study is needed to protect a product from over-exploitation. Another problem with extraction can be the loss of nutrients from the ecosystem, especially where the soils are poor. Some products remove more essential nutrients than others and this always needs to be taken into consideration. Nutrient loss is far more likely to occur on the upland soils of Amazonia than in lowland alluvial soils, where the nutrients are replaced annually through the flooding. The fruits studied by Peters & Hammond (1990), such as camu camu (*Myrciaria dubia*) and sacha mangua (*Grias peruviana*), both occur in large natural stands in alluvial soils and are ideal for extractivism.

The process of extraction of a product may modify the ecosystem in a way that effects other organisms that depend upon the extracted product or its species for their survival. The hoarded brazil nuts are a vital food for agoutis during the dry season, when other food is scarce. If too many brazil nuts are removed from the forest, it could affect the population of agoutis.

Another difficulty is that the production of a product can be highly variable from year to year, yet the market demands a constant supply of a product. Many tropical trees have unusual phenological patterns and flower and fruit irregularly or only once every two or more years. The brazil nut tends to produce abundantly only every second year. The market finds this sort of product hard to accommodate.

It is for these sorts of reasons that local peoples have often found alternative land uses, such as swidden agriculture, more attractive. This is particularly true when they depend upon the land for their subsistence. Many of these peoples turn the land over to agroforestry systems, which, while not helping conservation of wild species, do store a considerable amount of carbon. For analysis of such a system amongst the Bora Indians of Peru, see Denevan *et al.* (1984) and Denevan & Padoch (1988), and for the Huastec in Mexico, Alcorn (1984, 1989).

Conclusion

There are many difficulties with using extractive reserves as a means of conservation and many people have questioned its validity as a method (e.g. Anderson 1990; Browder 1992; Fearnside 1989). However, there is no doubt that the establishment of extractive reserves in Amazonia has slowed the rate of deforestation in some areas. Extractivism cannot cope well with price fluctuations of the commodity market, the rising demands of products through a growth economy and also the chain of intermediaries between the extractor and the final buyer, which means that the extractor receives a pittance for his work. Where this chain of middlemen is eliminated, extraction is more likely to succeed.

It is also important to note that, quite apart from the marketing of products and the issues of carbon sinks, it is essential to conserve forest because of the dependence of so many people, both indigenous and non-indigenous, on it for their own subsistence. Forest ecosystems provide food for many local peoples and produce products and employment that enable people to buy food.

References

Alcorn, J. B. 1984 *Huastec Mayan ethnobotany.* Austin, TX: University of Texas Press.

Alcorn, J. B. 1989 An economic analysis of Huastec Mayan forest management. In *Fragile lands of Latin America: strategies for sustainable development* (ed. J. O. Browder), pp. 182–206. Boulder, CO: Westview Press.

Allegretti, M. H. 1990 Extractive reserves: an alternative for reconciling development and environmental conservation in Amazonia. In *Alternatives to deforestation* (ed. A. B. Anderson), pp. 252–264. New York: Columbia University Press.

Anderson, A. B. 1988 Use and management of native forests dominated by açaí palm (*Euterpe oleracea* Mart.) in the Amazon estuary. *Adv. Econ. Bot.* **6**, 144–154.

Anderson, A. B. 1990 Extractivism and forest management by inhabitants in the Amazon estuary. In *Alternatives to deforestation: steps towards sustainable use of the Amazon rainforest* (ed. A. B. Anderson), pp. 65–85. New York: Columbia University Press.

Anderson, A. B. & Ioris, E. M. 1992 Valuing the rainforest: economic strategies by small-scale forest extractivists in the Amazon estuary. *Human Ecol.* **20**, 337–369.

Anderson, A. B. & Ioris, E. M. 1994 The logic of extraction: resource management and income generation by extractive producers in the Amazon estuary. In *Traditional resource use in Neotropical forests* (ed. K. H. Redford & C. Padoch). New York: Columbia University Press.

Appasamy, P. 1993 Role of non-timber forest products in a subsistence economy: the case of a joint forestry project in India. *Econ. Bot.* **47**, 258–267.

Balick, M. J. 1986 *Systematics and economic botany of the Oenocarpus-Jessenia (Palmae) complex.* Advances in Econonomic Botany Series, vol. 3. New York: New York Botanical Garden.

Balick, M. J. 1987 The economic utilisation of the Babaçu palm: a conservation strategy for sustaining tropical forest resources. *J. Wash. Acad. Sci.* **77**, 215–223.

Balick, M. J. & Gershoff, S. N. 1981 Nutritional evaluation of the *Jessenia bataua* palm: source of high-quality protein oil from tropical America. *Econ. Bot.* **35**, 261–271.

Balick, M. J. & Mendelsohn, R. 1992 Assessing the economic value of traditional medicines from tropical rainforests. *Conserv. Biol.* **6**, 128–130.

Browder, J. O. 1992 The limits of extractivism: tropical forest strategies beyond extractive reserves. *Bioscience* **42**, 174–182.

Castner, J. L. 1990 *Rainforests: a guide to research and tourist facilities at selected tropical forest sites in Central and South America.* Gainesville, FL: Feline Press.

Costanza, R. L. (and 12 others) 1997 The value of the world's ecosystem services and natural capital. *Nature* **387**, 253–260.

Daily, G. C. (ed.) 1997 *Nature's services. Societal dependence on natural ecosystems.* Washington, DC: Island Press.

Denevan, W. M. & Padoch, C. (eds) 1988 Indigenous agroforestry in the Peruvian Amazon. *Adv. Econ. Bot.* **5**, 1–107.

Denevan, W. M., Treacy, J. M., Alcorn, J. B., Padoch, C., Denslow, J. & Paiton, S. F. 1984 Indigenous agroforestry in the Peruvian Amazon: Bora Indian management of swidden fallows. *Interciencia* **9**, 346–357.

Dransfield, J. 1988 Prospects for rattan cultivation. *Adv. Econ. Bot.* **6**, 190–200.

FAO 1991 Non-wood forest products: the way ahead. FAO Forestry Paper no. 97.

Fearnside, P. M. 1989 Extractive reserves in Brazilian Amazonia. *Bioscience* **39**, 387–393.

Florschutz, G. H. H. 1983 Análise econômica de establicimentos rurais do Município de Tomé-açu, Pará: Um estudo de caso. EMBRAPA/CPATU Documentos 19, Belém, Brazil.

Ganesan, B. 1993 Extraction of non-timber forest products, including fodder and fuelwood in Mudumalai, India. *Econ. Bot.* **47**, 268–274.

Gentry, A. H. 1988 Tree species richness of upper Amazonian forests. *Proc. Natl Acad. Sci. USA* **85**, 156–159.

Godoy, R., Wilkie, D., Overman, H., Cubas, A., Cubas, G., Demmer, J., McSweeney, K. & Brokaw, N. 2000 Valuation of consumption and sale of forest goods from a Central America rainforest. *Nature* **406**, 62–63.

Grimes, A. (and 11 others) 1994 Valuing the rainforest: the economic value of non-timber forest products in Ecuador. *Ambio* **23**, 405–410.

Gunatilake, H. M., Senartne, D. M. A. H. & Abeygunawardena, P. 1993 Role of non-timber forest products in the economy of peripheral communities of Knuckles National Wilderness Area of Sri Lanka. *Econ. Bot.* **47**, 282–290.

Heinzman, R. & Reining, C. 1988 Desarrollo rural sostenido: reservas forestales de extracción en el Norte de el Petén en Guatemala. Guatemala: USAID.

Homma, A. K. O. 1989 Reserva extractavistas: uma opção de desenvolvimento viável para a Amazônia. *Pará Desenvolvimento* **25**, 35–48.

Lisboa, P. L. B., Maciel, U. N. & Prance, G. T. 1987 Perdendo Rondônia. *Ciência Hoje* **6**, 48–56.

Lisboa, P. L. B., Maciel, U. N. & Prance, G. T. 1991 Some effects of colonisation on the tropical flora of Amazonia: a case study for Rondônia. *Kew Bull.* **16**, 187–204.

Melnyk, M. & Bell, N. 1996 The direct-use values of tropical moist forest foods: the Huottoja (Piaroa) Amerindians of Venezuela. *Ambio* **25**, 468–472.

Nepstad, D. & Schwartzman, S. 1992 Introduction to non-timber product extraction from tropical forests: evaluation of a conservation and development strategy. *Adv. Econ. Bot.* **9**, 7–12.

Padoch, C. & de Jong, W. 1989 Production and profit in agroforestry: an example from the Peruvian Amazon. In *Fragile lands of Latin America* (ed. J. O. Browder), pp. 102–112. Boulder, CO: Westview Press.

Panayotou, T. & Ashton, P. 1993 *Not by timber alone*. Washington, DC: Island Press.

Pearce, D. W. 1990 An economic approach to saving the tropical forests. LEEC. Discussion Paper 90-06. London: IIED.

Pearce, D., Markandya, A. & Barbier, E. 1989 *Blueprint for a green economy*. London: Earthscan.

Pearson, D. L. & Beletsky, L. 2001 *The eco-traveller's wildlife guide: Brazil Amazon and Pantanal*. Academic.

Peluso, N. L. 1992 The rattan trade in East Kalimantan, Indonesia. *Adv. Econ. Bot.* **9**, 115–127.

Peters, C. M. 1992 The ecology and economics of oligarchic forests. *Adv. Econ. Bot.* **9**, 15–22.

Peters, C. M. & Hammond, E. J. 1990 Fruits from the flooded forests of Peruvian Amazonia: yield estimates for natural populations of three promising species. *Adv. Econ. Bot.* **8**, 159–176.

Peters, C. M. & Vasquez, A. 1987 Estudios ecológicos de Camu-camu (*Myrciaria dubia*) I. Producción de frutos en poblaciones naturales. *Acta Amazonica* **16**, 161–173.

Peters, C. M., Gentry, A. H. & Mendelsohn, R. 1989a Valuation of an Amazonian rainforest. *Nature* **339**, 655–656.

Peters, C. M., Balick, M. J., Kahn, F. & Anderson, A. B. 1989b Oligarchic forests of economic plants in Amazonia: utilisation and conservation of an important tropical resource. *Conserv. Biol.* **3**, 341–361.

Piñedo-Vasquez, M., Zarin, D. & Jipp, P. 1990a Land use in the Amazon. *Nature* **348**, 397.

Piñedo-Vasquez, M., Zarin, D., Jipp, P. & Chota-Inuna, J. 1990b Use values of tree species in a communal forest reserve in Northeast Peru. *Conserv. Biol.* **4**, 405–416.

Piñedo-Vasquez, M., Zarin, D. & Jipp, P. 1992 Economic returns from forest conversion in the Peruvian Amazon. *Ecol. Econ.* **6**, 163–173.

Prance, G. T., Balée, W., Boom, B. M. & Carneiro, R. L. 1987 Quantitative ethnobotany and the case for conservation in Amazonia. *Conserv. Biol.* **1**, 296–310.

Richards, E. M. 1993 *Commercialisation of non-timber forest products in Amazonia*. Socio-economic Series 2. Chatham: Natural Resources Institute.

Ros-Tonen, M., Dijkman, W. & Lammerts van Bueren, E. 1995 *Commercial and sustainable extraction of non-timber forest products*. Wageningen: Tropenbos.

Ruitenbeek, H. J. 1989 Appendix 13: Korup National Park social cost benefit analysis. In *WWF, Republic of Cameroon, Korup Project: plan for developing the park and its support zone.* London: WWF.

Schwartzman, S. 1989 Extractive reserves: the rubber tappers' strategy for sustainable use of the Amazonian rainforest. In *Fragile lands of Latin America: strategies for sustainable development* (ed. J. O. Browder), pp. 150–165. Boulder, CO: Westview Press.

Schwartzman, S. 1992 Land distribution and social costs of frontier development in Brazil: social and historical context of extractive reserves. In *Non-timber products from tropical forests: evaluation of a conservation and development strategy* (ed. D. Nepstad & S. Schwartzman), pp. 51–66. New York: New York Botanical Garden.

Smith, N. J. H. 2001 Land use dynamics in the Amazon estuary and implications for natural resource management. *Amazoniana* **16**, 517–537.

Tewari, D. D. 1994 Developing and sustaining non-timber forest products: policy issues and concerns with special reference to India. *J. World Forest Res. Manag.* **7**, 151–177.

Torres, H. & Martine, G. 1991 Amazonian extractivism: prospects and pitfalls. In *Documento de Trabalho*, vol. 5. Brazil: Instituto Sociedade, População e Natureza.

Valencia, R., Balslev, H., Paz, Y. & Mino, G. 1994 High tree alpha diversity in Amazonian Ecuador. *Biodiversity Conserv.* **3**, 21–28.

Chapter 14

Animal conservation, carbon and sustainability

NIGEL LEADER-WILLIAMS

Introduction

This chapter seeks to examine how approaches to conserving species of animals can help enhance the conservation of ecosystems upon which the United Nations Framework Convention on Climate Change (UNFCCC) focuses. Article 4(d) of the UNFCCC sets out commitments to:

> promote and co-operate in the conservation and enhancement of sinks and reservoirs of all greenhouse gases including biomass, forests and oceans, as well as other terrestrial, coastal and marine ecosystems.

Cited in Chapter 17 of this book

Thus, the UNFCCC and the ensuing Kyoto Protocol place no direct emphasis on animal conservation. Nevertheless, the United Nations Conference on Environment and Development (UNCED, also known as the Earth Summit) focused on a wide range of global issues related to sustainable growth and development, including conserving species and their habitats. Indeed, several other globally focused 'multilateral environmental agreements' (MEAs) fully or partly embrace this objective. For example, the Convention on Wetlands of International Importance Especially as Waterfowl Habitat (negotiated in Ramsar, Iran, in 1971 and therefore known as the Ramsar Convention) was an important forerunner in this regard. The Ramsar Convention sought to balance sustainable development with incentives to protect and wisely use species of concern to particular interest groups, and therefore to continued habitat and ecosystem conservation (Lyster 1985). In contrast, tourism is one of the main free-market approaches to promoting conservation, yet was not included in the global dialogue on sustainable development at the Earth Summit.

This chapter will consider how and why species conservation has relevance to the objectives of ecosystem conservation, and the different routes by which conservation is achieved, and some of the limitations of different systems. It then looks at two key MEAs that fully or partly bear on species conservation and how these relate to wider issues of globalization and, finally, it analyses how the use of species is an important focus for market-based approaches to conservation.

Equally, market approaches are not fully achieving their objectives, and throughout the chapter, the stress is on problems and solutions.

What is the relevance of species conservation?

Our planet now faces an unprecedented human-induced extinction spasm (Ehrlich & Ehrlich 1981; Diamond 1989; Lawton & May 1995), and species are becoming increasingly threatened (Hilton-Taylor 2000). However, academic conservation biologists and practising conservationists debate whether conservation goals are best achieved by promoting management of single species as opposed to management of whole ecosystems. Critics suggest that managing populations of particular species will not allow the challenges of conserving whole ecosystems to be met. More and more species are falling below a threshold of imperilment, and funding for conservation, which is already short (James *et al.* 2000), cannot keep pace with their individual needs. Hence, some argue that ecosystem management, usually at a landscape scale, remains the best possible solution to the problems of single-species management (Simberloff 1998). Equally, how clear cut can and should this distinction be? Any practical measures that prevent or reduce forest, or other key, ecosystem loss will make a contribution to reducing carbon dioxide (CO_2) increases in the atmosphere. This in turn seems to provide a very important reason to conserve animals, for at least six key points, some ecological, some strategic.

1 The goals of ecosystem and biosphere management are unattainable without the continued survival of many species, which are the fundamental building blocks of nature and ecology (Ehrlich & Ehrlich 1981). While there may be some redundancy in ecosystems (Lawton & Brown 1993), this remains a subject of debate (Naeem *et al.* 1994). However, so-called 'keystone species' may occur at many trophic levels, and their loss has a disproportionate effect on their ecosystems (Bond 1993). Therefore, a key question for ecology, and indeed for humanity, is the extent to which the increasing loss of species may compromise the resilience of ecosystems and the consequent delivery of ecosystem services (Ehrlich & Ehrlich 1992; Heywood 1995; Daily 1997), including the maintenance of atmospheric CO_2 levels.

2 Isolated populations of species are also the fundamental units of the evolutionary process and the units upon which natural selection operates (Darwin 1859). Populations comprise individuals, which contain genetic information, and it is this genetic diversity that determines their survival and evolutionary fate, which therefore underlies species diversity. The increasing loss of species due to anthropogenic causes represents an irreversible depletion of genetic material upon which evolutionary potential can work in the future (Wilson 1988).

3 Species are also the basic unit of whole-organism classification, and the most practical and commonly used currency when referring to biodiversity. Species diversity provides some of the most commonly used, best-understood and most readily repeatable measures of biological diversity, e.g. species richness or endemism, which in turn indicate where conservation efforts need to be focused (Gaston 1996).

4 Data on species provide some of the most readily available, repeatable and explicit monitoring and analytic systems with which to assess the success or otherwise of conservation efforts. This may be through direct counts of indicator species (Heywood 1995) or through assessments of threat (Hilton-Taylor 2000).

5 'Fuzzy' ideas like ecosystem management and genetic diversity hold little appeal for, and are little understood by, the general public, who prefer to grasp simpler messages conveyed by so-called 'flagship species'. For the concerned public in the developed world, flagships usually comprise charismatic species such as tigers, elephants and primates (Leader-Williams & Dublin 2000).

6 The enormous financial values of ecosystems are rarely fully captured, because many ecosystem services appear 'free' at the point of use (Costanza *et al.* 1997). Thus, relatively few of the indirect-use values of ecosystems—such as their ecological, protection, waste-assimilation, microclimate-stabilization and carbon-storage functions—can be captured in traditional markets (Munasinghe 1992). However, the direct use of animals within ecosystems for consumption or to stimulate production provides a way of capturing at least some values of ecosystems within traditional markets, providing the systems under which resources are managed allow this to happen effectively.

This last point forms the main focus of this chapter, which next considers the different routes by which conservation can be achieved.

What tenurial systems are available for conservation?

Protected areas

Many conservationists promote state-run national parks and protected areas as their core activity, with varying levels of human exclusion to protect species, habitat and wilderness values (Brandon & Wells 1992; Brandon *et al.* 1998). Such approaches exemplify a state-property regime based on considerations of collective societal interest in common pool resources. Somewhat arbitrary international targets seek to achieve a 10% coverage of each country's land surface within such protected areas. At the last reckoning, some 8.3% of the world was covered with protected areas (IUCN 1998). Others argue that this is not sufficient and that we should seek to achieve close to 50% if all species are to be conserved (Soulé & Sanjayan 1998). On the other hand, others believe that the separation of humans and nature is a false objective, as nature is rarely pristine, and the so-called 'wilderness myth' is a fallacy (Adams & McShane 1992). Furthermore, island parks become surrounded by degraded land and rural poverty, where exclusion equates to alienation and hardship. In a world with less and less room for conservation, the continuing challenge is not to seek single solutions, but rather to seek partnerships that promote conservation as a competitive form of land use (McNeely 1995).

Different property regimes

In reality, natural resources can be held under a variety of property regimes (Berkes 1989; Bromley 1991), although in practice such resources are rarely managed solely within any one regime. Thus enclosed public land in protected areas may be surrounded by private land and/or communal land. However, the different regimes are important in determining who is the manager, although what is formal may differ from what is actual.

A *private-property regime* rests on long-term security of tenure by a private individual and market dynamics. The establishment of full private-property rights requires each herder to now play a game against nature in a smaller terrain. Such a regime requires private investment, and must include self-imposed limits on equipment, season, time, place and, particularly, allocation. Private ownership has been a strong impetus for management of species, but it has produced inequities because prices for participation have forced some segments of society from the market. For example, the private sector may favour a higher-paying tourist hunter or game viewer over a local resident. In addition, it is difficult to manage fugitive, non-stationary resources such as migratory species in private-property regimes.

The *open-access* condition is one where the resources are the property of no one and are available to everyone. Hence, this is not strictly a property regime at all. Nor is it a management regime, since people use the resources opportunistically but do not manage them, as occurs in the 'Tragedy of the Commons' (Hardin 1968). In such situations, people free-ride on resources (Ostrom 1990).

A *common-property regime* is quite different, and occurs where use rights for the resource are controlled by an identifiable group and are not privately owned or managed by governments. There exist rules concerning who may use the resource, who is excluded from the resource, and how the resource should be used (Berkes 1989). A common-property regime assumes that individuals can act collectively, through cooperatives or self-organized enterprises, to limit offtakes, to distribute harvests, to sustain food supplies, and to protect cultural symbols, totemic animals and religious sites (Berkes & Folke 1998).

Options for conservation

Of these different regimes, both private and state natural-resource-management regimes have their strengths and may be appropriate for given resources in given contexts. Equally, both have their weaknesses, particularly if they are underfunded, large scale and managerially distanced from the resources in question, as is the case with many protected-area networks. In such circumstances the state, or the private owner, purports to be the manager. However, de facto use and management are in the hands of others: the people living with the resources. Hence, most state-property regimes are examples of the state's reach exceeding its grasp (Bromley & Cernea 1989). Many states, in seeking to meet percentage targets for the coverage of protected areas within their jurisdictions (IUCN 1998), have taken on far more resource-management authority than they can be expected to carry out effectively. More critically, this approach sets the government against the rural poor, and results in marginalization of local resource management and antagonism, when successful resource management requires the opposite (Ghimire & Pimbert 1997).

Conservation action must be carried out where people live and work, and is an activity that occupies social space (Ghimire & Pimbert 1997). Unless local communities have the incentives, the capacity and the latitude to manage species and ecosystems sustainably, national and international actions are unlikely to produce results. Local conservation efforts cannot succeed unless communities receive a fair share of the benefits and assume a greater role in managing their biotic resources, be they species, protected areas, coastal fisheries or forests. Equally, many purported common-property regimes are not now operating under conditions defined for their success (Berkes & Folke 1998). Traditional structures and leadership have often been broken down by government and colonial regimes, such that they can no longer play an effective role in land and resource management. Furthermore, their tenurial status has often changed such that they are now on state land with usufruct rights only, without the powers of exclusion and access to certain natural resources now denied. Thus the conditions for a genuine common-property regime (Berkes 1989; Berkes & Folke 1998) have been removed. With the state also unable to manage the resource, resource use has tended to acquire the characteristics of de facto open access. Therefore, many areas of communal land have been seriously degraded and many attempts at community management have failed, unfortunately for conservation, giving this type of property regime an undeservedly bad reputation.

Future approaches

Are conserving species and habitats on different property regimes in fact separate solutions? Policy myopia usually only results in consideration of state- and private-property regimes as vehicles for effective resource management, ignoring the further option of a common-property regime. The challenge is that the 'traditional-protectionist' or 'fortress-conservation' approach often has not been working fully effectively (IIED 1994; Roe *et al.* 2000) and is now becoming less feasible as space becomes limiting. This challenge has been increasingly met over the last 20 years by community-based conservation in all its varying forms (Barrow & Murphree 1998). Enforcement of protected-area legislation is becoming less acceptable because of increased pressures from growing rural populations, increased attention to peoples' rights and similar equity considerations, and inadequate resources because governments have other priorities in addition to conservation. In any case, most protected areas are too small and do not encompass self-contained, sustainable ecosystems. Therefore, the future requires a combined approach to resource management that ensures that state-, private- and common-property regimes work collectively to prevent the de facto open-access situation. In contrast, discussion about which system is and is not the most effective (Barrett & Arcese 1995; Bruner *et al.* 2001) seems futile, when in many instances neither system is operating under ideal conditions.

Serious consideration of the communal option requires far more than decentralization, involving people in planning, promoting participation in project implementation, and increasing the economic benefits to the people from the resource. Requirements for successful common-property regimes comprise defined groups in defined areas with powers of inclusion and exclusion, and proprietorship of the natural resources concerned. In turn, proprietorship means a sustained sanctioned use right, including the right to decide whether to use the resources at all; the right to determine the mode and extent of use; and the right to benefit fully from their exploitation in the way they choose (Berkes *et al.* 1989). The delegation of proprietorship over natural resources to communities involves relinquishing considerable authority and responsibility on the part of the state, although never more than to privatization, but this runs contrary to bureaucratic tendency to centralize authority and monopolize power (Gibson 1999).

The chapter now moves on to consider how these varying considerations are provided for under two of the key MEAs that form the focus of global support for conservation.

MEAs relevant to animal conservation

The Convention on International Trade in Endangered Species of Wild Fauna and Flora (known as CITES), and the Convention on Biological Diversity (CBD) are two key, globally focused MEAs that fully or partly bear on species conservation. To date, there have been relatively few environmental disputes under the World Trade Organization (WTO) regime. Furthermore, these disputes have not yet involved the jurisdiction of any MEA, where indeed the WTO recognizes it does not have the competence to deal with issues arising out of MEAs. Equally, it is important to recognize where the intentions of these treaties may be at odds with the WTO regime.

CITES

CITES was adopted in 1973 and came into force in 1975, some 20 years before the Earth Summit. CITES was designed to reduce threats to wild species posed by international trade, by restricting that trade (Lyster 1985; Wijnstekers 2001). Appendix I of CITES includes the most seriously threatened species in which no commercial international trade is allowed, while Appendix II includes the less seriously threatened species in which limited commercial trade is allowed. CITES has enjoyed some success in achieving its conservation objectives through a trade-restriction regime. In situations where issues related to demand have been successfully addressed, CITES has been successful, with spotted cats and the wearing of fur coats as perhaps the best example (Nowell & Jackson 1996). CITES also has an active secretariat and generally open voting at its regular Conferences of the Parties. CITES must also be applauded for its flexibility in moving away from the fairly simple trade-restriction regime outlined in its articles to a more inclusive national proactive management-and-benefit process, particularly through positive measures such as Resolution Conf. 8.9, and the significant trade process (Wijnstekers 2001).

Despite these successes, it is also important to recognize where CITES has not been able to fully address problems that it may also face in future. Already contentious issues can be the subject of a secret ballot, compromising the usual openness of conferences. CITES has also attracted the attention of non-governmental organizations (NGOs) in the developed world that are focused on minimizing the sustainable use of animals, particularly of charismatic megavertebrates. To date, CITES has hardly tackled economically important issues such as tropical-forest loss or depletion of marine fish stocks. Coming at this last point from another direction, nor has CITES really tackled open-access marine issues, although it has been bloodied by issues of de facto open access on land, for example in the battles over elephants and rhinos (Hutton & Dickson 2002). Furthermore, implementation, particularly of Article IV, the so-called non-detriment finding, by many producer states has proved problematic. Thus, certain range countries or groupings of countries in the developed world, notably the US and the EC, have justified unilateral positions to impose stricter domestic measures, which are equally unjustified in the view of many more responsible producing states (Hutton & Dickson 2002), and certainly at odds with the WTO regime.

The CBD

CBD was, like the UNFCCC, opened for signature in 1992 as part of the Earth Summit. The CBD focuses more widely on biological diversity (commonly contracted to biodiversity) without reference to any particular threat, yet to explicitly recognize the link between biodiversity conservation and sustainable development (Glowka *et al.* 1994). Article 2 of the CBD acknowledges that biological diversity is more than just species, and encompasses the variety, variability and uniqueness of genes and species and the environments in which they occur, and so is relevant to this and to later chapters in this book (see Chapter 15). The CBD's overall objectives include the conservation of biological diversity, the sustainable use of all its components, and the fair and equitable sharing of the benefits arising from its use (Article 1). Two features of the CBD are particularly important to sustainable development. First, the CBD recognizes that conservation and management are not just an ecological concern. For many countries, sustainable use and conservation are an inherent component of economic development. Especially for the rural poor, biological resources often provide the single most important contribution to their livelihoods and welfare in the form of food supplies, medicines, shelter, income, employment and cultural integrity. Second, successful biodiversity conservation depends on sound policies—such as pricing, taxation and land tenure—and effective institutional and social arrangements including laws, regulations and the respective roles of the state, the private sector, NGOs, local communities and indigenous people. Such concerns normally lie outside the domain of the traditional conservation endeavours of resource-management agencies, and of protected-area administrations and systems.

Links between CITES and the CBD

Despite the fact that both CITES and the CBD are concerned with the protection of species from potentially all habitats and ecosystems, there are significant differences between the treaties, and cooperation has so far been very limited (Dickson 2002; Cooney 2002). The two treaties have very different origins. CITES was negotiated at a time when the nature of threats to species was not well understood, when the idea of sustainable development had not been formulated, and when the voices of developing countries were rarely heard in the international arena. In contrast, the CBD explicitly differentiates developing from developed countries, and envisages both resource transfers and the equitable sharing of benefits from the use of resources. On the other hand, CITES makes its decisions by a two-thirds majority vote of parties, and has a sophisticated compliance procedure, while the CBD exhorts actions through consensus and does not have procedures for voting or compliance. However, there is tremendous potential for the two conventions to cooperate. For example, successful outcomes for many issues in animal conservation will require joint work on elements both of international regulation of trade, and of effective action at the national and local levels. The latter will recognize livelihood, tenurial and incentive issues, and the importance of management by the resource's users themselves. A current example that would benefit from such an approach is the unsustainable hunting for bushmeat in tropical forests (Robinson & Bennett 2000).

Links between species conservation and the WTO

On a related point, it is important to note the possible conflicts in the aims and intent of CITES and the CBD with the trade liberalization regime of the WTO, which could cause future difficulties for conservationists. Ironically, and despite their apparently opposite intent, there may well be situations in which the trade-restriction regime of the CITES plays right into the hands of the WTO regime, although perhaps unintentionally and against long-term conservation interests! Take the case of a depleted tortoise population in which commercial exports from the range states are banned, either through an Appendix I listing or through a recommendation of the significant trade process. If there still remains demand among pet owners for the species, this provides the opportunity for a developed country to establish a captive-breeding operation. Besides liberalizing opportunities for trade among nations other than the original resource owner, this situation also fulfils the protectionist agenda of reducing offtake from the wild, and the animal-welfare agenda of seeing fewer dead animals during capture and transit. However, this situation will keep all benefits with the captive-breeding operation and pet-owning states, and provide no incentive in the range states for habitat or species conservation. This result is totally out of step with modern conservation thinking and the intent of the CBD. In other words, a hollow victory may result in the long term.

Equally, in a conservation context, the WTO aims to allow cancer sufferers access to as yet undiscovered cures in the rainforest, without trade-protection measures being applied. However, allowing local indigenous knowledge to provide the potential chemicals that, with slight modification by a pharmaceutical company based in a developed country, can become the subject of a patent is not equitable either. Of course, trade is liberalized in line with WTO objectives, but largely to the benefit of the pharmaceutical company's shareholders. However, such an approach provides no equity to those possessing the original indigenous knowledge, given that a modification protected under patent stipulates no obligations to repatriate royalties. Thus, in this case, the WTO regime flies completely in the face of CBD intentions on sustainability, not to mention other poverty-elimination targets agreed under other regimes. This potential mismatch between MEA and WTO regimes seems to arise largely from issues of scale and differences in value systems. Reconciliation between the different objectives of the various regimes, and of the value systems underlying these objectives, will need to occur at very different levels, if indeed they can be reconciled at all.

The role of tourism in conservation provides a clear example of the mismatch between free-market globalization and conservation objectives. Non-consumptive tourism is not an issue that falls under CITES. Indeed, it may be considered as the option of choice to provide incentives for conservation by those who oppose consumptive use. Nevertheless, non-consumptive tourism is bedevilled by many of the same structural problems as consumptive use. Indeed, it shows equally well that, unless some action is taken, the world will become increasingly dominated by multinational interests that do not meet the local costs of their activities. However, most solutions to conservation and sustainability issues, on land at least, rest with ownership at the national, sub-national and local levels.

How can nature-based tourism and ecotourism provide incentives for conservation?

The scale of nature-based tourism

Tourism is a complex industry driven by the private sector and often by large international companies, and is an important part of the global economy. According to the World Tourism Organization, the industry directly and indirectly generates *ca.* 11% of global gross domestic product (GDP), and accounts for some 8% of the world's employment. Nature-based tourism encompasses all forms and scales of tourism that result from the enjoyment of natural areas and wildlife. This sector comprises some 40–60% of international tourist expenditures, and is increasing at 10–30% annually. If domestic nature-based tourism is taken into account, the scale of nature-based tourism is even more important (Anonymous 2001). In the wider development framework, tourism can stimulate private-sector support for species and habitat conservation. It can also provide an essential economic justification for improved management of conservation, both within and outside protected areas, in the context of both private-property and of community-based programmes. Conservationists can point to numerous examples where world-class attractions have been saved because of tourism, from national parks in Africa, to the Galapagos Islands, to the cloud forests and turtle beaches of Costa Rica, to Khao Yai National Park in Thailand (Honey 1999).

Some natural areas, however, are generally better suited for generating significant tourism revenue than others, especially because major attractions for nature-based tourists usually include large and charismatic species (Goodwin & Leader-Williams 2000). Thus open savannahs and woodlands in East and Southern Africa, with abundant game in landscapes with high visibility, are well suited to attracting large volumes of non-consumptive game-viewing tourists. Wetlands can be attractive areas for birdwatching, anglers and waterfowlers: witness the early and inspired thinking behind the Ramsar Convention. Coastal ecosystems also have high potential for recreational nature-based tourism. Indeed, the combination of coast and charisma now makes whale watching one of the fastest growing types of nature-based tourism. In contrast, despite their high biodiversity, forests and closed woodland generally have low recreational value because charismatic species are not easily seen. Equally, such areas can be attractive, either for specialist tourism, such as sport hunting or birdwatching, and for shorter visits as part of a package incorporating more popular destinations (Roe *et al.* 1997).

Is nature-based tourism sustainable?

By its very size and earning power, nature-based-tourism benefits could be used to encourage and support conservation and sustainable management through a market-driven approach. Nevertheless, conservationists remain concerned that nature-based tourism is often used to promote an international industry and national development objectives without due consideration of long-term conservation objectives for the animal species and habitats that attract the tourists. Large and increasing numbers of tourists often create heavy impacts, both direct and indirect, on natural environments (as well as on the culture of local people). One example is commercial tourism to the Galapagos Islands (made famous by Charles Darwin's studies of evolution) which started in 1969. A typical visit comprises spending a week on a boat to visit various sites on different islands and view the endemic species of animals and birds. Islands within the national park that can be visited are laid out with well-marked trails. A park master plan in 1974 called for a cap on visitor numbers to 12 000 per year. This cap was based on numbers of visitors that guides could manage, distance between groups on the trails, tourist space needed along trails, management capabilities and available resources.

However, this cap was revised to 25 000 in 1981 (Wallace 1993), while actual visitor numbers increased from 7000 in 1975 to 41 000 in 1988 and to 66 000 today (Parra-Bozzano 2001). Thus, increased pressures from the private sector, reduced park budgets and lack of political backing for park officials, and at times inadequate leadership, have combined with increased visitation to cause concerns about the sustainability of tourism. Many potential impacts remain well managed, and some islands are still off limits to prevent introduction of exotic species (Wallace 1993). Equally, impacts are evident, of which three are illustrative. Heavy use of trails has altered the nesting locations and disrupted displays of nesting blue- and red-footed boobies (Burger & Gochfield 1993). Artificial feeding by tourists caused the territorial breeding system of land iguanas to break down. Territories on the island of South Plaza were abandoned in favour of sites where food could be begged from tourists, and this had a negative effect on the breeding success of iguanas (Edington & Edington 1986). Finally, impacts from boats mooring in bays have increased with increased tourist traffic. Additional problems arise because of the increase in permitted private-sector tour operators. Immigration and urban development therefore continue at a rapid rate next to the park and bring new challenges. Towns have difficulty supplying potable water, treatment for human waste, adequate medical facilities, and port facilities. Fishery resources, once just used for local consumption, have now come under heavy pressure to satisfy wider national, as well as international, markets (Wallace 1993). Thus, in Galapagos, as indeed elsewhere, market forces driven by the private sector and providing for industry growth can override the needs for conserving the resources upon which the long-term survival of the industry depends.

Another major concern of the heavily globalized tourism industry is the extensive leakage of tourism-generated foreign exchange (Lundberg *et al.* 1995). As a result, nature-based tourism has not realized its full potential to support habitat- and species-conservation objectives, or the rural poor, for two main reasons. First, host countries do not receive the full benefit of the revenues that tourists pay to visit the attraction. Second, relatively little of the revenue generated goes directly or indirectly as an incentive either to protected-area managers or to local communities. Thus the fees and charges for tourism attractions fail to capture the full willingness of the tourist to pay, and may fail to capture much of the value visitors place on natural attractions and protected areas. Furthermore, the full economic potential of tourism spending in national and local economies is not realized. Leakage arises from the use of skilled labour and luxury products, the repatriation of profits by owners, and the considerable role of marketing, transport and other services based in the originating country. Indeed, The World Bank estimates that, on average, 55% of tourist expenditure remains outside destination countries in the developing world. Detailed studies indicate that the figure may be as high as 90% in some cases (Koch 1994). The flow of money spent for a package tour to a natural area in a developing country has been analysed (Figure 14.1). This shows that only *ca.* 0.1–1% of total tourism expenditure is captured by the attractions in entrance fees and charges; less than 10% is kept within the local economy; and only 20–40% is kept within the national economy.

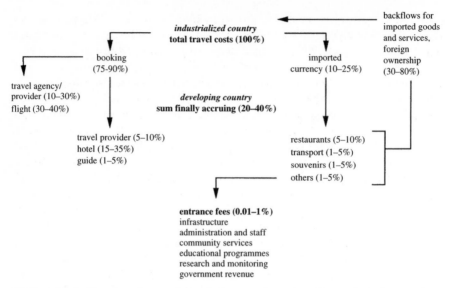

Figure 14.1. Revenue flows arising from a package tour to protected areas in a developing country (based on Gossling (1999)). All percentages are percentages of the total travel costs (100%). Higher sums accrue to the developing country if it has a national airline.

The remainder stays with the industrialized countries in the form of booking fees, aeroplane flights, hotels and backflows for imported goods and services (Gossling 1999).

Making nature-based tourism more sustainable

Two main approaches are needed to correct this situation and create a more effective incentive structure for conserving species and habitats through nature-based tourism. The first is to set tourism fees at market prices that tourists are willing to pay. The second is to expand local benefits through reducing leakage and increasing linkages. In Kenya, for example, nature-based tourism is an important industry, and the protected areas that support much of that industry cover some 8% of Kenya's land surface, also making important contributions both to animal conservation and the maintenance of ecosystems. Equally, benefits accruing to resource managers and communities living with wildlife were limited to a fraction of those that could be captured from tourists (Moran 1994). Demonstrating and appropriating full economic benefits was vital, especially where demographic pressures on land and economic constraints tied up in conservation are associated with increasing opportunity costs. If benefits remain skewed nationally, in favour of hotel owners and tour operators, and globally, in favour of foreign tourists, then local people and resource managers, who bear the costs of conservation, have little stake in maintenance of protected areas. Foreign tourists were willing to pay a mean of $72 per day, and produced a large consumer surplus of $46–$450 million per year that exceeded the $203 million for the opportunity costs of being able to convert land to other uses (Moran 1994). Therefore, it was recommended that the wildlife authority capture more revenue. Entrance fees to national parks have since been raised for non-nationals and are paid in foreign exchange. In turn, this creates more revenue both for protected-area management, and for sharing with local communities through protected-area outreach programmes (Leader-Williams *et al.* 1996). Equally, the wildlife authority has not opted for full profit maximization, and offers a lesser differential fee in local currency for nationals, in order to retain the support of Kenyans wishing to visit their national parks. Likewise, foreign tourists visiting Komodo National Park in Indonesia, home to the world's largest lizard, the Komodo dragon, were willing to pay over 10 times more than the previous entrance fee, providing there was evidence this was reinvested in management (Walpole *et al.* 2001). The wildlife authority has since raised the fee. In turn, local people must see greater benefits from Komodo dragons through tourism, in order that they view the species as a local flagship rather than a nuisance that eats local livestock (Walpole & Leader-Williams 2002).

The very nature of the tourism industry will cause it to remain subject to high leakage because of factors such as high marketing and travel costs (Lundberg *et al.* 1995). However, there is still considerable scope to ensure that local benefits are expanded, in order to reduce poverty in local communities, which in turn encourages local support for biodiversity conservation and sustainable management. Therefore, from both conservation and human-poverty perspectives it is necessary to place pro-poor tourism at the heart of the tourism agenda (Ashley *et al.* 2000). Some key mechanisms to achieve this objective include ensuring local ownership and management; leasing or partial-ownership arrangements; profit-sharing arrangements between the tourism industry and local residents; direct payments to local communities from tourism revenues; or high local employment in the tourism industry. Implementing these mechanisms is one of the key challenges if nature-based tourism is going to operate successfully as a form of incentive-based conservation. This will be much easier in situations where the following conditions hold.

- Relatively secure access or tenure rights are retained or established, including the power to exclude, over both land and other biological resources. Indeed, this is fundamental to the ability of local people to participate in decision making and gain benefits from tourism, as with any other form of incentive-based conservation.

- Local communities are given the management and marketing skills to participate in tourism.

- There are direct links to the local economy, through either employment of local labour or the purchase of local goods and services.

The latter is also especially important as it can help stimulate the local economy through multipliers, especially if local businesses and services are linked (see Lundberg *et al.* 1995). Wherever possible, there should be improved linkages:

- within the tourism industry, such that local labour is employed and local residents are trained to fill skilled positions such as guides and managers;

- to the local transport industry, such that existing modes of transport are used where possible, including boats, canoes, mules and porters—equally, expensive modes of transport can be bought and managed by local cooperatives;

- to local agriculture and fishing, such that imports of food are minimized;

- to local construction, equipment and maintenance sectors, so that local labour and materials are used where possible; and, finally,

- to local handicraft and souvenir selling, which is often a good way for local residents to benefit from tourist spending. Conversely, however, this linkage can have important perverse effects for animal conservation, for example through over harvesting of ostrich eggs or coral.

A role for consumptive tourism?

Consumptive tourism, such as hunting and sport fishing, is assumed by many to have negative implications for conservation through overuse of the target species, and secondary impacts on non-target species. However, such tourism, if well managed, properly monitored and based on an understanding of sustainable use, can generate significant funds, and provide incentives for habitat and species conservation among local communities. Furthermore, consumptive tourism can also be one of the few options for realizing the value of remote or low-visibility ecosystems where other forms of tourism are not viable (see Leader-Williams *et al.* 1996). Indeed, the economic contribution of consumptive tourism to such areas can be important. For example, over 30 District Councils have been granted *Appropriate Authority* status in Zimbabwe's CAMPFIRE programme. The economic engine house for CAMPFIRE has been sport hunting, which has contributed 90% of CAMPFIRE's revenue, and particularly hunting of elephants, which has contributed over 60% of those hunting revenues (Bond 1994), without any evidence that this offtake has reduced the ongoing increase in elephant numbers in Zimbabwe. Equally, for those who do not support consumptive use, this approach poses considerable moral difficulty, and this has brought tension to debates about listed species, such as elephants, within CITES conferences. In contrast, proponents believe that well-managed consumptive tourism counts as one of the ultimate forms of ecotourism.

The development of ecotourism

The many problems that are associated with tourism generically, and with nature-based tourism specifically, has led to the emergence of 'ecotourism' (Ceballos-Lascurain 1996). This is a greener and friendlier sounding term, the definitions for which are continually evolving. The International Ecotourism Society now defines ecotourism as 'travel to natural areas that conserves the environment and sustains the well-being of local people'. When correctly practised, such a definition requires ecotourism to encompass four key ideals: it must be of low environmental impact; it must contribute to conservation, whether directly through protected areas, or indirectly through providing benefits to local communities; it must be of low social impact; and it must raise awareness through conservation education. While many in the industry strive to achieve these ideals, many efforts fall short. The structure of the industry, and institutional problems and issues in the host country, are important reasons for this failure. Particular difficulties remain in involving local communities in ecotourism, given that most forms of tourism require easy access and infrastructure, and marketing skills that can tap into international markets (Ashley & Roe 1998).

The World Tourism Organization has a similarly large membership to CITES and the CBD, as well as 350 affiliate members representing local government, tourist associations and private-sector companies. It is an intergovernmental body entrusted by the United Nations to promote and develop tourism, and through which to stimulate economic growth and job creation, and provide incentives for protection of the environment and heritage of destinations. In contrast to CITES, the World Tourism Organization has no powers of sanction over its national members. However, since the 1990s, the route by which the industry has sought to regulate itself is through voluntary agreements that incorporate standards for social, economic and environmental concerns (Honey 2001). Some 250 voluntary initiatives have been documented, which include codes of conduct, awards, benchmarking, best practices and eco-labelling and certification programmes. These range from local initiatives that have received some impetus through Agenda 21 for the Travel and Tourism Industry, through to state, national and global programmes such as Green Globe 21. Because tourism is such a multi-faceted industry, certification programmes face complex challenges. Thus most schemes to date have focused on the easiest component, which is accommodation. However, schemes are increasingly covering other sectors, including the Blue Flag scheme for beaches and PAN Parks for protected areas (Honey 2001). Australia's Nature and Ecotourism Accreditation Program scheme covers attractions, tours and tour guides (Newson 2001), while the SmartVoyager scheme in the Galapagos Islands focuses on certifying tour boats that tread lightly on the environment (Sanabria 2001). A key distinction in certification is whether the programme uses process-based or performance-based methodologies. The former use management systems, while the latter use benchmarks. Increasingly, certification programmes are moving towards performance-based methodologies, as these focus on what a business does in various environmental, sociocultural and economic arenas.

In 2002, the year of the World Summit on Sustainable Development (WSSD), the United Nations General Assembly also wished to draw the attention of governments and the international community to the potential impacts, both positive and negative, of ecotourism on the natural environment, on biodiversity conservation, and on the social and cultural fabric of host communities. Hence 2002 was also designated as the International Year of Ecotourism

(IYE), in which the UNEP and the World Tourism Organization undertook various activities, including holding the World Ecotourism Summit in May in Quebec City, Canada. One of the greatest contributions that can emerge from the IYE is the establishment of a single global accreditation programme for sustainable tourism and ecotourism businesses, which in turn will ensure that the free market provides adequate incentives for conservation.

Conclusions

An effective link between local communities and their economic development can alter the pattern of incentives to improve conservation. Where local people earn significant income through participation in nature-based tourism or sustainable use, livelihood strategies can shift away from unsustainable use. However, where tourism and other forms of incentive-based use cannot give local communities what they need in the way of livelihoods, they will continue to invest in activities that do not support conservation efforts or even threaten them, for example by investing in livestock in areas of wildlife–livestock conflict. If some local groups benefit more than others, serious disagreements may arise. Tourism can also reduce local access to resources, for example where game viewing leads to tighter access restrictions on the areas where resources are harvested by local people. This could have serious impacts on conservation by concentrating harvesting in smaller areas and undermining local management systems. Thus the scope for improving livelihoods through tourism and other forms of consumptive use is therefore very variable, as are its impacts. Yet, as with all the other challenges of conservation, it is here where the war to conserve species and habitats will be won and lost.

Appendix A. Annexe

With no explicit links to carbon sequestration, concerns about conserving animals might be mistaken for an emotionally irrelevant attempt to protect fluffy and charismatic species. Equally, animal conservation provides clear opportunities to address ways of conserving ecosystems. First, species conservation is really about the long-term maintenance of the Earth's life-support systems. Species are the building blocks of ecosystems, and while there is some redundancy, the loss of keystone species can have a disproportionate effect. Furthermore, isolated populations of species form the future evolutionary potential of ecosystems. Second, species conservation can make an overly complex conservation agenda relating to carbon and ecosystem conservation appealing to the general public through simpler mechanisms such as flagship species. Third, species provide routes to capture some of the value of ecosystems through direct and indirect uses, and to create market-based incentives for conserving habitats and ecosystems. Use of species can be achieved through non-consumptive means such as nature-based tourism and ecotourism, or through consumptive means such as hunting and sport fishing. Fourth, the successes and failures in conserving indicator species shows where effort needs to be invested to ensure that market-driven approaches become fully effective as incentives for conservation. The recommendations that follow are inevitably coloured by the view from my own particular anthill, and will be approached by using and modifying a well-known stock phrase.

Think global, act local

Solutions to issues of conservation and sustainability inevitably rest at national and sub-national levels, through systems of rights, tenure, benefits and incentives that promote conservation-friendly over conservation-unfriendly approaches.

1 CITES is increasingly shifting its thinking from trade-regulation approaches to wider benefit- and incentive-based approaches operationalized through management planning. This approach is welcome and can hopefully be extended.

2 The CBD must increasingly operationalize its good intent with regard to systems of rights, tenure, benefits and incentives for those holding the opportunity cost of living among natural resources. The voices of local communities too often go unheard.

3 Local conservation efforts need to avoid becoming focused on the merits or demerits of particular systems of conservation such as protected areas versus a community-based approach, but instead focus on the common goals of preventing de facto open access and making conservation a competitive form of land use.

4 Globalized free-market industries such as tourism need to focus on direct and indirect means of reducing leakage and capture rent in local economies, such that conservation can achieve its objectives.

Think global, by thinking laterally

Conservationists mostly wish to reach the same endpoint, but the route maps and value systems by which they wish to get there frequently differ. There is not sufficient interdisciplinary thinking on how to achieve a balance between the objectives of conservation through protection versus incentive-based mechanisms.

1 Within CITES, parties should increasingly seek to reconcile, if possible, the views of protectionists and animal welfarists with those of economists concerned with incentive flows and social scientists concerned with the rights of local people.

2 Between the CBD and the WTO, there must be concerted thought devoted to overcoming selfish business and multinational interests in the developed world over the interests of local people in the resource-rich developing world. This is of particular concern when countries like the US behave in such a self-centred way within the WTO, yet do not accede to the CBD, while also being a frequent proponent of stricter domestic measures within the CITES.

3 The World Tourism Organization, likewise, must ensure the same objective through uptake and enhancement of its certification schemes.

Think global by acting long term

To succeed it is vital that the differential in power between trade and environmental concerns is reconciled and reversed to achieve parity, both nationally and globally.

1 Governments must promote increasingly joined-up governance at national and sub-national levels, allowing long-term environmental interests to balance shorter-term trade interests of turnover, production and discount rates.

2 While global interests aim to develop mechanisms that allow trade to be equitable and free, these must recognize that this does not only constitute allowing shareholders in the developed world access to profits from resources held in the resource-rich developing world. Instead, global interests must encompass in their thinking rights and benefits for local-resource owners, and their other legitimate goals such as poverty alleviation, as espoused by the CBD and other international instruments.

References

Adams, J. S. & McShane, T. O. 1992 *The myth of wild Africa: conservation without illusion.* New York: Norton.

Anonymous 2001 Ecotourism: facts and figures. *Ind. Environ.* **24**, 5–9.

Ashley, C. & Roe, D. 1998 *Enhancing community involvement in wildlife tourism: issues and challenges.* London: International Institute for Environment and Development.

Ashley, C., Boyd, C. & Goodwin, H. J. 2000 *Pro-poor tourism: putting poverty at the heart of the tourism agenda.* Natural Resource Perspectives, no. 51. London: Overseas Development Institute.

Barrett, C. & Arcese, P. 1995 Are integrated conservation and development projects (ICDPs) sustainable? On the conservation of large mammals in sub-Saharan Africa. *World Dev.* **23**, 1073–1084.

Barrow, E. & Murphree, M. 1998 *Community conservation from concept to practice: a practical framework.* Manchester: Institute for Development Policy and Management.

Berkes, F. 1989 *Common property resources: ecology and community-based sustainable development.* London: Belhaven Press.

Berkes, F. & Folke, C. 1998 *Linking social and ecological systems: management practices and social mechanisms for building resilience.* Cambridge University Press.

Berkes, F., Feeny, D., McCay, B. J. & Acheson, J. M. 1989 The benefits of the commons. *Nature* **340**, 91–93.

Bond, I. 1994 Importance of elephant hunting to CAMPFIRE revenue in Zimbabwe. *Traffic Bull.* **14**, 117–119.

Bond, W. J. 1993 Keystone species. In *Biodiversity and ecosystem function* (ed. E.-D. Schulze & H. A. Mooney), pp. 237–253. Springer.

Brandon, K. E. & Wells, M. P. 1992 Planning for people and parks: design dilemmas. *World Dev.* **20**, 557–570.

Brandon, K. E., Redford, K. H. & Sanderson, S. E. 1998 *Parks in peril: people, politics and protected areas*. Washington, DC: The Nature Conservancy and Island Press.

Bromley, D. W. 1991 *Environment and economy: property rights and public property*. Oxford: Blackwell.

Bromley, D. W. & Cernea, M. M. 1989 *The management of common property natural resources and some conceptual and operational fallacies*. World Bank Discussion Papers, no. 7. Washington, DC: World Bank.

Bruner, A. G., Gullison, R. E., Rice, R. E. & Fonseca, G. A. B. 2001 Effectiveness of parks in protecting tropical biodiversity. *Science* **291**, 125–128.

Burger, J. & Gochfield, M. 1993 Tourism and short-term behavioural responses of nesting masked, red footed and blue footed boobies in the Galapagos. *Environ. Conserv.* **20**, 255–259.

Ceballos-Lascurain, H. 1996 *Tourism, ecotourism and protected areas*. Gland, Switzerland: International Union for the Conservation of Nature.

Cooney, R. 2002 CITES and CBD: tensions and synergies. *Rev. Eur. Community Int. Environ. Law* **10**, 259–267.

Costanza, R. (and 12 others) 1997 The value of the world's ecosystem services and natural capital. *Nature* **387**, 253–260.

Daily, G. C. 1997 *Nature's services: societal dependence on natural ecosystems*. Washington, DC: Island Press.

Darwin, C. 1859 *The origin of species by means of natural selection*. London: John Murray.

Diamond, J. M. 1989 Overview of recent extinctions. In *Conservation for the twenty-first century* (ed. D. Western & M. Pearl), pp. 37–75. Oxford University Press.

Dickson, B. 2002 *International conservation treaties, poverty and development: the case of CITES*. Natural Resource Perspectives, no. 74. London: Overseas Development Institute.

Edington, J. M. & Edington, M. A. 1986 *Ecology, recreation and tourism*. Cambridge University Press.

Ehrlich, P. R. & Ehrlich, A. H. 1981 *Extinction: the causes and consequences of the disappearance of species*. New York: Random House.

Ehrlich, P. R. & Ehrlich, A. H. 1992 The value of biodiversity. *Ambio* **21**, 219–226.

Gaston, K. J. 1996 *Biodiversity: biology of difference and numbers*. Oxford: Blackwell.

Ghimire, K. B. & Pimbert, M. P. 1997 *Social change and conservation: environmental politics and impacts of national parks and protected areas*. London: Earthscan.

Gibson, C. C. 1999 *Politicians and poachers: the political economy of wildlife policy in Africa*. Cambridge University Press.

Glowka, L., Burhenne-Guilmin, F. & Synge, H. 1994 *A guide to the convention on biological diversity*. Gland, Switzerland: International Union for the Conservation of Nature.

Goodwin, H. J. & Leader-Williams, N. 2000 Tourism and protected areas: distorting conservation priorities towards charismatic megafauna? In *Priorities for the conservation of mammalian diversity: has the panda had its day?* (ed. A. Entwistle & N. Dunstone), pp. 257–275. Cambridge University Press.

Gossling, S. 1999 Ecotourism: a means to safeguard biodiversity and ecosystem functions. *Ecol. Econ.* **29**, 303–320.

Hardin, G. 1968 The tragedy of the commons. *Science* **162**, 1243–1248.

Heywood, V. H. 1995 *Global biodiversity assessment.* Cambridge University Press.

Hilton-Taylor, C. 2000 *2000 IUCN Red List of threatened species.* Gland, Switzerland: International Union for the Conservation of Nature.

Honey, M. 1999 *Ecotourism and sustainable development: who owns paradise?* Washington, DC: Island Press.

Honey, M. 2001 Certification programmes in the tourism industry. *Ind. Environ.* **24**, 28–29.

Hutton, J. M. & Dickson, B. 2000 *Endangered species, threatened convention: the past, present and future of CITES.* London: Earthscan.

IIED 1994 *Whose Eden? An overview of community approaches to wildlife management.* London: International Institute for Environment and Development.

IUCN 1998 *1997 United Nations list of protected areas.* Gland, Switzerland: International Union for the Conservation of Nature.

James, A., Gaston, K. J. & Balmford, A. 2000 Balancing the Earth's accounts. *Nature* **401**, 323–324.

Koch, E. 1994 *Ecotourism: a tool for rural reconstruction in South Africa.* Geneva: United Nations Research Institute for Social Development.

Lawton, J. H. & Brown, V. K. 1993 Redundancy in ecosystems. In *Biodiversity and ecosystem function* (ed. E.-D. Schulze & H. A. Mooney), pp. 255–270. Springer.

Lawton, J. H. & May, R. M. 1995 *Extinction rates.* Oxford University Press.

Leader-Williams, N. & Dublin, H. T. 2000 Charismatic megafauna as 'flagship species'. In *Priorities for the conservation of mammalian diversity: has the panda had its day?* (ed. A. Entwistle & N. Dunstone), pp. 53–81. Cambridge University Press.

Leader-Williams, N., Kayera, J. A. & Overton, G. L. 1996 *Community-based conservation in Tanzania.* Gland, Switzerland: International Union for the Conservation of Nature.

Lundberg, D. E., Stavenga, M. H. & Krishnamoorthy, M. 1995 *Tourism economics.* Wiley.

Lyster, S. 1985 *International wildlife law.* Cambridge: Grotius.

McNeely, J. 1995 *Expanding partnerships in conservation.* Washington, DC: Island Press.

Moran, D. 1994 Contingent valuation and biodiversity: measuring the user surplus in Kenyan protected areas. *Biodiversity Conserv.* **3**, 663–684.

Munasinghe, M. 1992 Biodiversity protection policy: environmental valuation and distribution issues. *Ambio* **21**, 227–236.

Naeem, S., Thompson, L. J., Lawler, S. P., Lawton, J. H. & Woodfin, R. M. 1994 Declining biodiversity can alter the performance of ecosystems. *Nature* **368**, 734–737.

Newson, H. 2001 Encouraging and rewarding best practice: Australia's Nature and Accreditation Programme (NEAP). *Ind. Environ.* **24**, 24–27.

Nowell, K. & Jackson, P. 1996 *Wild cats: status survey and conservation action plan.* Gland, Switzerland: International Union for the Conservation of Nature.

Ostrom, E. 1990 *Governing the commons.* Cambridge University Press.

Parra-Bozzano, D. 2001 Galapagos: ecotourismo versus conservacion. *Ind. Environ.* **24**, 30–32.

Robinson, J. R. & Bennett, E. 2000 *Hunting for sustainability in tropical forests.* New York: Columbia University Press.

Roe, D., Leader-Williams, N. & Dalal-Clayton, D. B. 1997 *Take only photographs, leave only footprints: the environmental impacts of wildlife tourism.* London: International Institute for Environment and Development.

Roe, D., Mayers, J., Grieg-Gran, M., Kothari, A., Fabricius, C. & Hughes, R. 2000 *Evaluating Eden: exploring the myths and realities of community-based wildlife management.* London: International Institute for Environment and Development.

Sanabria, R. 2001 Evolving ecotourism alliances conserve biodiversity in the Galapagos Islands. *Ind. Environ.* **24**, 33–37.

Simberloff, D. 1998 Flagships, umbrellas, and keystones: is single-species management passé in the landscape era? *Biol. Conserv.* **83**, 247–257.

Soulé, M. E. & Sanjayan, M. A. 1998 Ecology and conservation targets: do they help? *Science* **279**, 2060–2061.

Wallace, G. N. 1993 Visitor management: lessons from the Galapagos National Park. In *Ecotourism: a guide for planners and managers* (ed. K. Lindberg & D. E. Hawkins), pp. 55–81. North Bennington, VT: The Ecotourism Society.

Walpole, M. J. & Leader-Williams, N. 2002 Ecotourism and flagship species in conservation. *Biodiversity Conserv.* **11**, 543–547.

Walpole, M. J., Goodwin, H. J. & Ward, K. J. G. 2001 Pricing policy for tourism in protected areas: lessons from Komodo National Park, Indonesia. *Conserv. Biol.* **15**, 218–227.

Wijnstekers, W. 2001 *The evolution of CITES: a reference to the Convention on International Trade in Endangered Species of Wild Fauna and Flora.* Lausanne, Switzerland: CITES Secretariat.

Wilson, E. O. 1988 The current state of biodiversity. In *Biodiversity* (ed. E. O. Wilson), pp. 3–18. Washington, DC: National Academy Press.

Chapter 15

Collateral biodiversity benefits associated with 'free-market' approaches to sustainable land use and forestry activities

IZABELLA KOZIELL AND IAN R. SWINGLAND

Introduction

Biodiversity yields many sustainable development benefits yet, paradoxically, human societies continue to undermine this valuable resource base, instigating large-scale biodiversity losses and species extinctions. Most worrying, however, is that the situation is actually deteriorating faster than resources can be mobilized to counteract the destructive processes, hence the commonly expressed view that we are heading towards a sixth 'mass extinction'.

In the past, remedial action has focused on *in situ* and *ex situ* conservation approaches. The establishment of protected areas has been the primary focus of *in situ* conservation, although there are now also moves to protect valuable agricultural zones. *Ex situ* conservation has focused on conservation of, for example, germplasm or certain plants or animals, away from their site of origin, e.g. in a botanical garden, zoo or a genebank. Until recently, the financing and management of conservation activity remained the responsibility of the public sector; however, over the last few decades, severe cutbacks in the availability of public resources has severely undermined the effectiveness of such strategies. This, coupled with ever-increasing pressures on the land and resources held within protected areas, especially in developing countries, has constrained the lasting success of such approaches.

Consequently, the conservation sector has been forced to look at alternative methods of biodiversity conservation, and especially such methods that can generate viable and desired livelihood or development returns, while at the same time conserving biodiversity. Given that the root causes of biodiversity loss are linked to poverty on one hand and high levels of consumption, or economic development, on the other, finding such alternatives is not an easy task. In spite of this enormous challenge, the last decade has spawned a series of innovative approaches that focus on providing suitable social and economic incentives for conservation. It is now widely recognized that, given the lack of public funding, biodiversity conservation must start to pay for itself, otherwise it is most likely doomed. Hence the growing interest in opportunities for biodiversity conservation that might arise from 'free-market' approaches to sustainable land use and management.

Biodiversity and its 'political' context

Biodiversity, as a word, dates back only to the mid 1980s, but it has gained rapid political acceptance. Growing awareness of the immense value of biodiversity, and the ever-increasing rate of human-induced biodiversity loss, such as deforestation, has instigated some commitment towards corrective action. By 1992, the Convention on Biological Diversity (CBD) was open for signing at the United Nations Conference on Environment and Development (UNCED, also known as the Earth Summit), together with the United Nations Framework Convention on Climate Change (UNFCCC). The three main objectives of the CBD were articulated as 'the conservation of biological diversity, the sustainable use of its components and the fair and equitable sharing of benefits arising from the use of genetic resources'. The CBD has now been ratified by over 180 countries (with the notable exception of the United States, as with the UNFCCC).

The CBD is now the main framework for articulating policies and actions on biodiversity at international and national level.[1] However, the CBD, as with many of the other biodiversity-related conventions, has not yet gained the same level of global political and private-sector interest as the UNFCCC. This, together with the many difficult conceptual and operational challenges that biodiversity presents, has hampered its more widespread implementation. Given the UNFCCC's much higher international profile, there is some potential for using it to help advance CBD objectives, and provide the much-needed economic incentives for conservation, through some of the market-based mechanisms presented under the Kyoto Protocol.

According to the CBD definition, biological diversity (also known as biodiversity) encompasses the 'variability of all organisms from all sources. . . and the ecological complexes of which they are part. . . this includes diversity within species, between species and of ecosystems'. Some have questioned the relevance of introducing yet another ecological concept, and one that seems, in the first instance, closely related to 'nature' and synonymous with biological or natural resources. However, introducing the term has helped raise the political profile, especially at the international level, of a critical and previously overlooked aspect of biological science. It has also formed a more detailed and comprehensive way of understanding the value of the variety of life on Earth.

---

[1] There are also many other biodiversity-related conventions that deal with specific issues, such as Ramsar, focusing on wetlands, and CITES, on trade in endangered species.

'Biodiversity benefits'

Biodiversity is of enormous value to human development—an estimated 40% of the world's economy is based on biological goods and services that emanate from biodiverse systems. Biodiversity (and the genetic resources it harbours) has made possible the massive increases in the production of food and other natural materials, which have fed the growth and development of human societies. It is also the basis of innumerable environmental services that keep us alive, from the provision of clean water to pollination.

The consensus internationally is that the various biodiversity benefits, i.e. goods and services that arise from biodiverse systems, fall into three useful categories (direct, indirect and non-use), though views on what precisely each of these includes can vary (Koziell 2001):

1 Direct-use benefits accrue from *the range* of raw materials that biodiversity provides (e.g. different foodstuffs, medicines, building materials and fodder for livestock). One of the most valuable aspects of biodiversity as a direct use is associated with the choices and alternatives it supports. Thus it acts as a 'buffer' if customary resource-use preferences change (e.g. during periods of stress such as drought). Another is the application of genetic resources in artificial selection and adaptation of agricultural crops and livestock breeds for improved yield and/or pest resistance.

2 Indirect-use benefits are mostly associated with environmental services. Biodiversity is the medium through which air, water, gases and chemicals are moderated and exchanged to create environmental services (e.g. watershed protection, pollination and soil aeration). There is much to be done to improve understanding of the relationship between different levels and types of biodiversity and the effectiveness of environmental services. A perhaps underestimated indirect-use benefit of biodiversity is protection from pests and diseases.

3 Non-use benefits consist primarily of the option to use biological resources in the future. Maintaining diverse communities of plants and animals offer a greater variety of potential future uses as well as a greater capacity to evolve new forms and processes. There is also the notion of intrinsic benefit, which relates to biodiversity's existence but not for any utilitarian purpose. Sometimes this might be for spiritual reasons, or for aesthetic purposes.

Identifying which land- or water-management regimes yield the greatest biodiversity benefits is not an easy task. Firstly, as described above, there are so many different biodiversity benefits that no single land use can provide them all: hence arguments for multiple-use landscapes. Secondly, different people will prioritize different biodiversity benefits, depending on, for instance, their level of poverty (or affluence), their culture or religion, the nature of their interaction with it, or belief about what their interaction should be. Therefore, a rural agricultural community's perception of benefit often lies in stark contrast to that of an urban dwelling community. Thirdly, scientific understanding of precisely which biodiversity yields what sort of benefits remains patchy, e.g. which species or ecosystem configurations lead to more stable yields or more effective watershed protection, and uncertainty about the future means that it is virtually impossible to predict which biological resources might one day be of value.

To help provide some clarity, it has been necessary to identify proxies for biodiversity that are supposed to reflect overall biodiversity and hence identify areas where biodiversity benefits might be greatest. Species diversity has been one of the most commonly used units of measurement, mainly because of the ease with which some species can be recognized and also due to the recognized roles in ecosystem function that some species are known to play. There is now a bewildering array of tried and suggested techniques for assessing species-level diversity, many of which try to represent the relative importance of certain species by multiplying their individual abundances according to some preset criteria, e.g. global rarity, endemism, degree of endangerment or keystone functions. However, the goal of biodiversity conservation should be not just about maintaining the greatest number of species, but also ensuring that ecosystem and genetic diversity is sustained.

For the time being, these methods are the best available; however, whether or not these proxies and methods are truly able to reflect the range of biodiversity benefits remains a moot point. Whether or not any chosen proxy is the right one is always open to debate: selection is predicated on value judgements about which facets of biodiversity matter more and which matter less and which proxies best represent them. It is important to recognize that the way in which biodiversity is viewed and assessed, and the land-use decisions that are based on these assessments, are subjective choices and only as robust as the available information. They are also liable to change, as our scientific understanding and knowledge of the relationship between land use and biodiversity benefit improves (Vermeulen & Koziell 2002).

In any discussion on biodiversity benefits, it is important to be explicit about the precise nature of biodiversity benefits arising and for whom they matter most.

Free-market approaches to sustainable land use and biodiversity benefits

Markets for carbon offsets

The management of the land-based components of the carbon cycle could be an important part of the solution to the climate-change problem. This is because natural forests and certain other ecosystems, such as peatlands, are major stores of carbon. Alteration of such habitats means release of carbon into the atmosphere and the loss of storage functions; it also means loss of biodiversity. Expanding and improving the quality of these ecosystems can help sequester carbon. The fact that such 'carbon-rich' areas are also 'biodiversity rich' offers some potential for simultaneous action on biodiversity and carbon issues. However, biodiversity enhancement is not always a corollary of carbon sequestration, as the latter activities have often involved planting of biodiversity-poor monocultures.

The 1997 Kyoto Protocol recognizes forest and land-use change as both part of the problem and part of the solution to greenhouse-gas reductions. It has introduced a series of market-based measures (flexibility mechanisms), which, while highly contentious, have provided a framework within which land- and forestry-based markets in carbon offsets could start to evolve (Trexler *et al*. 1999). These mechanisms include the following:

- Article 3: Domestic Greenhouse Emission by Industrialized Countries. This article defines which domestic emissions should be inventoried by industrialized countries during the 2008–2012 commitment period. Currently, it requires tracking greenhouse-gas removals and emissions from human-induced afforestation, reforestation and deforestation that has occurred since 1990. Forest harvesting and management has been omitted for now, but may still get included by later Conferences of the Parties (COPs).

- Articles 6 and 17: Joint Implementation and Emission Trading between Industrialized Countries. These articles define two market mechanisms that allow industrialized countries to trade emission reductions with other industrialized countries. Article-3 restrictions on forest activities may apply to these mechanisms. Article 6 specifies project-based credit trading and explicitly refers to enhancing carbon storage and reducing emissions, such as by slowing forest degradation, and tree planting.

- Article 12: Clean Development Mechanism. Allows industrialized countries to meet their reductions through projects in developing countries. There is no explicit mention of land-use change and forest projects, but to invoke the mechanism, it must contribute to sustainable development (WRI 1998).

Given the coincidence between carbon and biodiversity issues, these mechanisms, if implemented with the necessary 'clauses' in place, have some potential to help advance biodiversity conservation objectives through private-sector activity. Further still, the high level of international interest and concern in climate change, especially from economic interests, as compared with biodiversity conservation, could help provide the otherwise absent incentives for biodiversity conservation amongst political and economic decision makers.

There have been many fierce debates over whether or not 'sinks' should count towards emissions-reduction targets. Concerns have focused around the fact that developed countries may simply turn to carbon-offset projects, without taking domestic action at source, and around how to monitor and measure compliance. However, despite the many concerns, COP-6 decided to give the go-ahead to 'sinks' even if the concept remains somehow flawed. It was also clearly stipulated that the sustainable development criteria relating to the Clean Development Mechanism are to be articulated and defined by the host country. COP-7 went on to define 'sinks' as the afforestation and reforestation of lands degraded prior to 1990: forest conservation was not included.

The latter decisions has severely limited the potential for using the Kyoto Protocol to provide biodiversity benefits, as afforestation biodiversity benefits are likely to be minimal when compared with forest conservation activities; however, this decision is not set in stone and is due to be revisited at COP-9 after the Subsidiary Body on Scientific, Technical and Technological Advice has studied the issue in greater detail.

While the legal basis for carbon-offset projects is still being finalized, there have been various carbon-offset projects already implemented within the land-use and forestry sector, as countries and companies move to take advantage of lower prices. There are some clear biodiversity benefits arising from some, but not all, of these projects, as follows:

- Reforestation or afforestation, e.g. through plantations, agroforestry or restoration of natural forests, to increase carbon sequestration. Where these activities include reforestation of pasture, cropland or degraded lands with monoculture plantations, there is a chance that valuable non-forest species and habitats found within the ecosystems to be reforested will become severely threatened. The level of biodiversity loss will, however, depend on the state and nature of the original ecosystem. For example, there are pasture lands that continue to maintain a high diversity of grass and insect species, so tree planting within such areas will result in obvious biodiversity losses. Furthermore, while there may be no biodiversity loss when degraded lands are reforested, the potential for recreating the original ecosystem will be lost, as will the original biodiversity that went with it. Restoration of natural forests may, on the contrary, offer biodiversity benefits.

- Improved forest management, e.g. through reduced-impact logging (RIL), to both increase sequestration and reduce emissions. Reduced-impact logging is far less damaging on other local plant and animal species—hence local biodiversity—than conventional logging practice. Methods such as pre-cutting vines, directional felling and planned extraction of timber on properly constructed skid trails all help reduces damage to other non-commercial trees, help prevent soil erosion and vine infestation. In some forests, research suggests that harvesting damage can be reduced by up to 50%! The biodiversity benefits resulting from RIL are obvious.

- Conservation and protection against deforestation, e.g. through the expansion of protected areas and improved fire control, to cut emissions. Such activities could offer biodiversity benefits by providing additional incentives for the enhanced protection of large tracts of forest. However, given the strong link between forest protection and reduced carbon emissions, forest areas will take precedence over other ecosystems (e.g. inland aquatic ecosystems). The latter may provide fewer carbon benefits but might be more critical for furthering global biodiversity-conservation objectives. Furthermore, forests are quite well protected globally, as compared with some other ecosystems, so unless other ecosystems are factored into the carbon equation, such activities may result in yet further skewing of the global protected areas system towards forests. There is also concern that, given the strong levels of dependence on forest resources in many parts of the developing world, if certain forest areas are made off limits to local people, the problem is only likely to be displaced, leading to exceptionally high rates of deforestation in nearby areas.

- Substitution of fossil fuels with sustainably produced biomass and improved fuelwood management to cut emissions. As with the discussion in (i) above, such substitution is likely to involve biomass plantations and the effects on biodiversity are likely to be affected by the location of any such plantation (i.e. the quality and uniqueness of the original ecosystem).

- Improved soil conservation and agricultural practices, e.g. through encouraging practices such as non-burning, minimum tillage and the use of natural fertilizers and mulching, to cut emissions. Such activities all help to improve the level of on-farm biodiversity, above and below the ground, i.e. insects, soil microbes and other microorganisms. They can also help stabilize the agricultural frontier, thus slowing deforestation and concomitant biodiversity loss.

Land-based carbon-offset projects have some potential to provide some biodiversity benefits, as long as the biodiversity issues are mainstreamed into the various accounting, definitional and management strategies that will arise. However, as long as forests are the prime focus of attention for such projects, this will result in forest biodiversity benefits alone. While this is clearly a major step forward, as analyses have shown that species diversity is exceptionally high in forest ecosystems, improvements in scientific understanding are rapidly revealing that other previously unexplored ecosystems, such as deep-sea environments, are also very rich in biodiversity. Thus carbon-offset projects should be seen as an important part of the conservation solution, but only as part of it.

Markets for genetic resources and traditional knowledge

A few years ago, bio-prospecting (the exploration of biodiversity for commercially valuable genetic and biochemical resources[1]) was heralded as a possible win–win opportunity for bolstering commercial, livelihood and biodiversity-conservation goals. The recognition that these resources are of obvious importance to the agro-chemical, food, pharmaceutical and cosmetic industries in developed countries, but had been collected freely in developing countries over the past few hundred years, triggered the third objective of the CBD. This provided a new regulatory instrument that aimed to promote more equitable exchange, on mutually agreed terms, of benefits from access to genetic resources and associated knowledge.

---

[1]This can include, for example, prospecting for useful genes for crop development, medicines, insecticides, enzymes, micro-organisms, fragrances and fungicides. To date, it has been dominated by the search for pharmaceutical products.

These provisions are proving controversial and difficult to implement; they relate closely to (and sometimes conflict with) many other policy and legislative frameworks—such as those on trade and investment, intellectual property, constitutional law and indigenous peoples' rights. Furthermore, the likelihood of finding a useful extract has been put at 1000–10 000 to 1 (Crook & Clapp 1998) and the increasing moves to synthesis means that there are fewer searches for raw materials occurring now (although this may change in future). Furthermore, for material that has been sourced from the 'wild', there are still many complex debates over the level of benefits that the original holders of the unimproved material should receive and who within the source community should receive the benefits (Reid *et al.* 1993; Ten Kate 1995). All in all, actual revenues are likely to be low, and unlikely to produce sufficient incentive to conserve if there are other income-generating opportunities available.

That said, there have been some major deals signed. Probably the most well known is that between the government of Costa Rica (through the National Biodiversity Institute) and Merck Pharmaceuticals. A major deal was signed between the two parties that covered payments for the collection of species samples and sometimes for refining them, and to provide royalty payments on any products that might be developed from such samples. There are, however, not many major deals of this nature that have been replicated in other countries, although there have been quite a significant number of smaller-scale initiatives.

Markets for 'green' products

The recent upsurge in consumer interest in 'natural', 'green' or 'organic' food and other products and services (e.g. ecotourism) has provided some stimulus for markets in such products. More markets for such products has meant a greater proportion of land devoted to such sustainable management regimes. Various accreditation schemes have been established to address this, such as the Forest Stewardship Council's timber-certification scheme, the Marine Stewardship Council's evolving fish certification scheme and a plethora of organic agriculture and tourism schemes. However, many of these schemes still face implementation challenges. Organic and sustainable timber or fish production should yield some obvious *in situ* biodiversity benefits, especially where high-chemical-input agricultural methods are replaced by lower-input regimes, or where high-intensity logging is replaced by RIL. However, the lack of empirical research on the relationship between such regimes and biodiversity, and the difficulties in identifying suitable proxies for biodiversity, means that specific conclusions still cannot be drawn as to the precise nature of biodiversity benefits. Furthermore, much remains to be done in terms of identifying suitable indicators for biodiversity, within the range of certification schemes.

Conclusions

The increasing emphasis on private, as opposed to public, goods and services in development paradigms is leading to significant changes in the original biodiversity. It also means that many of the conventional approaches to biodiversity conservation are struggling to survive. While it would certainly not be appropriate to write off these conventional approaches, there is a real need to look at how they can begin to evolve and compete within in a world increasing dominated by private enterprise. This will inevitably require trade-offs between biodiversity and livelihood benefits across much of the landscape. The challenge will lie in ensuring that these trade-offs are suitably balanced. In order to provide adequate safeguards, we need to be much clearer on where trade-offs are simply not appropriate, for instance, where biodiversity is of such 'absolute' value that it warrants no development activity at all. While some conservationists would argue that areas of absolute value have already been identified, e.g. through Conservation International's hotspot mapping, or WWF's eco-regions, such exercises now need to occur on a much smaller scale to be relevant for practical planning purposes. They also need to keep in tune with new insights on biodiversity provided by science.

In order to ensure that free-market approaches provide suitable biodiversity benefits, the following actions are proposed.

- Greater investment in research to improve the quality of information on the relationship between land use and biodiversity benefits.

- Establish inclusive and transparent process for articulating and identifying suitable proxies and indicators that can be incorporated in the range of verification, monitoring and evaluation processes associated with free-market approaches to sustainable land use and forestry.

- Identify and enhance synergies between the UNFCCC, the CBD and the Convention to Combat Desertification (CCD) and other international trade and economic agreements. This might involve the following.

  - Ensuring that biodiversity issues are fully mainstreamed into discussions relating to the accounting methods, mitigation frameworks, definitions and implementation, occurring under the Kyoto Protocol.

  - Strengthening capacity at national level, especially in developing countries, to tackle and manage these synergies 'on the ground'. This might involve identifying areas under national jurisdiction that are of both high biodiversity and high carbon value. Projects and activities aimed at maximizing both objectives could then be targeted specifically within such areas.

References

Crook, C. & Clapp, R. A. 1998 Is market-oriented forest conservation a contradiction in terms? *Environ. Conserv.* **25**, 131–145.

Koziell, I. 2001 *Diversity not adversity: sustaining livelihoods with biodiversity.* London: International Institute for Environment and Development.

Reid, W. V., Laird, S. A., Meyer, C. A., Gamez, R., Sittenfeld, A., Janzen, D. H., Collin, M. A. & Juma, C. 1993 Biodiversity prospecting: using genetic resources for sustainable development. Washington, DC: World Resources Institute.

Ten Kate, K. 1995 *Biopiracy or green petroleum? Expectations and best practice in bioprospecting.* London: Overseas Development Administration.

Trexler, M., Kosloff, L. & Gibbons, R. 1999 Overview of forestry ad land-use projects pursued under the pilot. In *The UN Framework Convention on Climate Change Activities Implemented Jointly (AIJ) pilot: experiences and lessons learned* (ed. R. K. Dixon). Dordrecht: Kluwer.

Vermeulen, S. & Koziell, I. 2002 *Integrating local and global biodiversity values: a review of biodiversity assessment.* London: International Institute for Environment and Development.

WRI 1998 *Climate, biodiversity and forests.* Washington, DC: World Resources Institute.

Chapter 16

Developing markets for forest environmental services: an opportunity for promoting equity while securing efficiency?

Natasha Landell-Mills

Introduction

In May 2001, Sustainable Forestry Management Ltd, a London-based private-investment fund, purchased 48 000 t of carbon dioxide (CO_2) from native American Confederated Salish and Kootenai tribes generated through the reforestation of 100 hectares of their Montana reservation. In 1999, Botanical Garden Trading Company Ltd, a start-up company aiming to compete for worldwide flower delivery, offered to return 2.5% of its turnover to conservation initiatives in biodiversity 'hotspots' of horticultural interest and to pay for access to these areas. In the Philippines, the Makiling Forest Reserve is negotiating with major local water users for the implementation of a watershed protection and conservation fee to pay for watershed services received.

All over the world, similar stories of path-breaking deals involving payments for forest environmental services are emerging. Free-market economists are quick to point to such stories as evidence that markets can offer effective solutions to environmental problems. Cash-strapped governments looking for innovative mechanisms for transferring responsibilities for forest protection to the private sector are increasingly interested in what markets have to offer.

Yet, despite spreading enthusiasm, there is a surprising lack of knowledge as to why such markets are emerging where none existed before, the process through which they evolve and whether markets are always desirable. For governments charged with ensuring equity as well as economic efficiency and environmental sustainability, a critical question that needs to be asked is how the rise of markets for environmental services impacts on the poor? Do markets for environmental services involve equity trade-offs? Or can markets be crafted to promote poverty reduction as well as improved efficiency in environmental service provision?

In this chapter, an effort is made to draw on a recent review of markets for forest environmental services undertaken by the International Institute for Environment and Development (IIED) in 2000/2001 to explore the specific question of what markets might mean for the poor. The aim is not to be negative about what markets have to offer, but to heighten awareness of possible trade-offs and the need for greater attention to how markets may be shaped to maximize efficiency and equity gains. The chapter ends with some preliminary thoughts on how governments might begin to level the playing field and increase market benefits for the poor.

Commercializing forest environmental services: a diversity of experience

Forests provide an array of environmental services. The critical role of trees in soaking up carbon and helping to reduce the build-up of greenhouse gases in the Earth's atmosphere is well recorded and a major focus of this book. Forest ecosystems are also widely recognized as harbouring a significant share of the world's biodiversity, critical for maintaining ecosystem balance, evolutionary processes and natural resilience to shocks. At the local level, forests are credited with maintaining a wide range of watershed services, from soil-erosion control, stream-flow regulation to flood prevention and the maintenance of aquatic productivity. From a distance forests are appreciated by millions of people for what they add to landscape beauty.

While forest environmental services are important, and often essential, to human welfare, they tend to be undervalued. This is because they often fall outside the market system and have no price. Consequently, 'producers' of forest environmental services rarely get paid, and 'consumers' are rarely asked to pay. The result is under-investment in forest protection. Governments have traditionally responded to the problem of 'missing markets' for environmental services by taking responsibility for the provision of these services, often through public ownership of forests.

Recently, however, there has been growing evidence that in the right conditions consumers of environmental services are willing to pay for the benefits they experience. Several factors have conspired to make payments more feasible. Increased awareness amongst consumers of the economic importance of environmental services as well as a growing awareness of threats to supply have been critical drivers. At the same time, improved methods for monitoring the status, impact and consumption of environmental services has made it possible to link payments to consumption and reduced the costs of controlling non-payment and 'free-riding'.

While evidence that markets for environmental services are gaining ground is widespread, understanding of these markets is hazy. To gain a clearer idea of the types of markets that are emerging, IIED undertook a global review of markets for four forest environmental services—biodiversity protection, carbon sequestration, watershed protection and landscape beauty—between February 2000 and July 2001 (Landell-Mills & Porras 2002). A total of 287

Table 16.1. *Commercializing forest environmental services*

Environmental service	Commodity
watershed protection (e.g. reduced flooding, increased dry-season flows, improved water quality, maintained aquatic habitat, soil-contaminant control, reduced downstream sedimentation)	watershed management contracts, water-quality credits, water rights, land acquisition/lease, salinity credits, transpiration credits, conservation easements, certified watershed-friendly products, stream-flow-reduction licenses, salmon habitat credits, reforestation contracts, protected areas
landscape beauty (i.e. protection of scenic 'view-scapes' for recreation or local residents)	entrance rights, long-term-access permits, package-tourism services, natural-resource management agreements, ecotourism concessions, photographic permits, land acquisition, land lease
biodiversity conservation (e.g. role in maintaining ecosystem functioning, maintaining options for future use, insurance against shocks, improved choice, existence values)	protected areas, bio-prospecting rights, biodiversity-friendly products, biodiversity company shares, debt-for-nature swaps, biodiversity credits, conservation concession, land acquisition, biodiversity-management contracts, logging-rights acquisition, tradeable development rights, conservation easements
carbon sequestration (i.e. absorption and storage of carbon in forest vegetation and soils)	assigned-amount units, certified emission reductions, emission-reduction units, carbon offsets/credits, tradeable development rights, conservation easements

Source: Landell-Mills & Porras (2002).

cases were reviewed from a range of developed and developing countries. In what follows some of the broad insights of this review are highlighted.

Markets are diverse phenomena

Apart from emphasizing the considerable number of initiatives underway around the world, the review offers critical insights into the variety of experience. Markets differ not just in terms of the commodities being bought and sold (and these differ even for the same environmental service; see Table 16.1), but they differ with respect to the character of their participants, geographical extent, payment mechanism employed, drivers, maturity, the process through which they evolve and their impacts. The sheer diversity of experiences makes any attempt to generalize extremely difficult and simple arguments in favour of markets for forest environmental services are misleading. The challenge is to identify the market structure that is optimal for a given situation.

Markets are intertwined in broader institutional landscapes

In addition to highlighting the considerable diversity between different market forms, the review points to the fallacy of simplistic debates around whether regulatory or market approaches are more desirable when dealing with forest environmental problems. Markets do not evolve in a void, but are intimately tied up with the regulatory environment in which they exist. Far from being competing arrangements, markets and regulatory approaches are often mutually reinforcing. In many instances, the establishment of new regulations and associated property rights spurs market creation. The emerging international market for carbon offsets, water-quality-permit trading in the US and pilots in salinity credit trading in Australia, for instance, are all rooted in new government regulations.

Markets are also closely intertwined with informal cooperative arrangements. In many situations, cooperation is strengthened by benefit-sharing mechanisms that ensure broad-based support. Payment systems, for instance, have played a key role in shoring up cooperative arrangements for watershed protection in India by offering a new tool for sharing benefits with disadvantaged groups. The successful operation of markets may itself depend on the strength of informal systems of monitoring and enforcement that minimize requirements for costly formal alternatives.

Market development and operation is costly

Markets are expensive to establish and run. Proponents of market approaches have often overlooked this fact, yet costs of setting up and managing markets may be significant enough to outweigh their benefits. Costs of market creation are associated with defining property rights, setting up exchange systems, educating market participants, establishing monitoring and enforcement mechanisms, etc. Market operation involves costs of information gathering, negotiation, contract formation, monitoring and enforcement, and renegotiating contracts where they prove unsatisfactory. Any judgement as to the desirability of markets must account for these market-creation and transaction costs.

Power relations are key

A central message from the IIED's review is that power relations are critical. As highlighted above, markets are a product of their environment. Power relations are a key facet of that environment and impact on the development of legal and regulatory systems, cooperative arrangements and markets. Drivers behind market establishment inevitably have their own interests and will make efforts to shape markets that fit these. Where weaker parties wish to influence market development, their success will depend heavily on gaining the support of more powerful entities.

Taken together, the points highlighted above emphasize the dangers of excessive faith in the optimality of markets. Markets are diverse phenomenon which need to be unpacked. Their ability to raise welfare will depend on the institutional context in which they evolve, power relations and associated transaction costs. Moreover, market performance will vary depending on whether we consider economic efficiency, social equity or environmental sustainability. In this chapter I am particularly concerned with market implica-

Table 16.2. *Potential opportunities and risks of markets for assets of the poor*

Opportunities	Risks
natural assets	
increased forest value associated with new market opportunities	new markets are inaccessible by the poor due to unclear property rights, insufficient marketing skills and education, inadequate information, lack of contacts, lacking communication infrastructure, inappropriate commodity design, e.g. long-term contracts inappropriate to livelihood strategies that require short-term flexibility
positive spin-offs for timber and NTFPs where sustainable forest exploitation permitted	
positive impacts for other natural assets: (i) soil fertility and agriculture (ii) water flows and quality (iii) air quality due to reduced forest fires	
	opportunity costs where delivery of environmental services precludes production of timber and/or NTFPs
social assets	
market may spur the formalization of resource tenure and clarification of property rights over environmental services	increased competition for control over forests and loss of rights by the poor
	erosion of community cohesiveness due to increased divisions between those who gain and lose from markets
increased organizational and management capacity of community-based organizations through collaboration in delivery of, or payment for, environmental service	threats to local culture as environmental services become commercial assets
protection of forest-based cultural heritage	
human assets	
improved education and skill base relating to forest management for environmental services, cooperation, project management, marketing, negotiation, enterprise development, etc.	the poor are excluded from market or given only menial jobs, while necessary skills are brought in
	reduced health due to lost access to NTFPs and associated nutrition and reduced disposable income
improved health due to more varied diets, improved water supply (quantity and quality), improved air quality, increased disposable income for medical treatment	
physical assets	
investment in improved communication links to remote forest areas	investment in improved communication links are targeted at certain market participants with few spin-offs for the wider community, leading to increased inequality

tions for the poor. This is not only of concern for ethical reasons, but because marginalization of the poor from the market-development process could have critical implications for the sustainability of market systems and undermine their effectiveness in achieving environmental objectives.

Table 16.2. (*Cont.*)

Opportunities	Risks
financial assets	
more diversified income base increases security and helps to build up financial assets	where markets lead to exclusion of the poor from forest areas, they will have negative repercussions for financial assets
	poor buyers of services (e.g. downstream communities paying for watershed services) will have unsustainable demands on their limited financial resources
political assets	
improved community-based organization provides a firmer basis for gaining political representation and voice	where markets lead to further marginalization, the poor have even fewer channels for influencing policy decision-making

Markets and the poor

In evaluating the impacts of markets for the poor, it is useful to frame the evaluation in terms of how markets impact on the assets on which the poor depend. A number of asset-based approaches to evaluating welfare have been developed (Carney *et al.* (1999) provide a useful overview). For the purposes of this chapter I will consider impacts for six assets: natural, physical (infrastructure and other man-made capital), financial, social (informal cooperative, family- or community-based support structures), human (educational and skill base), and political (access to and influence over policy-making structures). Opportunities offered by markets in building up the poor's asset base are set against risks that markets will devalue key assets. Table 16.2 provides a summary of the key potential impacts.

Table 16.2 highlights a number of channels through which markets may benefit the poor. It also identifies significant risks. Whether the poor realize the potential, or fall victim to the risks, depends on a number of factors. Seven stand out as follows.

1 **Security of tenure.** A clear prerequisite for the poor to benefit is that they have property rights over forests, and rights to income generated by environmental-service sales. Where the poor lack secure tenure, a critical concern is that markets raise competition for control over forest assets and lead to exclusion and further marginalization of the poor.

2 **Skills and education.** Where the poor have clear property rights, the extent to which they benefit from market opportunities depends on their ability to participate and compete for business. This in turn requires, amongst other things, managerial skills for organizing supply—especially when a large number of landholders is involved—negotiation and contracting skills for structuring deals, and technical skills relating to the delivery of environmental services. Low levels of education and inadequate marketing skills will place a serious handicap on participation.

3 **Market information.** Access to information on potential buyers and current prices being paid for environmental services is key for sellers to be in a position to negotiate a fair deal.

4 **Market contacts.** At present, environmental-service markets tend to be segmented, largely unregulated and highly dependent on directly negotiated deals. Knowing where to go to initiate a trade and where to find support and advice is critical. Finding an intermediary that can be trusted is essential. Market contacts take time to develop and are most easily made and solidified through regular communication. This may prove difficult to achieve for poor rural communities.

5 **Communication infrastructure.** Linked to the above, an important determinant of costs of negotiating and concluding deals will relate to how accessible sellers are to buyers. Transportation and communication infrastructure is important in bringing parties together.

6 **Contract design.** In general the provision of environmental services is a long-term commitment (e.g. carbon offset deals tend to span decades rather than months or years). However, poor communities rely on livelihood strategies that are flexible and able to cope with unexpected shocks. Thus, even where new markets offer opportunities for increasing income, if they require extended commitments they are unlikely to attract participation of the poor. Where the poor accept long-term contracts, there are serious risks that by locking them into a single land use for extended periods these contracts will decrease the poor's ability to respond to shocks and thereby damage welfare.

7 **Financial resources.** Participating in markets for forest environmental services is expensive. Transaction costs will tend to be even higher for the poor. Not only will the poor tend to require greater investment in skill development, but they are also more likely to suffer from inadequate communication, information, market contacts, and insecure property rights. In addition, because the poor tend to have only small plots they will generally need to join forces to attract business.[1] Collaboration requires time and effort.

Concluding thoughts: making markets work for the poor

From the above it is clear that, while the potential rewards from market development are significant, poor people are likely to face an uphill battle in realizing these. Governments are critical in establishing the legal underpinnings to monitoring and enforcement mechanisms for markets. They thus have a key role to play in making markets work for poor groups. Following on from the above assessment of constraints, four key ways in which governments may help to shape more equitable and inclusive markets are set out below.

---

[1] Threshold effects associated with the delivery of certain environmental services (e.g. biodiversity or watershed protection) often require that a minimum area is protected.

1 **Assign forest service property rights.** For poor forest-based communities to be able to participate in a market for environmental services they need to be able to offer credible commitments for supply. Secure property rights are key.

2 **Strengthen capacity for market participation, e.g. through training and education.** While requirements will vary depending on the context, general training programmes in marketing, negotiation, management, financial accounting, contract formulation and conflict resolution will tend to be important. Technical skills relating to forest management for environmental services will also be needed. In some instances it may be most cost effective for government to support the emergence of specialized ancillary service providers and intermediaries who can offer necessary services to poor communities. A key consideration will be how to ensure service providers do not exploit their position and retain the trust of poor communities.

3 **Market support centre.** Information is power. To improve poor people's ability to participate in emerging markets, a central market support centre could offer a number of key services:

- free access to information on recent prices and transactions;

- a contact point for potential buyers, sellers and intermediaries;

- an advice bureau to support the design and implementation of contracts; and

- research which draws together emerging best practice with respect to contract design and implementation and feeds this back through its advice bureau. This could be particularly important in the development of flexible contracts which are suitable to poor communities' needs.

4 **Access to finance.** Where finance is needed to negotiate and conclude environmental service deals, the government may have a role to play in supporting access to funds. This is especially true where banks and other formal lending institutions are failing to provide loan facilities due to their lack of expertise in emerging markets, inflexible collateral laws and/or the non-existence of reliable credit registries. The government has a key role to play in providing supportive legislation and stimulating competition amongst private financial intermediaries, which can result is significant increases in lending to the poor. To the extent that markets for forest environmental services increases the value of poor people's asset base, financial institutions should be encouraged to take these assets as collateral in securing loans.

Markets for forest environmental services are emerging throughout the world and the trend is set to continue. As markets evolve, governments have a critical role to play in crafting the legislative and regulatory environment to guide this process. Equity must be a key consideration; not just for moral reasons, but also to ensure markets work efficiently and are sustainable. The poor control vast areas of forests, which offer valuable environmental services to both local and global communities. Finding mechanisms to ensure that the poor have access to and participate in evolving market systems is key.

Acknowledgements

This chapter draws heavily on a global review of markets for forest environmental services and their impacts on the poor undertaken by the IIED between February 2000 and July 2001 (Landell-Mills & Porras 2002). Support for this research was provided by the UK Department for International Development, the European Commission, the Danish Ministry of Foreign Affairs and the Swiss Agency for Development and Cooperation. The opinions expressed here are those of the author and do not represent the views of the sponsoring agencies.

References

Carney, D., Drinkwater, M., Rusinow, T., Neefjes, K., Wanmali, S. & Singh, N. 1999 *Livelihoods approaches compared. A brief comparison of the livelihoods approaches of the UK Department for International Development (DFID), CARE, Oxfam and the United Nations Development Programme (UNDP).* London: Department for International Development.

Landell-Mills, N. & Porras, I. 2002 *Silver bullet or fools' gold? A global review of markets for forest environmental services and their impacts on the poor.* London: International Institute for Environment and Development.

Part 3

THE FUTURE MODEL

Chapter 17

Carbon sinks and emissions trading under the Kyoto Protocol: a legal analysis

ERIC C. BETTELHEIM AND GILONNE D'ORIGNY

Background and structure

The United Nations Framework Convention on Climate Change (UNFCCC, hereafter referred to as 'Convention') was adopted in 1992, at the Rio Earth Summit to address the adverse effects of climate change.[1] It was the conclusion of work done by the Meteorological Organization and that of the Intergovernmental Panel on Climate Change (IPCC), which developed the scientific consensus on climate change (see IPCC 1990a–c). The Convention came into force on 21 March 1994 and has been ratified by 188 countries as of February 2003.

As its name indicates, the Convention is a framework document. This means that it is intended to provide a structure for the Parties to develop laws aimed at achieving the Convention's objectives at regularly scheduled Conferences of the Parties (COPs). The Convention establishes a legal infrastructure, a deliberative process and the administrative bodies to be used to develop and adopt substantive protocols.[2] Article 7(2) establishes the COP as 'the supreme body of this Convention... [which] shall make, within its mandate, the decisions necessary to promote the effective implementation of the Convention'. Article 17(1) provides that the COP 'may... adopt protocols to the Convention'. Thus protocols adopted by and decisions made 'under any protocol' (see Article 17(5)) form the Convention's secondary legislation. Once ratified, and on coming into force, parties to the Convention implement the protocols by adopting national legislation. Rule making is delegated to subsidiary bodies such as the CDM Executive Board. The principles of law and interpretation in this context are no different from those of administrative law in national or multinational treaty regimes (see, for example, Lasok & Lasok 2001). Interpretation should be conducted, 'in good faith in accordance with the ordinary meaning to be given to the terms of the treaty in their context and in the light of its object and purpose' (1969 Vienna Convention on the Law of Treaties, Article 31).

The legal and administrative process initiated under the Convention to protect the Earth's climate should therefore be analysed on its own terms and in the context in which it arose, namely, a summit meeting on sustainable growth and development.[3] The deliberations focused not only on the Convention itself but also on the 1992 Convention on Biological Diversity, which was also promulgated at the Rio Earth Summit, on the 1971 Ramsar Convention on Wetlands and on the 1994 Convention to Combat Desertification. Each of them contemplates conservation in the context of sustainable economic growth and development. Progress over the intervening decade on the achievement of the goals embodied in these Conventions is to be assessed at the World Summit on Sustainable Development (WSSD) in Johannesburg in Autumn 2002.

Objective, principles and commitments

The recitals, Objective (Article 2) and Principles (Article 3) articulate the Convention's primary purpose and objectives and constitute its primary legislation to which the various instruments, such as the protocols, are subject. The objective of the 'Convention and any related legal instruments that the Conference of the Parties may adopt' is to achieve 'stabilization of greenhouse-gas (GHG)[4] concentrations in the atmosphere at a level that would prevent dangerous anthropogenic interference with the climate system[5]'. This is to be achieved in such a way that enables 'economic development to proceed in a sustainable manner (Convention Article 2).

The Convention's Principles, set out in Article 3, include the following:

- Intergenerational equity and common but differentiated responsibility between developed and developing countries (Convention Article 3(1)) with special attention given to countries particularly vulnerable to climate change's adverse effects and those that would bear a disproportionate or abnormal cost under the Convention (Convention Article 3(2)).

- The precautionary principle whereby, despite scientific uncertainty, action must be taken to adopt cost-effective measures and policies to 'anticipate, prevent or minimize the causes of climate change'. These measures and policies must be 'comprehensive, cover all relevant sources, sinks and reservoirs of greenhouse gases' and 'should be cost-effective so as to ensure global benefits at the lowest possible cost' (Convention Article 3(3)).

- 'The Parties have a right to, and should, promote sustainable development... taking into account that economic development is essential for adopting measures to address climate change' (Convention Article 3(4)).

- 'A supportive and open international economic system that would lead to sustainable economic growth and development in all Parties, particularly developing countries [and] measures taken to combat climate change. . . should not constitute a means of arbitrary or unjustifiable discrimination or a disguised restriction on international trade' (Convention Article 3(5)).

The objectives and principles set out in Convention Articles 2, 3 and 4(7) specifically link the developed world's compliance with emission-reduction commitments to promoting sustainable economic development in and transfer of technology to developing countries. Convention Article 4(1)(d) provides, *inter alia*, that the Parties are to promote sustainable development and cooperation in the conservation and enhancement of sinks including 'biomass, forests. . . as well as other terrestrial. . . ecosystems'. Article 4(2)(g)(7) enjoins the Parties to '. . . take fully into account that economic and social development and poverty eradication are the first and overriding priorities of the developing country Parties'.

It is these primary objectives, principles and commitments to which the protocols, decisions taken under them, and rules made pursuant to them are to conform. It is at least arguable that recent interpretations of, and decisions taken under, the Protocol discussed here, the Kyoto Protocol, and directions to subsidiary bodies made under it, are inconsistent with the Convention and the terms of the Protocol itself and thus *ultra vires* (Wade & Bradley 1993). It is, in particular, questionable whether decisions which effectively amend the Protocol by excluding 'the conservation and enhancement of' certain terrestrial sinks and which arbitrarily limit and discriminate against developing countries' participation in the economic benefits of emissions trading are legally binding. The exclusion of avoided deforestation as a source of carbon credits from developing countries during the first commitment period, the creation of a new carbon credit exclusively available to Annex I countries and the implementation of a regulatory system which discriminates against developing countries by limiting their access to credits from carbon sequestration are all doubtful in light of the express purposes of the Convention and the express language of the Protocol.

COP-3: the Kyoto Protocol

The principal achievements of the third COP held in Kyoto in December 1997 were, first, to agree that Convention Annex I countries would be bound to quantitative GHG-emissions limitations and reductions commitments specified in Protocol Annex B for the first commitment period (2008–2012) and, second, to provide flexible mechanisms (including carbon sequestration and emissions trading) to help achieve these commitments in an economically efficient manner. Protocol Article 3 assigns to each Annex I Party an individual emissions-reduction target based on its 1990 level of domestic emissions: its '1990 baseline'. Annex I[6] Parties agreed to 'ensure that their aggregate anthropogenic carbon dioxide equivalent emissions of greenhouse gases. . . do not exceed their assigned amounts,. . . with a view to reducing their overall emissions of such gases by at least 5% below 1990 levels in the commitment period 2008–2012'.[7] Articles 7 and 8 provide for accounting for assigned amount units (AAUs) of emissions.[8]

Convention Article 4(1) contains all of the Parties' general commitments and Article 4(2) refers to specific commitments by Annex I Parties, most notably to revert to 1990 GHG emissions by 2000. (This, of course, was not achieved. With very few exceptions, all Annex I countries' level of emissions exceeded the specified levels. See national communications to the UNFCCC.) Finally, the objectives and principles laid out in Convention Articles 2[9] and 3 (see Appendix A) and Article 4(7)[10] specifically link the meeting of emissions-reduction commitments by the developed world with promoting sustainable economic development and transfer of technology to developing countries.

The Protocol will come into force when at least 55 of the Parties representing at least 55% of the 1990 GHG emissions have ratified it (Protocol Article 25). As of February 2003 the Protocol had been signed by 84 Parties and ratified by 105 (including the European Union and Japan) representing 43.9% of 1990 emissions. To achieve the required percentage in the absence of US participation,[11] compromises on carbon sinks were made, which are discussed in detail later in this chapter (see pages 293–294 and 296).

Flexibility mechanisms

To enable Annex I Parties to fulfil their commitments in a financially efficient way, the Protocol provides three 'flexibility mechanisms' (Articles 6 ('Joint Implementation'), 12 ('Clean Development Mechanism'), and 17 ('Emissions Trading')) that Annex I countries may use to meet part of their carbon-emissions commitments by reducing or removing atmospheric carbon dioxide (CO_2) in accordance with Articles 3(3) and 3(4) (see Kyoto Article 3).

Two mechanisms, Joint Implementation (JI, Article 6 (see Appendix B)) and the Clean Development Mechanism (CDM, Article 12 (see Appendix C)) are similar in concept. An Annex I legal (public or private) entity finances emissions reduction or removals in another Annex I country (JI), or non-Annex I country (CDM) and acquires emissions-reduction units (ERUs) for JI or certified emissions reductions (CERs) for CDM projects that count towards fulfilling the financing country's national emission-reduction commitment. The use of different names and acronyms, 'ERUs' for JI projects and 'CERs' for CDM projects, reflects not only the determination to distinguish responsibilities between Annex 1 and non-Annex 1 countries but a persistent debate as to the role, if any, that carbon sinks and the third mechanism, emissions trading, should be permitted to play.

Article 6: Joint Implementation

JI projects occur between two Annex I countries: a host and an investor, with the view to reducing anthropogenic emissions by sources or enhancing anthropogenic removals by sinks (Protocol Article 6(1)). The conditions include, in addition to overall compliance with the Convention, that these reductions in emissions and removals be both additional to what would otherwise have occurred and be supplemental to domestic actions aimed at meeting the Parties' respective reduction commitments. The requirements of 'additionality'[12] and 'supplementarity'[13] reflect concerns that credits only be given for a net overall improvement with respect to emissions. They also help to ensure that the primary focus is on technological change 'domestic action' leading to reduced emissions. In recent COP decisions, such alleged issues of 'integrity' have dominated, to virtual exclusion, issues of sustainable economic growth and practicality of implementation (see page 296).

Article 6 provides that '[a]ny Party included in Annex I may transfer to, or acquire from, any other such Party emission reduction units resulting from projects aimed at reducing anthropogenic emissions[14] by sources (Convention Article 1(9): ' "Source" means any process or activity which releases a greenhouse gas, an aerosol or a precursor of a greenhouse gas into the atmosphere'.) or enhancing anthropogenic removals by sinks of greenhouse gases (Protocol Article 6(1)). The ERUs acquired from another party under JI are added to the acquiring party's assigned amount (Protocol Article 3(10)) (thus providing it with the right to emit more than its original assigned amount) and subtracted from the transferring party's assigned amounts (thereby reducing its permitted emissions; Protocol Article 3(11)). These transfers are, in essence, simply a form of emissions trading (see pages 289–290) between Annex I countries although not expressed as such.

Article 6, like Article 3, refers specifically to 'removals by sinks' as well as to reductions by source. Article 3(3) provides that 'removals by sinks resulting from human-induced land-use change and forestry activities, limited to afforestation, reforestation and deforestation since 1990 shall be used to meet' each Annex I Party commitment. Article 3(4) provides that '...additional human-induced activities related to...removals by sinks in the agricultural soils and the land-use change and forestry categories shall be added to, or subtracted from, the assigned amounts for Parties included in Annex I...'. Article 3 also provides for adjustments in assigned amounts based on such acquisitions and transfers (Articles 3(10) and 3(11)).

Article 12: Clean Development Mechanism

> The purpose of the clean development mechanism shall be to assist Parties not included in Annex I in achieving sustainable development and in contributing to the ultimate objective of the Convention, and to assist Parties included in Annex I in achieving compliance with their quantified emission limitation and reduction commitments under Article 3.
>
> Protocol Article 12(2)

Article 3(12) provides that '[A]ny certified emission reductions which a Party acquires...in accordance with the provisions of Article 12 shall be added to the assigned amount for the acquiring Party'. As only Annex I countries are intended acquirers of such reductions, this introduced a relationship, albeit asymmetrical, between the developed and developing worlds, which had not been originally contemplated. The meaning of the words quoted above could hardly be clearer: any certified reduction that contributed to the ultimate objective of the Convention (reducing atmospheric GHG concentrations), assisted Annex I countries to meet their commitments as specified in Article 3 and assisted non-Annex 1 countries to achieve sustainable development shall be given credit. Yet this is not the outcome of recent negotiations.

The CDM came about as a late development (see Werksman 1998) in the Kyoto negotiations, in response to mainly US pressure to make non-Annex I countries participate in achieving the Convention's objectives. By creating incentives for developing countries it not only encouraged their participation but also laid the foundation for global, as opposed to only intra-Annex I country, emissions trading. It did not, however, contemplate the possibility that developing countries might wish to acquire CERs from other developing countries. Developing countries will need to do so if they become subject to emission limits and experience economic growth (it is expected by some that developing countries will ultimately become subject to emission limits under the Convention by means of 'convergence' or otherwise to ensure that 'inter-generational equity' is achieved). The debate failed to deal with the objective of economic growth just as it failed to deal with alternative economic scenarios such as developed countries (like the former Soviet Union) experiencing a rapid contraction of their economies after 1990. The result thus far has been a series of distortions that creates perverse incentives and unexpected results including the US withdrawal from the Kyoto negotiations (see White House 2002).

Protocol Article 12(3) creates 'certified emission reductions' and allows them to be used to meet Annex I Parties' emissions-reduction commitments under Article 3 but the Article is otherwise silent on carbon sinks. It also does not explicitly refer to trading. Article 12 does refer, in Article 12(9), to including activities in paragraph 3(a), i.e. 'project activities resulting in certified emission reductions' and to the 'acquisition' of CERs for purposes of meeting Article 3 'emission limitation and reduction commitments' (Article 12(3)(b)). From an analytical point of view Article 12 must be read in its entirety and read together with Articles 3, 6 and 17 within the overall clearly expressed purposes of the Convention. The logical conclusion is free trade in emissions reductions generated by carbon sinks in developing countries. Yet the debate proceeded with medieval scholasticism in which language was parsed (so that *any* CER became *some* CERs) and the lack of express reference in one Article (although containing unambiguous reference to other Articles) became a 'silence'; a silence which could be interpreted to include particular agendas unrelated to achieving the goals of the Convention.

If, as was apparently the case, it was intended that CERs be used in accordance with Article 3 (which provides for all 'land use, land-use change and forestry' (LULUCF) activities and for acquisition of CERs by Annex I Parties) and that Article recognized Article 6, which not only provided for trading ('transfer') but for 'removals by sinks', it follows that CERs are intended both to be tradeable and to include all sinks or at least all sinks explicitly provided for in the Protocol and those additional ones approved under Article 3(4). By treating the fungibility of credits and LULUCF projects issues as separate and allowing stand-alone interpretation of clearly related Articles, the negotiators managed to create a hierarchy of units that is inherently biased against developing countries and arbitrarily and artificially increases the cost of compliance by developing countries. It is not surprising that the struggle over the intended scope and meaning of Article 12 nearly caused the collapse of the negotiations of the Protocol in November 2001 and the ultimate withdrawal of the United States from those negotiations.

At COP-6 (see page 293) a compromise was reached limiting LULUCF activities under the CDM to afforestation and reforestation for the first commitment period, postponing consideration of including forest preservation in the CDM and by creating a new non-bankable unit, the Removal Unit (RMU), to deal with forest management in Annex I countries in the first commitment period. This served to increase the asymmetry of treatment of LULUCF activities between developed and developing countries. The principal effect was to exclude, at least for the first commitment period, forest preservation from the CDM, although it is included in JI projects, and to significantly increase the supply of forestry-based credits from Annex I countries, through RMUs (which include avoided deforestation), to the detriment of developing nations. There is no reason in equity or in respect of sustainable development for this result and it is contrary to the text of the Protocol and to the fundamental principles of the Convention. On the contrary it frustrates the object of the Convention, which is to reduce GHGs in the atmosphere. Even ignoring the obvious conservation benefits of forest conservation in the developing world, sustainable development could, and to many observers should, include reductions in deforestation in developing countries not least as deforestation in such countries is the second largest source of GHG emissions (see IPCC 2001a–c). The denial of investment and emissions-trading revenue from such activity, particularly its denial to poor rural areas, is directly contrary to the 'overriding concern of developing countries' namely poverty eradication. The rationale for increasing sink activity in Annex I countries and reducing incentives for it in developing countries is, to say the least, unclear and according to many commentators, perverse (see Chapters 12, 13, 18 and 19).

What Article 12 is clear about, however, is that both public and private entities may participate in CDM projects (Protocol Article 12(3)(a)), which must produce measurable long-term benefits related to the mitigation of climate change (Protocol Article 12(5)(b)), are additional to any that would have otherwise occurred (Protocol Article 12(5)(c)), are certified by operational entities supervised by an Executive Board (Protocol Articles 12(5) and (4)), and are independently audited and verified (Protocol Article 12(7)). This apparently straightforward language later provided the basis for an elaborate set of requirements imposed on CDM projects but not on JI projects (see page 296).

Article 17: emissions trading

Emissions trading, like carbon sinks, was a key area of controversy. As mentioned above, Articles 3 and 6 refer to 'transfers' and Articles 3, 6 and 12 refer to 'acquisition' of units: the former two in respect to ERUs and the latter in respect to CERs. What was intended by these phrases in practical terms is unclear. Why, for example, would any Annex I country that expected economic growth, and hence growth in emissions, transfer its credits to another Annex I country? (The one exception to this, which was the focus of much discussion, were those countries, such as Russia, which, due to the arbitrary selection of a baseline of 1990 emissions and to the collapse of its economy thereafter, had an unforeseen windfall of so-called 'hot-air' credits.) The ambiguity is addressed, at least in part, by the introduction of the broader concept of 'trading' in Protocol Article 17. Article 17[15] provides that 'Parties included in Annex B may participate in 'emissions trading' for the purpose of fulfilling their commitments under Article 3. The language of Article 17 does not refer either to ERUs or to CERs nor does it refer to Articles 6 or 12. It does, however, refer to meeting both emission-limitation and reduction commitments, as do Articles 3 and 12. (Article 6(1) refers to 'reducing...emissions' and 'enhancing...removals by sinks'.) This language is taken to be broad enough to cover both ERUs and CERs and the subsequently created RMUs.

One potential difficulty with this interpretation is that Articles 3(10) and 3(11), dealing with ERUs acquired and transferred in accordance with either Article 6 or Article 17, contrast with Article 3(12), dealing with CERs, which refers only to acquisitions and not to transfers or to Articles 6 or 17. The inconsistency in drafting could therefore lead to the conclusion that an Annex I Party could acquire and transfer, i.e. 'trade', ERUs freely but would have to first 'acquire' CERs, add them to its assigned amount and then trade the result or a derivative thereof as ERUs. Following decisions taken at COP-7 in response to these debates, ERUs are expected to be recorded in national registries, while CERs are to registered separately under the auspices of the CDM Executive Board (see page 296). The decision at COP-7 to reject limits on emissions trading and to treat all units as equivalent, i.e. 'fungible' and tradeable seems to have resolved what would otherwise be an unwieldy lack of consistency of treatment between credits and Parties (see page 296). It would be of equal, if not greater, help if a similar, common sense, resolution could be reached soon in respect to carbon sinks.

Carbon sinks

Under the Convention, GHG sinks refer to 'human-induced'[16] or 'direct human induced' land use, land-use change, and forestry (LULUCF) activities, including afforestation[17], reforestation[18] and deforestation[19]. The three activities combined are also referred to as ARD. The Parties to the Convention recognized that *all* sinks and reservoirs of GHGs have an important impact on terrestrial and marine ecosystems (Convention Preamble, paragraph 4). Sink capacity to reduce the concentration of GHGs in the atmosphere contributes towards reaching the Convention's objective of 'stabilization of greenhouse-gas concentrations in the atmosphere at a level that would prevent dangerous anthropogenic interference with the climate system' (Convention, Article 2).

Each Annex I country Party to the Protocol agrees that it shall, 'in achieving its quantified emission limitation and reduction commitments under

Article 3, in order to promote sustainable development [Protocol Article 2(1)]...protect and enhance sinks and reservoirs[20] of greenhouse gases not controlled by the Montreal Protocol[21], taking into account its commitments under relevant international environmental agreements[22]; promotion of sustainable forest-management practices, afforestation and reforestation' (Protocol Article 2(1)(a)(ii)).

COP-3 requested from the SBSTA advice on what LULUCF activities should be 'additional[23] human-induced activities related to changes in greenhouse-gas emissions by sources and removals by sinks in the agricultural soils and the land-use change and forestry categories... added to, or subtracted from, the assigned amounts for Parties to the Protocol included in Annex I' (Decision 1/CP.3 paragraph 5(a)).

The Kyoto Protocol: Article 3

Protocol Article 3(3) provides that Annex I Parties may use 'direct human induced'[24] 'net changes' in GHG emissions and removals by sinks since 1990 to meet part of their emissions commitments, provided they are 'measured as verifiable changes in carbon stocks in each commitment period' (the first commitment period is between 2008 and 2012). While Article 3.3 applies expressly to sinks from 'direct human-induced land-use change and forestry activities, limited to afforestation, reforestation, and deforestation', Protocol Article 3(4) requests the COP[25] to choose whether and how additional human-induced activities related to changes in GHG emissions and removals in agricultural soils and LULUCF categories should be accounted for in meeting assigned amounts. Importantly, neither Article 3(4) nor any other Article provide for excluding any of these activities.

The IPCC noted in 2000 that '[t]o implement the Kyoto Protocol, issues related to LULUCF will have to be considered' (IPCC 2000), something that the Parties failed to do until COP-7. Until this matter is addressed, the Protocol's Articles 3.1, 3.3 and 3.4, which indicate how LULUCF activities (or sinks) may count towards meeting targets, and Articles 6, 12 and 17, which provide for creating sinks to count towards meeting targets and for trading rights to emit GHGs, cannot become functional. In short, agreement on the role of sinks in calculating the basis of assigned amounts and on accounting for acquiring reduction credits based on sinks is critical to the entire undertaking.

Article 3(4)

Article 3(4) provides that each party must submit data to the SBSTA to establish carbon stocks and assigned amounts in 1990 and in subsequent years prior to the next COP. These were to include 'additional human-induced activities related to changes in greenhouse-gas emissions by sources and removals by sinks in the agricultural soils and the land-use change and forestry categories...'. The language can only meaningfully be read as referring to activities *additional* to the three categories already recognized in Article 3(3). The question of what these additional activities should include was unresolved until

COP-7. It was then decided that, for the purposes of Article 12 (the CDM), the additional activities would include afforestation, reforestation and forest and land-management activities but not avoided deforestation (i.e. conservation). This is clearly inconsistent with the express language of the Convention (which requires both protection and enhancement of sinks) and Article 3(3) (which specifically includes deforestation). There is nothing in Article 3(4) or anywhere else in the Protocol that suggests that any decision made under it as to *additional* activities could result in the exclusion of deforestation or either of the two other activities specifically included in the provisions of Article 3(3). The decision at COP-7 may have been politically expedient and may be ameliorated to some extent by its terms of implementation[26] but it cannot be justified in terms of the express language of the Protocol, the Principles and Objective of the Convention or accepted principles of construction (see Mackay 1995).

Article 3(7)

Article 3(7) provides, *inter alia*, that:

> [I]n the first quantified emission limitation and reduction commitment period, from 2008–2012... Those Parties included in Annex I for whom land-use change and forestry constituted a net source of greenhouse-gas emissions in 1990 shall include in their 1990 emissions base year or period the aggregate anthropogenic carbon dioxide equivalent emissions by sources minus removals by sinks in 1990 from land-use change for the purposes of calculating their assigned amount.

Removals by sink must result from 'direct human-induced land-use change and forestry activities, limited to afforestation, reforestation and deforestation since 1990, measured as verifiable changes in carbon stocks in each commitment period' (Protocol Article 3(3)). In accordance with Article 3(4) they would also include such additional activities specified by the COP, provided that all such activities would be additional to those that would otherwise occur and be supplemental to domestic action. Interpreted in this way, Article 3(7) naturally follows on from Article 3(3), which included three specific activities, and Article 3(4), which provided for the addition of further such activities in calculating carbon stocks and meeting reduction commitments. In other words, what is clearly expressed as a firm basis for included-sink activity (in Article 3(3)), to be extended upon further scientific study (in Article 3(4)) and subject to clearly expressed criteria (in Article 6), leads, in Article 3(7), to the formula for calculating each Annex I Party's assigned amount—the basis on which everything else rests. Nothing in Article 3 provides for the elimination, in any compliance period, of any of the three basis sink activities specified in Article 3(3) or for any distinct treatment of them under Article 6 or under the Protocol as a whole.

COP-4

The Buenos Aires Plan of Action is the political agreement reached at COP-4; it constrains the Parties to demonstrate substantial progress on several issues, including the flexibility mechanisms. COP-4 reached several decisions relevant to them. Decision 7/CP.4 provides for a work programme on mechanisms (priority being given to the CDM) to lead to a decision on the three mechanisms at COP-6, and recommendations on guidelines for JI, modalities and procedures for the CDM, and '[r]elevant principles, modalities, rules and guidelines, in particular for verification, reporting and accountability of emissions trading, pursuant to Article 17 of the Kyoto Protocol'.

Decision 9/CP.4 is specifically dedicated to land-use, land-use change, and forestry. In this decision, the COP noted 'with appreciation' the IPCC's decision to prepare a special report on LULUCF. The COP confirmed that Protocol Article 3(3) means:

> the adjustment to a Party's assigned amount shall be equal to verifiable changes in carbon stocks during the period 2008–2012 resulting from direct human-induced activities of afforestation, reforestation and deforestation since 1 January 1990. Where the result of this calculation is a net sink, this value shall be added to the Party's assigned amount. Where the result of this calculation is a net emission, this value shall be subtracted from the Party's assigned amount.

> Decision 9/CP.4 paragraph 1

The COP then recommended draft decisions for adoption at the COP's first session, on definitions related to Protocol Article 3(3) activities and on 'modalities, rules, and guidelines as to how, and which, additional human-induced activities related to changes in greenhouse-gas emissions by sources and removals by sinks in the agricultural soils and the land-use change and forestry categories might be included under Article 3.4 of the Kyoto Protocol' (Decision 9/CP.4 paragraph 4). This set the scene for the final debates and compromises prior to ratification.

COP-6

The intense disagreements, particularly between the European Union and the United States, over the role of carbon sinks and emissions trading caused the first round of COP-6 held in The Hague in November 2000 to fail. The shock of that failure, and the subsequent announcement by the Bush Administration that the US would not ratify the Protocol, had the unexpected effect of intensifying efforts to put the negotiations back on track. Negotiations were resumed in Bonn in July 2001 and several important compromises relating to LULUCF were agreed. Essentially, increased use of sinks by Japan, Russia, Australia and Canada (including what amounts to avoided deforestation) was conceded to ensure that Annex I countries, representing an adequate percentage of 1990 emissions to bring the Protocol into force, agreed to ratify it.

The 'quid pro quo' was restriction on the scope of sinks in the CDM. A proposal that an option be included providing for CDM to incorporate all sink projects of all types was rejected. This was the result of the vehement assertion by some environmentalists that CDM sinks created a 'loophole' in the Convention. Although this and related arguments put forward in opposition to CDM sinks, particularly avoiding deforestation, do not bear scrutiny (Chapter 2), it was agreed that for the first commitment period the COP limited all LULUCF activities under the CDM to afforestation and reforestation projects (Decision 5/CP.6, Annex VII(7)). The Parties agreed that 'the treatment of land use, land-use change and forestry projects under the clean development mechanism in future commitment periods shall be decided as part of the negotiations on the second commitment period' (Decision 5/CP.6 Annex VI, Article 3(9)).

The Bonn Agreement did provide, however, that during the first commitment period, each Party may engage in additional activities under Article 3(4), and thus adjust its assigned amount, provided the activities are human induced and undertaken and accounted for since 1990.[27] For the purposes of Article 3(4), 'forest management', 'cropland management', 'grazing land management' and 'revegetation' are eligible LULUCF activities during the first commitment period, provided the activities occurred since 1990 and are human induced. 'Such activities should not account for emissions and removals resulting from afforestation, reforestation and deforestation as determined under Article 3, paragraph 3' (Decision 5/CP.6 Annex VII(5)).

Draft decisions to develop definitions and modalities to include LULUCF in the CDM were forwarded to COP-7, the SBSTA having been requested to provide biome specific 'forest' definitions (FCCC/CP/2001/L.11/Rev.1). There were also agreements on key technical issues: baselines, additionality, small-scale CDM-project activities, environmental-impact assessment (EIA), public participation, and the executive board review. 'The modalities to be addressed shall include non-permanence, additionality, leakage, scale, uncertainties, socio-economic and environmental impacts (including impacts on biodiversity and natural ecosystems)' (5/CP.6 Annex VI, Article 3(8)).

COP-6 nevertheless affirmed that 'it is the host Party's prerogative to confirm whether an Article 6 project activity assists it in achieving sustainable development' (Decision 5/CP.6 Annex VI, Article 2(1)) and recommended that 'the COP establish a supervisory committee to supervise, *inter alia*, the verification of emission-reduction units generated by Article 6 project activities' (5/CP.6 Annex VI, Article 2(3)). Similarly, the COP affirmed, 'the host Party's prerogative is to confirm whether a clean development mechanism project activity assists it in achieving sustainable development' (Decision 5/CP.6 Annex VI, Article 3(1)). A CDM executive board was created and the details of its composition and role were elaborated. Critically, this body's responsibilities, unlike the JI Supervisory Board, include an active role in approval of CDM projects pursuant to regulations to be developed by it. In contrast the JI Supervisory Board's role is essentially only one of oversight (see COP-7(I) J(2) Annex 1(C)).

LULUCF agreements

COP-6 also reached an important agreement on the principles guiding LULUCF activities, listed here.

- These activities are to be treated on a 'sound science' basis (Decision 5/CP.6 Annex VII(1)(a)). This suggests that the science must have reached a high level of certainty, and therefore, that the precautionary principle, which requires that preventive action be taken despite the absence of absolute scientific certainty, does not apply.

- LULUCF activities must contribute to biodiversity and environmental sustainability (Decision 5/CP.6 Annex VII(1)(e)); therefore some activities, although they contribute to reducing the atmosphere's total GHG concentration, would still not be eligible if they do not pass the biodiversity and sustainability tests.

- 'Accounting for LULUCF does not imply a transfer of commitments to a future commitment period' (Decision 5/CP.6 Annex VII(1)(f)).

- 'Reversal of any removal due to LULUCF activities [must] be accounted for at the appropriate point in time' (Decision 5/CP.6 Annex VII(1)(g)).

- Accounting excludes removals resulting from elevated CO_2 concentrations above their preindustrial level.

- The COP also agreed on definitions relating to forestry as they appear in the IPCC report on LULUCF. The Parties agreed to define 'forest', 'afforestation', 'reforestation' and 'deforestation' for the purposes of Protocol Article 3(3) on the basis of land-use change (Decision 5/CP.6 Annex VII(2)).

Unresolved issues

Despite these agreements, a number of issues remained unresolved and the Parties forwarded to COP-7 draft decisions on the flexibility mechanisms:

(1) principles, nature and scope;

(2) JI: implementation guidelines;

(3) CDM: modalities and procedures;

(4) emissions trading: modalities, rules and guidelines,

requiring from the IPCC methods to estimate, measure, monitor, and report changes in carbon stocks for the purposes of JI and the CDM relevant to Articles 3.3 and 3.4 and LULUCF; and to produce a report on good practice and uncertainty management.

COP-7

Accordingly, COP-7's agenda regarding sinks took the shape of a work programme on mechanisms (Decisions 7/CP.4 and 14/CP.4). Principles, nature and scope of the mechanisms pursuant to Articles 6, 12 and 17 were the subject of the Kyoto Protocol Decision 15-/CP.7. The COP recommended the adoption of a draft decision on mechanisms, which reiterates the principle that 'the use of the mechanisms shall be supplemental to domestic action and that domestic action shall thus constitute a significant element of' Annex I countries' efforts in meeting their commitments. It also made clear that Parties may only avail themselves of the flexibility mechanisms if they are in compliance with their obligations under Article 3 of the Protocol (COP-7, Decision 1J). The compliance committee's enforcement branch is to be responsible for supervising compliance. COP-7 established that a Party complies with its commitments under the Protocol if 'it has established its assigned amount pursuant to Article 3 and in compliance with the methodological and reporting requirements under Article 5'.

Article 6: Joint Implementation

COP-7 agreed that the COP 'shall provide guidance regarding the implementation of Article 6 and exercise authority over an Article 6 supervisory committee' (COP-7, Draft Decision-/CMP.1 (Article 6) Annex B(2)), which 'shall supervise, *inter alia*, the verification of ERUs generated by Article 6 project activities' (COP-7, Article 3). It provided rules for the qualifications, nomination, election and removal of committee members (COP-7, Draft Decision-/CMP.1 (Article 6) Annexes C(4), (5), (6), (7)). The COP also agreed on a list of standards and procedures for the accreditation of independent entities to provide accounting, monitoring, verification and related services on which the supervisory board can rely in supervising verification of emission reductions (COP-7, J(2), Appendix A(1)(a)). Self-verification of additionality by eligible participating Annex I Parties is also provided for (COP-7, Draft Decision-/CMP.1 (Article 6) Annex D(22)).

Among the issues that COP-7 resolved is the definition of baselines for Article 6 projects, which it defined as:

> the scenario that reasonably represents the anthropogenic emissions by sources or anthropogenic removals by sinks of greenhouse gases that would occur in the absence of the proposed project. A baseline shall cover emissions from all gases, sectors and source categories listed in Annex A and anthropogenic removals by sinks within the project boundary.

COP-7, Draft Decision-/CMP.1 (Article 6) Appendices B(1) and B(2)

Defining the baseline is important as it provides the basis on which the calculation of GHG emissions and removals rests. Requirements for a monitoring plan for all JI projects were also specified (COP-7, Draft Decision-/CMP.1 (Article 6) Appendix B(3)).

Article 12: Clean Development Mechanism

COP-7 designated the COP as having authority over and being authorized to provide guidance to the CDM Executive Board (COP-7, Draft Decision-/CMP.1 (Article 12) Annex 13(2), 3(a), (b) and (c)). It also provides participation requirements parallel to those for Article 6, but importantly is extended to all Parties, including non-Annex I Parties, to the Protocol (COP-7, Draft Decision-/CMP.1 (Article 12) Annex B(4)). No provision is made for self-validation. The CDM Executive Board has been delegated the task of approving all CDM projects according to detailed criteria and directed to develop rules for such approval consistent with the extensive guidance provided by COP-7. Parties participating in the CDM are to designate a national authority for the CDM, which is subject to rules drawn up by COP-7 (COP-7, Draft Decision-/CMP.1 (Article 12) Annex C).

Those rules will need to conform to detailed guidelines, modalities and procedures for the CDM determined at COP-7, which include definitions of LULUCF activities and the technical terms related to CDM, and administrative roles and procedures. In contrast to the four pages of such guidelines for JI projects, the decision in respect to the guidelines, modalities and procedures for CDM projects runs to some 14 pages. The matters required of CDM projects but not of JI projects include: a CDM registry; a publicly available database; public comment procedure; periodic reviews of methodologies; validation and registration requirements, which include comments by local stakeholders and UNFCCC accredited non-governmental organizations; environmental impact analysis; use of executive-board-approved methodology; written approval of voluntary participation from each Party involved; baselines that take into account national and/or sectoral policies and circumstances; limited crediting periods; adjustments for and periodic recalculation of leakage; a monitoring plan that requires collecting and archiving of all relevant data and all potential sources of emissions and project boundaries; and an extensive project design document (COP-7, Draft Decision-/CMP.1 (Article 12) Annex G and Appendix B).

A critical part of the compromise struck at COP-7 was to limit the total additions to a Party's assigned amounts from LULUCF activities in the first commitment period to 20% of the total (COP-7, Draft Decision-/CMP.1 (Modalities for the accounting of assigned amounts) Annex I(B)(5)). COP-7 did not address directly the details of using LULUCF in the CDM; it requested that the following COP develop definitions and modalities for 'including afforestation and reforestation project activities under Article 12 in the first commitment period, taking into account the issues of non-permanence, additionality, leakage, uncertainties and socio-economic and environmental impacts, including impacts on biodiversity and natural ecosystems' (COP-7, Decision 17/CP.7 10(b)). Further regulation is therefore inevitable.

Article 17: emissions trading

In comparison with the guidance on CDM projects, the COP-7 decision on emissions trading is brevity itself. Aside from eligibility requirements parallel to those under Article 6 and the establishment of a national registry, the only matter of note was the decision to make it clear that Annex I Parties are 'eligible to transfer and/or acquire ERUs, CERs, AAUs or RMUs issued in accordance with the relevant provisions...' (COP-7, Draft Decision-/CMP.1 (Article 17) Annex 2) and to adjust the accounting rules accordingly (COP-7, Draft Decision-/CMP.1 (Modalities for the accounting of assigned amounts)).

Summary

COP-6 and COP-7 confirmed emissions trading of all classes of carbon-credit unit, increased the range and scale of forestry and land-use-change credits to Annex I countries and severely curtailed the availability of such credits to the developing world, decreased the benefits to developing countries of emissions trading and reduced the likelihood, by raising the regulatory cost, of investment in their rural areas. These results are contrary to the Convention's overriding objectives, and its own and the Kyoto Protocol's express provisions. The directions given to the CDM Executive Board, like the decisions on which they are based, are arguably *ultra vires* the Convention and the Protocol. More importantly they tend to defeat the very purpose of the Convention.

Summary for policy makers

The policy debates and compromises over the participation of developing countries, the role of carbon sinks and of emissions trading have resulted in regulatory complexity, in legal uncertainty and in discriminatory treatment of developing countries. The regulatory complexity is illustrated by the creation of four units of account, three of acquisition and transfer where one would suffice, and the proposed regime for certification of CDM projects. Legal uncertainty is illustrated by the decisions of COP-6 and COP-7 that ignored the founding principles of the Convention, of companion international agreements, and of sustainable economic growth and development, and the express terms of the Protocol.

It is at least arguable that the COP has sought to exercise powers not granted to it and to act *ultra vires* the Convention and the Protocol. It has done so particularly by seeking to eliminate from the crediting system avoided deforestation in developing countries during the first commitment period. To that end it created new units of account not available to developing countries and attempted to add regulatory requirements that discriminate against carbon sequestration in developing countries. In the intense effort to reach agreement it seems to have been forgotten that the climate does not care where or how atmospheric concentrations of CO_2 are reduced and, more importantly, that this is the Convention's overriding goal.

Policy makers have burdened the process with qualitative judgements that have nothing to do with efficiently accomplishing the Convention's dual goals: mitigation of global warming and sustainable development in developing countries, particularly the alleviation of poverty.

The detailed regulation imposed on CDM projects under Article 12 and bifurcation of those provisions from those applicable to JI projects, including arbitrary limitations on transfers to Annex I countries, has introduced unnecessary complexity, increased costs of both compliance and administration, and reduced the usefulness of the flexibility mechanisms under the Convention. Arguably these regulations reduce the likelihood of achieving the goals of the Convention. The rationale for all of this is threadbare.

The discriminatory effect of the limitations on carbon sinks in developing countries is inconsistent with the Convention's core principles, including its emphasis on the primacy of economic development in the developing world, on poverty eradication, on an open international economic system, on the clear concern to protect and enhance all carbon sinks and reservoirs wherever located, and on achieving climate stabilization at the lowest possible cost. The administrative bodies, now charged with implementing the Protocol's provisions, must concentrate on simplifying compliance with the rules and reducing the costs of doing so. They should also interpret the COP decisions to be consistent with the Protocol and the Convention and restore to its proper, leading position the overriding goal of sustainable economic growth and development.

Lexicon

Definitions, modalities, rules and guidelines relate to land use, land-use change and forestry activities under the Kyoto Protocol. 'Article' in this chapter refers to an Article of the Kyoto Protocol, unless otherwise specified.

General definitions

Additionality.   Reduction in emissions by sources or enhancement of removals by sinks that is additional to any that would occur in the absence of a Joint Implementation or a Clean Development Mechanism project activity as defined in the Kyoto Protocol Articles on Joint Implementation and the Clean Development Mechanism. This definition may be further broadened to include financial, investment, and technology additionality. Under financial additionality, the project activity funding shall be additional to existing Global Environmental Facility, other financial commitments of Parties included in Annex I, Official Development Assistance, and other systems of cooperation. Under investment additionality, the value of the emissions-reduction Unit/Certified Emission Reduction Unit shall significantly improve the financial and/or commercial viability of the project activity. Under technology additionality, the technology used for the project activity shall be the best available for the circumstances of the host Party.

Baseline.   A non-intervention scenario used as a base in the analysis of intervention scenarios (www.ipcc.ch/pub/tar/wg3/456.htm).

Carbon offset. Carbon offsets are analogous to tradeable carbon-emissions permits. Carbon offsets are typically carbon sequestration services, such as afforestation/reforestation or preventing deforestation.

Leakage. 'The part of emissions reductions in Annex B countries that may be offset by an increase of the emission in the non-constrained countries above their baseline levels. This can occur through

(1) relocation of energy-intensive production in non-constrained regions;

(2) increased consumption of fossil fuels in these regions through decline in the international price of oil and gas triggered by lower demand for these energies; and

(3) changes in incomes (and thus in energy demand) because of better terms of trade. Leakage also refers to the situation in which a carbon sequestration activity (e.g. tree planting) on one piece of land inadvertently, directly or indirectly, triggers an activity, which in whole or part, counteracts the carbon effects of the initial activity' (www.ipcc.ch/pub/tar/wg3/465.htm).

Alternatively, leakage can also refer 'to the situation in which a carbon sequestration activity (e.g. tree planting) on one piece of land inadvertently, directly or indirectly, triggers an activity which, in whole or part, counteracts the carbon effects of the initial activity' (www.ipcc.ch/pub/tar/wg3/174.htm).

Reservoir (Convention Article 1(7)). A component or components of the climate system where a greenhouse gas or a precursor of a greenhouse gas is stored.

Sink (Convention Article 1(8)). Any process, activity or mechanism that removes a greenhouse gas, an aerosol or a precursor of a greenhouse gas from the atmosphere.

Stakeholder (COP-7 Provisional report, Sect. J, Para. 2, Annex A). The public, including individuals, groups or communities affected, or likely to be affected, by the project.

Supplementarity. 'The Kyoto Protocol states that emissions trading and Joint Implementation activities are to be supplemental to domestic actions (e.g. energy taxes, fuel efficiency standards, etc.) taken by developed countries to reduce their greenhouse-gas emissions. Under some proposed definitions of supplementarity (e.g. a concrete ceiling on level of use), developed countries could be restricted in their use of the Kyoto mechanisms to achieve their reduction targets. This is a subject for further negotiation and clarification by the parties' (www.ipcc.ch/pub/tar/wg3/472.htm).

Acronyms

An 'assigned amount unit' (COP-7 Provisional report, Sect. J, Para. 2, Annex A) or 'AAU' is a unit issued pursuant to the relevant provisions on registries in Draft Decision-/CMP.1 21/CP.7 (Article 5.2). (Modalities for the accounting of assigned amounts), and is equal to one metric tonne of carbon dioxide equivalent, calculated using global warming potentials defined by decision 2/CP.3 or as subsequently revised in accordance with Article 5.

A 'certified emission reduction' (COP-7 Provisional report, Sect. J, Para. 2, Annex A) or 'CER' is a unit issued pursuant to Article 12 and requirements thereunder, and is equal to one metric tonne of carbon dioxide equivalent, calculated using global warming potentials defined by decision 2/CP.3 or as subsequently revised in accordance with Article 5.

An 'emission-reduction unit' (COP-7 Provisional report, Sect. J, Para. 2, Annex A) or 'ERU' is a unit issued pursuant to Article 6 and requirements thereunder and is equal to one metric tonne of carbon dioxide equivalent, calculated using global warming potentials defined by decision 2/CP.3 or as subsequently revised in accordance with Article 5.

A 'removal unit' (COP-7 Provisional report, Sect. J, Para. 2, Annex A) or 'RMU' is a unit issued pursuant to the relevant provisions on registries in decision -/CMP.1 (modalities for the accounting of assigned amounts), and is equal to one tonne of carbon dioxide equivalent, calculated using global warming potentials defined by decision 2/CP.3 or as subsequently revised in accordance with Article 5.

Forest-related definitions

As established (IPCC 2001*a*–*c*) under Articles 2, 3.3 and 3.4, the following definitions shall apply:

(a) 'Afforestation' is the direct human-induced conversion of land that has not been forested for a period of at least 50 years to forested land through planting, seeding and/or the human-induced promotion of natural seed sources.

(b) 'Cropland management' is the system of practices on land on which agricultural crops are grown and on land that is set aside or temporarily not being used for crop production.

(c) 'Deforestation' is the direct human-induced conversion of forested land to nonforested land.

(d) 'Forest' is a minimum area of land of 0.05–1.0 ha with tree-crown cover (or equivalent stocking level) of more than 10–30% with trees with the potential to reach a minimum height of 2–5 m at maturity *in situ*. A forest may consist of either closed-forest formations, where trees of various stories and undergrowth cover a high proportion of the ground, or open forest. Young natural stands and all plantations which have yet to reach a crown density of 10–30% or tree height of 2–5 m are included under forest, as are areas normally forming part of the forest area which are temporarily unstocked as a result of human intervention, such as harvesting or natural causes, but which are expected to revert to forest.

An alternative definition of forest is a 'vegetation type dominated by trees. Many definitions of the term forest are in use throughout the world, reflecting wide differences in bio-geophysical conditions, social structure, and economics' (see IPCC 2000).

(e)   'Forest management' is a system of practices for stewardship and use of forest land aimed at fulfilling relevant ecological (including biological diversity), economic and social functions of the forest in a sustainable manner.

(f)   'Grazing land management' is the system of practices on land used for livestock production aimed at manipulating the amount and type of vegetation and livestock produced.

(g)   'Reforestation' is the direct human-induced conversion of non-forested land to forested land through planting, seeding and/or the human-induced promotion of natural seed sources, on land that was forested but that has been converted to non-forested land. For the first commitment period, reforestation activities will be limited to reforestation occurring on those lands that did not contain forest on 31 December 1989.

(h)   'Revegetation' is a direct human-induced activity to increase carbon stocks on sites through the establishment of vegetation that covers a minimum area of 0.05 ha and does not meet the definitions of afforestation and reforestation contained here.

Acknowledgements

The authors thank Karen Szerkowski of Mishcon de Reya for her help in researching this chapter.

Appendix A. Convention Article 3 principles

In their actions to achieve the objective of the Convention and to implement its provisions, the Parties shall be guided, *inter alia*, by the following:

(1)   ...The Parties should protect the climate system for the benefit of present and future generations of humankind, on the basis of equity and in accordance with their common but differentiated responsibilities and respective capabilities. Accordingly, the developed country Parties should take the lead in combating climate change and the adverse effects thereof.

(2)   ...The specific needs and special circumstances of developing country Parties, especially those that are particularly vulnerable to the adverse

effects of climate change, and of those Parties, especially developing country Parties, that would have to bear a disproportionate or abnormal burden under the Convention, should be given full consideration.

(3) ... The Parties should take precautionary measures to anticipate, prevent or minimize the causes of climate change and mitigate its adverse effects. Where there are threats of serious or irreversible damage, lack of full scientific certainty should not be used as a reason for postponing such measures, taking into account that policies and measures to deal with climate change should be cost-effective so as to ensure global benefits at the lowest possible cost. To achieve this, such policies and measures should take into account different socio-economic contexts, be comprehensive, cover all relevant sources, sinks and reservoirs of greenhouse gases and adaptation, and comprise all economic sectors. Efforts to address climate change may be carried out cooperatively by interested Parties.

(4) ... The Parties have a right to, and should, promote sustainable development. Policies and measures to protect the climate system against human-induced change should be appropriate for the specific conditions of each Party and should be integrated with national development programmes, taking into account that economic development is essential for adopting measures to address climate change.

(5) ... The Parties should cooperate to promote a supportive and open international economic system that would lead to sustainable economic growth and development in all Parties, particularly developing country Parties, thus enabling them better to address the problems of climate change. Measures taken to combat climate change, including unilateral ones, should not constitute a means of arbitrary or unjustifiable discrimination or a disguised restriction on international trade.

Appendix B. Protocol Article 6

(1) For the purpose of meeting its commitments under Article 3, any Party included in Annex I may transfer to, or acquire from, any other such Party emission-reduction units resulting from projects aimed at reducing anthropogenic emissions by sources or enhancing anthropogenic removals by sinks of greenhouse gases in any sector of the economy, provided that:

(a) any such project has the approval of the Parties involved;

(b) any such project provides a reduction in emissions by sources, or an enhancement of removals by sinks, that is additional to any that would otherwise occur;

(c) it does not acquire any emission-reduction units if it is not in compliance with its obligations under Articles 5 and 7; and

(d) the acquisition of emission-reduction units shall be supplemental to domestic actions for the purposes of meeting commitments under Article 3.

(2) The Conference of the Parties serving as the meeting of the Parties to this Protocol may, at its first session or as soon as practicable thereafter, further elaborate guidelines for the implementation of this Article, including for verification and reporting.

(3) A Party included in Annex I may authorize legal entities to participate, under its responsibility, in actions leading to the generation, transfer or acquisition under this Article of emission-reduction units.

(4) If a question of implementation by a Party included in Annex I of the requirements referred to in this Article is identified in accordance with the relevant provisions of Article 8, transfers and acquisitions of emission-reduction units may continue to be made after the question has been identified, provided that any such units may not be used by a Party to meet its commitments under Article 3 until any issue of compliance is resolved.

Appendix C. Protocol Article 12

(1) A clean development mechanism is hereby defined.

(2) The purpose of the clean development mechanism shall be to assist Parties not included in Annex I in achieving sustainable development and in contributing to the ultimate objective of the Convention, and to assist Parties included in Annex I in achieving compliance with their quantified emission limitation and reduction commitments under Article 3.

(3) Under the clean development mechanism:

   (a) Parties not included in Annex I will benefit from project activities resulting in certified emission reductions; and

   (b) Parties included in Annex I may use the certified emission reductions accruing from such project activities to contribute to compliance with part of their quantified emission limitation and reduction commitments under Article 3, as determined by the Conference of the Parties serving as the meeting of the Parties to this Protocol.

(4) The clean development mechanism shall be subject to the authority and guidance of the Conference of the Parties serving as the meeting of the Parties to this Protocol and be supervised by an executive board of the clean development mechanism.

(5) Emission reductions resulting from each project activity shall be certified by operational entities to be designated by the Conference of the Parties serving as the meeting of the Parties to this Protocol, on the basis of:

   (a) voluntary participation approved by each Party involved;

   (b) real, measurable, and long-term benefits related to the mitigation of climate change; and

(c) reductions in emissions that are additional to any that would occur in the absence of the certified project activity.

(6) The clean development mechanism shall assist in arranging funding of certified project activities as necessary.

Endnotes

[1] Convention Article 1(1): ' "Adverse effects of climate change" means changes in the physical environment or biota resulting from climate change which have significant deleterious effects on the composition, resilience or productivity of natural and managed ecosystems or on the operation of socio-economic systems or on human health and welfare.'

[2] The principal structural elements of the Convention for present purposes are the following: Article 1 defines relevant terms, such as 'climate change', 'emissions' and 'greenhouse gases'; Article 7 establishes the Conference of the Parties as the Convention's supreme body, which may create subsidiary bodies; Article 8 establishes a Secretariat to manage the COP's and its subsidiary bodies' activities; Article 9 establishes a Subsidiary Body for Scientific and Technological advice (SBSTA) to provide scientific and technological advice to the COP; Article 10 establishes a Subsidiary Body for Implementation (SBI) to 'assist the Conference of the Parties in the assessment and review of the effective implementation of the Convention'; and Article 17 establishes that only parties to the Convention may adopt a protocol to the Convention and that only Parties to a particular protocol may take decisions under that protocol.

[3] The 1987 Brundtland Report introduced the term 'sustainable development', which it defined as 'development that meets the needs of the present without compromising the ability of future generations to meet their own needs'. It is noteworthy how often the goal of sustainable 'economic growth' is omitted in much of the literature.

[4] Convention Article 1(5): ' "Greenhouse gases" means those gaseous constituents of the atmosphere, both natural and anthropogenic, that absorb and re-emit infrared radiation'. They include: carbon dioxide (CO_2), methane (CH_4), nitrous oxide (N_2O), hydrofluorocarbons, perfluorocarbons, and sulphur hexafluoride (SF_6).

[5] Convention Article 1(3): ' "Climate system" means the totality of the atmosphere, hydrosphere, biosphere and geosphere and their interactions.'

[6] The Convention lists in Annex I the economically developed parties and parties with economies in transition which agree to commit to the Convention's objectives and principles.

[7] Article 3(1): 'The Parties included in Annex I shall, individually or jointly, ensure that their aggregate anthropogenic carbon dioxide equivalent emissions of the greenhouse gases listed in Annex A do not exceed their assigned amounts, calculated pursuant to their quantified emission limitation and reduction commitments inscribed in Annex B and in accordance with the provisions of this Article, with a view to reducing their overall emissions of such gases by at least 5% below 1990 levels in the commitment period 2008–2012.'

[8] Protocol Article 7(4): 'The Conference of the Parties serving as the meeting of the Parties to this Protocol shall adopt at its first session, and review periodically

thereafter, guidelines for the preparation of the information required under this Article, taking into account guidelines for the preparation of national communications by Parties included in Annex I adopted by the Conference of the Parties. The Conference of the Parties serving as the meeting of the Parties to this Protocol shall also, prior to the first commitment period, decide upon modalities for the accounting of assigned amounts.'

[9]'The ultimate objective of this Convention and any related legal instruments that the Conference of the Parties may adopt is to achieve, in accordance with the relevant provisions of the Convention, stabilization of greenhouse-gas concentrations in the atmosphere at a level that would prevent dangerous anthropogenic interference with the climate system. Such a level should be achieved within a time-frame sufficient to allow ecosystems to adapt naturally to climate change, to ensure that food production is not threatened and to enable economic development to proceed in a sustainable manner.'

[10]Article 4(7) Commitments: 'The extent to which developing country Parties will effectively implement their commitments under the Convention will depend on the effective implementation by developed country Parties of their commitments under the Convention related to financial resources and transfer of technology and will take fully into account that economic and social development and poverty eradication are the first and overriding priorities of the developing country Parties.'

[11]The United States announced on 28 March 2001 that it would not ratify the Protocol (Environment News Network 2001; CNN 2001).

[12]Protocol Article 6(1)(b); additionality tests whether projects reduce or remove emissions in addition to what would have been reduced or removed had the project not taken place (action versus business as usual).

[13]Protocol Article 6(1)(d); '[t]he acquisition of emission-reduction units shall be supplemental to domestic action for the purposes of meeting commitments under Article 3.'

[14]Convention Article 1(4): ' "Emissions" means the release of greenhouse gases and/or their precursors into the atmosphere over a specified area and period of time'.

[15]Article 17: 'The Conference of the Parties shall define the relevant principles, modalities, rules and guidelines, in particular for verification, reporting and accountability for emissions trading. The Parties included in Annex B may participate in emissions trading for the purposes of fulfilling their commitments under Article 3. Any such trading shall be supplemental to domestic actions for the purpose of meeting quantified emission limitation and reduction commitments under that Article.'

[16]Kyoto Article 3(4). While Parties have not yet defined 'human-induced', it is understood to mean that humans could have indirectly provoked a land-use change, for instance by not farming deforested land and letting it reforest naturally without direct human interference to plant a new forest.

[17]The proposed definition for afforestation is 'the direct human-induced conversion of land that has not been forested for a period of at least 50 years to forested land through planting, seeding, and/or the human induced promotion of natural resources' (FCCC/CP/2001/5/Add.2 Part Four, p. 9).

[18]The proposed definition for reforestation is 'the direct human-induced conversion of non-forested land to forested land through planting, seeding, and/or the

human-induced promotion of natural seed sources, on land that was forested but that has been converted to non-forested land. For the first commitment period, reforestation activities will be limited to reforestation occurring on those lands that did not contain forest on 31 December 1989' (FCCC/CP/2001/5/Add.2 Part Four, p. 9).

[19]The proposed definition for deforestation is 'the direct human-induced conversion of forested land to non-forested land'. Kyoto Article 3.3: 'direct human-induced' is understood to mean that humans willingly and actively changed the land's use (FCCC/CP/2001/5/Add.2 Part Four, p. 9).

[20]Convention Article 1(7) 'Reservoir' means a component or components of the climate system where a GHG or a precursor of a GHG is stored.

[21]The 1989 Montreal Protocol on Substances that Deplete the Ozone Layer 1987 (as adjusted and amended on 29 June 1990) to the 1985 Vienna Convention for the Protection of the Ozone Layer, banned the use of a number of ozone-layer-depleting substances, some of which are also GHGs.

[22]The Convention cites: the Declaration of the United Nations Conference on the Human Environment, adopted at Stockholm on 16 June 1972; General Assembly resolutions 44/228 (22 December 1989) on the United Nations Conference on Environment and Development, 43/53 (6 December 1988), 44/207 (22 December 1989), 45/212 (21 December 1990), 46/169 (19 December 1991) on protection of global climate for present and future generations of mankind, resolution 44/206 (22 December 1989) on the possible adverse effects of sea-level rise on islands and coastal areas, particularly low-lying coastal areas, and 44/172 (19 December 1989) on the implementation of the Plan of Action to Combat Desertification; the Vienna Convention for the Protection of the Ozone Layer 1985, and the Montreal Protocol on Substances that Deplete the Ozone Layer 1987 (adjusted and amended on 29 June 1990); the Ministerial Declaration of the Second World Climate Conference adopted on 7 November 1990.

[23]Protocol Article 3(4).

[24]'Direct human-induced' is used in distinction from 'human-induced'.

[25]Convention Article 7 establishes the Conference of the Parties. Kyoto Article 13.1 establishes that 'the Conference of the Parties, the supreme body of the Convention, shall serve as the meeting of the Parties to this Protocol'; Parties to the Convention who are not Parties to the Protocol may attend the COP/MOP only as observers (Kyoto Article 13.2).

[26]Article 3(4) provides that the decision shall apply at the second and subsequent commitment periods although parties may choose to apply it to activities for the first commitment period, provided the activities have occurred after 1990.

[27]Appendix Z, in relation to forest management, provides: 'the COP is to establish how these emission rights will be allocated at least two years prior to the commitment period; accounting methods; cropland management; grazing land management; revegetation'.

References

CNN 2001 Bush firm over Kyoto stance. Cable News Network report, 29 March 2001. (Available at http://asia.cnn.com/2001/US/03/29/schroeder.bush/.)

Environment News Network 2001 Bush likely to get fast track trade authority. Environmental News Service report, 28 March 2001. (Available at http://ens.lycos.com/ens/mar2001/2001L-03-28-09.html.)

IPCC 1990*a* Scientific assessment of climate change. Report of IPCC Working Group I (ed. J. T. Houghton, G. J. Jenkins & J. J. Ephraums). First Assessment Report. Canberra: Australian Government Publishing Service.

IPCC 1990*b* Impacts assessment of climate change. Report of Working Group II (ed. W. J. McG. Tegart, G. W. Sheldon & D. C. Griffiths). First Assessment Report, vol. II. Canberra: Australian Government Publishing Service.

IPCC 1990*c* The IPCC response strategies. Report of Working Group III. First Assessment Report, vol. III, pp. 270. Covelo, CA: Island Press.

IPCC 2000 Summary for Policy Makers. In *Land use, land-use change and forestry: IPCC special report.* Cambridge University Press. (Available at www.grida.no/climate/ipcc/land_use/001.htm.)

IPCC 2001*a Climate Change 2001: the scientific basis. Contribution of Working Group I to the Third Annual Report of the IPCC* (ed. J. T. Houghton, Y. Ding, D. J. Griggs, M. Noguer, P. J. van der Linden & D. Xiaosu). Cambridge University Press. (Summary for Policymakers (SPM) and Technical Summary (ST) available at www.ipcc.ch/pub/spm22-01.pdf.)

IPCC 2001*b Climate Change 2001: impacts, adaptation and vulnerability. Contribution of Working Group II to the Third Assessment Report of the Intergovernmental Panel on Climate Change*, Third Assessment Report, vol. II (ed. J. J. McCarthy, O. F. Canziani, N. A. Leary, D. J. Dokken & K. S. White). Cambridge University Press. (Summary for Policymakers (SPM) and Technical Summary (ST) available at www.ipcc.ch/pub/wg2SPMfinal.pdf.)

IPCC 2001*c Climate Change 2001: mitigation. Contribution of Working Group III to the Third Assessment Report of the Intergovernmental Panel on Climate Change* (ed. B. Metz, O. Davidson, R. Swart & J. Pan), Third Assessment Report, vol. III. Cambridge University Press. (Summary for Policymakers (SPM) and Technical Summary (ST) available at www.ipcc.ch/pub/wg3spm.pdf.)

Lasok, D. & Lasok, K. P. E. 2001 *Law and institutions of the European Union*, 7th edn, ch. 5. Markham, Ontario: LexisNexis Butterworth.

Mackay, Lord (ed.) 1995 *Halsbury's laws of England*, 4th edn, vol. 44(1), para. 1369ff. Markham, Ontario: LexisNexis Butterworths.

United Nations International Law Commission 1969 *Vienna Convention on the Law of Treaties*, United Nations Teraty Series, 22 May 1969, art. 31.1, vol. 1155, p. 331.

Wade, E. C. S. & Bradley, A. W. 1993 *Constitutional and administrative law*, 11th edn, pp. 673ff. London: Longmans.

Werksman, J. 1998 The Clean Development Mechanism: unwrapping the Kyoto Surprise. *Rev. Eur. Community Int. Enivron. Law* **7**, 147–158.

White House 2002 President announces clear skies & global climate change initiatives. Statement, 14 February 2002. (Available at www.whitehouse.gov/news/releases/2002/02/20020214-5.html.)

Chapter 18

Protecting terrestrial ecosystems and the climate through a global carbon market

ROBERT BONNIE, MELISSA CAREY AND ANNIE PETSONK

Introduction

This chapter examines the efficacy of existing international legal frameworks to protect terrestrial ecosystems, analyses the Kyoto Protocol's provisions governing the atmospheric impacts of land use and suggests improvements to Kyoto's market framework to further both conservation and protection of the climate. A single premise provides context for our entire analysis: protecting terrestrial ecosystems and the climate requires the development of economic institutions that value the Earth's natural systems. To be effective, international environmental laws must create mechanisms to finance protection of the climate and natural ecosystems.

We begin by examining the major international legal instruments that address ecosystem conservation. While we recognize the important contributions these treaties have made, we find in general that they lack the financial mechanisms necessary to catalyse environmental protection at a globally significant scale. We then turn towards market mechanisms, emissions trading in particular, and its potential to create incentives for cost-effective environmental protection.

We next undertake an extended discussion of the Kyoto Protocol's emissions-trading framework and the opportunity to weave land-based carbon-sequestration activities into the global market for greenhouse-gas (GHG) emissions-reduction credits. Land-use activities, particularly emissions from tropical deforestation, are an important part of the global carbon cycle. Including land-use activities in an international emissions-trading framework would provide a potentially cost-effective means to address climate change while providing significant ancillary environmental benefits.

The lack of robust carbon inventory data from the world's forests and agricultural lands hurt efforts to structure effective land-use provisions during

negotiations in Kyoto in 1997. While the Kyoto Protocol will, if ratified, substantially advance environmental protection through market institutions, its
land-use provisions are problematic. In particular, articles governing land-use
activities in industrialized nations made it difficult in subsequent negotiations
to create incentives for enhanced carbon sequestration and ecosystem protection without potentially undermining the stringency of Kyoto's emissions
caps.

In Bonn and Marrakech in 2001, the Parties to the Protocol agreed upon
rules implementing most aspects of the Kyoto framework. Broadly, the Parties preserved and strengthened the treaty. However, in the case of land-use
activities, they failed to provide meaningful incentives for improved forest
management in industrialized nations and missed a significant opportunity to
use market mechanisms to address tropical deforestation.

We conclude by offering three recommendations for improving the structure and operation of the Kyoto Protocol's carbon-sequestration provisions.
First, both industrialized and non-industrialized nations must invest in
improved terrestrial carbon inventory systems. Second, for future commitment
periods (2013 and beyond), the Protocol must require full carbon accounting (i.e. measurement and accounting for all land-based GHG emissions and
sequestration) in all countries subject to emissions caps, thereby fully integrating land-use activities into the Kyoto framework. Full carbon accounting
provides the most accurate accounting system, creates incentives for improved
land management and will ensure that GHG emissions from loss and degradation of tropical forests are captured as developing countries adopt future
emissions-reduction targets. Finally, developing countries need assistance to
gain experience in reducing rates of deforestation while improving the livelihoods of their peoples before these countries can be expected to adopt emissions budgets under a full carbon accounting framework.

International environmental treaties

This section examines relevant provisions and programmes under the major
biodiversity protection treaties, including the Convention on International
Trade in Endangered Species of Wild Fauna and Flora (CITES), the Convention on Biological Diversity (CBD), the Convention to Combat Desertification
(CCD) and the Convention on Wetlands of International Importance (known
as the Ramsar Convention). Our purpose is to comment on their success and
limitations in establishing international frameworks that lead to the conservation of natural ecosystems.

The Convention on International Trade in Endangered Species

The 1972 United Nations Conference on the Human Environment, held
in Stockholm, launched the development of a major set of international
environmental instruments. Foremost among these was CITES, adopted in
1973. CITES regulates, monitors and limits commercial international trade
in endangered species. When first adopted, CITES was quite innovative in

classifying species according to their degree of vulnerability and rarity and in tailoring restrictions accordingly (Bean & Rowland 1997). Lyster (1985, p. 240) calls CITES, in which some 150 nations now participate, 'perhaps the most successful of all international treaties concerned with the conservation of wildlife'. However, compliance with the treaty has faltered in several countries since the 1980s (Weiss & Jacobson 1999).

Parties to CITES regulate wildlife trade through controls on species listed in three appendices to the treaty. CITES requires each Party to adopt national legislation designating a national Management Authority, which issues permits for trade in listed species. CITES also requires each Party to designate a national Scientific Authority responsible for advising the Management Authority on the issuance of permits. Parties are required to maintain trade records and forward those annually to the CITES Secretariat, enabling the Secretariat to compile statistical information on the global volume of trade in listed species. The treaty is enforced through presentations of reports on alleged infractions; national authorities enhance CITES enforcement through cooperation with customs, police or appropriate agencies. Bean & Rowland (1997) note the lack of effective enforcement mechanisms and the resulting variance in how the treaty is implemented by different Parties.

While CITES has made substantial contributions to the protection of wildlife, the treaty's reach is necessarily limited. CITES focuses narrowly on international trade and, thus, on the direct taking (e.g. shooting, capturing) of endangered wildlife. While direct taking is an important contributor to the loss of species, the greatest threat to biological diversity is the destruction of habitat, particularly in species-rich environments such as tropical rainforests (Wilson 1992). Given its exclusive focus on trade, CITES has had limited impact on the conservation of habitat and hence the considerable loss of biodiversity attributable to habitat loss.

The Convention on Biological Diversity

In 1987, the World Commission on Environment and Development released the Brundtland Report. Entitled *Our Common Future*, the report emphasized the importance of sustainable development and catalysed the 1992 United Nations Conference on Environment and Development (UNCED, also known as the Earth Summit), held in Rio de Janeiro, Brazil, on the 20th anniversary of the Stockholm Conference. At Rio, nations signed not only the United Nations Framework Convention on Climate Change (UNFCCC), but also the CBD, negotiated under the auspices of the United Nations Environment Programme (UNEP). Within weeks of the Earth Summit, over 150 nations had signed the CBD and it entered into force in 1993. Notably, the US did not ratify the CBD, arguing that its benefit-sharing provisions jeopardized private industry's claims to intellectual-property rights in products derived from ecosystems.

The CBD has three broad objectives: to promote (1) the conservation of biodiversity, (2) the sustainable use of its components and (3) the fair and equitable sharing of benefits arising out of the use of genetic resources. While the CBD is legally binding on contracting Parties, its provisions relating to a variety of measures (e.g. impact assessments, establishment of protected areas, etc.) typically require Parties to take actions 'as far as possible and as appropriate'. Importantly, unlike the more narrow focus of CITES, the CBD explicitly recognizes and seeks to address the primary cause of species loss: habitat destruction (Bean & Rowland 1997). The Conference of the Parties (COP) to the CBD and the CBD's Subsidiary Body on Scientific, Technical and Technological Advice (SBSTTA) develop recommendations on a wide range of habitats, including inland water systems, marine and coastal environments, agricultural systems and forests. Recommendations on biosafety have matured into a binding protocol on biosafety adopted by the CBD's COP.

Perhaps the most interest in the CBD has centred around the treatment of intellectual-property rights in bio-prospecting. Species hold great promise in providing undiscovered compounds that could advance medical science or prove useful to humans in other ways. As such, conservationists have been keenly interested in the prospects of financing the protection of biodiversity through the sale of intellectual-property rights to unique genetic compounds. The CBD does not seek to create new property rights in biodiversity, but does seek to help guide bio-prospecting through advocating, for example, equitable sharing of the proceeds from the discovery of important natural compounds. Equity, particularly the ability of local people to share in the proceeds from valuable compounds, has been one of the more prevalent criticisms of bio-prospecting (e.g. Parry 2001). Given the range of opinions on bio-prospecting, the CBD has had to pursue policies that accommodate those nations that view trade in intellectual-property rights as part of the threat to biodiversity and those who view it as a potential solution (Bean & Rowland 1997).

Whether intellectual-property rights can provide a stable and effective source of revenue for the creation and maintenance of protected areas remains to be seen. Various factors will dictate whether a meaningful market emerges, leading to large-scale conservation, including the likelihood of finding a major marketable compound or set of compounds in any particular region, the extent to which the active compounds can be synthesized in the laboratory, their usefulness, their marketability and the ability to capture proceeds from bio-prospecting for conservation. While some, most notably Costa Rica's INBio programme, have secured agreements with pharmaceutical companies that have yielded revenues for conservation activities, arrangements allowing for access to genetic resources and benefit sharing have not yet produced the capital necessary to affect conservation on a globally significant scale.

Indeed, the economics of bio-prospecting may not provide the incentive necessary for widespread conservation. Simpson (1997) argues, for example, that, given the vast numbers of species and regions from which to choose, pharmaceutical companies place a low value on protecting any single species. Because they can gain access to many species-rich areas, these companies have a seemingly limitless supply of potential compounds; in other words, they have access to many substitutes, and any one specific land area, therefore, has little value. Consequently, Simpson (1997) argues, pharmaceutical companies have a low willingness to pay for land conservation even if the area is species-rich and threatened. This observation suggests that conservationists should rely on other strategies to conserve natural ecosystems and that, therefore, the CBD's bio-prospecting provisions will be likely to have limited influence on the protection of habitat.

The Convention to Combat Desertification

Desertification is an acute problem with grave human consequences in developing countries, particularly in Africa. The 1994 CCD uses a 'bottom-up' approach to combat desertification, on the assumption that involving people who are affected by desertification in decision making is most effective in addressing and mitigating the problem. The CCD entered into force in 1996 and now has 186 participating Parties.

The CCD is governed by a COP, and it also works via a Committee on Science and Technology (CST), which advises and meets simultaneously with the COP. At the CST's recommendation, the COP has established an ad hoc panel to oversee the continuation of the process of surveying benchmarks and indicators, and has undertaken consideration of linkages between traditional knowledge and modern technology.

Articles 4, 6, 20 and 21 of the Convention recognize the importance of financial mechanisms in confronting the problem, particularly since most of the countries affected by desertification have few resources of their own. The CCD establishes a Global Mechanism, whose function is to guide and channel resources to activities, programmes and projects combating desertification. The Mechanism is housed in the International Fund for Agricultural Development (IFAD), an agency of the United Nations, is funded by the COP and seeks to leverage funds from the Global Environmental Facility (GEF), The World Bank, other development banks and voluntary donor nations.

Given the complex nature of the problem, it may well be too early to pass judgement on the effectiveness of the CCD. The CCD has, particularly through the Global Mechanism, clearly focused financial resources and attention on the problem. One potential weakness of the CCD, however, could be its reliance on development banks, the GEF and other nations for funding that is in high demand from a host of other competing interests.

The Convention on Wetlands of International Importance

The Convention on Wetlands, negotiated in Ramsar, Iran, in 1971, provides a framework for national action and international cooperation for the conservation of wetlands and, as such, was the first international treaty focusing on wildlife habitat. The Convention encourages Parties to ensure the wise use of wetlands, though there are no associated legal obligations to do so. The Parties meet periodically to establish a Convention work plan and to review wetland conservation efforts. Most importantly, the Ramsar treaty establishes the List of Wetlands of International Importance (the 'Ramsar list'). Parties commit to designate at least one wetland to the list and to ensure the maintenance of the ecological character of each listed site. One hundred and thirty-six nations are Party to the treaty and 1263 sites covering 107.5 million hectares have been included on the Ramsar list. Criteria for listing include, *inter alia*, the presence of rare species, important wildlife populations and unique wetland types.

A wetland's inclusion on the Ramsar list may boost efforts to protect it. Lyster (1985) provides several examples of wetlands whose status on the Ramsar list increased the political pressure for national action to conserve the sites. Other listed wetlands have not fared so well. Indeed, Ramsar includes no binding obligation to protect any listed site. Further, it contains no financial mechanism to fund conservation, the absence of which may make it particularly difficult for developing countries to conserve listed wetlands (Lyster 1985). Such a mechanism might also help to finance protection of wetlands in industrialized nations where opportunity costs of conservation are high.

At the eighth meeting of the Conference of the Ramsar Parties, held in Valencia, Spain, in November 2002, the Parties considered, among other things, the use of economic incentives to protect wetlands. Resolution VIII.23 adopted by the Conference reiterated the need for Parties to continue review of existing legislation and practices in order to identify and remove perverse incentives that encourage the destruction of wetlands. The resolution merely encourages the Scientific and Technical Review Panel to investigate linkages among incentives and related topics, including financial mechanisms and trade (Ramsar Convention on Wetlands 2002). Thus Ramsar's most significant contribution to wetlands protection will continue to be focusing international attention on the importance of particular recognized sites. In the absence of legal obligations or comprehensive financing, such an approach will be limited in its effect.

Towards a market for ecosystem services

CITES, CBD, CCD and Ramsar have each been successful in creating international institutions and, in some cases, bolstering national efforts to protect biodiversity and natural resources. However, these treaties suffer from a lack of binding obligations (CITES excepted), and from the absence of meaningful funding mechanisms. Of the four treaties discussed, the CBD, though we are pessimistic about its potential to effect significant conservation, is instructive in two important ways. First, while bio-prospecting is unlikely to steer substantial financial resources towards ecosystem protection, the CBD is daring in its effort to harness (or, at least, to help direct) private capital for conservation. Governments in industrialized nations will continue to fund environmental protection in varying degrees, but the potential of private businesses to do the same, particularly in the developing world, could be enormously important.

Second, the CBD's provisions related to genetic resources acknowledge the value of the unique services, in this case useful chemical compounds, provided to humans by natural systems. There is growing interest in valuing, through market mechanisms, the services provided by natural ecosystems, and there are many emerging applications of market solutions, including trade in water rights to benefit rare fish (Willey 1992), banking of endangered species habitat

(Bonnie 1997) and certification of sustainably grown wood products. Likewise, in the context of GHG emissions, the creation of property rights in the form of these tradable commodities could potentially provide financial incentives for the conservation and improved management of ecosystems at a globally significant scale.

Emissions trading: theory and practice

In 1990, the US began what amounted to a large-scale experiment with emissions trading, a concept that economists had discussed for years, but which was largely untested. The acid-rain programme, Title IV of the Clean Air Act Amendments of 1990, employed for the first time a cap-and-trade framework to halve sulphur dioxide emissions over a large geographic region.

While a traditional command and control regulatory approach mandates particular emission reductions by each source or use of a particular pollution control technology, emissions trading mandates only a fixed limit on aggregate emissions by the regulated sector. Under a cap-and-trade system, each unit of allowable emissions is associated with a permit, or allowance, that authorizes the bearer to emit that unit of emissions. Individual sources may buy or sell these emission allowances, but must tender for compliance allowances equal to their actual emissions. If a source can reduce emissions below its cap, then the surplus reductions may be banked or sold to another source, thereby creating economic incentives for surplus emissions reductions.

Similarly, under the Title IV system, the US Congress set a cap on sulphur dioxide emissions, allocated allowances to utilities on the basis of historic emissions, required utilities to possess one allowance for each ton of sulphur dioxide emitted each year and allowed them to buy, sell or bank allowances. If a utility's emissions exceed the number of allowances held, a stiff penalty of more than $2000 per ton of excess emissions is imposed, and the utility must surrender allowances equal to the number of tons of excess emissions (USEPA 2001a). The programme has resulted in 100% compliance and, through 1999, has seen an average of 22% over-compliance due to the banking provisions, resulting in greater emissions reductions than legally required (USEPA 2001b; Swift 2000). Allowance prices have averaged approximately $150 per ton (USEPA 2001b; Swift 2000; Ellerman *et al.* 2000), well below anticipated costs of $300–$1000 per ton (Hahn & May 1994).

Three critical elements of the Title IV programme account, in large part, for its success. First, the programme specifies a mandatory ('hard') cap on emissions in the regulated sector. Alternatives such as rate-based emissions caps, for example, or caps on emissions that limit the price of allowances will typically allow emissions to rise indefinitely into the future (Weitzman 1974; Baumol & Oates 1988). Second, emission units must be fully fungible and bankable into the future. If allowances cannot be banked for future use, businesses will seek to use all of them before they expire, thereby increasing actual emissions. With banking, however, sources have a strong economic incentive to reduce emissions below the level needed for compliance (Ellerman *et al.* 1997, 2000). Third, any legitimate cap-and-trade system must contain provisions to ensure strict compliance with the cap, including transparent measurement and reporting of emissions and penalties that are sufficiently high so that sources do not opt to exceed the cap and simply accept the penalty or fine associated with non-compliance (Ellerman *et al.* 1997, 2000; Swift 2000).

The Kyoto Protocol and emissions trading

The Kyoto Protocol places legally binding limits or caps on the emissions of six GHGs from 31 industrialized nations for the five-year period 2008–2012 (UNFCCC COP 1997). Nations with emissions caps are listed in Annex B of the Protocol and are frequently referred to as 'Annex-B Parties'. The Protocol implements its legally binding commitments by issuing Annex-B Parties emissions budgets denominated in 'assigned amounts' of GHG emissions allowances for the five-year period. These budgets are calculated from the baseline of the nations' GHG emissions in 1990. For example, under the Protocol, member states of the European Union adopted emissions budgets for the 2008–2012 period at levels 8% less than their 1990 emissions. The Russian Federation adopted an emissions budget set at a level equal to its 1990 emissions. Annex-B Parties are required to ensure that their actual emissions do not exceed their emissions budgets. In the 2001 Marrakech Accords, the Parties signalled their intent to require that any Party exceeding its emissions budget at the end of 2012 must surrender emissions allowances in the next commitment period in an amount equal to excess emissions multiplied by a factor of 1.3 (UNFCCC COP 2001).

The Protocol includes four market-based mechanisms that may be used by nations to meet their emissions caps during the compliance period: emissions trading among nations with emissions caps, joint investment projects in nations with caps, reductions from joint investment projects in uncapped nations through the Protocol's Clean Development Mechanism (CDM), and reallocation of targets among groups of nations (UNFCCC COP 1997). Using these mechanisms, a nation with a cap on emissions may meet the requirements of the Kyoto Protocol in several different ways: it may adjust its emissions cap up or down by trading units of the cap with another capped nation (international emissions trading and reallocation of targets), by undertaking a project with another capped nation to reduce emissions within that nation's borders (joint implementation), or by undertaking a project to reduce emissions in an uncapped nation below what would have otherwise occurred (CDM).

The Kyoto Protocol also includes provisions for the inclusion of GHG emissions and sequestration from land-use activities in its emissions-trading framework. Before we turn to an explanation of those provisions, we first explain the rationale for including land-use activities in an international treaty addressing climate change. We then address the challenges of incorporating land-use activities in a GHG-emissions-trading framework. Only then do we turn to the treatment of land-use activities in the Protocol.

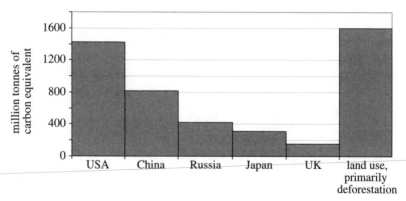

Figure 18.1. Comparison of mean annual deforestation emissions (1989–1995) to fossil-fuel emissions from major emitting countries (1995). Source: UNEP (1996); IPCC (2000).

Valuing the ecosystem services of forests

Global carbon cycle

Land-use activities, and the management of forests in particular, have a significant effect on concentrations of GHGs in the atmosphere. Terrestrial ecosystems are estimated to provide a sink (or flux out of the atmosphere) of 2.3 ± 1.3 GtC yr^{-1} (IPCC 2000). A significant proportion of this carbon sink results from the regrowth of forests in the Northern Hemisphere (Caspersen *et al*. 2000). Emissions from land-use activities, primarily tropical deforestation, on the other hand, are estimated to be 1.6 ± 0.8 GtC yr^{-1} (IPCC 2000).

When tropical forests are clearcut, burned or destroyed, a significant proportion of the carbon stored in leaves, wood and soils is emitted into the atmosphere as carbon dioxide (CO_2). Globally, 14.2 million hectares of tropical forest are lost annually (Food and Agricultural Organization of the United Nations 2001). Using IPCC data, emissions from land-use change, primarily tropical deforestation, comprise *ca.* 20% of total anthropogenic CO_2 emissions, and are comparable to CO_2 emissions from fossil-fuel combustion in the US, the world's largest emitter of GHGs (Figure 18.1).

The contribution of tropical deforestation to climate change is equally dramatic when compared with the contributions from combustion of petroleum, coal and natural gas (Figure 18.2). Thus addressing tropical deforestation must be fundamental component of an effective international climate policy.

Ecosystem services provided by terrestrial ecosystems

Terrestrial ecosystems provide enormous benefits to society (Costanza *et al*. 1997), including carbon sequestration, watershed protection, erosion control, biodiversity conservation and others. Yet the traditional marketplace has typically proven inadequate at valuing ecosystem services (Bonnie *et al*. 2000). For example, forestlands typically have market values for the production of wood products or for the supply of potential agricultural land. Capturing

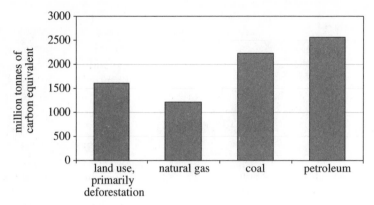

Figure 18.2. Comparison of mean annual deforestation emissions (1989–1995) to emissions from petroleum, natural gas and coal (1990–1999). Source: IPCC (2000); US Department of Energy (1999).

these values requires harvesting timber or converting the forest to cropland or rangeland, both of which diminish at least some of the ecosystem services otherwise produced. Because markets do not yet broadly exist for ecosystem services, forest owners are often unable to reap financial rewards from conservation activities or non-consumptive uses of forests.

Creating a marketable value for the GHG benefits of standing forests would provide a potentially powerful incentive for forest protection. Further, in many ecosystems, valuing GHG benefits would serve as a useful proxy for the other ecosystem services produced by the ecosystem. Protecting carbon stores in mature tropical rainforests, for example, simultaneously protects a diversity of wildlife species that use the rainforest. Kremen *et al.* (2000) demonstrated that if monetary compensation were given for reduced carbon emissions from curtailed deforestation in Madagascar, forest preservation would become a financially profitable endeavour for that country relative to timber harvest. Other non-forest-carbon-sequestration activities such as grassland restoration and conservation-tillage practices can increase carbon stocks while also providing ancillary environmental benefits such as erosion control and wildlife conservation. GHG-emissions-trading systems that incorporate land-use activities have the potential to alter the way ecosystems are valued in a potentially significant way.

Many potential participants in such a market have already begun to explore opportunities for purchasing GHG offsets in the land-use sector. BP, American Electric Power and other companies, in partnership with The Nature Conservancy (an NGO), have invested approximately $10 million in a project to preserve 600 000 hectares of Bolivian rainforest. The project is anticipated to provide substantial GHG emissions reductions through reduced rates of deforestation in the region. In the US Mississippi River Delta, electric utilities have funded reforestation and permanent retirement of marginal agricultural lands, providing atmospheric benefits, improved water quality and enhanced wildlife habitat, including for the Louisiana black bear (*Ursus americanus luteolus*), a threatened species. McCarl & Schneider (2001) examined the potential of US farmers to respond to a market for carbon-sequestration credits. At a price of $50 per tonne of carbon, farmers would in time produce over 150 million tonnes of carbon equivalent in annual sequestration through changes in cropping practices, reforestation of cropland and other activities.

While carbon-sequestration activities generally provide substantial ancillary environmental benefits, there are instances where such activities may result in undesirable land-use practices. Poorly designed sequestration rules, for example, could allow for the 'off-book' liquidation of mature forests, with resulting emissions being unaccounted for, and then 'on-book' replacement, for credit, with younger trees. This threat, however, is easily solvable with rules that require establishment of carbon stock baselines based on historic data prior to forest liquidation.

A more difficult issue relates to fire-adapted ecosystems. Fire suppression in such ecosystems can increase carbon stores in the short term through an increase in a forest's shrub layer. However, fire suppression appears to be a very risky medium- to long-term sequestration strategy, as it increases the odds of catastrophic fires and the resultant significant GHG emissions. Nonetheless, the effect of carbon crediting on fire-adapted ecosystems bears watching.

Socio-economic issues are also an important consideration in the establishment of carbon markets, particularly in developing countries where land tenure regimes may be ill defined. Without appropriate safeguards, local residents may not benefit financially from market transactions. As with bioprospecting, equity is an important issue both from an ethical standpoint and a practical one as support from local populations is important to ensure that conservation measures are enduring. With appropriate safeguards to protect land tenure of local people, however, local populations could stand to gain significantly from a carbon market.

The additional non-atmospheric benefits associated with carbon-sequestration activities tend to be quite positive. Emissions trading offers the possibility of placing a marketable value on the ecosystem services provided by improved land-use practices, thereby creating incentives for the conservation of biodiversity, watersheds and soils.

Incorporating land-use activities in an emissions-trading framework

While there is a compelling environmental rationale for the inclusion of land-use activities in a GHG-emissions-trading framework, two fundamental issues must still be addressed. First, can carbon stock changes in forests, vegetation and soils be accurately measured? Second, are credits produced in the land sector fully fungible with emissions-reduction credits produced through other means?

Land-based carbon stocks can be measured through statistical analyses of direct measurements in forests, vegetation and soils. In forest projects, measurement costs have been reported as low as $0.28 per tonne of carbon with precision levels greater than 95% (Kadyszewski 2001). However, many countries do not currently have a nationwide measurement system with the precision necessary to provide for emissions trading. While project-based activities are still an option, the absence of comprehensive, national carbon-measurement systems in many countries remain a significant obstacle to fully incorporating land-use activities in an international emissions-trading systems.

For a market to operate effectively, carbon-sequestration credits must not only be measurable, they must also be fungible with credits produced in other sectors of the economy. During the negotiations surrounding inclusion of land-use activities in the Kyoto Protocol, the question of fungibility was intensely debated, and centred largely on the reversibility, or so-called permanence, of carbon stocks. The IPCC notes that 'enhancement of carbon stocks resulting from land use, land-use change and forestry activities is potentially reversible through human activities, disturbances, or environmental change, including climate change' (IPCC 2000, p. 9).

The potential reversibility of carbon stocks requires on-going monitoring of carbon stocks that are included in an emissions-trading framework. If carbon stocks that have been credited in the system are later re-released, then they must be replaced from some other source. It matters not whether sequestration activities enter the market through project-based activities or a comprehensive nationwide measurement system. As long as all emissions of credited carbon stocks are accounted for and required to be replaced when lost, then the potential reversibility of carbon stocks will affect neither a nation's emissions cap nor atmospheric concentrations of GHGs. The requirement for ongoing measurement and liability of credited carbon stocks in the land-use sector will add to the costs of carbon-sequestration activities. Nonetheless, such an accounting system effectively renders moot any obstacle to emissions trading based on the reversibility of land-based carbon stocks.

The Kyoto Protocol's carbon-sequestration framework

The Parties to the Kyoto Protocol were, and still are, sharply divided on the appropriate role of carbon-sequestration activities in the Protocol. Adding to the political complexity, the negotiations have been plagued by a dearth of information regarding the magnitude of emissions and sequestration in the land-use sector in both industrialized and non-industrialized nations. In negotiating the Kyoto Protocol in 1997, negotiators had little information on net sequestration rates for Annex-B Parties, which made it difficult for climate negotiators to assess the impacts of including land-use activities in emissions budgets established in Kyoto. Since 1997, there are still significant gaps in the quality of carbon inventory data. This lack of scientific data was clearly detrimental to negotiations in Kyoto, The Hague, Bonn and Marrakech.

Article 3.3: afforestation, reforestation and deforestation

Article 3.3 of the Protocol requires Annex-B Parties to account for net emissions (or sequestration) from afforestation, reforestation and deforestation since 1990. Accounting under Article 3.3 is highly dependent upon the definitions of these three activities. For example, a definition of reforestation that includes re-establishment of a forest following timber harvest combined with a definition of deforestation that excludes emissions from timber harvesting would allow countries with large areas of managed forest land to receive a large volume of credit towards meeting their emissions budget without having to account for the emissions associated with harvesting. Such accounting anomalies could occur through a variety of definitional scenarios.

Alternatively, a system that requires accounting for carbon stock changes for land-use changes only (conversions of forest land to non-forest land and vice versa) would yield a framework that is most representative of atmospheric changes in GHGs resulting from afforestation, reforestation and deforestation. Even this interpretation of Article 3.3 could lead to some counterintuitive outcomes. For example, an Annex-B Party with roughly equal amounts of deforestation and reforestation (and, thus, a relatively stable forest land base) would be likely to have net emissions under Article 3.3, because deforestation of mature forests results in significant pulses of emissions, while afforestation and reforestation activities result in small sequestration gains because the volume of annual sequestration in young forests is low. More broadly, Article 3.3 produces this anomaly because it only accounts for a small portion of the forest-management activities affecting carbon-sequestration rates in Annex-B countries. Accurately capturing the atmospheric fluxes of GHGs resulting from land-use activities requires comprehensive accounting.

Article 3.4: other sequestration activities

Beyond afforestation, reforestation and deforestation, the Kyoto Protocol failed to resolve whether and how other land-use activities would be treated in Annex-B countries. Article 3.4 of the Protocol directs the negotiators to decide upon rules by which the inclusion of 'additional human-induced activities related to changes in greenhouse gas emissions by sources and removals by sinks in the agricultural soils and the land-use change and forestry categories' in the Protocol could be 'added to, or subtracted from' an Annex-B Party's assigned amount. Thus treatment of land-use activities under Article 3.4 could have potentially significant implications for the assigned amounts of Annex-B nations. This can best be illustrated with a practical example. Here, we use the case of the US. Though the current US Administration has chosen not to participate in the Protocol, the case of the US nonetheless provides insight into the problems inherent in Article 3.4.

Table 18.1 depicts the potential impact of inclusion of all land-use activities under Article 3.4 on the effective reductions required by the US to comply with its assigned amount. Allowable annual GHG emissions for the US under the Kyoto Protocol during the first commitment period (2008–2012) are 1530 million tonnes of carbon equivalent (MMTCE) (based on figures from the USEPA (2001*b*)). Under an assumed annual emissions growth of 1.2%, the US would emit *ca.* 2039–2139 MMTCE annually from 2008–2012, thus requiring annual reductions of 509–609 MMTCE to meet its Kyoto target. Prior to climate

Table 18.1. *Ramifications of including land-use activities under Article 3.4 on the GHG emission reductions required by the US during the first commitment period of the Kyoto Protocol*

US allowable emissions under Kyoto Protocol (USEPA 2001b)	Annual US fossil-fuel emissions 2008–2012	Projected reductions under Kyoto Protocol	Projected business-as-usual sink under Article 3.4	Required reductions met with BAU sinks
		Million metric tonnes of carbon equivalent (MMTCE).		
1530	2039–2139	509–609	310	51–61%

negotiations in The Hague in 2001, the US projected mean net carbon sequestration in the land-use sector of 310 MMTCE for the years 2008–2012 under business-as-usual assumptions (i.e. no substantial change in current US land-management practices). Consequently, by including all carbon-sequestration activities under Article 3.4 without any restrictions, the US could, through business-as-usual practices in the land sector, meet 51–61% of its required emissions reductions.

This outcome results not from inherent problems associated with accounting for land-use activities under an international framework, but instead from the architecture of the Kyoto Protocol and, especially, Article 3.4 itself. The Kyoto Protocol did not require Parties to include emissions and sequestration from land-use activities (other than from a limited set of agricultural activities, see Kyoto Protocol Annex A) in the calculation of their 1990 base year emissions (unless their land-use change and forestry in 1990 constituted a net source, see Kyoto Protocol Article 3.7). Thus, when the Protocol provided that the allowable total GHG emissions budgets for Parties would be set as a multiple of the base year emissions, emissions and sequestration from land-use activities were not subject to a baseline. Had the data been available on carbon stocks in Annex-B countries and had negotiators agreed to account for GHG sequestration (or emissions) from all land-use activities, then the targets might have been structured quite differently. Countries with large net sequestration would be likely to have been pressured to lower their targets substantially in order to reflect the expected sequestration. That clearly did not happen and, given the paucity of data, could not have happened in Kyoto.

Instead, the emissions budgets established in Kyoto did not explicitly recognize the potential contribution of business-as-usual land-use trends in Annex-B countries, and Article 3.4 left open the question of whether and how land-use activities would be treated. As such, efforts to include sequestration activities in Article 3.4 were viewed by many as an attempt to weaken the Kyoto targets. It is important to note, however, that the inclusion of sequestration activities in Article 3.4 could also stimulate enhanced sequestration through an emissions-trading framework.

Negotiators focused on two approaches for limiting the impact of Article 3.4 activities on the Kyoto emissions budgets. The first approach was to limit the activities that would be eligible under Article 3.4. For example, narrowly defined activities, such as reduced-impact logging, grassland restoration and use of cover crops in croplands, would necessarily reduce the impact of Article 3.4 on emissions budgets because of these activities would result in fewer tonnes of carbon entering the system. But, as negotiators realized, such activities would face the same definitional problems noted in our earlier discussion of Article 3.3. Defining narrow activities would be difficult and could lead to gaming by nations that hoped to exclude emissions in the land-use sector while accounting only for sequestration activities (IPCC 2000).

The second approach to limiting the impact of Article 3.4 on the Kyoto was to focus on an over-arching limitation across all Article 3.4 activities. Three general variants of this approach were discussed: discounting, cap and 'threshold' methods. All three would limit the impact of Article 3.4 activities on the Kyoto targets, but each would create quite different incentives with respect to the management of the land-use sector.

The first option, discounting, would reduce all carbon-sequestration credits earned under Article 3.4 by some percentage (e.g. 90%). Discounting would reduce total sequestration tonnes markedly but would also dramatically reduce incentives for Annex-B nations to adopt policies that would enhance carbon sequestration. The second option, a cap, would place a numerical cap on the number of tonnes that Annex-B nations could earn under Article 3.4. Like discounting, a cap can create perverse incentives depending upon the level at which the cap is set. For example, assume an Annex-B nation is projected under business-as-usual trends to sequester 10 MMTCE of carbon annually through Article 3.4. If a cap were placed at 5 MMTCE for this nation, its entire allotment of carbon-sequestration credits would be fulfilled with business-as-usual sequestration, leaving neither room nor incentive for the country to adopt policies to further enhance its carbon stores.

The third option, a threshold approach, would provide a more environmentally beneficial way to limit credit under Article 3.4, if the threshold is set appropriately. Under this approach, an Annex-B country would only be allowed to claim credit for sequestration activities after surpassing some threshold level of carbon storage. For example, an Annex-B country might be assigned a threshold of 5 MMTCE, meaning that it would only receive credit for sequestration tonnes produced beyond this threshold amount. The threshold method would limit the amount of credit that can be claimed by Parties for carbon sequestration produced under business-as-usual projections, while maintaining incentives for countries to undertake additional activities to increase carbon stores.

The choice of policy instruments to limit crediting under Article 3.4 has significant ramifications for the effective stringency of the Kyoto targets and for the incentives provided to Annex-B nations to manage their forests and agricultural lands. As we will elaborate more fully in our discussion of the Bonn Agreement and the Marrakech Accords, it was the structure of Article 3.4 and the different political and economic aims of the negotiating Parties, rather than anything inherent in the nature of carbon sequestration, that made it difficult for negotiators to find a solution that both preserved the stringency of the Kyoto targets and maintained incentives for improved carbon management in the land-use sector.

Article 12 and tropical deforestation

The world's tropical rainforests are concentrated in Latin America, Africa and southeast Asia, regions not represented in Annex B of the Protocol. Thus Articles 3.3 and 3.4, which apply only to Annex-B nations, will not, in large part, affect the substantial GHG emissions from tropical deforestation during the first commitment period. However, if non-industrialized nations are subject to emissions budgets in subsequent commitment periods under the Kyoto Protocol, as one would expect, treatment of carbon-sequestration activities under Articles 3.3 and 3.4 will become a crucial factor in determining whether or not emissions from deforestation are indeed addressed in a comprehensive manner.

In the short term, tropical deforestation can only be addressed through Article 12 of the Kyoto Protocol, the CDM. Article 12 itself does not explicitly include or exclude land-use projects from eligibility. As such, inclusion of land-use projects in the CDM was hotly contested following the negotiations in Kyoto.

Under Article 12, industrialized nations may purchase 'certified emissions reductions' (CERs) from non-Annex-B nations. CERs are generated through projects that reduce emissions below what would have occurred in the absence of the project. In the case of tropical deforestation, this could potentially allow for projects designed to reduce rates of deforestation in the tropics, financed by the sale of CERs.

By definition, the CDM allows emissions trading between Annex-B nations (with emissions caps) and non-Annex-B nations (without emissions caps). The challenge in trading between sources in capped nations and sources in uncapped nations is in ensuring that reductions from uncapped nations, are, in fact, real. This requires accounting for two key factors. First, guidelines must be established to select an emissions (or sequestration) baseline from which to measure emissions reductions. Article 12 requires that CERs be issued only if 'reductions in emissions. . . are additional to any that would occur in the absence of the certified project activity'. This so-called 'additionality' provision requires project proponents to establish 'without-project' emissions baselines against which emissions reductions are measured. In the case of tropical deforestation, this would require the projection of without-project deforestation rates for the project area. Establishing such baselines should not be overly challenging, since tropical deforestation is a relatively predictable phenomenon (Bonnie *et al.* 2000).

Second, trading between capped and uncapped nations can result in leakage of GHG benefits if the project activities cause a shift of emissions-producing activities to areas outside the project boundaries. In the case of the forest sector, leakage could occur when timber harvesting is reduced on one tract, but the reduction of timber supply causes increased harvests on other forest land, thereby nullifying any gains to the atmosphere. To ensure that projects with uncapped nations result in real GHG reductions, project proponents must measure and account for leakage in calculating creditable GHG emissions reductions.

Most importantly, neither the challenge of baseline calculation nor the issues associated with leakage pertain solely to carbon-sequestration projects. They are characteristic instead of all emissions-reduction projects in uncapped nations and, thus, provide no rationale for excluding land-use activities from Article 12.

Treatment of land-use activities under the Bonn Agreement and the Marrakech Accords

Adoption of the Kyoto Protocol in 1997 provided only a bare framework for the treatment of land-use activities. Significant unresolved issues remained, requiring decisions by the Parties ultimately resolved in Bonn and Marrakech in 2001. With respect to Article 3.3, negotiators were to decide upon definitions of afforestation, reforestation and deforestation. Negotiators also had to decide which activities to include under Article 3.4 and how to mitigate the impact of the provision's potential impacts on the stringency of the Kyoto targets. Lastly, the Parties had to decide whether or not carbon-sequestration projects would be eligible under the CDM.

The negotiations in Bonn and Marrakech were successful on many fronts in solidifying the emissions-trading framework in the Protocol and thereby promoting the potential establishment of an international market in GHG emissions-reduction credits. Unfortunately, the rules adopted for the carbon-sequestration provisions of the Protocol missed a number of opportunities to create positive incentives for countries to improve their environmental performance for the management of forests and agricultural lands. In some cases, the rules adopted encourage precisely the opposite behaviour.

Parties adopted definitions under Article 3.3 that account for the GHG emissions and sequestration from afforestation, reforestation and deforestation only in the context of land-use conversions. As such, the rules provide an accounting system that accurately reflects the atmospheric impacts from these three activities. However, as noted below, any such incentive to increase carbon stores provided by the elaboration of these definitions is greatly reduced by the treatment of forest management in Article 3.4.

Under the Bonn Agreement and the Marrakech Accords, Article 3.4 allows Annex-B parties to elect to account for the GHG impacts from forest management, cropland management, grazing-land management and revegetation. Inclusion of the first three of these activities moves the Protocol towards a comprehensive accounting framework that avoids gaming, leakage and definitional problems associated with more narrowly defined activities. The inclusion of revegetation as an eligible activity, however, is problematic. The term appears intended to include re-establishment of non-forest vegetation in areas that do not meet the minimum specifications that define a forest. However, the exclusion of 'devegetation' as a required eligible activity for parties electing to include revegetation under Article 3.4 means that emissions associated with the clearing of such lands will not be recorded.

A far more serious problem is the method chosen to limit the amount of credit that Annex-B Parties can claim under Article 3.4. The Parties chose to place country-specific caps on the forest-management activities of all Annex-B nations. As noted earlier, a cap on forest sector crediting under Article 3.4 would be very likely to exclude credit for activities undertaken during the commitment period that enhance carbon sequestration. The effect of a cap, therefore, is at once to reduce the stringency of the Kyoto targets while robbing Annex-B nations of any incentive to increase carbon storage in the forest sector.

Ironically, in the case of cropland and grazing-land management, negotiators elected to apply the threshold method of accounting. The threshold chosen is the sequestration rate for that Party in 1990. This provision maintains incentives for Parties to adopt policies that increase sequestration rates in the agricultural sector. Such an approach would have been environmentally preferable for forest-management activities under Article 3.4.

The perverse incentive for forest-management activities under Article 3.4 is made worse by two other provisions in the Bonn Agreement and the Marrakech Accords. First, if a Party has excess forest-management sequestration after application of cap in Article 3.4, it may use those tonnes to cover any deficit it incurs in Article 3.3 up to 9 MMTCE annually. As such, nations with projections of sequestration in the forest sector that exceed the cap on Article 3.4 have little incentive to reduce rates of deforestation or increase rates of reforestation and afforestation.

Second, in Marrakech, Parties agreed to prohibit banking of unused forest-management tonnes in Article 3.4 (that is, unused tonnes in excess of the cap). The absence of banking is damaging both to forests and the climate. For example, assume a Party expects to have 10 MMTCE of unused forest-management tonnes after accounting for its Article 3.4 cap. With banking, the country has an incentive to ensure that it, in fact, produces those unused tonnes during the commitment period as they have value in subsequent commitment periods. Without banking provisions, no such incentive exists and, arguably, the nation might benefit by speeding forest harvests now, because it will not be penalized for lowering its forest-management sequestration to the level of the cap. Moreover, harvesting those forests earlier would enable the Party to earn credits for the regrowth of carbon stocks in regenerated areas in subsequent periods. Of course, many factors will dictate whether such forest liquidation does indeed occur, including the domestic policies of Annex-B countries in implementing the Protocol, forest products markets, forest ownership patters and others. Regardless, the incentives created by the rules governing Article 3.4 are very troubling.

Parties also chose to exclude projects addressing tropical deforestation from the CDM, seriously hampering efforts to address the *ca.* 20% of global CO_2 emissions from this source. The decision to forgo a potentially powerful financial incentive to value the ecosystem services associated with the conservation of tropical rainforests is perhaps the most vexing to advocates for tropical forest protection.

Making sense of the Marrakech decisions is difficult, but one factor in particular appears to have contributed substantially to the decision-making process of all Annex-B nations. All Annex-B Parties sought, for different reasons, certainty as to the number of available credits that could be garnered through carbon-sequestration activities. Some desired certainty that sequestration tonnes would be limited; others desired certainty that they would receive a specified number of sequestration tonnes. A country's particular stance on carbon sequestration was driven in part by whether it expected to be a net seller or net purchaser of emissions-reduction credits under the Protocol. For countries that expect to purchase emissions-reduction credits on the international market, a cap allowing credit of tonnes expected under business-as-usual trends provides certainty that they will receive a certain number of tonnes through Article 3.4 and will, therefore, have an easier job complying with the Protocol. These net purchasers also probably realized that there was no easy way to predict the number of sequestration tonnes that would be available for purchase under the CDM. Consequently, these net purchasers were not adamant in their support for the inclusion of projects addressing tropical deforestation in the CDM.

Nations that might be net sellers of emissions-reduction credits may have sought more guaranteed tonnes under Article 3.4 in order to ensure a predictable revenue stream. It was also in the interest of these countries to restrict tonnes entering the market from the CDM. Given the enormous GHG emissions from tropical deforestation, excluding such projects would make economic sense by restricting the supply of available credits on the world market and thereby receiving a higher price for their tonnes.

Those countries who stood to gain little from a liberal interpretation of Article 3.4, and who expected not to have to rely on carbon-sequestration tonnes for compliance, typically sought during the negotiations to limit the number of forest-management tonnes that other nations could use. A potential reason for this is that doing so would boost their economic competitiveness relative to other nations, as they could spend less national income on compliance with Kyoto. A cap under Article 3.4 and exclusion of projects addressing tropical deforestation in the CDM provided them with certainty that sequestration tonnes used by other nations would have an absolute limit.

Of course, nations may have been swayed by other factors than self-interest, though the above explanation is consistent with the positions of most Annex-B nations. In any case, the shortcomings of the decisions made in Bonn and Marrakech are likely to increase the costs, reduce the environmental effectiveness and potentially weaken forest protection under an otherwise well-designed emissions-trading framework under the Kyoto Protocol.

Creating an emissions-trading framework that protects biodiversity and the atmosphere

The Bonn Agreement and the Marrakech Accords failed to develop rules for land-use activities that create positive incentives for management of terrestrial sinks in Annex-B and non-Annex-B countries. Emissions from land-use activities have contributed significantly to climate change. Recognizing that improved land-management practices and, in particular, effective measures to reduce rates of deforestation are critical to overall efforts to reduce GHG emissions, how can the Kyoto framework be improved to create incentives for enhanced carbon sequestration and reduced GHG emissions through improved land management?

Compilation of comprehensive scientific data

An effective emissions-trading system requires comprehensive data on GHG emissions and sequestration. The Kyoto negotiations on carbon-sequestration activities have taken place in the absence of robust data on terrestrial carbon stocks from Annex-B nations. Annex-B nations must improve their carbon-measurement systems. Equally importantly, non-Annex-B nations must begin to develop better inventory systems, especially if the Protocol is to adequately address tropical deforestation. Such inventory systems in developing countries could be financed by industrialized nations in exchange for GHG credits produced through carbon-sequestration activities.

Move towards mandatory full carbon accounting for all nations

A system of full carbon accounting (FCA) measures all changes, positive and negative, in all carbon stocks from all lands continuously. Under FCA, once lands enter the emissions-trading system, all carbon stocks on those lands are monitored permanently over contiguous commitment periods. FCA works within an emissions-trading framework because ultimately the atmosphere does not differentiate (and neither should climate policy) between CO_2 molecules produced by fossil-fuel combustion and such molecules produced through forest destruction. FCA is the only way to provide a balanced accounting system that accurately reflects the relationship between land-use activities and the atmosphere. FCA avoids the definitional issues, in evidence in Article 3.3 of the Protocol, associated with partial accounting systems.

In addition, FCA avoids the complexities, such as gaming, leakage and permanence of GHG benefits, associated with partial accounting systems. Gaming, for example, could result through a partial accounting system if some additional land-use activities are made eligible under Article 3.4, while others are not. Similarly, leakage of GHG benefits may occur through partial accounting systems. Where demand for agricultural land is high, for example, reforestation of agricultural lands could lead to agricultural intensification elsewhere. This transfer of activity could result in soil-carbon losses not captured by a partial accounting system.

FCA offers a superior approach to the permanence issue because it requires continuous monitoring of carbon stocks over contiguous commitment periods. As such, FCA will capture fluctuations in carbon stocks and, where necessary, require GHG emissions from the land-use sectors to be offset. In short, because all emissions on managed lands are captured over contiguous commitment periods under FCA, the reversibility of GHG benefits from land-use activities is not an obstacle to emissions trading.

Adoption of FCA would move the Kyoto Protocol towards a system in which projected emissions and sequestration from the land-use sector would be explicitly considered in the context of adopting assigned amounts for subsequent commitment periods. This avoids the difficulties associated with limiting business-as-usual crediting under the current configuration of Article 3.4. Under FCA, business-as-usual activities can be figured into the establishment of Kyoto emissions budgets. This is of central importance because it alleviates the tension between land-use activities and the stringency of Kyoto targets under Article 3.4, thereby resolving the perception (and an important political problem) that inclusion of carbon-sequestration activities are intended to weaken the Kyoto treaty. Done properly, inclusion of land-use activities will strengthen it.

Finally, in contrast to the current structure of Article 3.4, FCA must be mandatory for all Parties. This is crucial for addressing tropical deforestation as well as for emissions from other land-use activities. Tropical deforestation is the primary source of GHG emissions from many developing nations (e.g. Brazil). As developing countries enter Annex B by adopting emissions budgets, it is vital that they be given incentives to reduce deforestation. Allowing countries with significant land-use emissions to exclude large portions of the land sector would seriously undermine the effectiveness of the Kyoto Protocol. If accounting for land-use activities is to be reflective of atmospheric GHG concentrations and if tropical deforestation is to be confronted in a comprehensive way, FCA cannot be discretionary.

Capacity building in developing countries

It is unlikely that developing countries will be willing to take emissions budgets that require FCA unless they gain experience in successfully curbing tropical deforestation while also providing for the needs of their citizens. The CDM provides a unique opportunity for developing countries to gain experience in addressing tropical deforestation. Projects addressing tropical deforestation must be made eligible for the CDM beyond the first commitment period. Negotiators should also consider revisiting the question of forest conservation project eligibility for the first commitment period.

The two greatest threats to the global environment are climate change and loss of biodiversity, the later of which is most severe in areas experiencing high rates of tropical deforestation. The inclusion of land-use activities in a GHG-emissions-trading framework through full carbon accounting can potentially leverage substantial financial resources to reduce atmospheric GHGs and protect the Earth's terrestrial ecosystems.

References

Baumol, W. J. & Oates, W. E. 1988 *Theory of environmental policy*, 2nd edn, pp. 57–78. Cambridge University Press.

Bean, M. & Rowland, M. 1997 *The evolution of national wildlife law*, 3rd edn. Westport, CT: Praeger.

Bonnie, R. 1997 Safe harbor for the red-cockaded woodpecker. *J. Forestry* **95**, 17–22.

Bonnie, R., Schwartzman, S., Oppenheimer, M. & Bloomfield, J. 2000 Counting the costs of deforestation. *Science* **288**, 1763–1764.

Caspersen, J., Pacala, S., Jenkins, J., Hurtt, G., Moorcroft, P. & Birdsey, R. 2000 Contributions of land-use to carbon accumulation in US forests. *Science* **290**, 1148–1151.

Costanza, R. (and 12 others) 1997 The value of the world's ecosystem services and natural capital. *Nature* **387**, 253–260.

Ellerman, A. D., Schmalensee, R., Joskow, P. L., Montero, J.-P. & Bailey, E. M. 1997 *Sulphur dioxide emissions trading under title IV of the 1990 clean air act amendments: evaluation of compliance costs and allowance market performance.* Cambridge, MA: Massachusetts Institute of Technology.

Ellerman, A. D., Schmalensee, R., Bailey, E. M., Joskow, P. L. & Montero, J.-P. 2000 *Markets of clean air: the US acid rain program.* Cambridge University Press.

Food and Agricultural Organization of the United Nations 2001 *State of the world's forests.* (Available at www.fao.org/forestry/fo/sofo/sofo-e.stm.)

Hahn, R. W. & May, C. A. 1994 The behavior of the allowance market: theory and evidence. *Electricity J.* **7**, 28–33.

International Panel on Climate Change (IPCC) 2000 *Land use, land-use change and forestry.* Cambridge University Press.

Kadyszewski, J. 2001 Testimony before the Senate Committee on agriculture, nutrition and forestry, March 29.

Kremen, C., Niles, J., Dalton, M., Daily, G., Ehrlich, P., Fay, J., Grewal, D. & Guillery, R. 2000 Economic incentives for rain forest conservation across different scales. *Science* **288**, 1828–1832.

Lyster, S. 1985 *International wildlife law.* Cambridge: Grotius.

McCarl, B. A. & Schneider, U. A. 2001 Greenhouse gas mitigation in US agriculture and forestry. *Science* **294**, 2481–2482.

Parry, R. L. 2001 Bio-pirates raid trees in the swamps of Borneo. *The Independent*, 2 August 2001.

Ramsar Convention on Wetlands 2002 'Resolution VIII.23 Incentive measures as tools for achieving the wise use of wetlands', adopted at the eighth meeting of the Conference of the Contracting Parties to the Convention on Wetlands (Ramsar, Iran, 1971), Valencia, Spain, 18–26 November 2002. (Available at www.ramsar.org/key_res_viii_23_e.htm.)

Simpson, R. 1997 Biodiversity prospecting: shopping the wilds is not the key to conservation. *Resources*, Winter, pp. 12–15.

Swift, B. 2000 Allowance trading and potential hot spots—good news from the acid rain program. *BNA Environ. Reporter* **31**, 954–959.

United Nations Conference of the Parties (COP) to the Framework Convention on Climate Change (UNFCCC): Kyoto Protocol 1997 37 ILM 22. (Available at www.unffccc.de/fccc/docs/cop3/107a01.pdf.)

United Nations Conference of the Parties (COP) to the Framework Convention (UNFCCC): Marrakech Accords 2001. (Available at www.unfccc.de/fccc/docs/cop7.)

United Nations Environment Program (UNEP) 1996 Vital climate graphics. (Available at www.grida.no/climate/vital/11.htm.)

US Department of Energy 1999 www.eia.doe.gov/emeu/international/total.html.

US Environmental Protection Agency (USEPA) 2001*a* Acid rain program compliance report. (Available at www.epa.gov/airmarkt/arp/overview.html.)

US Environmental Protection Agency (USEPA) 2001*b* Inventory of US greenhouse gas emissions and sinks: 1990–1999. Washington, DC.

Weiss, E. B. & Jacobson, H. K. 1999 Getting countries to comply with international agreements. *Environment* **41**, 16–29.

Weitzman, M. L. 1974 Prices vs. quantities. *Rev. Econ. Stud.* **41**, 477–491.

Willey, Z. 1992 Behind schedule and over budget: the case of markets, water, and environment. *Harvard J. Law Public Policy* **15**, 391–425.

Wilson, E. O. 1992 *The diversity of life*. Cambridge, MA: Harvard University Press.

Chapter 19

Designing a carbon market that protects forests in developing countries

EDUARD NIESTEN, PETER C. FRUMHOFF,
MICHELLE M. MANION AND JARED J. HARDNER

Introduction

The Kyoto Protocol to the United Nations Framework Convention on Climate Change (UNFCCC) strongly emphasizes the role of market mechanisms in reducing atmospheric concentrations of greenhouse gases (GHGs), and has prompted the development of an international trading scheme for carbon credits to this end. Though incorporating many elements of a 'free-market approach', the efficient, equitable, and effective functioning of this market will require careful construction of principles and rules that govern market operations and participation, to ensure both reduced net carbon emissions and a minimum of economic dislocation and environmental and social impacts. The agreements reached at COP-6*bis* and COP-7 in 2001 made significant strides in refining this trading mechanism and designing the rules that are to govern trading of carbon emissions quotas.

The parties reached several key decisions to define the menu of land-use, land-use change and forestry (LULUCF) options available to Annex I (industrialized) countries to meet their emissions–reductions obligations. They also affirmed as a core guiding principle that the implementation of LULUCF activities 'contributes to the conservation of biodiversity and sustainable use of natural resources' (UNFCCC 2002*a*). However, possible interpretations and application of some available LULUCF options may contribute to biodiversity loss by exacerbating deforestation and forest degradation trends in non-Annex I (developing) countries. Such outcomes also would increase GHG emissions and negatively impact forest-dependent communities. Here, we examine the potential seriousness of these threats and recommend steps that climate policymakers can take to address them.

Concerns about potentially large impacts on native forests in developing countries arise from two quite different decisions. The first and most conspicuous decision entails the LULUCF project activities in developing countries that are eligible for carbon crediting under the Clean Development Mechanism

(CDM). Parties at COP-7 restricted eligible project activities to afforestation and reforestation (A&R). At least for the first commitment period, 2008–2012, project activities designed to slow deforestation were not deemed eligible for crediting. The result of a complex political negotiation,[1] this decision eliminates for the near-term any carbon market incentive to address the *ca.* 20% of annual anthropogenic carbon dioxide (CO_2) emissions caused by forest conversion in the tropics (Prentice *et al.* 2001). In addition, it also raises concerns about whether CDM crediting for A&R will act as an incentive to clear natural forest for the purposes of establishing carbon plantations. Biodiversity considerations aside, such a process would undermine the carbon sequestration benefits from plantation efforts. Moreover, land that might be suitable for natural forest restoration could face competition from plantation efforts subsidized by carbon premiums, again leading to both biodiversity and GHG emissions additionality concerns. Climate negotiators have an important near-term opportunity to address these concerns, as the Subsidiary Body for Scientific and Technological Advice was tasked at COP-7 with developing more specific guidance by COP-9 on the treatment of additionality, environmental impacts (including 'impacts on biodiversity and natural ecosystems') and other key issues affecting the implementation of A&R projects in the CDM (UNFCCC 2002*b*).

The second potential impact on native forests in developing countries stems from the decision to credit forest management activities in Annex I countries under Article 3.4. This provides a carbon premium for standing natural forests in industrialized countries that, in effect, increases the opportunity cost of harvesting Annex I timber and makes timber in developing countries, which have no cap on emissions, relatively cheaper. This creates a potential carbon market incentive for 'inter-annex leakage' by redirecting timber harvests from industrialized to developing countries. For the first commitment period, such leakage may be minimal, as Article 3.4 sets country-specific caps for forest management at levels that allow carbon credits to be gained largely through business-as-usual activities (see Chapter 18). But several lines of evidence explored in this chapter suggest that it is a potentially serious concern for future commitment periods, for which the rules have yet to be written.

Afforestation and reforestation in the CDM

Potential A&R project activities eligible for crediting under the CDM could range from small-scale agroforestry and native forest restoration to large-scale industrial plantations. The type of activities, and their geographic distribution, magnitude, and environmental and social impacts will depend on the rules governing A&R project implementation and eventual market-clearing prices for carbon credits. They will also depend on the interests of developing countries in soliciting particular types of projects, and the interests of prospective investors in seeking CDM project credits. Large-scale plantations, for example, may be of substantial interest to project investors because of their potential to generate profitable financial returns as well as carbon credits (Frumhoff *et al.* 1998; Brown *et al.* 2000).

Plantation forestry projects motivated by CDM carbon crediting need not have negative impacts on biodiversity. Plantations established on degraded lands and managed according to internationally recognized certification standards can, for example, provide both environmental and social co-benefits. In some cases, non-permanent plantations of exotic or native species can be designed to jump-start the process of native forest restoration and hence directly support forest and biodiversity conservation objectives (Parotta 1997*a, b*; Brown *et al.* 2000).

However, despite a widespread belief to the contrary, plantations in the tropics do not typically reduce pressure on natural forests. This stems from the fact that forests generally are not logged or cleared for the sawn wood, pulpwood or other products that plantations provide (Kanowski *et al.* 1992). Rather, natural forests supply a range of products that have yet to be reproduced in tropical plantations; in particular, the potential contribution of plantations to the global supply of tropical hardwoods remains insignificant (Sawyer 1993).

Poorly designed or located plantations can have significant negative impacts on biodiversity (Brown *et al.* 2000). For instance, permanent plantations in areas adjacent to natural forests eliminate in those locations the prospect of restoring native forests and their biodiversity. With specific regard to the CDM, of greatest concern is the potential for carbon premiums to accelerate deforestation by financing the clearing of forests to be replaced with plantation monocultures. This concern arises because the emissions associated with deforestation would not be constrained by a national cap (WBGU 1998; Brown *et al.* 2000).

Accelerated rates of forest degradation and deforestation may occur wherever carbon payments can sway the balance between financial costs and benefits of particular enterprises in forested areas. Substantial oil-palm investments in Indonesia, for example, are rendered viable only by the income from logging of natural forests that precedes plantation establishment (Casson 1999; LaFranchi 2000). A carbon premium linked to such plantations could expand still further the geographic range over which conversion of natural forest to oil palm is financially viable.

Indeed, precedents exist in which timber companies have pursued plans to clear native vegetation and establish timber plantations that generate carbon credits. In February 2000, for example, the Rio Foyel S.A. timber company proposed to harvest four thousand hectares of native forest in southern Argentina, to be followed by reforestation with exotic pine species. The stated objectives of the project were carbon sequestration and sustainable timber production. Regional authorities, local community members, and environmental organizations objected to the deforestation of native species, introduction of exotic species, and potential damage to the watershed. The company eventually withdrew the project proposal. While this particular project thus was averted, it illustrates how the prospect of income from carbon sequestration can encourage the timber sector to clear native forests (Biodiversidad en América Latina 2000).

Similarly, the Tokyo Electric Power Company (TEPCO) has been involved in efforts to clear native forests in Tasmania for the purpose of establishing carbon plantations (Cadman 2000). In a joint venture with Australian timber company North Forest Products, TEPCO has sought to generate of the order of 130 000 tonnes of carbon credits in this fashion. Although taking place in an Annex I country, this joint venture is again illustrative of the means by which a carbon market could fuel deforestation in developing countries through CDM A&R projects.

The potential scale of impacts to native forests and biodiversity in developing countries is not clear. To evaluate the scale accurately, one must first assess the extent to which carbon financing through the CDM is likely to lead more generally to an expansion of plantations in non-Annex 1 countries. This is difficult to predict. The area dedicated to timber plantations in developing countries and their contribution to the world timber supply are already increasing rapidly (Table 19.1), an expansion that is expected to continue even in the absence of a carbon market.[2]

Not simply a function of market forces, these rapid rates of plantation expansion in many developing countries, particularly in the tropics, result from generous government subsidies. Such subsidies often reflect government efforts to spur employment and economic development in areas able to support forests for industrial and fuelwood production (FAO 1997, 2001). In areas where a carbon premium is truly additional to existing subsidies or other incentives, growth in plantation coverage seems likely to continue on an upward continuum.

However, some developing country governments might seek carbon financing for plantations through the CDM as an alternative to existing subsidies for plantation establishment and hence reduce or eliminate subsidies as the carbon market financing develops. In these cases, a carbon premium would not accelerate plantation establishment over baseline rates. CDM financed plantations that merely replace those that would have funded by other sources would also not sequester carbon above baseline rates, however, and hence would not meet strict tests of additionality.

Carbon premiums for A&R plantation projects in the CDM thus give rise to serious concerns over potential impacts on native forests and biodiversity. While the potential scale of the problem is difficult to predict, the fact that carbon financing enhances incentives for accelerated forest degradation and deforestation strongly suggests that parties should act to eliminate these incentives. A straightforward way to do so would be through the selection of an appropriate base year, such that land cleared after that year would be ineligible for A&R crediting under the CDM. For example, setting 1990 as a base year would imply that only lands that were demonstrably deforested prior to 1990 would be eligible for A&R projects. This would neatly eliminate the potential for carbon crediting to accelerate negative impacts to native forests. However, such a base-year rule would come at a cost. As noted above, well-designed A&R projects under the CDM have the potential to provide positive biodiversity co-benefits by promoting the restoration of natural forests. But restoration projects need to be established in close proximity to standing for-

Table 19.1. *Extent and rate of plantation establishment*

	Total plantation (kha)	Annual rate establishment (kha)	Proportion for industrial roundwood (%)
developed countries	81 224	2560 (4%)	100
non-tropical developing countries	30 213	2358 (5%)	73
tropical countries	27 505	1654 (6%)	58
subtotals for tropical regions			
tropical Africa	2 434	120 (5%)	52
tropical America	5 973	230 (4%)	76
tropical Asia	19 098	1304 (7%)	45
totals	138 942	6572 (5%)	87

Source: Pandey & Ball (1998).

est, that is, on lands that are likely to have been recently deforested. Hence, a tightly enforced rule setting an early base year would also effectively eliminate crediting for many A&R projects with substantial potential for positive impacts on biodiversity. This perverse outcome could be reduced by setting a relatively recent base year (e.g. 2000) for projects that are explicitly designed to promote native forest restoration and pass rigorous environmental impact review.

Inter-annex market leakage

Market-driven leakage of carbon emissions arises when emissions reductions require a change in economic activity, but the market signal that elicited the original activity persists. It is a problem facing both the energy and LULUCF sectors (Chomitz 2000). For the LULUCF sector, the concern is that, by crediting key LULUCF interventions in industrialized countries in the absence of caps on emissions from timber harvests and deforestation in developing countries, a carbon market could redirect harvests and associated emissions to the latter. That is, if carbon premiums alter forest management systems and harvest patterns such that the timber supply from Annex I regions declines, developing countries may respond by increasing their share of global timber markets. Carbon benefits from LULUCF measures in Annex I countries would then be reduced or negated by accelerated harvests in developing countries, with substantial impacts to biodiversity should these harvests be directed to natural forests.

What is the potential for such inter-annex leakage? Timber markets can respond rapidly to policy changes by changing supply sources. For example, timber market leakage has been documented following forest protection in the Pacific Northwest (PNW) region of the US (Washington and Oregon), displacing harvests to the southern US, Canada, and, to a lesser extent, newer plantation producers such as New Zealand and Chile (see Figure 19.1). Similar displacement from industrialized to developing countries may be expected should carbon premiums reduce Annex I timber harvests. In particular, soft-

Table 19.2. *Global and Annex I industrial roundwood production and trade*

	Softwoods (m³)			Hardwoods (m³)		
	1990	1995	1999	1990	1995	1999
world						
production	1 159 805 920	944 876 350	936 735 789	541 641 424	567 918 190	568 672 261
imports	41 942 796	50 179 248	60 042 493	40 651 080	44 364 468	40 584 406
exports	42 628 955	48 142 563	59 341 856	40 775 275	40 674 689	37 078 771
Annex I						
production	695 469 000	732 811 000	747 751 242	216 317 000	270 206 000	304 218 353
imports	29 455 988	38 105 500	47 505 500	27 969 670	29 968 900	26 896 500
exports	32 806 945	42 565 900	56 245 900	8 446 850	20 761 600	20 843 300
Annex I share of world						
production	60%	78%	80%	40%	48%	53%
imports	70%	76%	79%	69%	68%	66%
exports	77%	88%	95%	21%	51%	56%

Source: Data reproduced from the UN Food and Agriculture Organization's FAOSTAT database at www.fao.org/forestry.

wood products, as opposed to hardwoods, are the segment of the world timber market that exhibits significant overlap between Annex I and non-Annex I production (Brooks 1995; Leslie 1999). This is because softwoods generally are more likely to be transformed into highly substitutable intermediate products, such as pulp and fibre, whereas hardwoods tend to yield more-differentiated end products. Thus, reduced softwood harvests in Annex I regions would be replaced to some degree by equivalent products from the non-Annex I regions.

As noted above, such leakage is likely to be minimal for the first Kyoto Protocol commitment period of 2008–2012, since Article 3.4 sets country-specific caps for forest management at levels that allow carbon credits to be gained largely through business-as-usual activities (see Chapter 18). For future commitment periods, the degree to which carbon markets would prompt relocation of harvest pressure from Annex I to non-Annex I countries will depend on a range of factors. These include each region's share of the global timber market, emissions–reductions targets, and carbon crediting rules for future commitment periods and their impacts on carbon prices.

Annex I countries dominate global production and trade, accounting for four-fifths of softwood production and just over half of hardwood production (see Table 19.2). This dominant position of Annex I countries in global timber output indicates that, if biotic carbon sequestration projects significantly reduce harvests in Annex I countries, the impact will be felt in international timber markets.

Carbon market prices under Kyoto may well be sufficient to exert an impact on timber harvests in Annex I countries. Various analyses estimate that market clearing carbon prices would settle in the neighbourhood of $20, $40 or as much as $80 per tonne (Fankhauser 1995; Roughgarden & Schneider 1999; Totten 1999). In a survey of several sophisticated modelling efforts, EIA (1998) presents estimates ranging from about $100–200 per tonne. These could be high-end estimates, as they assume that the US, a large potential source of demand for carbon credits, participates in the international carbon market. The role played by the US in a future carbon market remains uncertain, however. Without US participation, lower aggregate demand for carbon credits will result in lower carbon prices than anticipated by these studies.

Carbon market prices within the range of projections reported above would most likely motivate both decreased harvests from natural forests and increased afforestation in industrialized countries. Analyses of Douglas fir exploitation in the Pacific Northwest and Loblolly pine exploitation in the southeast US indicate that the price of carbon needs to be at least $20 per tonne to encourage increased retention of land for forest or retention of trees during harvests (Van Kooten *et al.* 1995; Murray 2000; Wayburn *et al.* 2000). Wayburn *et al.* (2000) find that prices over $100 per tonne allow carbon to compete directly with alternative development and short rotation harvest schedules. In marginally productive areas, lower carbon prices may be sufficient to promote afforestation efforts (Parks & Hardie 1995, 1996; Stavins 1999; Plantinga *et al.* 1999). McCarl & Schneider (2001) calculate that a carbon price of $50 per tonne could prompt nearly 5 million hectares of afforestation efforts in the US.

Taken together, these lines of evidence provide strong cause for concern that Kyoto carbon market incentives to reduce timber harvests in Annex I industrialized countries could motivate increased harvests in developing countries, particularly those producing softwoods at competitive market prices. Sophisticated modelling efforts building on the work of Sedjo & Sohngen (2000) are needed to more precisely anticipate the prospective scale of inter-annex leakage resulting from stronger incentives to reduce industrialized country forest-carbon emissions.

Modelling inter-annex leakage will also help clarify the extent to which it may lead to increased harvests from natural forests or plantations. Where leakage leads to expanded harvests from plantations, it has the worrisome potential to motivate the further expansion of plantations in areas most appropriate for the conservation and restoration of natural forests. This parallels the potential impact of carbon crediting for A&R plantation projects under the CDM discussed in the preceding section. One key difference is that the scope for constraining such negative impacts is more limited. Redirected plantation investments will not be subject to any carbon market rules, whereas A&R projects will be subject to CDM rules on additionality and environmental impact.

Where leakage leads to expanded harvests in natural forests, it generally will have sharply negative impacts on biodiversity. The logging practices that currently predominate in tropical forests characteristically result in substantial collateral damage to non-commercial trees during harvest, increased frequency and intensity of fire compared with unlogged forests, and, in some regions, sharply increased rates of bushmeat hunting and colonization along logging roads. These impacts substantially reduce biodiversity by altering the

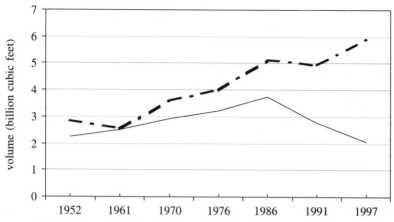

Figure 19.1. Timber harvests in forests in the Pacific Northwest and the southern US, 1952–1997. In 1989, a significant area of national forest in Washington and Oregon was set aside as critical habitat for the northern spotted owl. This figure depicts the marked decline of timber harvests in this region after 1989. The harvest response in the southern US (broken line) conformed to predictions of timber market models. While softwood removals in the PNW (solid line) fell between 1986 and 1997, annual softwood removals in the south increased from 5.13 billion cubic feet to 5.9 billion cubic feet over the same time period (1 cubic foot equals 0.0283 m^3). By the mid-1990s, eastern Canada and the southern US had increased softwood production enough to offset most of the decrease in timber harvests resulting from restrictions in the western US. Note that softwood removals in the South did not immediately increase in response to the decline in harvests in PNW forests, due to the economic recession of 1988–1991. Meanwhile, increased exports from New Zealand, Chile, and Russia compensated for the decline in PNW exports to the Pacific Basin (Haynes *et al.* 1995; USDA Forest Service 2001; Guan & Munn 2000; Sedjo 1995; Brooks 1995). Data for southern US reflects softwood timber harvest only.

structure, function and species composition of forests relative to undisturbed or carefully managed natural forests (Frumhoff 1995; Putz *et al.* 2000a; Bennett & Gumal 2001).

   Leakage of timber harvests from industrialized to developing country forests will also tend to increase net carbon emissions to the atmosphere. Tropical forests generally have higher carbon densities than temperate forests (Olson *et al.* 1983; Dixon *et al.* 1994; Nilsson & Schopfhauser 1995; Prentice *et al.* 2001) but lower densities of commercial species, and conventional logging practices in many tropical countries result in high collateral damage to non-commercial species (Holmes *et al.* 2000; Putz *et al.* 2000b; Pulkki 1998; Gullison *et al.* 1997). Thus, increasing timber supplies from tropical, non-Annex I forests to replace supplies from Annex I countries will in general raise the average amount of carbon released per volume of harvested timber (Houghton & Hackler 1999, 2000).

   Climate policymakers need to recognize the potential for inter-annex leakage and the consequent substantial negative impacts on forest biodiversity and carbon emissions in developing countries. For the second and subsequent commitment periods, they can act to restrain such leakage and its impacts by ensuring that crediting for forest management in industrialized countries is informed by modelling efforts to anticipate the scale of leakage associated with different Annex I LULUCF policy options, and coupled with effective measures to protect natural forests in developing countries. The latter should include expanding the options permitted under the CDM to carbon crediting for projects that protect threatened forests from deforestation and forest degradation. Ultimately, inter-annex leakage can be most effectively mitigated by fully capturing carbon emissions associated with deforestation and forest degradation in developing countries under a future emissions cap.

Conclusion

In the near-term, LULUCF activities undertaken through the Kyoto carbon market pose little prospect of contributing substantially to the conservation of biodiversity. This is because Parties chose, for the first commitment period, to render ineligible for CDM crediting projects that slow deforestation in developing countries. Moreover, their decision to allow crediting for A&R projects in the CDM raises the prospect of net negative impacts to biodiversity by increasing the financial attractiveness of plantations relative to maintaining or restoring native forests. Such impacts may be exacerbated in the second and subsequent commitment periods by inter-annex leakage resulting from decreased timber harvests in industrialized countries.

As climate policymakers refine the first commitment period rules governing crediting for A&R projects in the CDM, they can substantially reduce the incentive for conversion of native forests to carbon plantations by restricting A&R plantation activities to locations not recently cleared. This can be accomplished through a carefully designed 'base year' rule that also allows for CDM project financing of native forest restoration in these same areas. But as long as threatened native forests in developing countries are excluded from an international market that values carbon sequestered in forests in Annex I countries and plantations everywhere, market biases will tend to accelerate their harvests and conversion.

Climate policymakers can take a significant step towards correcting this market bias by fully crediting forest conservation in the CDM in the second and subsequent commitment periods. Ultimately, carbon market incentives for forest clearing can be reduced and incentives for forest conservation most effectively strengthened by fully capturing carbon emissions associated with deforestation and forest degradation in developing countries under a future emissions cap.

A final comment relates to the role of the US. Following the US withdrawal from the Kyoto process, the impact on forests in developing countries will also depend on the course of domestic US climate-change mitigation policy. However it is constructed, US policy is likely to include a significant role for LULUCF measures to achieve net carbon emissions reduction (and, we hope, serious measures to reduce energy sector emissions). Hence, US policies could give rise to similar concerns. For example, should a US climate-mitigation strategy reduce domestic timber harvests, it would promote a dynamic similar to the inter-annex leakage issue discussed above. Conversely, sound US investments in forest conservation in developing countries can substantially reduce net emissions and protect high value biodiversity.

Acknowledgements

We thank Robert Bonnie for review of an early draft of this chapter, Julia Petipas for logistical support, and the David and Lucile Packard Foundation for partial financial support.

Endnotes

[1]This compromise decision reflected the diverse positions of influential parties and nongovernmental organizations (NGOs) (Fearnside 2001). These included: strong objections to any LULUCF projects in the CDM by several European Union negotiators seeking to minimize the extent to which industrialized countries could avoid domestic energy sector emissions reductions in meeting their emissions–reductions targets; effective lobbying by Brazil for inclusion of A&R, reflecting an interest in attracting plantation investment, and exclusion of avoided deforestation, reflecting in part a desire to minimize attention on the large contribution of Brazilian deforestation to global emissions; greater interest among several Annex I parties (e.g. Japan, Canada, Australia) in gaining credits for domestic LULUCF measures than for CDM investments; and a lack of consensus on LULUCF in the CDM by influential NGOs. Many forest-rich developing countries and NGOs, as well as leading climate, forest and other environmental scientists strongly supported the inclusion of sound forest conservation projects in the CDM (Cochabamba Declaration 1999; Belém Manifesto 2000; UCS 2000), but they lacked a sufficiently strong voice at the negotiations.

[2]The most recent comprehensive analysis of global plantation forestry estimates that forest plantations amounted to 187 million hectares worldwide in 2000. Of this global total, plantations located in tropical and other developing countries cover *ca.* 130–140 million hectares (FAO 2001; Pandey & Ball 1998), a substantial increase over estimated plantation coverage in tropical and other developing regions of roughly 80 million hectares in 1995, and 40 million hectares in 1980. The rate of increase is somewhat lower than these numbers suggest, as the 2000 data include rubberwood plantations that were not included in the earlier estimates (FAO 2001).

In order to meet growing world demand for timber and pressing needs for fuelwood, continued growth in the plantation sector is highly likely (FAO 2001; Hardcastle 1999). Growth in demand for wood proceeds at *ca.* 0.75–1% per year, although this growth rate is likely to fall in the long-term due to slowing population growth and changes in technology (Sohngen *et al.* 1998). Simulations by Sohngen *et al.* (1998) suggest that this growing demand will fuel average timber price increases of *ca.* 0.4% yr^{-1} in the near-term, and slower increases further in the future. Sohngen *et al.* (1998) further suggest that this price trend is sufficient to double the area of timber plantations over a period of *ca.* 150 years, without any premium or subsidy linked to carbon sequestration. Others estimate that contribution of plantations to global timber supply may increase even faster: projections in Carneiro & Brown (1999) imply a contribution from plantations anywhere from 29–55% of global supply by 2050, and ABARE–Jaakko Pöyry (1999) estimate that the plantation share may reach 44% as soon as 2020.

Preliminary estimates suggest that the geographic distribution of future plantation growth in the near-term is most likely to be concentrated in developing regions. Whereas Europe, Russia, and North America are anticipated to be largely self-sufficient in industrial timber, Africa and South America are expected to need *ca.* 2 million hectares, and Asia another 8 million hectares, both to meet industrial wood needs. Fuelwood requirements, however, are likely to dominate overall growth in tropical plantations, since it must be produced relatively close to the point of consumption. Hardcastle (1999) estimates that Africa will require 12–25 million hectares of fuelwood plantations and Asia another 22–44 million hectares. If recent trends in plantation establishment are indicative of near-term future expansion, then plantations in Asia are also likely to further expand. Asian plantations accounted for 40% of global industrial plantations in 1995 and nearly 60% of plantations established since 1985 (FAO 2001).

References

ABARE–Jaakko Pöyry 1999 Global out-look for plantations. Research Report 99.9. Australian Bureau of Agricultural and Resource Economics, Canberra.

Belém Manifesto 2000 Declaration of Brazilian Civil Society on the relations between forests and climate change and expectations for COP-6, Belém, Brazil, 24 October 2000. (Available at www.ipam.org.br/polamb/manbelemen.htm.)

Bennett, E. L. & Gumal, M. T. 2001 The interrelationships of commercial logging, hunting, and wildlife in Sarawak: recommendations for forest management. In *The cutting edge: conserving wildlife in logged tropical forests* (ed. R. A. Fimbel, A. Grajal & J. G. Robinson), pp. 359–374. New York: Columbia University Press.

Biodiversidad en América Latina 2000 Bajo la excusa de proteger el clima, proyecto forestal quiere destruir bosque patagónico. Noticias, 2 November 2000. (Available at www.biodiversidadla.org/noticias83.htm.)

Brooks, D. 1995 Federal timber supply reductions in the pacific northwest: international environmental effects. *J. Forestry* **93**(7), 29–33.

Brown, S. (and 13 others) 2000 *Land use, land-use change, and forestry. A special report of the Intergovernmental Panel on Climate Change.* (ed. R. T. Watson, I. R. Noble, B. Bolin, N. H. Ravindranath, D. J. Verardo & D. J. Dokken), pp. 283–338. Cambridge University Press.

Cadman, T. 2000 The Kyoto effect: how the push for carbon sinks by industry and government has become a driver for deforestation. Report by Greenpeace and WWF-International.

Carneiro, C. M. & Brown, C. 1999 Global Outlook for Plantations. In *Proc. FAO Advisory Committee on Paper and Wood Products, 40th Session, Sao Paulo, Brazil, 27–28 April 1999.* (Available at www.fao.org/forestry/fop/fopw/acpwp/40/Carne.htm.)

Casson, A. 1999 The hesitant boom: Indonesia's oil palm sector in an era of economic crisis and political change (1997–1999). Occasional Paper no. 29, Center for International Forestry Research, Bogor, Indonesia.

Chomitz, K. 2000 Evaluating carbon offsets from forestry and energy projects: how do they compare? Development Research Group report, World Bank, Washington, DC.

Cochabamba Declaration 1999 *Proc. of Meeting of Ministers of Environment & Forestry of the Amazonian Countries on the Clean Development Mechanism Cochabamba, Bolivia, 14–15 June 1999*. (Available at www.caf.com/espanol_old/cochabamba_1999.htm.)

Dixon, R., Brown, S., Houghton, R., Solomon, A., Trexler, M. & Wisniewski, J. 1994 Carbon pools and flux of global forest systems. *Science* **263**, 185–190.

EIA 1998 Impacts of the Kyoto Protocol on US Energy Markets and Economic Activity. Energy Information Administration report. Office of Integrated Analysis and Forecasting, US Department of Energy, Washington, DC.

Fankhauser, S. 1995 *Valuing climate change: the economics of the greenhouse*. London: Earthscan Publications.

FAO 1997 State of the world's forests. Report. Food and Agriculture Organization of the United Nations, Rome.

FAO 2001 Global Forest Resources Assessment 2000. FAO Forestry Paper no. 140. Food and Agricultural Organization of the United Nations, Rome.

Fearnside, P. M. 2001 Saving tropical forests as a global warming countermeasure: an issue that divides the environmental movement. *Ecol. Econ.* **39**, 167–184.

Frumhoff, P. C. 1995 Conserving wildlife in tropical forests managed for timber. *Bioscience* **45**, 456–464.

Frumhoff, P. C., Goetze, D. C. & Hardner, J. J. 1998 Linking solutions to climate change and biodiversity loss through the Kyoto Protocol's Clean Development Mechanism. Union of Concerned Scientists, Cambridge, MA. (Available at www.ucsusa.org/publications/cdm.pdf.)

Guan, H. & Munn, I. A. 2000 Harvest restrictions: an analysis of new capital expenditures in the Pacific Northwest and the South. *J. Forestry* **98**(4), 11–16.

Gullison, R. E., Hardner, J. J., & Shauer, A. 1997 The percentage use of felled mahogany trees in the Chimanes Forest. *J. Trop. For. Sci.* **10**, 94–100.

Hardcastle, P. D. 1999 Plantations: potential and limitations. Draft report for The World Bank Forest Policy Implementation Review and Strategy (Available at http://wbln0018.worldbank.org/essd/forestpol-e.nsf/HiddenDocView/ED54A1971D1352598525682D00713358?OpenDocument.)

Haynes, R., Adams, D. M. & Mills, J. R. 1995 The 1993 RPA timber assessment update. General technical report no. RM-259. USDA Forest Service, Rocky Mountain Forest and Range Experiment Station, Fort Collins, CO.

Holmes, T., Blate, G., Zweede, J., Pereira Jr, R., Barreto, P., Boltz, F. & Bauch, R. 2000 *Financial costs and benefits of reduced-impact logging relative to conventional logging in the Eastern Amazon*. Alexandria, VA: Tropical Forest Foundation.

Houghton, R. A. & Hackler, J. L. 1999 Emissions of carbon from forestry and land-use change in tropical Asia. *Glob. Change Biol.* **5**, 481–492.

Houghton, R. A. & Hackler, J. L. 2000 Changes in terrestrial carbon storage in the United States: the roles of agriculture and forestry. *Global. Ecol. Biogeogr.* **9**, 125–144.

Kanowski, P. J., Savill, P. S., Adlard, P. G., Burley, J., Evans, J., Palmer, J. R. & Wood, P. J. 1992 Plantation forestry. In *Managing the world's forests* (ed. N. P. Sharma), pp. 375–401. Dubuque, IA: Kendall/Hunt.

LaFranchi, C. 2000 Oil palm in Indonesia: dynamics of an industry threat to biodiversity. Center for Applied Biodiversity Science, Conservation International, Washington, DC.

Leslie, A. J. 1999 For whom the bell tolls: what is the future of the tropical timber trade in the face of a probable glut of plantation timber? In *Tropical Forest Update, the newsletter of the International Tropical Timber Organization*, vol. 9, issue 4. (Available at www.itto.or.jp/newsletter/v9n4/7.html.)

McCarl, B. A. & Schneider, U. A. 2001 Greenhouse gas mitigation in US agriculture and forestry. *Science* **294**, 2481–2482.

Murray, B. C. 2000 Carbon values, reforestation, and 'perverse' incentives under the Kyoto Protocol: an empirical analysis. *Mitigat. Adapt. Strategies Global Change* **5**(3), 271–295.

Nilsson, S. & Schopfhauser, W. 1995 The carbon sequestration potential of a global afforestation program. *Climatic Change* **30**, 267–293.

Olson, J. S., Watts, J. A. & Allison, L. J. 1983 Carbon in live vegetation of major world ecosystems. Report no. ORNL-5862. Oak Ridge National Laboratory, Oak Ridge, TN.

Pandey, D. & Ball, J. 1998 The role of industrial plantations in future global fibre supplies. *Unasylva* **49**(2), 37–43.

Parks, P. & Hardie, I. 1995 Least cost forest carbon reserves: cost-effective subsidies to convert marginal agricultural lands to forests. *Land Econ.* **71**, 122–136.

Parks, P. J. & Hardie, I. W. 1996 Forest carbon sinks: costs and effects of expanding the conservation reserve program. *Choices Mag.* **11**(2), 37.

Parrotta, J., Turnbull, J. & Jones, N. 1997*a* Catalyzing native forest regen-eration on degraded tropical lands. *For. Ecol. Manag.* **99**, 1–7.

Parrotta, J., Knowles, O. & Wunderle Jr, J. 1997*b* Development of floristic diversity in 10-year-old restoration forests on a bauxite mined site in Amazonia. *For. Ecol. Manag.* **99**, 21–42.

Plantinga, A., Mauldin, T. & Miller, D. 1999 An econometric analysis of the costs of sequestering carbon in forests. *Am. J. Agric. Econ.*, **81**, 812–824.

Prentice, I. C., Farquhar, G .D., Fasham, M. J. R., Goulden, M. L., Heimann, M., Jaramillo, V. J., Kheshgi, H. S., Le Quéré, C., Scholes, R. J. & Wallace, D. W. R. 2001 The carbon cycle and atmospheric carbon dioxide. In *Climate Change 2001: the Scientific Basis. Contribution of Working Group I to the Third Assessment Report of the Intergovernmental Panel on Climate Change* (ed. J. T. Houghton, Y. Dong, D. J. Griggs, M. Noguer, P. J. van der Linden, X. Dai, K. Maskell & C. A. Johnson), pp. 183–237. Cambridge University Press.

Pulkki, R. E. 1998 Conventional versus environmentally sound harvesting: impacts on non-coniferous tropical veneer log and sawlog supplies. *Unasylva* **40**, 23–30.

Putz, F. E., Redford, K. H., Robinson, J. G., Fimbel, R. & Blate, G. M. 2000*a* Biodiversity conservation in the context of tropical forest management. World Bank Environment Department report, Washington, DC.

Putz, F. E., Dykstra, D. P. & Heinrich, R. 2000*b* Why poor logging practices persist in the tropics. *Conserv. Biol.* **14**, 951–956.

Roughgarden, T. & Schneider, S. 1999 Climate change policy: quantifying uncer-tainties for damages and optimal carbon taxes. *Energy Policy* **27**, 415–429.

Sawyer, J. 1993 *Plantations in the Tropics: environmental concerns*. Gland, Switzer-land: IUCN.

Sedjo, R. 1995 Local logging, global effects. *J. Forestry* **93**(7), 25–28.

Sedjo, R. & Sohngen, B. 2000 Forestry sequestration of CO_2 and markets for timber. Discussion Paper no. 00-35. Resources for the Future, Washington, DC.

Sohngen, B., Mendelsohn, R. & Sedjo, R. 1998 The effectiveness of forest carbon sequestration strategies with system-wide adjustments. Draft paper. (Available at www.worldbank.org/research/abcde/pdfs/sohngen.pdf.)

Stavins, R. 1999 The costs of carbon sequestration: a revealed preference approach. *Am. Econ. Rev.* **89**, 994–1009.

Totten, M. 1999 *Getting it right: emerging markets for storing carbon in forests.* Washington, DC: Forest Trends, World Resources Institute.

UCS 2000 Scientists Call for Action on Forest Conservation in the Kyoto Protocol's Clean Development Mechanism. Statement. Union of Concerned Scientists, Cambridge, MA, USA. (Available at www.ucsusa.org/environment/cdmcall.html.)

UNFCCC 2002*a* United Nations Framework Convention on Climate Change Report no. FCCC/CP/2001/13/Add.1. (Available at www.unfccc.de/index.html.)

UNFCCC 2002*b* United Nations Framework Convention on Climate Change Report no. FCCC/CP/2001/13/Add.2. (Available at www.unfccc.de/index.html.)

USDA Forest Service 2001 2000 RPA assessment of forest and range lands, FS-687. Washington, DC: USDA Forest Service.

Van Kooten, G., Binkley, C. & Delcourt, G. 1995 Effect of carbon taxes and subsidies on optimal forest rotation ages and supply of carbon services. *Am. J. Agric. Econ.* **77**, 365–74.

Wayburn, L., Franklin, J., Gordon, J., Binkley, C., Mladenoff, D. & Christensen Jr, N. 2000 *Forest carbon in the united states: opportunities and options for private lands.* Santa Rosa, CA: Pacific Forest Trust, Inc.

WBGU 1998 The accounting of biological sinks and sources under the Kyoto Protocol: a step forwards or backwards for global environmental protection? Special report. German Advisory Council on Global Change, Bremerhaven, Germany.

Chapter 20

Greenhouse-gas-trading markets

RICHARD L. SANDOR, MICHAEL J. WALSH AND RAFAEL L. MARQUES

Introduction

This chapter provides a summary of the historical development patterns observed in newly organized markets, and an assessment of the status of the emerging greenhouse-gas (GHG) markets in the context of the inventive process. It discusses the logical extension of new market mechanisms for environmental services and presents the rationale and objectives for pilot GHG-trading markets. It goes on to explain the importance of generating price information indicative of the cost of mitigating GHGs and provides a summary of the steps being taken to define and launch pilot carbon markets in North America and Europe. It ends with a review of key issues related to incorporating environmental services associated with carbon sequestration into a carbon-trading market.

The history of new markets offers many examples where societal demand to deploy capital to address particular objectives helps stimulate the formation of organized markets. Increasing societal demand for cost-effective methods for improving environmental quality has ushered in a variety of successful market-based environmental-protection programmes. There is an emerging consensus to employ market mechanisms to help address the threat of human-induced climate changes.

Carbon-trading markets are now in development around the world. A UK market is set to launch in 2002, and the European Commission has called for a 2005 launch of an EU-wide market. The Chicago Climate Exchange (CCX) is a voluntary carbon market now in formation in North America. These markets represent an initial step in resolving a fundamental problem faced by those seeking to define and implement appropriate policy actions to address climate change. Policymakers currently suffer from two major information gaps. The first is that the scale of potential damages arising from climate changes is highly uncertain. The other important gap is a lack of understanding of the monetary costs associated with action to mitigate GHGs. These twin gaps significantly reduce the quality of the climate policy debate.

The CCX, for which the authors serve as lead designers, is intended to provide an organized carbon-trading market involving energy, industry and carbon sequestration in forests and farms. Trading among these diverse sectors will provide price discovery that helps clarify the cost of managing GHG concentrations and combating climate change when a wide range of mitigation options is employed. By closing the information gap on mitigation costs, society and policymakers will be far better prepared to identify and implement optimal policies for managing the risks associated with climate change.

Establishment of practical experience in providing tradeable credits for carbon-absorbing land-use practices, especially reforestation and conservation management of agricultural soils, will also help demonstrate the viability of a new tool for financing activities that improve water quality, support biodiversity and constitute important elements of long-term sustainability in land-use management.

Development patterns observed in newly organized markets

The historic pattern of successful implementation of various organized markets, including environmental markets, offers insights as to the feasible paths for development of markets established for the purpose of reducing GHG emissions (Sandor 1992, 1999). As discussed in Chapter 3, the first step is the emergence of demand for capital to flow to address a specific objective. The past decade has seen a crystallization of the sort of structural change that demands that resources be dedicated to protection against the risk of climate change. The international effort to formalize the demand for GHG mitigation through the United Nations Framework Convention on Climate Change (UNFCCC) has seen a multitude of parallel efforts through national and local policy actions, as well as in the private sector. Standards that can provide the foundation for widespread use of emissions trading as a tool for cost-effectively cutting GHGs are now emerging in both the public and private sectors. The establishment of legal trading instruments is underway, spot markets are being developed in numerous locations and derivative markets are already being considered.

From a higher-level perspective, if we apply Joseph Schumpeter's summary of the three phases of inventive activity—invention, innovation and replication into commercialized forms—then one can say that development of the GHG market is an example of the commercialization or extension stage (Schumpeter 1942). The early efforts during the 1970s to exploit cost efficiencies and gains from trade gave industry limited flexibility in the form of multi-plant 'bubbles' or emission-netting schemes. Following these attempts to 'invent' practical emissions-trading systems, innovation during the 1980s took the form of better-defined and more-easily-traded emission rights. These improvements were employed in the US programmes for reducing lead content in motor fuel, and in the highly successful acid-rain-reduction programme that introduced commodity-like trading in SO_2 allowances in the 1990s (Sandor & Walsh 2000). Having built a basis of experience, the hypothesis that the timeframe for designing and launching GHG markets can be accelerated will now be tested.

In any event, the challenges associated with incorporating carbon sequestration into the GHG markets makes it likely that these markets will go
through several iterations over the next two decades as experience is gained,
as measurement technology improves and as market participation and value
grows. The initial efforts to develop GHG-trading markets may produce successes, partial successes and failures. But all the efforts can be expected to
yield lessons that can help guide the formation of successful later-generation
markets.

Extension of new market mechanisms for environmental services

The international community has codified a climate-protection strategy that
allows for a broad range of market-based tools for managing and reducing
GHGs. As with all emissions-trading systems, the ultimate goal is to lower
overall mitigation cost by exploiting gains from trade, using price signals to
guide resources to their most efficient use and stimulating innovation.

The incorporation of a variety of market-based tools for managing GHG
emissions in part reflects the success in using these tools for managing other
environmental problems. Indeed, it is unlikely that the UNFCCC would have
contained its various emissions-trading mechanisms had there not been successful large-scale demonstration of the concept.

The agreement that has emerged from the UNFCCC and its Kyoto Protocol has also formally recognized the major influence of land-use management
on GHG concentrations. This represents a critically important extension of the
emissions-trading concept that potentially has profound benefits for ecosystems and biodiversity. This new dimension of emissions trading holds promise
to provide an additional tool for financing land-use practices and conservation
investment on a significant scale. If the opportunity can be successfully harnessed, society can simultaneously reduce the threat of climate change while
enhancing natural landscapes and realizing the co-benefits of habitat protection, improved water quality and increased aesthetic values. Importantly,
introduction of new tools for financing sustainable land use offers the potential to increase the viability of local economies and indigenous societies that
are dependent on healthy forest systems (Walsh 1999).

The Kyoto Protocol provides an initial approach for including the role
of biomass and soil carbon in its GHG limits and market mechanisms. Article 3.3 of the Kyoto Protocol calls for counting the net contribution of human-
induced afforestation, reforestation and deforestation since 1990 in the 38
industrialized countries for which the specified emission limits are intended
to apply. Article 3.4 directed that the climate conference to determine which
GHG removals by sinks in the agricultural soils and the land-use change and
forestry categories should be incorporated into the Protocol. The completion
of the Marrakech meetings of the UNFCCC provided guidance on these activities, the inclusion of which was a major concern for several countries such as
Canada and Australia. Importantly, the Marrakech Accords also provide for

recognition and crediting of afforestation and reforestation projects in developing countries via the Protocol's Clean Development Mechanism.

The objectives of the climate and biological diversity conventions are deeply intertwined. Habitat alteration, which some view to be associated with ongoing changes in the Earth's climate, is the principle cause of species loss and endangerment. At the same time, the market mechanisms established in the UNFCCC and Kyoto process introduce a new source of financial support for enhancement and protection of biological habitat. The challenge now is to implement practical market mechanisms that provide demonstration benefits while testing methods for handling the technical challenges that are inherent in all environmental protection programmes.

The Kyoto Protocol, as well as related initiatives being undertaken by national and local governments and the private and non-governmental sectors, provides the opportunity to incorporate the carbon-sequestration services realized through enhancement carbon 'sinks'. The various emerging markets for trading in carbon credits can be harnessed to enhance habitats by providing a new source of financing for reforestation and agricultural-management practices that can contribute to improved ecosystems.

Rationale and objectives for pilot GHG-trading markets

The argument that emissions-trading markets will help lower the cost of mitigating GHGs rests on the assumption that such markets can be established and integrated internationally, that their transaction costs can be kept low and that they can ultimately succeed in guiding global mitigation resources to the least-cost options. Considering the limited experience with emissions trading worldwide, the introduction of early pilot trading programmes represents a critically important step in the process of building, refining, spreading and integrating these markets. It is widely observed that the best way to advance the process is to promptly begin trading, even if on a limited scale, so that institutions and skills can be built on the basis of real-world experience. Pilot GHG markets can offer a means to do just that.

The formation of a pilot market requires resolution of a wide range of design questions and implementation challenges. These include: defining emissions, sources and offset projects to be included; monitoring and verification protocols; establishing registries and reporting procedures; enrolling participants; determining baselines; allotting allowances and enrolling offset projects; and assuring effective true-up of emissions and allowance and offset holdings. Each of the steps presents a number of challenges due to political, technical and institutional constraints, and many of the required steps introduce the need to create new approaches to solve the issue at hand. At the same time, practices used in other commodity and environmental markets do offer approaches that can be applied to formation of a GHG market.

As the myriad practical issues are resolved, the initial market architecture that emerges will represent a foundation upon which the market refinement and expansion process can be built. While the industrialized countries that start early can probably realize successful iteration within a decade, the spread of effective GHG trading to a large number of countries is likely to take significantly longer. The inevitability of the build, test and refine cycle makes it critically important to start soon. In order to begin realizing the benefits that a GHG market can produce for ecosystems in developing countries, it is important to include sequestration activities in the emerging markets as soon as possible.

To summarize, the rationale for pilot GHG trading is to:

- test methods and technologies;

- build expertise among emission sources and offset projects;

- initiate the process of managing GHG limitations as a conventional business practice;

- begin the process of harnessing GHG markets for the direct benefit of ecosystems; and

- generate price information indicative of the cost of GHG mitigation.

This final point is now discussed further.

Significance of price information indicative of the cost of mitigating GHGs

The long-running debate over the appropriate degree of GHG mitigation to be pursued will continue as individual countries consider signing on to near-term action, and as the international community prepares to consider Kyoto's second-round mitigation goals. However, this debate suffers from two major information gaps. The first is a lack of consensus regarding the damages that could occur if action to reduce GHG emissions is not taken. Stated another way, the benefits of taking mitigation actions are uncertain.

The second information gap is a lack of understanding of the monetary costs associated with mitigating GHGs. The implicit cost–benefit analysis underlying the climate debate dictates that for any particular level of benefits accruing from action to mitigate climate change, a high cost of mitigation will lead policymakers to take less action. If mitigation costs were known to be low, policymakers would be likely to support stronger action.

At this time, however, society does not have reliable data on the costs involved in pursuing climate-mitigation actions. Establishment of emissions-trading systems thus becomes imperative, since policy decisions are now being made. In addition, while many assume that enhancement of terrestrial carbon sinks offers one of the least-expensive GHG-mitigation options, the institutional capacity to properly include this option is not currently in place.

Generation of price information indicative of mitigation costs should be considered a primary objective of pilot GHG-trading programmes. However, as discussed below, the pilot markets being developed in the UK and the European Union (EU) do not include north–south international trade or carbon-sequestration activities. Because actions to increase carbon sequestered in soils, forests and other biomass is widely considered to be one of the least-cost mitigation options, this omission may cause the price information to be generated in the UK and EU markets to misrepresent the true cost of mitigation if all GHG-mitigation options were to be exploited. This omission is all the more perplexing given the explicit recognition of sequestration activities in the Kyoto Protocol.

Pilot carbon markets under development in North America and Europe

Pilot GHG-trading systems are emerging in North America and Europe. These programmes are intended to begin building institutions and skills needed to form broader markets in the coming years. It is important to note that, while the emissions-reduction commitments under the Kyoto Protocol (which the EU countries appear ready to accept) do not become binding until 2008 and later, the UK and EU pilot markets are planned for launch well in advance of the Kyoto time-frame. The early start will help to reveal strengths and weaknesses of the initial approaches taken, thus generating benefits from the 'learning by doing' approach. Regrettably, the long-standing hesitation of European countries to embrace the role of carbon sequestration as an important component of GHG management appears to have contributed to the omission of land use and sequestration from the first-generation markets in Europe and the UK.

At the national governmental level, the UK has recently launched an emissions-trading system for GHGs developed by the government and a consortium of businesses known as the Emissions Trading Group (DEFRA 2001). The British government has indicated that it will attempt to merge this initiative into the pilot EU programme with as little friction as possible. The programme is a voluntary pilot open to all sectors except transport and power generation. It covers all six categories of GHGs, employs allowance allocations and offers government-provided financial incentives to participate. At this time, the UK programme does not allow crediting for carbon-sequestration projects, but the issue is subject to review in the future. The programme was activated when emission sources signalled their intent to take on emissions-reduction commitments by 'bidding in' their proposed reduction quantities into an auction mechanism conducted in the first quarter of 2002.

The European Commission released a proposal at the end of October 2001 to establish an emissions-trading programme to start in 2005 (CEC 2001). Noting that carbon dioxide (CO_2) makes up 80% of the total GHG footprint in the EU, and citing its relative ease of monitoring, the proposal calls for including CO_2 only in the market's initial phase. The plan targets large facilities in the energy, metals, mineral-processing and forest-products sectors. The proposal is silent on the issue of carbon sequestration.

Efforts are also under way in the Netherlands, where the government plans to form a CO_2-trading system by 2004–2005. In Germany and Japan, working groups made up of members of the public and private sectors are discussing steps to establish GHG-emissions-trading markets. Denmark launched the first

Table 20.1. *Proposed salient features: Chicago Climate Exchange*

market design	cap-and-trade 'allowances' and project-based offsets
geographic coverage	emissions sources in the US starting in 2003, with expansion to sources in Canada and Mexico; offsets from projects in Brazil
emissions-reduction schedule	proposed cuts to 2% below baseline in 2003, further 1% cuts annually through 2006; baseline is proposed to be 1998–2000
offset projects	afforestation and reforestation, agricultural soil carbon and emission cuts, landfill methane destruction, renewable energy systems
trading system and auctions	web-based electronic trading platform, periodic auctions to generate price information and liquidity

national domestic GHG-emissions-trading market, but it was limited solely to the power sector. It is notable that the German Green Party, which is not generally known to support markets and industry, proposed the establishment of an early national GHG-trading programme.

Efforts in North America to form organized early pilot markets for GHG trading appear at this time to be limited to the preparations being undertaken by the CCX. The Joyce Foundation, through a grant to Northwestern University, has provided the funding to prepare a feasibility study for the exchange and to implement the design phase of the project under the direction of our Chicago-based company, Environmental Financial Products LLC. Market launch is targeted for late 2002.

The CCX is preparing a hybrid market architecture that will blend a cap-and-trade allowance system with project-based offsets, including sequestration projects. The exchange will issue annual allowances equal to each member-company's target level. A registry will be established with accounts containing each participant's allowance and offset holdings. Offsets from eligible projects, such as biomass sequestration in North America and energy or sequestration projects in Brazil, will also be registered and can be used for compliance. Companies will monitor and report actual emissions in a linked database. Just as in the SO_2 programme, subsequent to the end of each year, allowances plus offsets equal to actual emissions must be relinquished. Participating companies that have emitted more CO_2-equivalent emissions than the allowances they hold may purchase offsets or allowances to achieve compliance. Participants having excess allowances or offsets may sell or bank them. Table 20.1 presents the salient features of the CCX.

There are currently 46 entities participating in the formulation of rules for the CCX (see Table 20.2). They have expressed their intent to participate further by taking emissions-limitation commitments and trading if the final rules are compatible with their strategic objectives. The participating entities include the electric-power, oil and gas, forest-products, manufacturing and landfill-management industries, as well as two large municipalities. They also include offset providers from wind, solar and hydroelectric power compa-

Table 20.2. *Entities participating in the CCX design phase*

energy	Alliant Energy
	American Electric Power
	BP
	Cinergy
	CMS Generation
	DTE
	Exelon
	FirstEnergy
	Manitoba Hydro
	Midwest Generation
	NiSource
	Ontario Power Generation
	PG&E National Energy Group
	Pinnacle West Corporation (APS)
	Suncor Energy
	TXU Energy Trading
	Wisconsin Energy
industry	Baxter
	Cemex
	DuPont
	Ford Motor Company
	Grupo IMSA de Mexico
	Interface
	ST Microelectronics
	Waste Management Inc.
offset providers	Agriliance
	Cataguazes-Leopoldina
	Conservacion Mexico
	Ducks Unlimited
	Growmark
	Iowa Farm Bureau Federation
	National Council of Farmer Cooperatives
	Navitas Energy
	Nuon
	Ormat
	Pronatura Noreste
	The Nature Conservancy
service providers	American Agrisurance
	Det Norsk Veritas
	Edelman PR
	IT Group
	SCS Engineers
	Swiss Re Carr Futures/Crédit Agricole
	Winrock International
forest-products companies	International Paper
	Temple-Inland
	Mead Corp.
	Stora Enso
municipalities	City of Chicago
	Mexico City

nies, farmers' cooperatives and environmental and conservation organizations specializing in carbon-sequestration projects.

CCX participants include the two largest forest-products companies in the world, the largest electricity generator in the US and several leading-edge land-stewardship groups. Total annual emissions from the participating industrial entities are *ca.* 700 million tonnes CO_2 equivalent, nearly equal to those of Germany.

It is important to note that the inclusion of carbon-sequestration activities undertaken in the industrial-forest sector, in the agricultural sector and through projects undertaken by conservation groups offers the prospect of generating a more robust price signal compared with a market that excludes sequestration. Provisions to assure that sequestration offsets do not flood the market will be examined so that prices reflect a balance of industrial emissions reductions and sequestration. As discussed below, inclusion of a variety of sequestration activities introduces an array of technical and institutional challenges. Put another way, this diverse range of land-use activities presents a perfect opportunity to begin building methods and capacity to effectively include sequestration in GHG markets worldwide.

Key issues related to incorporating carbon sequestration into a GHG-trading market

By incorporating carbon sequestration in managed forests, as well as sequestration by specifically targeted project-based sequestration offsets from the outset, the CCX programme provides an early opportunity to begin building a broad portfolio of mitigation activities, and to learn through practice. This will help CCX participants and others learn more about the practical mechanics of implementing, quantifying, registering and trading offsets from land-use activities in the context of an organized carbon market.

Despite the massive amount of discussion and debate surrounding the inclusion of sequestration in GHG-mitigation efforts, there is relatively limited practical experience with sequestration crediting. In order to build experience with sequestration crediting, the CCX will include the following categories of carbon-sequestration activities in its first phase:

- Afforestation and reforestation and other revegetation projects.

- Soil sequestration through on-farm conservation practices.

- Net changes in carbon-storage balances realized by forest-product companies.

Early inclusion of these activities will help address questions that have to date been largely theoretical, such as the following:

- What are practical and cost-effective methods for quantifying carbon sequestration?

- How can multiple projects be aggregated to exploit economies of scale in trading?

- What environmental co-benefits are realized?

- What efforts are needed to assure sequestration effectiveness in the aggregate?

In order to improve the chances that answers to the above questions can be generated by the CCX pilot, the market design focuses on finding an initial balance between assuring confidence in the environmental effectiveness of sequestration projects and keeping transaction costs low enough to foster participation. The market design endeavours to establish standardized protocols whenever possible. In order to be confident that a standardized procedure does not overstate the true environmental effectiveness of a sequestration project, simplifications introduced for the purpose of lowering transaction costs will employ discounted sequestration values. For example, due to statistical factors and other considerations, it is extremely expensive to quantify increases in carbon sequestration in agricultural soils within reasonably narrow confidence bands. This expense grows for when the carbon increments occur over shorter time periods. To avoid this prohibitive cost, default values and model-based estimates of sequestration are being developed based on expert input. By adopting a specified quantitative relationship that links management practices to annual sequestration quantities, the CCX will mandate only that the management practice specified by contract is, in fact, undertaken.

In the course of developing protocols for the CCX, a number of important conceptual and technical questions have arisen. Among the more interesting ones are the following:

- Must forest-carbon quantification protocols be standardized across participants? How can this be done?

- How are afforestation and reforestation projects defined? Can avoided deforestation be defined, consistently quantified and included in a pilot market?

- What project-verification methods should be employed?

- How can increased carbon stocks in agricultural soils be quantified at acceptable cost?

- How can the market architecture help assure long-term carbon storage?

- How can multiple small projects be aggregated so that per-tonne transaction costs decline?

- How should long-term storage of carbon in wood products be reflected in the carbon accounts of forest-product companies?

- What methods for pooling and insuring sequestration projects offer cost-effective means for assuring that sequestration projects achieve and maintain progress in storing increased amounts of carbon?

The answers to these questions are being developed with industry input, expert advice of academics and forest and soil consultants, through incorporation of research findings reported in the literature, and by reference to international standards. While compromises between accuracy and cost must be made, the philosophy of using conservative discounted values whenever lower-cost quantification methods are used is expected to prove effective. The pilot will not realize the objective of having robust participation and a variety of sequestration activities unless a number of steps are taken to reduce transaction costs.

Inclusion of a variety of carbon-sequestration activities in the CCX is considered a first step in a series of efforts needed to help harness the emerging global market in GHG mitigation for the benefit of ecosystem enhancement and conservation. The ultimate success of this endeavour, which might take 10–20 years to realize, may represent a major new source of funding for land-use management practices that produce simultaneous benefits for local communities, water quality and wildlife.

Conclusions

The UNFCCC emerged from the 1992 Earth Summit at Rio de Janeiro, which also formally introduced the Convention on Biological Diversity (CBD). Given the potential for carbon sequestration and credit trading to significantly enhance land conservation and stewardship, it can be argued that the efforts to pursue the goals of the climate convention can also represent the most important set of actions that advance the goals of the CBD.

The UN process has introduced a framework for conducting international trade in GHG reductions and sequestration. However, implementation is largely left to national governments and others who can make these mechanisms operational around the world. The introduction of pilot GHG markets that include carbon sequestration is a first step in a sequence of efforts that will be needed to harness the carbon markets for the benefit of terrestrial ecosystems. The early pilot markets must be viewed as a test phase from which lessons can be drawn and necessary improvement identified. As practical experience is gained, and as technologies such as remote sensing mature, the ability to broaden the reach of benefits to ecosystems worldwide will grow.

References

CEC 2000 *Proposal for a Directive of the European Parliament and of the Council establishing a framework for greenhouse gas emissions trading within the European Community and amending Council Directive 96/61/EC*. Brussels: Commission of the European Communities.

DEFRA 2001 *A summary guide to the UK emissions trading scheme*. London: Department for Environment, Food and Rural Affairs. (Available at www.defra.gov.uk/environment/climatechange/trading/pdf/trading-summary.pdf.)

Sandor, R. L. 1992 In search of trees. In *Combating global warming: study on a global system of tradeable carbon emission entitlements*. Geneva: United Nations Conference on Trade and Development.

Sandor, R. L. 1999 The role of the United States in international environmental policy. In *Preparing America's foreign policy for the twenty-first century* (ed. D. L. Boren & E. J. Perkins). Norman, OK: University of Oklahoma Press.

Sandor, R. L. & Walsh, M. J. 2000 Some observations on the evolution of the international greenhouse gas emissions trading market. In *Emissions trading: environmental policy's new instruments* (ed. R. F. Kosobud). Wiley.

Schumpeter, J. A. 1942 *Capitalism, socialism and democracy.* New York: Harper and Brothers.

Walsh, M. J. 1999 Maximizing financial support for biodiversity in the emerging Kyoto Protocol markets. *Sci. Total Environ.* **240**, 145–146.

Index